Handbook of Modernity in South Asia

The Oxford India Handbooks are an important initiative in academic publishing.
Each volume offers a comprehensive survey of research in a critical subject area
and provides facts, figures, and analyses for a well-grounded perspective.
The series provides scholars, students, and policy planners
with a balanced understanding of a wide range of issues in the social sciences.

Other Titles in the Series

Handbook of Modernity in South Asia

Modern Makeovers

edited by

SAURABH DUBE

OXFORD
UNIVERSITY PRESS

OXFORD
UNIVERSITY PRESS

Oxford University Press is a department of the University of Oxford.
It furthers the University's objective of excellence in research, scholarship,
and education by publishing worldwide. Oxford is a registered trademark of
Oxford University Press in the UK and in certain other countries

Published in India by
Oxford University Press
YMCA Library Building, 1 Jai Singh Road, New Delhi 110 001, India

ISBN-13: 978-0-19-807404-5
ISBN-10: 0-19-807404-2

Typeset in Adobe Garamond Pro 11/13.6
by Sai Graphic Design, New Delhi 110 055

For the Sarkars
Sumit, Tanika, Aditya

Contents

Preface

The idea for this volume was hatched over tea in the New Delhi office of Oxford University Press (OUP) over four years ago. It was sustained by two international colloquia held at El Colegio de México in 2007 and 2008 as well as by diligent responses of contributors to calls for their chapters. Not everyone represented here was present at the colloquia. Yet, the contributors have each been met in distinct locations, from Baltimore to Bogotá, New Delhi to New York, Coyoacán to Kolkata, and lively conversations (and, often, fun times) have undergirded these encounters.

I would like to begin, then, by thanking the contributors for their efforts. These contributors include Prathama Banerjee, who began as a 'reader' of the volume and ended by contributing an 'Afterword' to the venture. Happy gratitude is due as well to Ishita Banerjee, who not only co-organized the colloquia, but has contributed in myriad ways to the realization of *Modern Makeovers*. Her endeavours equally underlie, including as co-editor, the somewhat different, Spanish version of this work, which is forthcoming soon. Thanks are due further to the staff and students, faculty and administrators of El Colegio de México for astutely supporting these different, entwined ventures. Among the research assistants who have helped in many ways is Atig Ghosh (now Dr Atig Ghosh). Our graduate student and a contributor to this volume, Atig was a co-conspirator in its planning, and extended able assistance towards the introduction to the work. As always, it has been a pleasure to work with the OUP team.

Finally, as a tiny acknowledgement of extended ties of affect and intellect, this volume is dedicated to three historians, two senior and one younger—Sumit, Tanika, and Aditya Sarkar.

Mexico City
April 2011

SAURABH DUBE

Abbreviations

ABC	American Board of Commissioners for Foreign Missions Records
AITBA	All India Tamang Buddhist Association
AIWC	All India Women's Conference
BAWS	*Babasaheb Ambedkar Writings and Speeches*
BC	Backward Class
CIAM	Congrès International d'Architecture Moderne
CPI	Communist Party of India
CWMG	*Collected Works of Mahatma Gandhi*
DMK	Dravida Munnetra Kazhagam
DSA	Department of Science and Art
DUAC	Delhi Urban Arts Commission
GIFP	Government of India, Foreign and Political Department
HLH	Houghton Library, Harvard University
ILP	Indian Labour Party
IMF	International Monetary Fund
IMG	*Indian Medical Gazette*
IPTA	Indian People's Theatre Association
IUD	Intrauterine Device
MCD	Municipal Corporation of Delhi
NAI	National Archives of India
NCR	National Capital Region
NMML	Nehru Memorial Museum and Library
OIOC	Oriental and India Office Collections
PWD	Public Works Department
RWA	Resident Welfare Association

SEBI	Securities and Exchange Board of India
ST	Scheduled Tribe
TNSA	Tamil Nadu State Archives
ULFA	United Liberation Front of Asom
USIN	United States Immigration and Naturalization Service
WBSA	West Bengal State Archives

Makeovers of Modernity

An Introduction*

Saurabh Dube

What is the relationship between modernity and India? Is modernity new to India, involving the transformation only in recent decades of an apparently timeless traditional society through global networks of banking and industry, migration and information, and trade and technology? Or have different groups on the Indian subcontinent variously participated in processes of modernity over a much longer time period? In brief, how is modernity itself to be understood and what forms have its expressions taken in India?

Approaching Modernity

To pose questions in this manner is to register that in everyday and academic understandings, being modern and enacting modernity repeatedly appear as the transcending of tradition, as a break with what existed before. Indeed, even those academic, literary, and political writings that argue for the coexistence of the traditional and the modern do so by treating the two as discrete domains, which are then seen as being variously conjoined with each other. All of this rests on powerful, contending, visceral images of tradition and modernity. To take a few examples: in architectural forms, adobe huts versus high-rise buildings; in performance arts, folkloric rhythms versus electronic extravaganzas; in cultural spaces, India versus Europe; and, in general, always unchanging customs versus already transforming technologies. Such images and

* With assistance from Atig Ghosh.

ideas have dense worldly, or ontological, attributes.[1]

Actually, there is even more to the picture. For, in commonplace and scholarly conceptions, modernity is equally pervasively projected as the condition of *being* modern that originated in the 'West' and was then carried over to the 'rest' as their process of *becoming* modern. If modernity's lore of origins insists upon a radical break with the all that is pre-modern, such rupture is initially inaugurated in an imaginary yet palpable West. Only after this primal break is modernity framed as unfolding through time and space, spreading across worlds that are transformed in its (European) image and (Western) wake. Arguably, the end to this script, if only in some (albeit, influential) hands, is arrived at with the onset of the postmodern and postmodernity.

Needless to say, the simplicity of these story lines is seductive. Yet, the simplicities, stories, and seductions also intimately inform, although heterogeneously, the ways in which social subjects across the global live today. All of this leads to the question: what are the conditions, limitations, and possibilities of modernity—and the modern—in contemporary contexts? *Modern Makeovers* asks and addresses such questions. It especially thinks through prior, inherited understandings of modernity that are based on pre-figured, modular projections of the traditional and the modern, the non-West and the West. Indeed, the volume approaches formations of modernity as always particular yet already global, all the

while drawing on a range of South Asian experiences.

Unfolding Modernity

Scholars might readily concede today that the modern and modernity are notoriously imprecise categories, variously elaborated and bitterly debated for a long time now. Yet, modernity and the modern—and the postmodern and postmodernity—continue to be regarded in intellectual arenas chiefly as concepts, whose validity or/and invalidity derives from particular political positions or intellectual persuasions. In contrast, the present project is premised on the recognition that modernity is at once a concept and an entity, bearing profoundly worldly dimensions. It further registers that if all concepts–entities with palpable social careers must have many avatars, varying from context to context and time through time, this is especially true of modernity and the modern.

This is to say that *Modern Makeovers* is marked by twin, contrasting imperatives. On the one hand, the work registers the acute limitations of efforts to readily define, delineate, and delimit modernity by framing themselves as the last words on the subject. On the other hand, it does not take a solipsistic, unframed view of modernity as an empty placeholder that can be then strategically filled in with meaning and purpose by academics and actors unto their own ends. Together, the volume approaches and understands modernity as a contradictory and contested concept and entity—one that, in spite of having been simply celebrated by many and merely written off by others, continues to have a

---

[1] Indeed, these key considerations are acutely evident in the title of this work, an issue discussed at the end of this introduction.

curious, contending force in popular self-reckonings and distinct political agendas.

The volume, then, attempts to critically call a series of bluffs, yet all the while engaging with these ruses carefully and prudently. Our collective endeavour is sustained by the recognition that there is no monolithic condition of being modern. To begin with, not even in Europe/West. Indeed, although the discourse of modernity has been ever expressed in terms of internal coherence and inherent unity, its processes have always entailed varied and contradictory histories. Registering this fact helps in performing two simultaneous tasks. To take seriously the imperious, central claims of discourses of modernity; *and* to emphasize the mix-ups and the margins that shore up modern worlds. In these ways, the volume hopes to hold up a mirror, as it were, to the mask of modernity as a potent, pervasive saga of progress, while keeping in view the truth that provisos of progress exist among social subjects as tissues of belief, structures of sentiment, and textures of experience.

As such, *Modern Makeovers* explores the checkered routes that have characterized the ongoing processes of the making of modernity and articulations of the modern in South Asia, their past and their present. To start off, aspirations towards becoming modern and the claims of being modern have been crucial to everyday world on the subcontinent for quite sometime now. On the one hand, such resilience is linked to widespread projections of societal and political modernization. On the other hand, the desires towards becoming/being modern, understood as identity and concept, have fused together with various other indices of everyday self-reckoning, some of which are

readily palpable and others that are more imperceptible. It only follows that processes of modernity are themselves sustained by their interconnectedness with such myriad, other tropes of self-making.

The present volume tracks the processes and networks through which modern institutions and selves, the one insinuated in the other, have been enabled and expressed on the subcontinent, entailing always the meanings and practices of subjects of modernity. Here are to be found apperceptions and actions that are individual and collective. These emerge entwined with everyday arenas of, for example, medicine and religion, gender and power, education and consumption, and aesthetics and advertising. They further reveal the protean expressions of the modern—a resilient force implicated in quotidian conceptualizations of colony and culture, ideology and identity, time and space, and state and nation. In brief, the contributions all explore the everyday articulations of modernity in South Asia and beyond as densely woven into the intimate lives of the popular and the political on the subcontinent.

All of this hinges on at least three critical tasks, which are conducted on different registers in *Modern Makeovers*. First, there is the urgency of thinking through the dichotomy of the traditional and the modern and its critical implications. At the same time, to undertake the endeavour is not to simply reject the opposition as an analytical error. Instead, it is to understand the reasons for the provenance, persuasion, and persistence of the antinomy. Second, taking this step sets the stage for the volume to explore modernity as involving processes of the past and the present, shaped not only by the Western modern subject but by diverse subjects of modernity, including especially the terms of self-making of different classes and communities in India. Third and finally, the work seeks to carefully unravel the distinct textures and many hues of modernity and its experiences on the subcontinent, also at once raising critical questions concerning the plural manifestations and key contentions of the modern in South Asia.

It was suggested earlier that formations of modernity have been always global yet already particular. Unsurprisingly, *Modern Makeovers* does not mark off considerations of India from Europe, of the colony from the metropolis, and of the non-West from the West. Similarly, the work desists from simply separating the present from the past, power from culture, affect from reason, and politics from religion. Rather, this introduction and the chapters draw together these distinct domains as parts of mutual fields of exploration and explication.

It is in such (several) senses, then, that this volume draws upon yet reaches beyond—at once explicitly and implicitly—distinct departures in recent discussions of modernity. I have in mind studies that have diversely explored issues of 'colonial', 'multiple', 'alternative', and 'early' modernity/modernities.[2] I keep in view also

works focusing on different articulations of modernity as historically grounded and/or culturally expressed.[3] The point is that

---

[2] Prathama Banerjee's incisive 'Afterword' to this volume critically considers such questions, especially interrogating and extending issues of 'early' modernity. Significantly, she takes up these tasks by seizing upon the terms of the 'non-modern' (and the 'extra-modern') as well as those of the 'contemporary' (and the 'untimely'). Writings on 'colonial', 'multiple', 'early', and 'alternative' modernity/modernities include, for example, Antoinette Burton (ed.), 1999, *Gender, Sexuality, and Colonial Modernities*, London: Routledge; Saurabh Dube and Ishita Banerjee–Dube

(eds), 2005, *Unbecoming Modern: Colonialism, Modernity, Colonial Modernities*, New Delhi and New York: Social Science Press and Berghahn Books; *Daedalus*, 1998, Special issue: *Early Modernities*, vol. 127, no. 3; *Daedalus*, 2000, Special issue: *Multiple Modernities*, vol. 129, no. 1; and Dilip P. Gaonkar (ed.), 2001, *Alternative Modernities*, Durham: Duke University Press.

[3] See, for instance, Laura Bear, 2007, *Lines of the Nation: Indian Railway Workers, Bureaucracy, and the Intimate Historical Self*, New York: Columbia University Press; Amanda J. Weidman, 2006, *Singing the Classical, Voicing the Modern: The Postcolonial Politics of Music in South India*, Durham: Duke University Press; Sibylle Fischer, 2004, *Modernity Disavowed: Haiti and the Cultures of Slavery in the Age of Revolution*, Durham: Duke University Press; James Ferguson, 1999, *Expectations of Modernity: Myths and Meanings of Urban Life on the Zambian Copperbelt*, Berkeley: University of California Press; Charles Piot, 1999, *Remotely Global: Village Modernity in West Africa*, Chicago: University of Chicago Press; Lisa Rofel, 1998, *Other Modernities: Gendered Yearnings in China after Socialism*, Berkeley: University of California Press; Harry Harootunian, 2000, *Overcome by Modernity: History, Culture, and Community in Interwar Japan*, Princeton: Princeton University Press; Donald Donham, 1999, *Marxist Modern: An Ethnographic History of the Ethiopian Revolution*, Berkeley: University of California Press; John Comaroff and Jean Comaroff, 1997, *Of Revelation and Revolution: The Dialectics of Modernity on the South African Frontier, Vol. 2*, Chicago: University of Chicago Press; Paul Gilroy, 1995, *Black Atlantic: Modernity and Double-Consciousness*, Cambridge, MA: Harvard University Press; Saurabh Dube (ed.), 2010, *Enchantments of Modernity: Empire, Nation, Globalization*, London: Routledge; Saurabh Dube, 2004, *Stitches on Time: Colonial Textures and Postcolonial Tangles*, Durham: Duke University Press; Sanjay Seth, 2007, *Subject Lessons: The Western Education of Colonial India*, Durham: Duke University Press; and Timothy Mitchell (ed.), 2000, *Questions of Modernity*, Minneapolis: University of Minnesota Press. See also, Anand Pandian, 2009, *Crooked Stalks: Cultivating Virtue in South India*, Durham: Duke University

Modern Makeovers engages and extends such concerns in its own manner. To begin with, the work approaches the multiple articulations of modernity by registering contingency and contradiction and contention and contestation as inhabiting the checkered core of modern worlds. Moreover, the terms, textures, and transformations of modernity—and the modern—each appear in this volume as marked by power as well as difference, authority as well as alterity, and the dominant as well as the subaltern. Finally, such scholarly procedures stay with the specific articulations of modernity yet all the while attending to their key implications,

Press; Anupama Rao, 2009, *The Caste Question: Dalits and the Politics of Modern India*, Berkeley: University of California Press; Ajantha Subramanian, 2009, *Shorelines: Spaces and Rights in South Asia*, Stanford: Stanford University Press; Véronique Bénéï, 2008, *Schooling Passions: Nation, History, and Language in Contemporary Western India*, Stanford: Stanford University Press; Simon During, 2004, *Modern Enchantments: The Cultural Power of Secular Magic*, Cambridge, MA: Harvard University Press; Birgit Meyer and Peter Pels (eds), 2003, *Magic and Modernity: Interfaces of Revelation and Concealment*, Stanford: Stanford University Press; Alex Owen, 2004, *The Place of Enchantment: British Occultism and the Culture of the Modern*, Chicago: University of Chicago Press; Michael Saler, 2006, 'Modernity and Enchantment: A Historiographic Review', *American Historical Review*, vol. 111, no. 3, pp. 692–716; Dipesh Chakrabarty, 2000, *Provincializing Europe: Postcolonial Thought and Historical Difference*, Princeton: Princeton University Press; Ritu Birla, 2009, *Stages of Capital: Law, Culture, and Market Governance in Late Colonial India*, Durham: Duke University Press; Dipesh Chakrabarty, 2002, *Habitations of Modernity: Essays in the Wake of Subaltern Studies*, Chicago: University of Chicago Press; Arjun Appadurai, 1996, *Modernity at Large: Cultural Dimensions of Globalization*, Minneapolis: University of Minnesota Press; and Vasant Kaiwar and Sucheta Majumdar (eds), 2003, *Antinomies of Modernity: Essays on Race, Orient, Nation*, Durham: Duke University Press.

reifying neither the one nor the other, but critically considering their everyday expressions and quotidian configurations—as enacted on the ground. Needless to say, such dispositions towards modernity shall be clarified in the pages ahead.

Unravelling Modernity

Not so long ago, two historical anthropologists wrote that, 'Perhaps the greatest virtue of the recent Western scholarly preoccupation with "postmodernity" is what it has revealed about "modernity" itself'.[4] Yet, even as they authored this assessment, Jean and John Comaroff were possibly getting ahead of themselves. For, in the two decades that have followed their diagnosis, there have been even wider, rather different, critical considerations of modernity. It is not only that a variety of scholarship has accessed yet exceeded the impact and influence of the linguistic turn and postmodern preoccupations in the social sciences. It is also that questions of modernity have been approached and unravelled as part of the careful querying of the categories and entities that are presupposed by distinct but typical ways of acting and understanding in contemporary worlds. Together, as Akeel Bilgrami has argued, 'the extensive debate in many related disciplines over the last few decades', turning on inherited ideas and ideologies, form part of 'our intellectual efforts at self-understanding—in particular, our efforts to come to a more or less precise

[4] Jean Comaroff and John Comaroff, 1993, 'Introduction', in Jean Comaroff and John Comaroff (eds), *Modernity and Its Malcontents: Ritual and Power in Postcolonial Africa*, Chicago: University of Chicago Press, p. xi.

grip on the sense in which we belong to a period, properly describable as our "modernity"".[5]

All this has meant that questions of modernity have increasingly escaped the limits of (purely) discursive derivation, scholarly formalism, and a priori abstraction.[6] Underscored instead has been the fact that if modernity acutely entails idea, ideal, and ideology, it equally involves the articulation of distinct historical processes over the last few centuries. Indeed, there has been keen recognition of the divergent expressions of modernity and contending intimations of the modern—shaped by particular pasts, defined by projects of power, and molded by provisos of progress. As a result, formations of modernity have been themselves revealed as contradictory and contingent processes of culture and control, as checkered and contested histories of meaning and mastery—in their constitution, sedimentation, and elaboration. On the one hand, it is within such contingency and contradiction that modernity's constitutive hierarchies and formative oppositions are framed and elaborated. On the other hand, these processes are not subject-less procedures, and emerge instead as expressed by subjects of modernity—and not only

modern subjects—that are non-Western and Western. I shall soon return to these questions.

For the moment, it is worth staying somewhat longer with the ambiguities that surround the concept–entity of modernity. In no small measure, the haziness derives from the manner in which modernity is often elided with modernization (and at other times, folded into modernism). As is generally known, the notion of modernization, as expressed by its different theorists/theories, refers to modular projections of material, organizational, and technological—as well as economic, political, and cultural—transformation(s), principally envisioned in the looking glass of Western development. Here, different, often hierarchically ordered, societies are seen as succeeding (or failing) to evolve from their traditional (or pre-modern) states through linear stages of succession to become modernized (or capitalist) arenas.[7] Now, the simplistic, step-by-step schemas and the reductively totalizing templates of modernization theories have always been far too tendentious.[8] And so, too, have they been decisively questioned and firmly rejected by critical scholarship for some time now. Yet, motifs of modernization have also

[5] Akeel Bilgrami, 2008, 'Occidentalism, the Very Idea: An Essay on the Enlightenment and Enchantment'. Available at http://3quarksdaily.blogs.com/3quarksdaily/2008/09/occidentalism-t.html (Last accessed on 19 November 2010).

[6] For a wider discussion of the ideas discussed in this paragraph, see Saurabh Dube, 2010, 'Critical Crossovers: Cultural Identities, Postcolonial Perspectives, and Subaltern Studies', in Margaret Wetherell and Chandra Talpade Mohanty (eds), *The Sage Handbook of Identities*, London: Sage Publications, pp. 136–7.

[7] Here, especially influential statements included, W.W. Rostow, 1960, *The Stages of Economic Growth: A Non-Communist Manifesto*, Cambridge: Cambridge University Press; David E. Apter, 1965, *The Politics of Modernization*, Chicago: University of Chicago Press.

[8] I acknowledge that reassessments of modernization have emphasized the place of 'tradition' in elaborations of 'development', for example. But such understandings continue to be based on the enduring oppositions—and teleological templates—of discourses of modernity.

crucially carried wide resonance, easily elided with mappings of modernity, such that each shores up the other.

Why should this be the case? To begin with, as was noted earlier, a crucial characteristic of dominant discourses of Western modernity has hinged on their positing of the phenomena as marked by a break with the past, a rupture with tradition, a surpassing of the medieval. Of course, there have been dense histories and contradictory claims at stake here, entailing contending strains of the Enlightenment, counter-Enlightenment, and post-Enlightenment traditions, all issues that I have discovered elsewhere.[9] At the same time, it is also the case that by the second half of the nineteenth century—through projections and ruses of teleological historical progress, stages of civilization, and social evolutionist schemas—an exclusive West gradually became the looking glass for the imagining of universal history. As worldly knowledge, oriented not merely towards ordering but simultaneously remaking the world, these neat proposals and their formative presumptions entered the lives of historical subjects—formidably disseminated as ways of approaching and modes of apprehending social worlds, they have appeared equally instituted as tissues of affect and textures of experience within everyday arenas. In this

scenario, the blueprints of modernization actually distilled the designs of modernity, the aggressive assumption of the latter holding in place the schematic prognosis of the former. Taken together, modernity's discourses and modernization theories, inextricably entwined, the one with the other, have articulated an imaginary but palpable, distended and aggrandizing West/Europe as history, modernity, and destiny—for each society, culture, and people.

Yet, there is more to the picture. Beyond routine representations, in artistic, intellectual, and aesthetic arenas, each understood broadly, modernity has often appeared in intimate association with its cognate (or conceptual cousin), modernism. Now, modernism is also an enormously contentious term that necessarily follows from the contested and contradictory character of the tendencies it describes. Here are to be found cultural movements, styles, and representations, going back to the mid-nineteenth century and extending into our own times, which have been diversely expressed and performed in different parts of the world. Following Theodor Adorno, modernism has been a principally 'qualitative' rather than a merely 'chronological' category:[10] but it is also the case that the internal endeavours within modernisms to surpass the past, articulate the present, and envision the future have been intrinsically heterogeneous ones. They have variously engaged and interrogated, accessed and exceeded Enlightenment thought and romantic tradition, abstract reason and religious truth, surface coherence and tonal

[9] Saurabh Dube, 2007, 'Anthropology, History, Historical Anthropology', in Saurabh Dube (ed.), *Historical Anthropology*, New Delhi: Oxford University Press, particularly pp. 6–7. I have discussed the complex pasts (in European intellectual history) of the term 'modern' and their easy yielding to the category 'modernity' (concerning Third World contexts) in Saurabh Dube, 2010, *After Conversion: Cultural Histories of Modern India*, New Delhi: Yoda Press, pp. 15–17.

[10] Theodor Adorno, 2005, *Minima Moralia*, London: Verso, p. 218.

depth, Western representations and pre-colonial narratives, the certainties of science and the presence of god, and governmental authority and popular politics.[11]

On the one hand, from Charles Baudelaire's avowal of the 'transitory' and the 'fleeting' through to modernist rejections of realism and replication in favour of discontinuity and disruption, and from Ezra Pound's invitation to art to 'make new' through to the many manifestations of modernisms flowing from the mid-twentieth century (and before), a key characteristic of these cultural tendencies has been to emphasize the difference of the contemporary present from past epochs. On the other hand, as Peter Childs has argued, modernism has always involved 'paradoxical if not opposed trends towards revolutionary and reactionary positions, fear of the new and delight at the disappearance of the old, nihilism and fanatical enthusiasm, creativity and despair'.[12] Now, to hold together the discourses of modernity and the articulations of modernism is not only to trace the distinct yet interleaving ways in which they each offer a cessation and overcoming of the past. It is also to register that the constitutive contradictions and contentions of modernism(s) can hold a mirror up to connected characteristics and contingencies

of that acutely universal of authoritative universals—modernity.

To approach the entanglements between modernity, modernism, and modernization in this manner, where the one is not simply folded into the other yet their mutual linkages are adequately acknowledged, might have critical consequences. Building on my own prior proposals, modernity is now understood not only as a forceful idea and ideology but as also entailing heterogeneous histories and plural processes.[13] These imaginings and procedures extend back to the last five centuries and interlock in critical ways, such that both models of modernization and movements of modernism appear as crucial components yet small parts in the broader articulation of modernity. There are at least two faces to the phenomena, each insinuated in the other.

On the one hand, as part of a familiar picture, constitutive of modernity are processes of reason and science, industry and technology, commerce and consumption, nation-state and citizen-subject, public spheres and private spaces, and secularized religion(s) and disenchanted knowledge(s). It warrants emphasis that vigilance is required regarding the endless unfolding of these developments as heroic histories. Indeed, instead of teleological tales of the march of modernization/modernity, such stories require being unravelled as rather more checkered narratives, even as models of modernization are registered as part of the protocols of modernity. On the other hand, although this is often overlooked, at the core

---

[11] A parallel here is the manner in which opposed tendencies of modern knowledge—defined as those of rationalism and historicism, of the analytical and the hermeneutical, and of the progressivist and the romantic—can frequently combine in intellectual practice, leading to contradictions and contentions and ambivalences and excesses. Dube, 'Anthropology, History, Historical Anthropology', pp. 10–15; see also, Dube, *After Conversion*.

[12] Peter Childs, 2000, *Modernism: The New Cultural Idiom*, New York: Routledge, p. 17.

[13] See, for example, Dube, *Stitches on Time*; Dube, *After Conversion*; and Dube (ed.), *Enchantments of Modernity*.

of modernity are also processes of empires and colonies, race and genocide, resurgent faiths and reified traditions, disciplinary regimes and subaltern subjects, and seductions of the state and enchantments of the modern. Lessons learned from the split, Janus-faced nature of modernism assume salience here. This is to say that even as modernity has been ceaselessly portrayed as embodying a singular, seamless trajectory, its principal procedures have been contradictory, contingent, and contested—protocols that are incessantly articulated yet also critically out of joint with themselves.[14]

It is precisely these procedures that emerge expressed by subjects of modernity. Here, my reference is to historical actors who have been active participants in processes of modernity: social actors who have been both *subject to* these processes but also *subjects shaping* these processes. Over the past few centuries, the subjects of modernity have included, to take just a few instances, peasants, artisans, and workers in South Asia that have diversely articulated processes of colony and post-colony; indigenous communities in the Americas under colonial and national rule; peoples of African descent not only on that continent but in different diasporas across the world; and, indeed, subaltern, marginal, and elite women and men in non-Western and Western theatres. Unsurprisingly, these subjects have registered within their measures and meanings the formative contradictions, contentions, and contingencies of modernity.[15]

All of this is to emphasize, too, the importance of affect and subjectivity—long privileged within modernism(s)—in explorations of modernity. Yet, it is to do so while refusing to approach affect(s) as the repressed other of the modern as well as eschewing an understanding of subject(s) as sovereign selves.[16] Needless to say, such measures are salient for unravelling the procedures of modernity. First, it is well known that conceptions of modernity generally proceed by envisioning the phenomenon in the image of the European and Euro-American (frequently, implicitly, male) modern subject.[17] On the contrary, I am indicating the inadequacy of conflating *the modern subject* with the *subject of modernity*. Is it perhaps the case then that my articulation of subjects of modernity productively widens the range of address of modernity and its participants? Moreover, mine is not a chronological claim that everyone living in the modern age counts as a modern subject. For, subjects of modernity have revealed, again and again, that there are different ways of being modern, now accessing and now exceeding the stipulations of the Western modern subject. Yet, all too often, in fashioning themselves, subjects of modernity have also barely bothered about the Western modern subject exactly while articulating the enduring terms of modernity. What are the implications of such recognition for weaving in distinct textures and transformations of affects and

---

[14] Dube, *Stitches on Time*, particularly p. 11.
[15] Dube, 'Modernity and Its Enchantments: An Introduction', in Dube (ed.), *Enchantments of Modernity*, pp. 1–43.

[16] On issues of affect, I have found illuminating William Mazarella, 2010, 'Affect: What Is It Good For?' in Dube (ed.), *Enchantments of Modernity*, pp. 291–309.
[17] I am developing here ideas that were first initiated in Dube, *Stitches on Time*.

subjectivities—including inherently plural experiences, articulations, and elaborations of time, space, and their enmeshments—in considerations of modernity? Finally, it bears emphasis that there are other modern subjects besides Western ones, embodying formidable heterogeneity. Does this not suggest the need in discussions of modernity to rethink exclusive images of the modern subject, both in non-Western arenas and in Western ones?[18]

At any rate, I hope it is clear that the dispositions to modernity that I am outlining do not claim to comprehensively define this category, entity, and process. Rather, my bid is to open up spaces and suggest resources for discussing procedures of modernity and their many persuasions. This sets the stage for the sections that follow, which foreground contemporary shifts in the humanities and social sciences in considerations of the modern, modernism, and modernity.

Imperial Implications

All too often, the ideas–entities of modernity and colonialism as well as those of Enlightenment and empire can appear as opposed elements. Here, if colonial domination in distant territories is seen as frequently representing the endless omission of the humanitarian potential of metropolitan modernity, so, too, does the exact image of empire usually appear as intimating innate anathema to an immaculate idea of the Enlightenment. At the same time, recent years have

seen wide-ranging discussions that have opened up imaginative issues turning on an intriguing interplay between the Enlightenment and empire and a far-reaching dynamic between modernity and colonialism.[19] The chapters in the first section of this volume extend such concerns in specific ways, in their own manner. On the one hand, they cast a new light on the linkages between empire and nation, the metropolis and the margins, the colony and the post-colony. On the other hand, they acutely unravel the unfamiliar implications of an imperial modernity and the critical contentions of a colonial modern.

Opening our deliberations, Mrinalini Sinha focuses on the powerful notion of *civis Britannicus* or British subjecthood, in order to query familiar projections of the linear trajectory of the nation-state. Here is a history that apparently extends uninterruptedly from the Treaty of Westphalia in 1648 to the United Nations' sanction of an inter-*national* order after World War II. Arguing that in its more politicized forms, civis Britannicus stood for imperial citizenship, Sinha shows that in the pre-World War II scenario, there were a number of multinational and supranational polities that rivalled the nation-state. Here, people often articulated their claims in terms of imperial identity—including the freedom of movement across all territories 'where the Union Jack is flying'—and transgressed thereby exclusively national identifications. In this context, resting upon the vast spread of the British Empire, civis Britannicus was

---

[18] These various modern subjects in the West and the non-West are also subjects of modernity. But, once more, not all subjects of modernity are modern subjects, of course.

[19] The literature here is vast. For two discussions of these questions see, Dube, 'Critical Crossovers'; and Dube and Banerjee–Dube (eds), *Unbecoming Modern*.

one, singular, compelling basis for staking political claims of a non-national character. There were two dimensions to such processes: on the one hand, there were to be found expansive political aspirations towards supranational British subjecthood; and on the other hand, lay the innate difficulty and the subsequent refusal of the British government to fulfil such aspirations of its subjects. Unsurprisingly, the claims of civis Britannicus as an empire-encompassing ideal of British citizenship foundered on the shoals of imperial *realpolitik*.

Significantly, in Sinha's hands, anti-colonial nationalism does not appear as an inherently coherent, inexorable, step-by-step movement towards the demand and achievement of national independence. It is unravelled instead as characterized by rather more checkered pasts, as imbued with contradictory histories. Indeed, claims to imperial subjecthood were frequently made in apparent infringement of the conventionally construed nationalist trajectory, at once political and legal, of the anti-colonial movement. As such, 'national independence in the colonial world may have as much to do with the demands of anti-colonial struggles themselves as with the imperial deflection of these demands onto the safer confines of the national–territorial space'.

Bodhisattva Kar takes forward such concerns of the intricate interplay between empire and nation in distinct ways, especially by extending these to the influence that the colonial casts on the postcolonial. His chapter opens with the forgotten history of Bengali racism that crucially unravelled during the (imperial) partition of Bengal in 1905 and the (nationalist) Swadeshi

movement that ensued in its wake. Put simply, the Bengali *bhadralok* (middle- and upper-classes–castes) were horrified to have been clubbed with the 'primitive' Assamese population in the eastern division of India. Here, paranoid pleas to the colonial state were articulated in terms of the sheer impossibility of a fit between the civilized, modern culture of the Bengali 'self' and the uncivilized, pre-modern barbarism of the Assamese 'other'.

This sets the stage for Kar to focus on the province of Assam and its claims to a national identity. In the region, Jawaharlal Nehru's exhortations to set aside particular provincial problems and to think in terms of national independence were severely challenged by various publicists and politicians. For example, Jnananath Bora argued that the putatively provincial problems evoked by Nehru were actually national issues for the Assamese population. Indeed, Assam had not formed part of India before colonialism. Until imperial rule, the population had thought of their land(s) as *des* (country/nation) rather than *prades* (province). In the context of this discussion, Kar poses the key question: can the postcolonial begin? In response, he construes a narrative around the inevitably hierarchical time of the Indian national, arguing that:

The earliest entrant into the imperial order is logically more modern than the belated. It is only by accepting the autobiographical time of capital which enables it to describe itself as a coherent, self-sufficient, and universal project that the nation can insert itself into *le domaine moderne* [the domain of modern], and insofar as it remains committed to capital's schemes of improvement, anachronistic spaces remain its vital condition of possibility.

This is to say that modern nation building is irredeemably embroiled in the identification of 'anachronistic spaces', especially of the provincial. The provincial, in its turn, articulates itself in terms of a national sensibility and thereby identifies its particular provincials, its own anachronistic spaces. Indeed, all attempts to apparently 'deprovincialize' political entities and identities are actually articulated in terms of becoming a nation. Unsurprisingly, at the other end of the spectrum, the nation comes to approximate its 'mythical other', namely, the prior empire. Indeed, the colonial territorial order lodges itself firmly at the core of the national spatial formation. If this serves to innately defer the commencement of the postcolonial, it equally underscores the centrality of anachronistic identifications to a national (or, nationalist) modernity.

Next, Rohan Deb Roy cycles back to the imperial order, narrating the pasts of a pathological symbiosis of drug and disease in order to imaginatively explore the intricate interleaving of medicine, 'malaria', and modernity. A common sense discursive etiology would hold that malaria in nineteenth-century Bengal was a diagnostic meta category that found its therapy in the mega-drug quinine. However, Deb Roy reverses this presupposition arguing instead that the promotion of quinine as a panacea for malaria engendered nothing less than the disease itself. This came about through two simultaneous, interwoven processes. First, governmental discourses drew together an absurdly wide range of symptoms—from 'daily bodily niggles' to cardiovascular arrests—spread over a vast geography under the singular sign of malarial affliction.

Second, precisely such endeavours called forth massive investments in information gathering and pathological prosopography. At the core of Deb Roy's layered narrative are these twin processes, revealing the manner in which imperial governmental exercises were not only organized and executed but impeded and subverted by a plethora of untamable data and hardheaded 'native' attitudes.

Yet Deb Roy's chapter does more, too, focusing on distinct detractors of this dominant epidemiology, which implicitly links his arguments with wider considerations of 'tensions of empire' that were constitutive of colonialism, modernity, and colonial modernities. On the one hand, both within and outside the spaces of 'scientific' discipline and institutions of colonial medicine, there existed a range of protagonists who plied 'alternative' medical practices, discourses, and trades, which disregarded the dominant epidemiological alarmism. On the other hand, there were to be found *within* the official medical establishment, insider–participants who dismissed the malaria mania as a medical overreaction and as an obstruction to the advancement of scientific knowledge. And so, modern medical knowledge itself unravelled haltingly—often along multiple, counterintuitive trajectories—presenting parallels with the progress of the dreaded disease, malaria.

Atig Ghosh also focuses on eastern India yet unto distinct purposes. He tracks the life and career of the relatively unfamiliar figure of 'Kangal' Harinath Majumdar. In the first phase of his life, Harinath was the editor of *Grambartaprokashika*, a popular newspaper of the mid-nineteenth century Bengali *mofussil*. Once the newspaper folded due to zamindar opposition and financial difficulty, Harinath turned to the life of a mystic, peripatetic songster—a *baul* as he sometimes called himself. In innovatively drawing together the two lives of 'Kangal' Harinath into a mutual field of analysis, Ghosh develops twin trajectories of argument.

To begin with, the chapter considers the constitution of the category of the baul, especially through the energies and interventions of Harinath. Prior to this curious character, the notion of the baul was conceptually fuzzy. His activities made the category substantive, even solid. And then, the legendary Rabindranath Tagore and the famous Ksitimohan Sen turned the baul into the romanticized image which is still popular in Bengal (and across the world) today. At the same time, working through these materials, Ghosh queries the notion of a colonial modernity. Against the grain of typologies of a 'Bengali colonial modern'—offered, notably, by Dipesh Chakrabarty—the chapter suggests distinct ways of engaging and exceeding the notion, a concept that can be valuable in other respects. Specifically, according to Ghosh, rather than proceeding from a preconceived idea of a colonial modern, it is more productive to think of Kangal Harinath's life without such a 'guarantee'. To take such a step is to articulate the protocols of a 'history without warranty', which unravels the subtle textures of Harinath's historical situation and his varied terms of self-articulation, without subsuming these under the sign of an a priori and totalizing narrative of the (Bengali) colonial modern.

Probing Politics

Imaginations and articulations of modernity have been irreducibly political. Over the past 500 years, these politics have variously turned on issues of (the nature of) the human and the individual, of selves and others, of order and truth, of reason and progress, of the private and the public, of freedom and equality, of the secular and the religious, of rights and governance, and of the economy and the universal. Reaching far beyond ready consensus, it is actually contention, critique, and contradiction that have, from the beginning, characterized each of these attributes of politics under modernity. Registering the contentious characteristics of these terrains, recent writing has critically engaged modern social imaginaries, querying their constitutive presumptions yet also affirming intellectual and political possibilities in the wake of such questioning.[20] The chapters in the section on politics severally build on such impulses

---

[20] Once more, the literature on these issues is enormous. For a few representative studies from distinct spectrums see, for instance, Wendy Brown, 2001, *Politics Out of History*, Princeton: Princeton University Press; John Gray, 2000, *Two Faces of Liberalism*, New York: The New Press; Stephen K. White, 2000, *Sustaining Affirmation: The Strengths of Weak Ontology in Political Theory*, Princeton: Princeton University Press; and David Scott, 2005, *Conscripts of Modernity: The Tragedy of Colonial Enlightenment*, Durham: Duke University Press. See also, Ian Baucom, 2005, *Specters of the Atlantic: Finance Capital, Slavery, and the Philosophy of History*, Durham: Duke University Press; David Scott, 1999, *Refashioning Futures: Criticism after Postcoloniality*, Princeton: Princeton University Press; and Charles Taylor, 2007, *A Secular Age*, Cambridge, MA: The Belknap Press of Harvard University Press.

towards interrogation and affirmation. They think through the terms of the individual and community, equivalence and exception, faith and reason, religious politics and secular principles, liberal politics and global Islam, fragmentation of power and democratization of authority, heresy and orthodoxy, and popular practices and institutional identities.

In the first chapter of this section, Anupama Rao forcefully foregrounds the figure of the Dalit as the subject who inaugurates India's political modernity. She does this by traversing the textures and tangles of the political thought and social activism of Bhimrao Ramji Ambedkar. As is generally known, before 1947, Ambedkar's political efforts concentrated on constituting the Dalits into a minority community that was on par with the Muslims, a response to the colonial understanding of communities as constituencies. Once fabricated into a minority community, the Dalits could then lay claim to being a political constituency in order to demand representation. These twin procedures of, first, constituting the Dalits as a minority community and then, investing the freshly fangled collectivity with political representation engendered a dual difficulty for Ambedkar.

On the one hand, the raising of the Dalits to the status of a minority community—on par with the Muslims—obviously opened up Ambedkar to the charge of fomenting separatism, as adding to the already existing Hindu–Muslim divide. He was concerned about this situation since separatism was not a viable political option for the Dalits, whose members were dispersed all over South Asia, unlike the concentration of Muslims in particular regions. On the other hand, a second more critical charge levelled against

Ambedkar, especially by M.K. Gandhi, turned on the following questions: if the Dalits were a degraded and underprivileged people, what was the political rationality behind constituting them as a minority community and granting them separate representation, especially since such an act could only reify their abject reality? Should not the right-minded, ethical strategy be directed, then, at ameliorating, overcoming, and surpassing their social debility and wretchedness?

Now, Ambedkar had theorized his 'minority community' as a historically debased, abused, and severely underprivileged section of society and polity in India. He had not only presented the caste order as a form of involution of class division, but had equally described untouchability as the central cohesive principle of caste society, suggesting that the shared hatred of the untouchable was the sole ground for the unity of otherwise antagonistic castes. This formulation imbued the untouchables with concreteness as a community and yet, conceived of them as a negative principle of the caste order. But could such a negatively construed community of suffering have political value? Did not their precise lack make the Dalits invisible, even as human beings, to the powers that be? According to Ambedkar, the situation could be rectified only by claiming a universal right to politics. Yet, his strident demands for political representation for Dalits required that such representation was *equal* as well as *separate*. It was in this way that Ambedkar braided together the conventional liberal logic of *equivalence* with a countervailing logic of *exception* on grounds of the Dalits' historical debasement.

Deftly weaving her way through Ambedkar's negotiation of the charges and challenges he faced, Rao persuasively presents the wider implications of the Dalit leader's endeavour to confer political value on his community. Put briefly, through his simultaneous recourse to the logics of equivalence and exception, Ambedkar exposed the 'animating fiction' of Euro-American political liberalism, of the universality of the individual rights-bearing subject as the elemental unit of politics.

Appropriately enough, in *Modern Makeovers*, the discussion of B.R. Ambedkar's politics is followed by an exploration of M.K. Gandhi's religion. Here, a putative puzzle provides the point of entry for Ajay Skaria's chapter. Throughout his political career, Gandhi had insisted that there could be 'no politics without religion'. Yet, towards the late 1940s, we find that Gandhi came to advocate the separation of state and religion. It is easy to map this change in orientation onto the political developments in the subcontinent and explain Gandhi's later position in relation to the religious violence and communal riots that preceded, accompanied, and followed the Partition. At the same time, Skaria suggests that such simultaneous insistence on religious politics and secular principles was not contradictory. To grasp such entwinement, he insists, we must engage with what may be termed Gandhi's religion.

For Gandhi, the 'secular concept of the human' is built upon a fundamental attribute of modern civilization, namely, to produce and live by rational, iterable truths. Within this definitional framework, modern civilization morally permits extreme violence to be carried out on distinct species as well as on other human beings, once the latter are found to contradict freedom and equality of humanity and, therefore, as being irrational. As such, 'even where secular traditions extend an abstract equality to the other, this abstract equality is always undercut by the insistence that full equality requires the exercise of reason'. Gandhi countered such hollow claims of equality that lay at the core of modern secular civilization with another conception. His was a distinct notion of equality, one that was inseparable from religion. Indeed, for Gandhi, equality could be properly conceptualized only religiously. Skaria terms this attempt at a novel reworking of the concept of equality as Gandhi's 'religious secularism', so that 'what Gandhi ventures in *Hind Swaraj* and elsewhere, is nothing less than another concept of religion itself, where religion names the practice of finitude. This finitude enables a very different equality, what might be called an immeasurable equality.'

In Skaria's incisive, imaginative, and intriguing analysis, the 'finitude' or limit (*hadh*) that Gandhi talks of is intimately related to absolute faith: the faith as 'an acknowledgement of the way that human agency is limited and can always be overcome by "acts of God"'. At the same time, such faith, although absolute, is marked by deep humility. It is constituted by—as well as itself constitutes—a singular relation to god, one that refuses to make epistemological and ontological claims. This is because such an epistemological and ontological grounding of faith would produce belligerent 'truths', further, inexorably, leading to feuds with other 'truths' of a similar provenance. Thus, in Gandhi's schema, the finitude of faith enables a singularity that is sustained by the limit, even as such singularity engenders equality. Gandhi does not jettison 'reason'. Far from it, he assiduously sustains reason, but to crucially refigure the relation between faith and reason. For Gandhi, 'faith begins where reason fails. That is to say, faith is beyond reason.' Reason must be sanctified by faith. Such is the task of an ethical religious politics, inserted into our contemporary horizons, in order to rethink the nature of modernity.

Faisal Devji explores related questions on different registers. He interrogates the a priori association between Islamic endeavours and fundamentalist politics, highlighting the tensions and limits of liberal politics. Devji argues that the founding principles of the nation-state and political liberalism have to do with a project of superseding religion. Yet, this brand of liberal nationalism—or, nationalist liberalism—appears marked by a curious understanding of principles such as tolerance, innate to liberal politics. Only those subjects are to be tolerated who were tolerant themselves. This is to say that the nation-state will tolerate only such minorities as are already, always tolerant of the national majority and its majoritarian social–legal directives. Thus, the liberal state expects a minority people to be perfectly tolerant even in front of provocations and insults to their faith. Here, Devji focuses on two contemporary events and a crucial text. The events are the global protests of Muslim peoples against the *Satanic Verses* by Salman Rushdie in 1989 and similar protests against the publication of caricatures of Prophet Muhammad in the Danish newspaper, *Jyllands-Posten*, in 2005. The text in turn is Ayatollah Khomeini's *Wasiyyat Namah*. Through the discussion, Devji reveals the

upstaging of familiar liberal assumption. To begin with, in the controversies in question, the protests employed a vocabulary not of religious fundamentalism but of political liberalism. They also assumed global dimensions. In both the *Satanic Verses* and the *Jyllands-Posten* affairs, the nation-state found itself outmanoeuvered: ahead of the global orchestration of Muslim dissent, it failed in its attempt to bully the national minority. Indeed, confronted by a Muslim citizenry *sans frontières*, it was paradoxically the nation-state that found itself pushed into the role of a minority.

Such emergence of a global citizenry of Muslims is intimately linked to processes of the world going global. Evocatively, Devji identifies this global moment with signal historical events of Neil Armstrong landing on the moon and the addition of nuclear weapons to the global arsenal. Under the peril of the potential abandonment of the planet and a nuclear holocaust, humanity came to be united in an unprecedented way through the shared global fear of total annihilation. This doomsday gloom oversaw the weakening of national boundaries, since the nation-states as narrowly circumscribed political entities could no longer be effective guarantors against a global apocalypse. Unsurprisingly, the prevalent apocalyptic mood invigorated world religions such as Islam. Islam's globalization was possible 'because it is anchored neither in an institutionalized religious authority like a church, nor in an institutionalized political authority like a state. Indeed, it is the continuing fragmentation and thus the democratization of authority in the world of Islam that might account for the militancy of its globalization.' Even more significantly, the demonstrations discussed by Devji were not so much about raising the clarion call of 'Islam in Danger' as they formidably expressed a sentiment of hurt, a sense of violation of liberal values. In fact, both the events sought to portray Muhammad not so much as the Prophet of Islam but as a world citizen and a family man whose civil propriety had been deliberately outraged. The demonstrations were democratic and legal in nature, using rhetoric drawn from pervasive idioms of political liberalism. At the same time, in situating such liberal categories of democracy and civil society in a global rather than a national context, the protests also extended and invested them with a universality that liberalism itself has aspired towards yet failed to accomplish. It followed that the conventional custodian of political liberalism, the nation-state, was challenged by its own liberal language, which was now articulated much more powerfully. Put differently, through the worldwide protests of a global Islam, liberal politics and the nation-state were being queried and confronted not by their pasts but by their futures.

In the following chapter, Ian Bedford puts a distinct spin on questions of a national modernity, drawing on materials from politics and society in modern Pakistan. He argues that following the dismemberment of the Ottoman Empire after World War I and the subsequent emergence of Turkey as a modern secular nation-state, the achievements of Mustafa Kemal 'Ataturk' became something of a 'model' to be emulated by Islamic states everywhere. At the same time, Bedford suggests that the secularization of Islamic national identity was accompanied under

Ataturk by an alternative emphasis on ethnic identity, such that Islam was replaced by a newfound pride in 'Turkish-ness' as part of a vigorous nation-building project. Against this background, the chapter turns to the ironies and ambivalences of politics in Pakistan. Here, the governments of General Ayub Khan as well as his democratically elected successor, Zulfikar Ali Bhutto, appear to approximate the Ataturk model, with both rulers promoting versions of secularism, albeit tepidly. In contrast, the regime of General Zia-ul-Haq seems to run counter to the model, especially since orthodox Sunni Islam received a shot in the arm under his governance. But Bedford proposes that such assumptions need to be rethought by approaching the Ataturk model as constituted both by attributes of secular dynamics as well as aspects of ethnic reconstitution.

It is well known that General Zia captured state power through a military coup in 1977. Exactly a year later, the Shah of Iran was deposed in a 'revolution' spearheaded by Ayatollah Khomeini. As such, General Zia foresaw the necessity to appease the hard-line *Ulama* and create a support base for himself among the minority orthodox faction in Pakistan, providing the latter with a long-awaited opportunity. Now, in religious belief, Pakistan was overwhelmingly represented by 'syncretic' Sufi-style modes of practice as well as a sizeable following of the Shia creed—a matrix of Islamic practices that Bedford calls 'popular Islam'. In this scenario, General Zia's initiative allowed the Sunni conservatives to challenge popular Islam as heretical, indeed Indian, and replace it with a new, orthodox state identity. General Zia did not wilfully rework the religious sociology of his country. Yet, this is what came to pass as Zia unleashed forces that he could not control thereafter. And so, in Pakistan, one Islam replaced another Islam: a brand of orthodox hard-line faith substituting amorphous forms of popular Muslim practice. Instead of a newfound ethnic pride in being Pakistani, a more rigid, conservative recasting of the already-existing basis of popular identity inaugurated the modern state in Pakistan. This is the irony underling the contemporary Pakistani state that we know today.

Critical Cultures

Alongside implications of politics, stipulations of culture have been critical to delineations of modernity. To begin with, spatial mappings and temporal measurements of the West and the non-West have rested on a trajectory of time and an axis of culture, the one entwined with the other, a matrix that claims to be normatively neutral but which is, in fact, profoundly hierarchical. Here, it is not only that the notion of modernity as a rupture with the past carves up social and historical worlds into the traditional and the modern, further objectifying other oppositions such as those between ritual and rationality, myth and history, and magic and modernity. It is also that the precise processes through which these oppositions are made ontological, or worldly ones, produces hierarchies of otherness: from varieties of savages, barbarians, and primitives, through to stages of civilization that yet lacked the key foundations of reason, and onwards thence to the mature state and rational stage of European modernity, representing the pinnacle of culture, the goals of time, and the ends of history.[21]

Unsurprisingly, scholarly disciplines—and their precise divisions—have played an important role in such procedures: for example, the implications of the social sciences in governmental rationalities; the coupling of history writing with the modern nation; and the central place of the 'savage slot' and the 'native niche' in elaborations of anthropology.[22] At the same time, the histories of these disciplines have not only been contradictory but also contested ones, shaped by the braiding of the analytical with the hermeneutic, the progressivist with the romantic, and the rationalist with the affective. Taking forward such contentions, the chapters in the section on 'Critical Cultures', all written by ethnographers, shift the focus of anthropology from terrains of tradition to subjects of modernity. They variously think through thereby the imperatives of maturity, maturation, and 'ripening'; of governmental seductions, national identities, and intimate 'identifications'; of state planning, its affective attributes, and an

---

[21] Dube, 'Modernity and Its Enchantments', particularly pp. 2–8.

[22] For instance, Immanuel Wallerstein, 1991, *Unthinking Social Science: The Limits of Nineteenth Century Paradigms*, London: Polity Press; Michel-Rolph Trouillot, 1991, 'Anthropology and the Savage Slot: The Poetics and Politics of Otherness', in Richard J. Fox (ed.), *Recapturing Anthropology: Working in the Present*, Santa Fe, NM: School of American Research Press, pp. 17–44; Dube, 'History, Anthropology, Historical Anthropology'. See also, Immanuel Wallerstein, 1996, *Open the Social Sciences: Report of the Gulbenkian Commission on the Restructuring of the Social Sciences*, Stanford: Stanford University Press.

'activist modernity'; and of anthropological knowledge, everyday identities, and contemporary cultures.

Since the European Enlightenment of the seventeenth and eighteenth centuries, modernity has been often associated with an inexorable, linear process of maturing and maturation. Following Kant, the state of being 'un-' or 'non-modern'—and, therefore, of being 'immature'—is marked by the inability to use one's own understanding without guidance from another. Furthermore, in keeping with Hegelian injunctions, maturation into modernity has to be dissociated from transformations in nature: the former entails human agency; and, unlike cycles of nature, it follows a linear, progressive trajectory of change. Here are to be found provisos of progress—as dictated by the telos of history—that take individuals, cultures, and civilizations to their eventual pinnacle, the salient stage of a mature modern. Anand Pandian queries these distinct projections of maturation to modernity, drawing on historical and ethnographic materials from the Cumbum Valley in southern India.

To begin with, the colonial situation itself produces critical conundrums: after all, following imperial logics, the colonized can only aspire to *mature* into modernity under the *guidance* of colonial regimes. If this inherently discredits for the colonies the Kantian criterion of modernity and maturity, Pandian proceeds to further explore the issue of maturation by juxtaposing it to the Tamil *pakkuvam* or 'ripening' in the particular agrarian and environmental contexts of his fieldwork. As a term and concept, ripening refers as much to the

quality of soil and its potential for crop bearing as it does to the moral maturation of human actors, an incessant interchange that is clearly demonstrated by popular proverbs. Here, by bringing 'the potential development of subject and nature into a common frame', the chapter equally exposes the weakness of the Hegelian distinction between natural cycles and human history. Far from being mutually exclusive, in Pandian's narrative, natural transformations and human developments reveal themselves as co-constitutive, together marked by an inescapable contingency, 'situations of encounter, accident, and chance'. Finally, in the context of the Cumbum Valley, there is no necessary value judgement attached to the process of maturation: 'Evidence of maturity or its absence call for neither the recognition of attainment, nor condemnations of failure'. Does this not indicate key considerations regarding the inescapable plurality of modern subjects—and subjects of modernity—in postcolonial worlds?

The shaping of modern subjects under the terms of a political modernity and postcolonial governance lie at the heart of the next chapter, Véronique Bénéï's excursus into the worlds of citizens and subjects, education and nation, and the school and the state in western India. The starting point for her chapter is the centrality of 'pedagogical missions' to projects of modernity, such that schools have been 'a privileged site for testing, even implementing projects—however utopian—of citizenship'. On the one hand, Bénéï proposes a critical dynamic between the productivity of power of the nation-state and the meaningful practices of citizen–subjects in the active construal of national identity. On the other, she posits an extended interplay between the fluid and contingent nature of identities with processes of 'identification' that produces—in the short term and the long run—'near crystallized', essentialist notions of collective belonging.

It is precisely such processes of identification with the nation that are fostered and fomented by the state schooling system, including through familiar procedures of ideological indoctrination as well as the assiduous inculcation of sensory faculties of sight and vision. At the same time, a crucial role in these terrains is played by the working over of a shared auditory world in order to produce the citizen–subject of the modern nation. Thus, songs glorifying the nationalist movement and the postcolonial nation seek to systematically inculcate a national identity in the young school-goers. According to Bénéï, these protocols destabilize the conventional modern binary of the 'public' and the 'private', since the relentless (re)shaping of the sensory universe of the child—as of an adult—often allows a powerful, nationalizing agenda to straddle the putative poles of the dichotomy. It follows, too, that the chapter points towards 'the ideological perils inherent to any institutional, and particularly educational, modern nation-state project, especially when the powerful sensory resources it plays upon remain unacknowledged'.[23]

Prudent planning by the state is the rational road to a nation's modernity through its modernization. Family planning—or, the restless rational organization by the nation-state of the ideal nuclear family—plays a crucial role here. Unsurprisingly, the independent Indian nation under Jawaharlal Nehru adopted family planning as an official state policy in 1951, leading to jubilation among planners and their ilk at the early arrival of modernity in India. At the same time, as the chapter by Kalpana Ram argues, the apparent impassivity of the rationalist scientific discourse of planning is interrupted—indeed, fractured—by the 'eruption of affect' among individual planners and demographers. Ram's attempt is to recover the hidden body of these 'intellectuals'—bureaucrats, planners, demographers—in the process of family planning. She deftly demonstrates that

---

[23] Atig Ghosh has drawn my attention to two further issues regarding Bénéï's arguments. On the one hand, the chapter has something of a formative tension built into it, since Bénéï's case indicates that, in assiduously pursuing its goal of producing a *national* citizenry, Marathi schooling often concurrently engenders a powerful feeling of *regional* identity, especially since the 'sensorium' of the citizen-in-making is intimately tied to a strident regional history and its concomitant symbolic system. On the other hand, Atig finds that the Bénéï chapter, especially at its end, carries chilling implications. These follow from the fact that in 'classical' analysis, processes of 'identification' are said to take place at three distinct levels: first, the family; second, 'the professional, confessional and other institutions in which we might include schools'; and third, the hegemonic community/nation. Here, fascism entails the compressing of the first and the third levels of identification into the second level. Following Bénéï's analysis, schooling as the second level of identification conjoins the familial (or the private) and the communal/national (or the public), collapsing these into itself, especially through its mobilization of the sensory world. Although Bénéï herself is reluctant to follow the implications of her argument, Atig wonders if her materials do not point toward a classic blueprint of fascist formations? (To all of which I only add: what senses of the 'classical'—and the 'everyday'—are we pursuing here?)

far from being a dispassionate process, family planning is riddled with individual actors' affective response to the population at hand. 'Affect' is understood here as the energy associated with projects of the most public kind, as the necessary moment of any institutional practice with aspirations to national efficacy, and therefore, as distinct from emotions embedded in the interiors of individual consciousness. Alongside, the tone and texture of affect are reliant on the 'mood' that pervades the planning process, innately underpinning its modalities.

On the eve of Indian independence, this mood was expressed as immense enthusiasm for a still distant yet immanently realizable future. Indeed, the state was sustained by the hope that its 'intellectuals' and its 'people' would work together towards the mutual realization of a distinctive modernity. However, as the euphoria of Nehru's era waned, the planners frequently found themselves at cross-purposes with the subjects at large. Their mood darkened into one of distrust. More and more, they felt that the people of India, its teeming millions, did not know what was best for them. An increasingly negative sensibility became the pervasive mood of family planning, its affective charge expressed as fear and frustration. At the same time, this changing mood of the planning process was far from being all pervasive. Now, the target populations of family planning quickly adapted and reworked ideological elements of modern state programmes to suit and serve their own interests, reshaping the meanings of marriage, maternity, and sexual relations, sustained by 'the contagious charge of activist modernity'.

It is not only state planning but anthropological knowledge that has become an integral element of everyday identities of citizens, subjects, and people at large, an issue imaginatively explored by Townsend Middleton in *Modern Makeovers*. Focusing on successful and unsuccessful claims made by a particular populace to be granted the status of a Scheduled Tribe (ST), his chapter considers both the ethnographic state of an imperial provenance and the key implications of such formations for a postcolonial imaginary. Here, processes of modernity are revealed as reifying the categories of tradition, religion, and community through 'ethno-logics': the assiduous absorption and unsteady articulation of anthropological knowledge in quotidian conceptions and everyday identifications. This is hardly surprising, since formations of modernity cannot be sustained without the imaginary yet tangible presence of 'traditional' identities as a continuous counterpoint, consisting of contrast and contraposition. Indeed, if the nineteenth century was an epoch when 'history' broke upon social worlds—as Sudipta Kaviraj, among others, has reminded us—Middleton wonders if the same is not true for 'anthropology' in our times. If today culture, tradition, and identity are apparently on every lip, is anthropology then not on every mind?

Affecting Arts

Modernity and modernism, it was noted earlier, should not be readily collapsed together: the former intimates wider processes of history and ideology, which incorporate the latter tendencies as one among their distinct, compelling constituents. At the same time, to hold together modernity and modernism as parts of mutual fields of exploration and understanding can have key consequences. On the one hand, the recognition that they are both characterized by contradiction, contention, and contingency, albeit of distinct if overlapping orders, suggests the requirement for more fractured and less seamless readings of these phenomena. On the other hand, to register that modernity and modernism also share substantial, common crossovers—turning on, for example, enticements of market and nation, claims of abstract–rational design and its undercutting–constitutive other, and formations of subjectivity and ambivalence—underscores the importance of raising unfamiliar questions and pursuing unexpected leads in contemporary analysis. Together, such congeries of considerations reveals that modernity and modernism are each constituted by the intriguing interplay between aesthetics and politics, identity and economy. Moreover, they both continue to be insinuated in developmental designs that are undone yet upheld by improvisational interruptions. Finally, at stake here are critical reconsiderations of subjectivity, affect, form, and the everyday that query familiar understandings of modernism and modernity—at once in Europe and South Asia, the West and the non-West. Some of these concerns come alive in the chapters that follow on advertising, design, and art in India.

Arvind Rajagopal historicizes the development of advertising in twentieth-century India, foregrounding its political and economic logics. During the protected economy of the Nehru era, the multinational advertisement agencies catered exclusively to the consumption capacities of the urban classes. There was no need for them to be sensitive to the aspirations and requirements of the indigenous market. Thus, the gulf that had existed during the colonial era between urban elite advertising and its vernacular equivalent was preserved right through to the 1980s. However, all this changed drastically due to two developments across the 1980s: first, the spread of the television; and second, the liberalization of the market. The intensification of competition in a market that was no longer protected, together with an exponential expansion of the target audience of advertising through television, led to a search for new strategies of marketing. This was also a time marked by the rise of the Hindu right, which challenged the political hegemony of the Congress party by forging a new language of popular politics that drew on Hindu religion and ritual. Considering its overwhelming dependence on political trends, the advertising industry relied upon such emergent indigenization of popular rhetoric, in order to forge its own repertoire of Hindu images as part of an expanded and unified visual regime.

Rajagopal argues that in the context of economic liberalization, the production of subjects into citizens is not only the concern of the nation but that of the market as well, especially through the means of advertising. At the same time, the scope of such a project has to be inherently limited since advertising is ultimately parasitic on national politics. It follows that even though advertisements are instrumental in promoting modern forms of consciousness and identity, in the last instance, it is in the arena of politics that 'the logic unleashed by them can ever find their resolution'.

Following on the intricate imbrications of the advertisement industry and political economy, Jaideep Chatterjee turns his attention to 'design', which is popularly projected as a transparent and neutral medium. Indeed, all too often design appears as the domain of the rational–scientific expert who conceives of it in abstract terms and ultimately, realizes it concretely through a materially built, improved environment. Chatterjee's scrutiny of design as a concept, however, reveals its formidably modernist import, one that is ideologically loaded and intimately implicated in the project of the national modern. With a potent 'develop-mentality' animating all modern nation-states, including the Indian one, design forms the core of such developmental visions. And so, far from being innocent and neutral, the modernizing imperatives of design intimately associate it with other, more obviously suspect, modern 'universals' such as development, progress, rationality, and nationalism. Here, considering its claims of linear progress and scientific rationality, design is constantly counterposed to ad hoc imperatives, extemporization, and improvisation, which are all seen as irrational, arbitrary, and useless for the development of the nation. These terms of the ad hoc, the extemporary, and the improvised—so denigrated by the discourse of design—are captured most effectively by the Hindi word *jugar* and its manifold usages. Here, the discourse of design seeks to vindicate its innately neutral, scientific, and rational bent by claiming to completely minimize or even purge jugar from the processes and practices of planning.

Against the grain of the legislative discourse of design, Jaideep Chatterjee finds other purposes and provenance for jugar and its expressions. Chatterjee was member of a team of 'developers' entrusted with the task of (re)designing 'Khirki', an urban village in Delhi. The project was based on the following presumption: if Delhi was to enter the league of global cities of New York, London, and Tokyo, then such bucolic embarrassments as Khirki had to be designed and developed anew. Now, as a participant in this state-sponsored project of development-by-design, Chatterjee discovered that the claims to scientific neutrality and rationality were severely compromised at each step and at every level of the planning bureaucracy. Quite simply, integral to the sustenance of a working environment was a range of measures towards accommodation and negotiation—of the vested interests of power brokers in 'Khirki'; of various political pressures; and of the immense egos of important architects. Thus, the edifice of design was constitutively shot through by improvisation and the requirements of thinking on the feet. This is to say that at the heart of the planning process and design imperatives of the 'Khirki' project lay the immense force and dense gravity of protocols of jugar.

Significantly, Chatterjee does not dismiss design as camouflaged jugar. Far from it, he fully registers the ideological force of design as concept and practice. Rather, the chapter makes a distinct plea: 'to recognize that in spite of claims to universality, scientificity, rigor and formality', what attends and informs 'design (whether as idea, a form of knowledge, or design-on-paper or design-as-built) is jugar'. This is to say that jugar is design's 'other'. At the end, Chatterjee pushes the implications of his arguments even further, suggesting that not only design but all that we recognize as identifiably 'modern'—as being linear, rational, progressive, scientific, and national—is riddled with importunate improvisation. Or, procedures of jugar are critically constitutive of processes of modernity.

In the final chapter of this section, Sanjukta Sunderason turns to questions of modernism in Indian art. She argues for the importance of acknowledging and engaging with the implicit interplay between art and the politics of location. The two claims defining international modernism—artistic subjectivity and pure form—have remained embedded in the lived and historical experience of Indian artists. It follows that the dialectics of identity, memory, and experience have marked modernism in Indian art, imbuing it with a certain ambivalence. She suggests that to 'address this ambivalence in Indian modernism' requires at least two measures: a 'need to loosen the fixities of "pure form" and "deep subjectivity"'; and a recognition of 'the persistence of the political, albeit in amorphous mutations', in the mapping of the 'modern' in Indian art.

Based on these considerations, Sunderason construes an imaginative narrative of the modern and modernism in Indian art. Focusing of the work of artists such as Somnath Hore and Tyeb Mehta, she unravels the productive overlap between the private and the public and the formal and the social. Indeed, her account deftly interweaves explorations of these individual artists with a close engagement with artistic collectivities such as the Calcutta Group of Artists and the Progressive Artists' Group of Bombay. Here, she further links up the genesis and functioning of these groups—and thereby of the artists themselves—to political and historical contexts defined by the Great Famine of 1943, the Partition of India, the Bangladesh War of Liberation, the Naxalbari movement, and the state of Emergency, revealing the marks and scars on the body politic of Indian modernism. Indeed, it is only by undertaking the necessary detours through the social, the historical, and the political that modernism and the modern in Indian art are revealed not only as deeply fissured but as formed and transformed by the grounded subjectivities of the artists themselves.

At the End

As the preceding discussion would have shown, this volume maps prior routes and charts novel pathways in discussions of modernity in South Asia. (This is powerfully brought home in an imaginative 'Afterword' by Prathama Banerjee, which I shall not seek to sum up here—the piece speaks for itself, independently.) The work also draws together the different regions of the subcontinent. At the same time, as its title indicates, the volume attends at once to depths and surfaces, which are constitutive of modernity and its representations. Thus, in invoking *Modern Makeovers*, the reference is simultaneously to structural reconstructions and historical renovations, cosmetic transformations and changed appearances, and the exact entwining of these attributes, each as critical to claims and procedures of modernity, the mapping and making of modern worlds. Indeed, it is by taking such steps that the volume extends and exceeds conventional notions of a 'handbook', understood as 'a concise reference book providing specific information about a subject or location'[24] as well as 'a scholarly book on a specific subject, often consisting of separate essays or articles'.[25] Rather, *Modern Makeovers* reveals that a *Handbook of Modernity in South Asia* is much better-off working upon distinct, heterogeneous registers as well as construing facts unexpected. Here are to be found unfamiliar registers and uneasy facts, which speak in the echoes of lingering doubt, giving a lie to dead certainties of the historical record.

[24] Available at http://www.thefreedictionary.com/handbook (Last accessed on 19 November 2010).

[25] Available at http://dictionary.reference.com/browse/handbook (Last accessed on 19 November 2010).

I

Imperial Implications

1

The Strange Death of an Imperial Ideal
The Case of *Civis Britannicus*

Mrinalini Sinha

On 24 August 1924, one Raka Singh Gherwal, a Rajput from Punjab who was thirteen years resident in Linton, Oregon, a naturalized United States (US) citizen and a US Army veteran from World War I, wrote a strange letter in response to Colonel Josiah Wedgewood. Wedgewood was a Liberal Member of Parliament in London, who already had something of a reputation as a British 'friend' of India and of Indians. Gherwal's letter of 24 August, written in ungrammatical English, was responding to what seemed to him was Wedgewood's almost flippant reply to his original request for help. The occasion that had prompted Gherwal's original request was the recent proceedings by the Attorney General of the US to strip Gherwal and others like him of their US citizenship by instituting denaturalization proceedings against them:

'You have stated in your letter Sir,' Gherwal wrote to Wedgewood,

loss of citizenship will not affect to me much, you can't understand Sir what mean U.S. citizenship to me. As a citizen of the U.S. I can go anywhere if I want to go, but when I lose my citizenship of U.S. after ever nobody let me go there where the Union Jack is flying. I mean to Canada or Australia also where I will be His Majesty's subject. I am thinking U.S. citizenship mean to me more than anything; reason it gave me right as man. And if there will be justice than I am entitled to citizenship: have served with American Army, and been in this country more than 13 years.[1]

---

[1] For details of the case, see Government of India, Foreign and Political Department, Proceedings G (hereafter GIFP, G), 1924, 346-G-G/24, National Archives of India (NAI); and GIFP, G, 1923, 886, NAI.

What are we to make of this somewhat odd petition? What standing could Gherwal have as an Indian–American citizen, and by extension only a *former* British subject, to appeal for help to the *British* Parliament? Why does Gherwal believe that the US citizenship, acquired by renouncing his British subjecthood, will enable him paradoxically to enjoy better the status of His Majesty's British subject with the right to travel freely where 'the Union Jack is flying'? This chapter is, in effect, an extended meditation on these questions. My aim is to sketch an outline of the historical trajectory of the concept of *civis Britannicus*—British subjecthood—that had once animated generations of Indians, like Gherwal, both within and outside India.

Indeed, as is well known, mainstream anti-colonialism in India had for long subsisted alongside an abiding faith in the British Empire: that is, anti-colonialism did not entail, until quite recently, a simultaneous demand for separation from the Empire. But to take this history seriously—that is, on its own terms—has consequences for our standard developmentalist account of anti-colonialism. For, first of all, it suggests that we refuse to plot the eventual demand for complete independence in 1929 within a teleological narrative in which the latter demand appears simply as the logical and natural development of anti-colonialism—an outcome of a moment of arrival, as it were, when anti-colonial Indian nationalism achieves full maturity.

The aim in my larger project, of which this chapter is a part, is precisely to turn this evolutionary narrative on its head, that is, to suggest that the demand for complete

independence was not natural, but it was, in fact, a *contingent*—and, dare I say, not necessarily benign—development in the history of Indian anti-colonialism that needs to be explained. One part of my explanation consists in exploring the global structural dynamics of the post-World War I period—that Erez Manela has recently evocatively called the 'Wilsonian moment'—and another part consists in tracing the political and legal trajectory of the concept of 'civis Britannicus' on the basis of which Gherwal premised his request for help to Wedgewood and to the British Parliament.[2] The larger question that animates my reconstruction of Gherwal's story, then, is this: why did a once-expansive conception of civis Britannicus—often, especially in its more politicized invocation, equated with imperial citizenship—give way eventually to a territorially confined conception of citizenship tied to an arguably more limited, and even limiting, polity: the nation-state?

East Indians as US Citizens

Let us return to Gherwal's story. The immediate context for Gherwal's woes, to be sure, lies in the history of restrictions against Indian immigration to the US. By 1924, when Gherwal was writing his letter, there was already a history of at least two decades of steady Indian immigration into the US (even though the documented presence of East Indians, the term commonly used for people from India, went back at least

[2] Erez Manela, 2007, *The Wilsonian Moment: Self-Determination and the International Origins of Anticolonial Nationalism*, New York: Oxford University Press.

to the eighteenth century).[3] The Indians in the US, a majority of whom were from Gherwal's state of Punjab, had come to the West Coast via British Columbia in Canada. Many of these early Indian immigrants—all referred to generically as 'Hindus' even though the majority were actually Sikhs and a good number were Punjabi Muslims—had come via other stops in the British Empire: many, for example, were veterans of the British Indian Army and of the British Indian Police deployed overseas in places like China, especially during the Boxer rebellion, or in Hong Kong and in the Straits settlements.[4] In the early 1900s—responding both to general anti-Asian sentiments and to particular anti-'Hindu' animosity in the western states—the US immigration commissioners had adopted what the British Ambassador in Washington, DC, confessed were blatantly 'unfair' administrative measures to send back new arrivals from India: at least two ship loads carrying Indians were turned away on grounds of medical unfitness; more than a dozen cases were rejected on grounds that the individuals were born into religions—Hinduism and Islam—that condoned polygamy; and roughly the same number on fear that they would become a charge on the state.[5] By 1914,

these measures had been so successful that the number of fresh arrivals from India—given that immigration into Canada had also been virtually closed to Indians—had pretty much died out.[6] Yet, the US immigration legislations, enacted in 1917 and then again in 1924, for the first time, included Indians for exclusion as Asiatics, effectively making all fresh immigration from India to the US illegal.

However, the status of Indians already domiciled in the US was a more complicated matter. In 1910, a long-time Parsi resident, H.B. Balsara, had become the first Indian to be naturalized as a US citizen.[7] By 1924, more than a hundred Indians had received naturalization papers as US citizens in accordance with S 2169 of the Revised Statute of the US Naturalization Act of 1870, by which 'free white persons' and those of 'African' descent were eligible for citizenship. The executive branch of the US government and the naturalization examiners repeatedly appealed against such cases, but the various judicial courts uniformly decided in favour of the Indians on the ground that the phrase 'free white persons' was to be interpreted as a member of the Caucasian race—and high-caste Hindus and other elite Indians, as Aryans, were Caucasians, just like the Semitic races of Western Asia.

However, the ambiguity surrounding the 'race' of the Indians, and consequently their eligibility for naturalization as US citizens, was never fully resolved and it came up repeatedly for debate in cases of Indian

---

[3] See H. Brett Melendy, 1971, *Asians in America*, Boston: Twayne Publishers; Joan Jensen, 1988, *Passage from India: Asian Indian Immigrants in North America*, New Haven and London: Yale University Press; and Ronald Takaki, 1989, *Strangers from a Different Shore*, Boston: Little, Brown and Company.

[4] See Melendy, *Asians in America*. Also, see Sharon M. Lee, 1993, 'Racial Classification in the U.S. Census 1890–1910', *Ethnic and Racial Studies*, vol. 16, no. 1, January, pp. 74–94.

[5] See GIFP, XA, December 1913, pp. 3–6; also see GIFP, GA, several files from 1906 to 1909.

[6] For example, in 1911, some 2,000 Indians had reportedly entered the US; the following year, the number had dwindled to 256; and in 1913, to a mere sixty-four. See USIN 50239/110B.

[7] GIFP, XA, January 1911, pp. 7–9.

naturalization in courts across the US.[8] In
the first such case that was appealed right
up to the US Supreme Court, the Court
on 19 February 1923 decided to reverse the
naturalization, the previous year, of Bhagat
Singh Thind, also a US army veteran. On
the question, 'Is a high caste Hindu of full
Indian blood born at Amritsar, Punjab, a
white person within the meaning of the S
2169 Revised Statutes?' the Court decided
that he was not.[9] The decision rested on
the extra-legal grounds that although
Thind was a Caucasian, he was not a 'white
person' in the ordinary or the common
meaning of the term as understood by
the man on the street. Following Thind's
case, therefore, the government initiated
denaturalization proceedings against some
thirty to fifty individuals from India,
who like Gherwal, had been naturalized
previously as US citizens. Gherwal's appeal to
Wedgewood was prompted precisely by the
initiative of the executive branch of the US
government, following the Thind decision,
to strip Gherwal and others like him of US
citizenship.

What does this struggle over the rights
of Indians as US citizens have to do with
the imperial ideal of civis Britannicus, the
claims of British subjects? After all, the
US, at best, was only a former member of
the British Empire. Typically, of course,
the story of Indian immigration to the US
has been studied within the framework of
Asian–American history or of migration
studies. By placing this story within a British
imperial framework, however, I wish to

gesture towards my larger argument about
the crucial role played by the US—and by
Britain's settler colonies—in the post-World
War I period in promoting the nation-state
form as the ideal type of modern polity
against both continental and overseas
empire-states. By the same token, the
struggle of Indians in the US, for a variety
of reasons, became the final straw that broke
the back of the once-cherished imperial ideal
of civis Britannicus.

Contours of British Subjecthood

Let us turn to the actual issues of political
belonging raised in Gherwal's letter.
Gherwal's appeal to the British Parliament
was premised on the ideals of 'imperial
citizenship' to which he was once rightfully
entitled as a natural-born British subject, a
status enjoyed by all those born in British
India. Technically, of course, there was no
such thing as imperial citizenship or, for that
matter, any such thing as *British* citizenship.
In fact, as several scholars have reminded us,
for a country as old as the United Kingdom
(UK), the legal category of the citizen arrived
very late.[10] The category did not enter British
legal discourse until 1948, and that too only
in the context of imperial and *not* national
citizenship: the Act of 1948, for example,

[8] GIFP, GA, July 1915, pp. 12–13.
[9] GIFP, XA, September 1923, pp. 9–11; and GIFP, XA, January 1924, p. 18.

[10] For an overview, see Mervyn Jones, 1947, *British Nationality Law and Practice*, London: Clarendon Press; Ann Dummett and Andrew Nicol, 1990, *Subjects, Citizens, Aliens and Others: Nationality and Immigration Law*, London: Weidenfeld and Nicolson; and Rieko Karatani, 2002, *Defining British Citizenship: Empire, Commonwealth and Modern Britain*, London: Routledge. For the ambiguity of the meaning of British subject right until the 1948 citizenship act, see India Office, Public and Judicial Department, L/P & J/8/4, British Library.

made Britains, Kenyans, Jamaicans, and so on, for the first time, citizens of the United Kingdom and Colonies. It was not until the Act of 1981 that Britain acquired a national citizenship that was exclusively for England, Scotland, and Wales. Yet, both political and popular discourses in Britain and in the Empire were littered with references to the rights and duties of the citizen.[11] Technically, however, there was no such thing as either British or imperial citizenship; everyone born under His/Her Majesty's dominions, whether in the British Isles or in British India, were British subjects, bound by their common allegiance to the British monarch. Yet, despite this technical lacuna, the vocabulary of imperial citizenship had great resonance across the political spectrum, at least until the period between the two world wars.[12] And this vocabulary—deliberately vague as it always had been—had begun to acquire formal parameters and some political

and legal teeth in the course of the early twentieth century as a result of empire-wide political struggles of Indians to claim their rights as imperial citizens.

All those born or naturalized in His or Her Majesty's Dominions anywhere in the world were all British subjects and entitled, theoretically, to the same protection of the state. Consider here Lord Palmerston's famous invocation of 'civis Britannicus sum'—invoking the apostle Paul—before the British Parliament in 1850 to defend his military action against the Greek government in supposed defence of Don Pacifico, a Portuguese Jew who happened to be born in British Gibraltar.[13] There were, of course, different classes of British subjects. Notwithstanding the staggering variety, however, the different classes of British subjects, at least theoretically, were *emphatically* not determined by either race or by creed.[14] The Queen's Proclamation on 1 November 1858, made in the aftermath of the Revolt of 1857, often referred to by contemporaries as the Magna Carta for India, reiterated this ostensible principle of

[11] See Keith McClelland and Sonya Rose, 2006, 'Citizenship and Empire, 1867–1928', in Catherine Hall and Sonya Rose (eds), *At Home with the Empire: Metropolitan Culture and the Imperial World*, Cambridge: Cambridge University Press, pp. 275–97.

[12] See Daniel Gorman, 2002, 'Wider and Wider Still? Racial Politics, Intra-Imperial Immigration and the Absence of an Imperial Citizenship in the British Empire', *Journal of Colonialism and Colonial History*, vol. 3, no. 3, Winter, available at http://muse.jhu.edu (Last accessed on 27 March 2004); Daniel Gorman, 2004, 'Lionel Curtis, Imperial Citizenship, and the Quest for Unity', *The Historian*, vol. 66, no. 1, March, pp. 67–96; and Daniel Gorman, 2007, *Imperial Citizenship: Empire and the Question of Belonging*, Manchester: Manchester University Press. At the other end was the Imperial Indian Citizenship Association in Bombay, which published the *India Abroad Bulletins*, nos 1–7, Bombay, 1923. Also, see Sukanaya Banerjea, 2005, 'Political Economy, Gothic, and the Question of Imperial Citizenship', *Victorian Studies*, vol. 47, no. 2, Winter, pp. 260–71.

[13] Cited in Gorman, 'Wider and Wider Still?'

[14] In practice, of course, immigration laws, first in the Dominion colonies and then in Britain, compromised equality for different classes of British subjects. For the Dominions, see especially Robert A. Huttenback, 1976, *Racism and Empire: White Settlers and Colored Immigrants in the British Self-Governing Colonies*, Ithaca, NY: Cornell University Press. For Britain, see Randall Hansen, 1999, 'The Politics of Citizenship in 1940s Britain: The British Nationality Act', *Twentieth Century British History*, vol. 10, no. 1, pp. 70–3; Kathleen Paul, 1995, '"British Subjects" and "British Stock": Labour's Postwar Imperialism', *Journal of British Studies*, vol. 34, no. 2, April, pp. 233–76; and Kathleen Paul, 1997, *Whitewashing Britain: Race and Citizenship in the Postwar Era*, Ithaca, NY: Cornell University Press.

non-discrimination between Britons and Indians alike as British subjects.[15] This was the political ideal of civis Britannicus—elaborated, to be sure, by imperial authorities to serve the particular needs of colonial governance, but, subsequently, given heft and substance by decades of political struggles by Indians themselves—on which Gherwal and Indian-American organizations like the North American Indian Association and the Khalsa Dewan Society of Stockton, California, staked their appeal to the British Parliament.

Had Gherwal, however, already abjured his standing as a British subject—and thus his entitlement to appeal to the British government—in becoming a naturalized US citizen? The legal implications of this loss were at first unclear. Being British, in legal terms, was defined as owing allegiance to the Crown; to be a *British* subject, then, was to be personally linked to the British monarch and not necessarily to the state; a distinction that suggested that in legal terms, allegiance—and by extension, British nationality—was derived from the person of the monarch and was thus indelible.[16] Until

the Naturalization Act of 1870, indeed, the common law regulations that had governed the rules for British nationality since 1608 had made no provisions for the loss or renunciation of one's status as a British subject.[17] Hence, interestingly, long after the American Revolution, even naturalized American citizens of British origin had remained British subjects. The provision for the loss of British nationality was first codified only in 1870, following the trial in 1866 of Feninans, who although naturalized American citizens, were convicted as British subjects in a Canadian court for treason against the British monarch.[18] By the terms of this 1870 Act, therefore, Gherwal had renounced his status as a British subject and his right to British protection when he was naturalized as a US citizen.

Yet a further legal twist ended putting the status of Gherwal and other former Indian-Americans in the US in limbo. The US government, in making its legal case for the denaturalization of Indian-US citizens, proceeded on the basis that the Thind decision had made all such prior cases of the naturalization of Indians as US citizens null and void *ab initio*, thus reverting all such individuals to their former status as British subjects as if they had never been naturalized.[19] To this extent, despite being naturalized as a US citizen, Gherwal

---

[15] Quoted in A. Berriedale Keith (ed.), 1922, *Speeches and Documents on Indian Policy, 1750–1921, Vol. 1*, London: Oxford University Press, pp. 382–6. It was on the strength of such a promise that Indians, while lacking the political rights of citizenship in India, could vote and be elected to the Parliament in Britain. Dadabhai Naoroji was the most well-known Indian to be elected to the British Parliament; for his election, see Antoinette Burton, 2000, 'Tongues Untied: Lord Salisbury's "Black Man" and the Boundaries of Imperial Democracy', *Comparative Studies in Society and History*, vol. 43, no. 2, pp. 632–59.

[16] I owe this point to M. Page Baldwin, 2001, 'Subject to Empire: Married Women and the British Nationality and Status of Aliens Act', *Journal of British Studies*, vol. 40, no. 4, October, pp. 522–56.

[17] See Jones, *British Nationality Law and Practice*; and Dummett and Nicol, *Subjects, Citizens, Aliens and Others*.

[18] Cited in Baldwin, 'Subject to Empire'. For the case, also see Dummett and Nicol, *Subjects, Citizens, Aliens and Others*, p. 87.

[19] Yet, British authorities were uncertain for a considerable period after the Thind decision as to whether denaturalized Indians reverted to their former status as British subjects. See GIFP, 1926, 5(46)-X.

and the Indians in the US were still the charge of the British government and, as such, were entitled to the privileges of imperial citizenship that accrued to them as natural-born British subjects. Under these circumstances, the metropolitan British government was starkly confronted with the thorny question of how far it was willing to go to uphold the rights of its natural-born non-European British subjects in comparison with its European British subjects.

Mobility within the Empire

The curious explanation that Gherwal gives for desiring the US citizenship is itself a reminder of the extent to which the concept of civis Britannicus for British Indians had already been considerably eviscerated by the early decades of the twentieth century. Recall in this context, Gherwal's contradictory explanation for his strong desire to retain his US citizenship. The possession of US citizenship, he argues, would allow him to enjoy the status of a subject of His Britannic Majesty in Canada, Australia, or any of the other self-governing colonies of settlement within the British Empire. Indeed, the status of Indians in the Empire, and particularly in the Dominion colonies, had already stretched to the limits the ideals of imperial citizenship.

While the history of restrictions against fellow British subjects from India, especially in the Dominion colonies, is well known, what is less known, perhaps, is that the Government of India and, to a lesser degree, the India Office and the Colonial Office in London were frequently some of the strongest advocates for the cause of the Indians in the Empire. The Government

of India, especially, could scarcely afford the political opprobrium of becoming itself *principes crimnalis* in the 'whites only' policies of the Dominions. Indeed, it was in supporting the struggles of Indians against immigration restrictions imposed by the Dominion colonies, that the colonial and imperial governments first became complicit in officially ratifying one of the most popular elaborations of the concept of civis Britannicus: the right of British subjects to free and unrestricted mobility within the Empire.[20] Repeated pronouncements and actions taken both by the Government of India and the British government in the course of the nineteenth century gave official recognition to this particular right of British subjects.

Eventually in 1911, however, the Government of India was forced to go back on this official policy: it conceded the right of the self-governing Dominions to determine the composition of their own populations, a dramatic shift that was subsequently ratified by the Reciprocity Resolution of the Imperial Conference of 1918.[21] Yet, even this shift in policy was made with the avowed aim of securing in exchange a commitment from the Dominion governments for the equal treatment of British Indian subjects already domiciled in the Dominions. Henceforth, however, imperial policy, for the first time, began to make a distinction between different forms of political belonging within the British

[20] For this history, see Mrinalini Sinha, 2005, 'Hindus, Aryans, and Caucasians: How Indians Became Black', Workshop paper for the Rutgers Center for Historical Analysis, Rutgers University, 13 December, unpublished manuscript.
[21] Ibid.

Empire: a pan-imperial British nationality, which ever since the British Nationality and Status of Aliens Act of 1914 was uniform empire-wide; and more local forms of national political belonging that were to be regulated by the self-governing Dominions themselves and, since 1918, at least in principle, also by India.[22] As such, the shift in official understanding of the meaning of civis Britannicus still continued to garner considerable political support in India.

To be sure, the abandonment of the principle of the unrestricted movement of British subjects within the Empire was a significant loss for the concept of civis Britannicus as it had come to be understood in the political struggles of Indians and in the official policies of the Government of India. Yet, the sacrifice of this principle was offset, at least partially, by official commitment to the equality of the treatment of British subjects already domiciled in the constituent parts of the Empire—an issue that now became the basis for a popular new understanding of civis Britannicus in India.

By the time Gherwal petitioned Wedgewood for help in retaining his US citizenship, one of the fundamental pillars of civis Britannicus—unrestricted movement within the Empire—had already been abandoned. Yet, the concept still retained its appeal in the new understanding of equal treatment for British subjects. Hence, the convoluted logic of Gherwal's letter: in Canada, Australia, New Zealand, and South Africa, but not in the US, he could still invoke his British nationality, his status as British subject, to make a case

against invidious racial discrimination. The Government of India was still very much at the forefront of championing the rights of Indians as British subjects already domiciled in the Dominions. For example, the Viceroy, Lord Hardinge's sympathy for Gandhi's struggle against the Government of the Union of South Africa in 1914 was so pronounced that there was talk among pro-South Africa elements in London to have the Viceroy recalled.[23] But the only way that was open to Gherwal to enter any of the Dominion colonies of the British Empire—where he could still count on the Government of India to take up his case for equal treatment—was paradoxically through renouncing British nationality, and allegiance, so as to secure the US citizenship! In short, Gherwal as a US citizen had little expectations of equal treatment in the US; but British subjecthood that promised him equal treatment was not enough to secure him entry into certain parts of the British Empire, which he could only enter as a US citizen.

Equality of British Subjects

Further compounding Gherwal's woes—and quite unbeknownst to him—at the very moment that the US authorities were instituting denaturalization proceedings against Indian-Americans, Whitehall was at the brink of further rolling back the status of the British subject that would make moot the very reason he gave for retaining his US citizenship: the ability to go where the Union Jack was flying where he could be assured,

---

[22] The distinction is from Baldwin, 'Subject to Empire'. Also see Mss. Eur. D 545/2, British Library.

[23] Ibid.

at least theoretically, equality as a British subject.

Shortly before Gherwal's letter to Wedgewood, however, the concept of civis Britannicus had received its second, and nearly fatal, blow. The latest retreat followed from the protracted struggle over the question of the status of British Indians in the Crown Colony of Kenya, which was administered directly by Whitehall instead of by the self-governing Dominion governments.[24] During the course of this struggle, the Viceroy, Lord Chelmsford, was forced into making, before the Legislative Assembly in India, the clearest official elaboration of the meaning of British subjecthood for Indians: Indians as British subjects, he declared unambiguously, were entitled absolutely to 'no better and no worse treatment than their fellow white subjects' anywhere in the Empire.[25] While neither the Government of India nor Whitehall could guarantee compliance to this principle from self-governing Dominion governments, both governments were committed to the principle wherever their writ had affect. This view was subsequently confirmed at the Imperial Conference of 1921, where V.S. Sastri's resolution on behalf of the Government of India was also accepted by the majority of the conference with only General Smuts of South Africa dissenting.[26]

With this resolution, imperial authorities were forced to give real substance to Queen Victoria's declaration and to confront officially, for the first time, its implications for the status of British subjecthood empire-wide.

The subsequent repudiation of this formal empire-wide principle in 1922 by Winston Churchill, then Colonial Secretary and himself signatory to the Imperial Conference Resolution of 1921, was arguably one of the biggest setbacks for the imperial ideal of civis Britannicus. The change in Churchill's attitude, already evident at the Imperial Conference in 1921 where his sympathy with General Smuts' position was unmistakable, had to do with the precedence that the declaration of equal rights for British Indian subjects created for the status of Africans in the African holdings of the Empire.[27] The early intimations of this impact were already being felt in Kenya colony, where indigenous Africans had begun mobilizing around the Indian question.[28] Reports from Kenya of Indian support for Africans, especially the alliance between East African Indians and Harry Thuku of the Young Kikuyu Association, were especially alarming. The South African government was the first to warn against this danger. The South African government had always maintained that while the 'Indian question' in South Africa was in itself not a serious problem, it became so in so far as it was inseparable from the 'native question': 'you could not give political rights to the Indians',

[24] For details, see Mrinalini Sinha, 2006, 'Why Did Churchill Blink? India, Africa and the Third British Empire', Keynote address, Annual Conference of Midwest Conference of British Studies, Indianapolis, October, unpublished manuscript.
[25] Quoted in Ibid.
[26] For behind the scene manoeuverings on the resolution, see Mss. Eur. F 112/307; 308; 309; and Mss. Eur. E 267/1.

[27] Sinha, 'Why Did Churchill Blink?'
[28] Ibid. Also see, Robert G. Gregory, 1971, *India and East Africa: A History of Race Relations within the British Empire, 1890–1939*, Oxford: Clarendon Press.

as Smuts argued, 'which you deny to the rest of your colored citizens in South Africa'.[29] As such, the South African government threw in its lot with the white settlers in Kenya to impress the Colonial Office and the prime minister in Britain on the dangerous precedence set by the Resolution of 1921 for the foundations of the South African state with implications for South Africa's desire to remain within the British Empire.[30] The ignominy of Churchill's retreat on Kenya, of course, was couched by his successor at the Colonial Office in nobler language. The Devonshire Declaration—named after Churchill's successor, Lord Devonshire— announced that imperial policy in Africa would henceforth be guided by the development of Africans. The Declaration, however, barely masked the fact that there was to be no equality for the two different classes of settlers in Africa: Indians and Europeans. While inaugurating a significant new phase in Britain's Africa policy, it could not conceal the origins of this policy in the attempt to deflect attention away from the important imperial capitulation on the question of equal rights of British subjects.[31] Africans, no less than Indians, were told that henceforth they could expect humanitarian concern but not equality as British subjects.

By 1923, indeed, the principle of equal rights for British subjects was fully dead. The Imperial Conference of 1923 confirmed this latest contraction in the elaboration of the concept of civis Britannicus. Smuts now submitted an important memorandum to the conference, which deliberately misinterpreted the resolution of 1921 as implying a common empire-wide imperial citizenship, to argue for the reversal of that resolution.[32] His argument bears quoting at some length:

The Indian claim for equal franchise rights in the Empire outside India arise, in my opinion, from a misconception of the nature of British citizenship. This misconception is not confined to India, but is fairly general, and the Conference would do not only India, but the whole Empire an important service by its removal. The misconception arises, not from the fact, but from the assumption that all subjects of the King are equal, that in an Empire where there is a common King there should be a common and equal citizenship, and that all differences and distinctions in citizen rights are wrong in principle…There is no common equal British citizenship in the Empire, and it is quite wrong for a British subject to claim equal rights in any part of the Empire to which he has migrated or where he happens to be living. There is no indignity or affront at all in the denial of such equality…The newer conception of the British Empire as a smaller League of Nations, as a partnership of free and equal nations under a common hereditary sovereign, involves an even further departure from the simple conception of a unitary citizenship. British citizenship has been variable in the past; it is bound to be even more so in the future. Each constituent part of the Empire will settle for itself the nature and incidents of its citizenship. The composition and character and rights of its people will be the concern of each free and equal State in the Empire. It will not only regulate immigration from other parts of the Empire as well as from

---

[29] Quoted in Mss. Eur. F 112/311.
[30] Ibid. Also, India Office Collections, Private Office Papers, 1/6 (i) (hereafter IOL/PO), British Library.
[31] See Gregory, *India and East Africa*; and Sinha, 'Why Did Churchill Blink?'

[32] I get this point from Marilyn Lake and Henry Reynolds, 2008, *Drawing the Global Color Line: White Men's Countries and the International Challenge of Racial Equality*, Cambridge: Cambridge University Press.

the outside world, but it will also settle the rights of its citizens as a matter of domestic concern. The common Kingship is the binding link between the parts of the Empire; it is not a source from which private citizens will derive their rights. They will derive their rights simply and solely from the authority of the State in which they live…From this point of view the Indian resolution passed at last conference was a big mistake. Not only is it impracticable, but it runs contrary to the new conception of the Empire, as not a unitary State, but a partnership of equal States. It has both theoretically and practically landed us in a false position, and the sooner we get out of it the better for the future good relations of the different States of the Empire.[33]

In a clever move, Smuts had succeeded in turning the issue of equality for British subjects to the question of equality for constituent states within the Empire: a turn with important consequences for the status of the British subject and for the future of the revised supranational polity that both supporters and critics of Empire still hoped it could become.

When Gherwal was pleading his case to Wedgewood, however, he had no way of knowing that the basis on which he was making his argument had changed: after the latest imperial about-turn on the status of the British subject, there would be no difference between the expectation of equality and fair treatment as a US citizen resident in the US or as a British subject in South Africa, Canada, Australia, or even any of the Crown colonies of the British Empire. The status of British subject, as the Imperial Conference of 1923 had now made clear, did not entitle a person to equal rights with other British subjects; it only

entitled a person to protection by His or Her Majesty's government against the actions of a foreign government. Even this newly shrunken version of the meaning of British subjecthood—the right to equal protection from the British government abroad—was soon to fall by the wayside as post-war Britain confronted its own reduced standing in the world in relation to some foreign governments, especially the US.

Protection for British Subjects

Before the war, the British Foreign Office, at the urging of the Government of India and of the India Office, had managed to gain limited concessions for Indians in the US through its consular representatives. For example, in 1913, and then again in 1914, the British Ambassador in Washington, DC, had succeeded in manoeuvering behind-the-scenes with the office of the US Secretary of State to get two 'Hindu Exclusion' Bills in the Congress abandoned that would have singled Indians out by name for exclusion.[34] The immigration law that followed in 1917 only included India in a more general list of countries in the 'Pacific Barred Zone' from where immigration was to be prohibited. British consular officials had also been proactive in the US before the war in responding to the anti-Hindu riots in the western states.[35] By the time of the Thind decision in 1923, and of the US immigration legislation of 1924, however, British clout with the US officials was considerably diminished. During the denaturalization crisis, for example, the British Ambassador,

---

[33] Mss. Eur. F 112/311.

[34] Sinha, 'Hindus, Aryans, and Caucasians'.
[35] Ibid.

Sir Esme Howard, complained that his letter to the State Department dated 22 September 1923, did not even receive a reply from that office for a full year until 2 April 1924.[36] The Secretary of State for the US further ignored the British Ambassador's request to be consulted informally on the bill that became the US Immigration Law of 1924 with its even greater restrictions on British Indians who were now, by the Thind case, also deemed ineligible for citizenship.[37]

To be sure, the British Foreign Office continued through its consular representatives in the US to lobby the State Department on behalf of Indians. Of particular concern to imperial authorities was the genuine hardship of resident Indians as a result of the impact of the denaturalization of Indian Americans on their ability to own land in California and in other states that had passed anti-alien land laws; of equal concern to the British was the fact that resident Indian businessmen and merchants in the US were also unable to travel on business outside the country without risking being debarred from re-entry.[38] There were some minor concessions that the British Foreign Office was able to secure for already domiciled Indian landowners and businessmen in the US; but the US authorities remained largely indifferent to British overtures on behalf of British Indians. And the British metropolitan government, anxious not to let the 'Asiatic question' sour

relations with its most powerful ally, declined to pursue all available options on behalf of British Indian subjects in the US.[39]

By contrast, the Government of India, under pressure from Indian public opinion, was eager for the home government to make public its correspondence on behalf of Indians in the US. Officials in India were sensitive not to give the impression of imperial indifference to the plight of Indian Americans, especially after the imperial betrayal on Kenya over which the Viceroy, Lord Reading, was almost fired for siding with Indian disappointment.[40] Yet, Whitehall immediately demurred. The Japanese Ambassador to the US, Baron Hanihara, had made formal protestation to the State Department on behalf of Japanese subjects, only to have his initiative boomerang on him. The State Department leaked the Japanese request just before the debate in Congress, angering US lawmakers who rejected external interference and subjected the Japanese to even harsher treatment than in the original bill. A similar airing of Britain's own weakness in relation to the US seemed too high a price to pay for assuaging Indian suspicions.[41] The imperial negotiations with the US government were thus never made public.

The government's silence was increasingly seen in India as apathy. Even at the height of the Kenya crisis, the strenuous advocacy of the Indian case in some quarters had gone at least some way in dampening anti-Empire sentiments in India. Not only was Lord Reading almost recalled for his pro-India

---

[36] GIFP, GA, December 1924, pp. 12–14.
[37] Sinha, 'Hindus, Aryans, and Caucasians'.
[38] GIFP, E, 40-X, 1928; GIFP, G, 346-G-G/24; GIFP, 5(46)-X, 1926; GIFP, E, 278-X, 1935; and India Office Collections, Economic and Overseas Department (hereafter IOL/E), 7/1332, file 676, British Library.

[39] Sinha, 'Hindus, Aryans and Caucasians'.
[40] See Gregory, *India and East Africa*.
[41] GIFP, XA, October 1924, pp. 22–6.

stance, but it was rumored that even the Secretary of State for India, E.S. Montagu, had threatened to resign over the Cabinet's decision on Kenya. Montagu resigned just a few months later on a different issue, but the Kenya debacle still rankled.[42] The official silence—and on occasion, total paralysis in dealing with the US, Britain's most vital political and economic partner—allowed a growing suspicion of imperial motives to fester in India; and, even more perhaps, it foregrounded the impotence of the concept of British subjecthood by the mid-1920s. Imperial reticence, combined with imperial impotence, in dealing with the situation of British Indians in the US meant that even the remaining anodyne conception of British subjecthood—the right to seek protection from the British state against a foreign government—was put to rest. How the mighty had fallen: by 1925, indeed, 'civis Britannicus sum' was just an empty phrase.

Gherwal's personal case fared no better than that of his countrymen. Wedgewood forwarded Gherwal's letter to the British Foreign Office, which on investigation of the case, concluded that his was not the most sympathetic case for his Majesty's government to take up individually with the US authorities. The decision rested in part on the report from the British consular official in Portland, Oregon, that Gherwal's lawyer had allegedly confided to him that Gherwal had been discharged from the US Army for having contracted a sexually transmitted disease, a charge that the lawyer himself denied and that was also contradicted by the US Army's official notice

of discharge.[43] The trumped-up charge of a sexually transmitted disease was a staple of anti-immigrant organizations in the US such as the Asiatic Exclusion League and the various anti-Hindu leagues that had sprung up all along the Pacific coast. The spectre of the seduction of innocent white women was still a powerful one. Issues of sexuality and gender, indeed, were deeply implicated in the Indian struggles over imperial citizenship and their outcome in the first few decades of the twentieth century.

Seduction of the Nation-State Form?

Let me conclude, however, by pointing to the concerns that have motivated my interest in the history of imperial citizenship. I see this work in conversation with a growing number of scholars from a variety of disciplines who are rethinking the tyranny of the nation-state form that has dominated the historical scholarship of the modern period. What these scholars are forcing us to reconsider is precisely the linear and unbroken history of the nation-state form from the Treaty of Westphalia in 1648 to the post-World War II United Nations-sanctioned world order of nation-states. For much of this period, in fact, a variety of multinational and supranational polities flourished as rivals to the nation-state; these other forms of polities also rivalled the nation-state as the object of people's political aspirations. The work of John Kelly and Martha Kaplan on Fiji and world decolonization has done most, perhaps, in reminding us of the radical novelty—after World War II, by their reckoning—of the

---

[42] Gregory, *India and East Africa.*

[43] GIFP, G, 346-G-G/24; GIFP, G, 886.

spread of the idea of the nation-state as the most, and only, optimum form of political belonging in the modern world.[44]

While my argument seems to quibble with Kelly and Kaplan on a matter of chronology, I have found incredibly suggestive their linking of the universality of the nation-state form with the moment of decolonization. Consider here the following implications that emerge out of a history of imperial citizenship: that it was the refusal and difficulty of fulfilling the expansive aspirations of citizenship rights of colonized people that prompted an imperial move towards containing the rights of citizenship within clearly demarcated nation-states—a prelude, perhaps, to a strategy that we now associate with the Bantustans. Consider, too,

the alternative histories of decolonization such a history suggests: that national independence in the colonized world may have as much to do with demands of anti-colonial struggles themselves as with an imperial deflection of these demands onto the safer confines of national–territorial space. Paul Kramer's new book on the US and the Philippines already points in this direction—support for Philippines independence in the US came in exchange for restricting Filipino entry and access to rights as American nationals (but not quite US citizens).[45] I throw out these ideas here as provocations—rather than fully worked out arguments—in the hope that they will invite conversation on a project that is still, I am afraid, very much a work-in-progress.

---

[44] John Kelly and Martha Kaplan, 2001, *Represented Communities: Fiji and World Decolonization*, Chicago: University of Chicago Press.

[45] Paul Kramer, 2006, *The Blood of Government: Race, Empire, the United States and the Philippines*, Chapel Hill, NC: University of North Carolina Press.

2

Can the Postcolonial Begin?

Deprovincializing Assam*

Bodhisattva Kar[†]

Bāngāl, Bāngāl—you bastards, you make my head spin—Why do you still call me a Bāngāl [a rustic from the eastern districts of Bengal]?—I have broken all food taboos—And still I am not like a Calcuttan? What have I not done to become like a Calcuttan? I have visited prostitutes' quarters, made my woman wear fine cloth, munched white men's biscuits, guzzled alcohol—and still, after all this, I cannot become like a Calcuttan! Then what is the point of preserving this sinful body? Let me dive into water, let sharks and crocs eat my body...[1]

Thus spoke Rammanikya, with a distinct Dhaka accent, and fell unconscious on the floor in front of a laughing Calcutta audience. Too drunk to be dishonest, Ram was summing up the frustrations of the first-generation provincial middle-class migrants to Calcutta, a sentiment too acutely known to Dinabandhu Mitra, the writer of the Bengali farce, *Sadhabār Ekādaśī*. In his famous epilogue to *Nationalist Thought and the Colonial World*, Partha Chatterjee advises us to read this fascinating nineteenth-century account of urban decadence as 'the story of Enlightenment in the colonies', where Nimchand, a well-read drunkard of Calcutta, recites 'Hail holy light' seeing a police sergeant's lamp. For Chatterjee, the farce becomes profoundly symptomatic of the tragic dissolution of the liberatory promise of the Enlightenment into the cruel

* Versions of this chapter were presented in the University of Guadalajara, Mexico, and the Maulana Abul Kalam Azad Institute of Asian Studies, Calcutta.

[†] I am particularly grateful to Neeladri Bhattacharya, Saurabh Dube, Walter Mignolo, Tanika Sarkar, Hari Vasudevan, and Benjamin Zachariah for their comments and criticisms. Translations from Assamese and Bengali are mine.

[1] Dinabandhu Mitra, 1970 [1866], *Sadhabār Ekādaśī*, Calcutta: Bangiya Sahitya Parishat, p. 30.

certitudes of colonial governmentality.[2] For us, however, the tragedy doubles with Rammanikya, Nimchand's unsuccessful *mofussil* imitator. What may it take, we choose to ask along with and through this mofussil character, to 'become like a Calcuttan?'—to dissolve the provincial into the metropolitan theatre of the colonial modern?

What Bengal Thinks Today

…what Bengal thinks tomorrow, India will be thinking tomorrow week.[3]

Few remember today that the famous one-liner of the Marathi Congress leader, Gopal Krishna Gokhale—'What Bengal thinks today, India will think tomorrow'—was actually a citation of the epigrammed statement of Aurobindo Ghosh, the Bengali revolutionary-turned-*yogi*. Seemingly, there is no need to remember. For the wounded *bhadralok* soul, it has remained a comforting catchphrase, a self-congratulating axiom that gently stirs the pleasant memories of early nationalism. The slogan, popularized among the Bengali middle class during its so-called anti-partition agitation in 1905, continues to command the power of a proverb and the potential of a programme. It does not matter who coined it first. It is already a part of the nationalist common sense, a fixture of the polite bhadralok salons. But what does the slogan mean?

Perhaps one needs to look closely at the very movement during which the slogan gained its currency. By and large described as the first organized attempt of the Indian middle class to take the nationalist campaign from drawing rooms on to streets and public halls of Calcutta and other towns in Bengal, the so-called anti-partition agitation has come to be celebrated as 'nothing less than a revolution in the political structure of Bengali society', which, in turn, had a profound impact on the emergent Indian nationalism, in all its constitutional and extra-constitutional varieties.[4] 'Its goal no longer remained the mere abrogation of the partition,' asserts a standard textbook, 'but complete independence or swaraj, and in this sense the movement could not be considered in any way to be an expression of narrow Bengali sub-nationalism'.[5] It is beyond the scope of this chapter to offer a detailed narrative of the bhadralok agitation against Curzon's Territorial Redistribution Scheme. Sumit Sarkar's masterful account provides almost a day-by-day description.[6] However, in drawing attention to a particular rhetorical pattern of the nationalist discourse produced within this movement, which continues to be routinely underplayed in the standard South Asian historiography, the first section

---

[2] Partha Chatterjee, 1986, *Nationalist Thought and the Colonial World: A Derivative Discourse?* New Delhi: Oxford University Press, pp. 167–8.

[3] Aurobindo Ghosh, 1964 [1894], *Bankim Chandra Chatterji*, Pondicherry: Sri Aurobindo Ashram, p. 38. In 1909, Ghosh again asserted that '…what Bengal does today the rest of India will do tomorrow'. Aurobindo Ghosh, 1974 [1909], *Speeches*, Pondicherry: Sri Aurobindo Ashram, p. 104.

[4] Rajat K. Ray, 1984, *Social Conflict and Political Unrest in Bengal, 1875–1927*, New Delhi: Oxford University Press, p. 150.

[5] Sekhar Bandyopadhyay, 2004, *From Plassey to Partition: A History of Modern India*, Hyderabad: Orient Longman, p. 256.

[6] Sumit Sarkar, 1973, *The Swadeshi Movement in Bengal: 1903–1908*, New Delhi: People's Publishing House.

of this chapter wishes to identify a structural dynamic of the provincial in the nationalist problematic.

The early twentieth-century Bengali bhadralok agitators described the realignment of administrative state space in the eastern part of the British Indian Empire as 'a partition of Bengal'. In choosing to stay with this appellation, the standard histories keep to the tenor of Gokhale's slogan. While every history book casually mentions that the scheme involved spatial shuffling in the administrative units of Madras, Central Provinces, and Assam,[7] none actually takes care to spell out the dispersed, complex, and connected careers of this moment. I argue that this inattention is far from incidental or innocent, because in forcing the competing narratives of the spatial realignment to vanish into a linear account of the 'Bengal Partition', the standard histories confirm metropolitan nationalism's claim as the authentic other of colonialism.

To recount the basic facts, a new province of Eastern Bengal and Assam was formally announced amidst intense bhadralok protest on 19 July 1905, consisting of the Chief Commissionership of Assam; the Divisions of Chittagong, Dhaka, and Rajshahi; and the districts of Hill Tripura and Malda. According to the bhadralok calculations of the time, 'the Bengali Hindus' were to be a religious minority in the new province ('Muslims' outnumbering them by more than 6 million) and a linguistic minority in the old (as a result of incorporating large numbers of 'Hindi and Oriya-speaking population'). Deciding to speak in the name of the indivisible Bengali nation, the bhadralok agitators strongly reacted to what they recognized as a colonial conspiracy. The famous Town Hall Meeting at Calcutta (18 March 1904) directly asked, 'Why Dacca, Mymensingh, and the Chittagong Division should agree to enrich Assam at the cost of themselves and their kith and kin?'[8] It is important to emphasize here, against the grain of the sanctioned histories, that the spite of the Bengali nationalist press was often directed more to the savage Assamese neighbours than to the civilized British masters.

The 27 December 1903 issue of *Dhākā Prakāsh* characteristically wrote, 'It makes one tremble and shudder to think that the highly cultured people of five East Bengal districts will be thrown into social combination with the naked barbarians of Assam, and brought under the rule of despotic Assam officials. What

---

[7] The details are available in Ibid. Bandyopadhyay, *From Plassey to Partition*, p. 252, offers a useful summary:

Curzon drew up a scheme in his Minute on Territorial Redistribution in India (19 May/1 June 1903), which… proposed the transfer of Chittagong Division, Dacca and Mymensingh districts to Assam and Chota Nagpur to the Central Provinces; Bengal would receive in return Sambalpur and the feudatory states from Central Provinces and Ganjam district and the Vizagapatnam agency tracts from Madras. In the subsequent months the scheme gradually expanded, although secretly, through additions to the list of transferred districts. The final scheme was embodied in Curzon's dispatch of 2 February 1905 to the Secretary of State Broderick, who reluctantly accepted it without even a proper parliamentary debate.

[8] 'The Humble Memorial of the Residents of Calcutta, its Suburbs and the Various District of Bengal to His Excellency the Governor General in Council', in 1906, *Papers Relating to the Reconstitution of the Provinces of Bengal and Assam*, Simla: Government Central Printing Office, p. 264.

a degradation! What a misfortune!'[9] From Mymensingh, *Chāru Mihir* quipped with absolute detestation, 'The half-educated Assamese will continue to be the lords of the administration of the country, and we shall be judged and tried by them. What a misfortune!'[10] A more logic-chopping *Tripurā Hitaishi* observed in 1904 that '[t]he Assam officials have to dispense justice among the coolies, the Garos, the Nagas, the Akas and other savages, so that their higher faculties get deteriorated and they become unfit to deal with higher and more civilized people'.[11] The influential *Sanjivanī* prayed with all seriousness, 'O Lord Curzon! O Sir Andrew Fraser!…Do not drive us from the bright and radiant land of Bengal into the dark and dire cave of Assam.'[12] As the Bengal National Chambers of Commerce, the mainstay of this anti-imperial nationalism, explained in its petition,

the prospect of being transferred from a highly progressive and cultured province like that of Bengal to a backward and primitive province like that of Assam, of breaking off with old associations, of the enforced disruption of immemorial ties, of being cut off from their kith and kin, and lastly, the prospect of being lowered in the estimation of their brethren in other parts of India by being merged into a people placed on a much lower place of civilisation and with whom they have nothing in common, cannot

fail to produce deep pain, sorrow and discontent amongst the several millions of His Majesty's subjects living in Eastern Bengal…[13]

The mere possibility of being placed with a place that was out of place in the national time of modernity and history revealed an intensely exclusionary profile of metropolitan nationalism even when it was at one of its 'anti-colonial' peaks. 'The Humble Memorial of the Inhabitants of the District of Dacca' similarly insisted that 'the land beyond the river Meghna has always been looked down upon as the land of the aborigines'. The inclusion of Dhaka

into the Administration of Assam, and its permanent administrative association with tracts which have always been looked down upon in a social point of view, will be considered as degrading in the eye of Hindu Society, and they will, in course of time, lose all touch with their kith and kin in the other districts of Bengal. The tract, a person resides in, has always a determining effect in the eye of Hindu Society as to his social status.[14]

Almost all the nationalists asserted that the anachronistic space of Assam—'the dark and dire cave'—was completely incompatible

---

[9] *Dhākā Prakāsh*, 27 December 1903 (translation from the Report on Native *Newspapers*, 1903, IOR/L/R/5/29, Oriental and India Office Collections [OIOC]).

[10] *Chāru Mihir*, 22 December 1903 (translation from the relevant year's *Report on Native Newspapers*).

[11] *Tripurā Hitaishi*, 26 January 1904 (translation from the relevant year's *Report on Native Newspapers*).

[12] *Sanjivanī*, 28 January 1904 (translation from the relevant year's *Report on Native Newspapers*).

[13] Sita Nath Roy, Honorary Secretary, Bengal National Chambers of Commerce, to the Chief Secretary to the Government of Bengal, Calcutta, dated 3 February 1904, in *Papers Relating to the Reconstitution*, p. 85.

[14] 'The Humble Memorial of the Inhabitants of the District of Dacca to Sir Andrew Fraser, Lieutenant-Governor of Bengal, 4 March 1904', in 'Reconstruction of the Province of Bengal and Constitution of a New Province to be called the North Eastern Provinces', Home Department, Public-A, February 1905, Proceeding No. 157 (Enclosures to Letter from Government of Bengal, No. 2556-J, dated 6 April 1904, to the Address of the Government of India, Home Department) (OIOC).

with 'the bright and radiant land of Bengal', the earliest British possession in South Asia. As the Sylhet landowners elaborated in their petition,

To invest the chief executive authority of the Province [that is, Chief Commissioner] with discretionary power in respect of matters which hitherto formed a subject of written law would be to place them beyond the pale of all laws. *This is a state of things which would be quite suitable for a Province inhabited by unruly savages.* Sylhet, Your memorialists submit, was always considered as one of the advanced districts of Bengal. The people—at least the major portion of them—are as educated, enlightened and polished as those of any other Bengal district. To deprive them of laws is to place them in the category of half-tutored savages.[15]

As must be clear from this tiny sample of the enormous nationalist literature produced during the movement, the defence of the unity of an administrative unit was coded as the defence of the social, while the temporal unity of the social could be ensured only through the ceaseless production of anachronistic spaces. Arguments after arguments emerged in the nationalist archive pointing towards the primitive and backward character of Assam: it was an uncivilized country of barbarous tongues and lax caste rules; it had no respectable history; it was a malarious terrain with 'an unhealthy and cheerless climate';[16] a land of evil magic and wicked charms; and a free zone for savage head-hunters and immoral opium-eaters.

As a leader said in a public meeting, 'I say it is no light matter for 11 millions of people to be driven to *a strange land*, of congenial clime, to the land of kala-joar or black fever and to be forced to form alliance with *a strange people with whom we have nothing in common*'.[17] The term 'denationalization' became popularized during the movement. To quote *Chāru Mihir* again:

In culture and education the Mymensingh people are inferior to none in Bengal and in matters social, domestic, and political; they have through centuries been bound by indissoluble ties with the inhabitants of the other districts of the province. But Mr. Risley [the Home Secretary, a prime mover of the Scheme] is going to break these ties. Of two brothers, one is going to be a Bengali, and the other an Assamese; the nemesis of one will be different from the interests of the other; and one will grow under the superior administration of Bengal, and the other will dwindle under the inferior administration of Assam. The very thought that, after 20 or 25 years, the Mymensingh people will be different men from Bengalis, is tormenting. In origin, race, and language we are different from the Assamese. Our national language will suffer great deterioration by contact with the Assamese language. We shudder at the very thought.[18]

'I cannot see, nor has anyone succeeded in explaining it to me,' replied the Viceroy in his public address in Mymensingh, 'why a Bengali should cease to speak Bengali because a Chief Commissioner or a Lieutenant-Governor came to reside at Dacca [the proposed capital of Eastern Bengal and Assam], or why, as I said at Dacca, 14½ millions of Bengalis should

---

[15] 'The Humble Memorial of the Zemindars, Talukdars, and Other Proprietors of Land in the District of Sylhet to His Excellency the Viceroy and Governor General of India in Council', in *Papers Relating to the Reconstitution*, p. 112; emphasis added.
[16] *Amrita Bazar Patrika*, 20 January 1904.

[17] Sitanath Raybahadur, quoted in Sarkar, *The Swadeshi Movement in Bengal*, p. 41; emphasis added.
[18] *Chāru Mihir*, 22 December 1903 (translation from the relevant year's *Report on Native Newspapers*).

abandon their tongue because they enter into partnership with 1½ millions of Assamese.' In an attempt to conciliate the Bengali nationalists, Curzon said, '[p]robability would seem to point entirely in opposite direction, and to suggest that Assamese, whether it be a dialect of Bengali or whether it be a separate language—as to which the experts appear to differ—will be the one to disappear'.[19] In his 1903 Minute, Curzon admitted that the new 'province would acquire a new and composite character; but this character would not be more composite than is found in many other Indian administrations'. Fantasizing about an 'unbroken connection by rail between the oil wells of Digboi and Margherita, the coal mines of Makum, and the tea plantations of the Upper Brahmaputra,—and the Bay of Bengal', Curzon was determined to break 'the parochialism of Assam'.[20]

The state–society binary through which the standard 'Bengal Partition' historiography invites us to approach the design of the empire often serves to lead us away from the larger question of mobile geographies of capitalism.[21] In leaving the claims of the social untroubled, these histories unfortunately fail to address certain crucial complexities of nationalist discourse. '[A]s I travelled in the railway train yesterday,' Curzon told his audience in Dhaka on 18 February 1904, 'I saw batches of well-organised schoolboys holding up placards, on which was written, "Do not turn us into Assamese".'

Surely I need not point out to an intelligent audience that no administrative rearrangement can possibly turn one people into another, or make 14½ millions of people to speak any language but their own: and really the alarms that I am describing seem almost too childish to deserve notice were it not that I have found them to be seriously stated, and apparently genuinely entertained.[22]

The Chief Secretary to the Government of Bengal summed up the official justification in one line: 'Mere administrative division does not produce social division, any more than administrative unity produces social

---

[19] 'Addresses at Mymensingh, 20 February, 1904', in private papers of George Nathaniel Curzon, IOR/Mss. Eur. F111/247a (OIOC). An anonymous author of a Bengali nationalist tract countered this claim saying that 'Assamese may disappear as a separate language but not before mixing up some of its dialect with the language of Eastern Bengal [leading to its deterioration]', 1904, 'One of the People', in *The Partition of Bengal: An Open Letter to Lord Curzon*, Dacca: B. Chakravarty, p. 16.

[20] 'It is owing to its contracted area, to its restricted opportunities, to its lack of commercial outlet, to its alien services, and to the unhealthy predominance in its life and administration of a single industrial interest depending in the main upon imported labour, that what may be described as the parochialism of Assam is due.' 'Minute by His Excellency the Viceroy on Territorial Redistribution in India, Part II, (June 1, 1903)', in private papers of George Nathaniel Curzon, IOR/Mss. Eur. F111/247a (OIOC).

[21] Indeed, in planning to erect 'Assam into a vigorous and self-contained administration, capable of playing the same part on the North-East Frontier of India that the Central Provinces have done in the centre, and that the Punjab formerly did on the North-West', Curzon proposed to name the new province the North-Eastern Provinces. He was immediately told that 'the important commercial interests represented by the tea industry would complain if the name of Assam, now so widely known in the markets of the world as the chief source of Indian tea, were to disappear from the list of Indian Provinces'. Brodrick to the Governor General in Council, Public, No. 75, India Office London, dated 9 June 1905, in Ibid.

[22] 'Addresses at Dacca, 18 February, 1904', in Ibid.

union'.[23] In underscoring the gap between the depth of the social and the surface of the administrative ('*Mere* administrative division'), the imperial government was, in effect, trying to turn the tables on the nationalist agitators. After all, as Chatterjee accomplishedly demonstrates, the strategic foregrounding of an 'inner domain' outside the ravages of 'westernization' and colonialism was the necessary condition of this very nationalism.[24] Who could have understood the precariousness of the social better than those who had the greatest affective and material investments in the British Indian state space?

As the Chittagong *babu*s pointed out, their district was 'in fact, the first British district in the province'. If 'amalgamated with the backward Assam, the advanced and progressive Chittagong and the other districts will naturally gravitate towards the lower level as an inevitable result of such an unequal combination'.[25] This is hardly the place to recount the long and rather consistent history of disapproval,

condemnation, and lampooning with which the dominant bhadralok culture in Calcutta addressed the varying mofussil cultures of Chittagong, Sylhet, Dhaka, and other '*Bāngāl*' districts all through the nineteenth century, traces of which still animate the urban culture in postcolonial West Bengal; but in the sudden, *fin-de-siècle* pledge of unity and brotherhood during the 'anti-partition' movement, signs of this anxious economy were unmistakable. As the Mymensingh bhadraloks pointed out, 'by any division of Bengal proper, the portion detached from the Metropolis must lose the benefit of the energy, culture, and enlightenment of the residents of the Metropolis'.

This practical cessation of intercourse between East Bengal and West Bengal must necessarily lead to a deterioration of the language of the former—a language which is being gradually improved and assimilated to that of West Bengal. In this respect, His Excellency seems to be labouring under a mistaken impression. What your memorialists urge is not their language will cease to exist but that its gradual improvement will be retarded, and that ultimately it will assume the form of an inferior dialect. It is this inferiority of dialect which formerly caused the people of West Bengal to look down upon East Bengal. Your memorialists naturally apprehend that the severance of this district from the Metropolis or, more properly speaking, from the Bengal Government with its seat in the Metropolis, will remove one of the most important factors in the advancement of that people.[26]

---

[23] From the Officiating Chief Secretary to the Government of Bengal to the Secretary to the Government of India, Home Department, Calcutta, 6 April 1904 (Confidential), Para 42, in Ibid.

[24] Partha Chatterjee, 1993, *Nation and Its Fragments: Colonial and Postcolonial Histories*, Princeton: Princeton University Press, p. 6.

[25] 'The Humble Memorial of the Residents of Chittagong Assembled at a Public Meeting Held on the 17th Day of January 1904' (to G.N. Curzon, George Nathaniel Curzon, Viceroy of India), in 'Reconstruction of the Province of Bengal and Constitution of a New Province to be called the North Eastern Provinces', Home Department, Public-A, February 1905, Proceeding No. 157 (Enclosures to Letter from Government of Bengal, No. 2556-J, dated 6 April 1904, to the Address of the Government of India, Home Department) (OIOC).

[26] 'The Humble Memorial of the Inhabitants of the District of Mymensing' (to Andrew H.L. Fraser, Lieutenant-Governor of Bengal, undated), in *Papers Relating to the Reconstitution*, p. 117. Similarly, 'One of the People', *Partition of Bengal*, p. 10, remarks that the detached districts' 'culture would fall off owing to

It is not incidental that we started this chapter with Rammanikya. 'The greater Calcutta,' noted the Government of India in 1905, 'ranks among the twelve largest cities in the world, while the population of Calcutta proper is more numerous than that of any other city in the British Empire except London'.[27] But the question, let us repeat, is not so much of Calcutta and Mymensingh or of Bengal and Assam as of the unending enchantment of the metropolis. The reproducibility of the improvement template, we insist, is potentially infinite. The point becomes clearer from the response of the Assamese *śrījut*s to their Bengali detractors.[28]

'What do our Bengali friends mean by saying that Assam is a backward province, the people are not enlightened, and therefore they do not like to be mixed up with the savages?' asked a wounded Manik Chandra Barua.

Indeed, it is impossible to conceive an argument more selfish, more narrow-minded, more dishonourable, or more dishonest...Do they not remember that, about 30 years ago, Assam was a part and parcel of Bengal, and that it was under the same Lieutenant-Governor? Do they also not remember that when that high-minded ruler, Sir George Campbell, introduced 'Assamese', the language of the people of Assam, into Assam, a hue and cry was raised by the Bengalees, saying that 'Assamese' was not a language, and that it was a mere jargon of Bengali, and do they not now, in the same breath, say that 'Assamese' is quite a separate language?

'Is it not practically saying this,' asked Barua, 'that because the Assamese are backward, let them remain so, and let them be trodden down by their more-advanced neighbours?'[29] His friend, Jagannath Barua, the President of Jorhat Sarbajanik Sabha, similarly observed that:

[w]hen the question of recognising the Assamese language was under consideration and when the appointments in the services of Assam are [were?] claimed by Bengalis, it was urged all along that

---

less frequent communication with the metropolis of India, the centre of education and culture'. And again, on page 16, the author resented 'the estrangement of the literary view of Eastern Bengal from the men of light and leading in the metropolis'. And as the Bengal National Chambers of Commerce put it, 'From a common language, a common metropolis, a common administration, a common University, common social ties and commerce and religion and several other things in common between Western and Eastern Bengal, the inhabitants of both parts, men of culture, men of light and leading, freely mix on a common platform in the metropolis, imbibe and impart thoughts, and gather ideas and informations [sic]. Consequently it would be nothing short of a calamity to dismember Bengal proper, to forcibly disrupt immortal ties and to divide the Bengali-speaking race into two sections, absorbing and merging one section into a backward race inhabiting Assam.' Sita Nath Roy, Honorary Secretary, Bengal National Chambers of Commerce, to the Chief Secretary to the Government of Bengal, Calcutta, dated 3 February 1904, in *Papers Relating to the Reconstitution*, p. 80.

[27] 'Letter from the Government of India, to the Right Hon'ble St. John Brodrick, His Majesty's Secretary of State for India, dated 2 February 1905', in *Papers Relating to the Reconstitution*, p. 3.

[28] It may be mentioned here that in protest against the racist rhetoric of the Bengali 'anti-partition' activists, Tarun Ram Phukan left his practice in the Calcutta High Court and return to Assam. Mahendra

Mohan Chaudhuri, 1977, 'deśbhakta tarunrām phukan, in *Tarunrām Phukan Smritigrantha*, Guwahati: Publication Board, Assam p. 4.

[29] 'Note by *Srijut* Manik Chandra Barua, Dated Gauhati, February 27, 1904' (to Chief Commissioner), annexure to 'Proposed Redistribution of Territory between Bengal and Assam', From F.J. Monahan, the Secretary to the Chief Commissioner of Assam to the Secretary to the Government of India, Home Department, 6 April 1904, Home Department, Public-A, February 1905, Proceeding No. 156 (OIOC).

the two languages were one and the two people were one, but now, when the question of uniting a portion of Bengal with Assam has arisen, the Assamese language is declared to be an entirely different language and the Assamese people are relegated to the levels of Lushais and other hill tribes.[30]

The bhadraloks' anxiety in being classed together with the savage Assamese and the śrījuts' pain in being 'relegated to the levels of Lushais and other hill tribes' were not strikingly different. Acceptance of the category of 'backwardness' for self-description was an acceptance of the linear time of capital, modernity, and nation. Even the most untiring advocate of the Kāmarūpa glory, Kanak Lal Baruah, acknowledged the force of this temporal schema.

The Assamese, who came under British rule eighty years ago, are naturally less advanced than their more fortunate brethren the Bengalis, who have enjoyed the blessings of British rule in a central locality for nearly a century and a half. They [that is, the Assamese] are, therefore, alarmed at the prospects of having to run the race of life tied to a more advanced community.[31]

Gokhale's one-liner points at this inevitably hierarchized time of the national. The earliest entrant into the imperial order is logically more modern than the belated. It is only by accepting the autobiographical time of capital which enables it to describe itself as a coherent, self-sufficient, and universal project that the nation can insert itself into *le domaine moderne*, and in so far

as it remains committed to capital's schemes of improvement, anachronistic spaces remain its vital condition of possibility. Without the tragedy of Rammanikya, there is little humour in the metropolis.

The Days after Yesterday

To begin for another time is senseless.[32]

'In a sense Assam is fortunate,' declared Jawaharlal Nehru in 1937, 'for the very fact that it has been somewhat neglected and its development has been slow opens out promising vistas of rapid development on a planned basis, greater production of wealth and a rising standard of living for her people'.[33] The president of the Indian National Congress was visiting Assam on a hectic, eight-day propaganda tour. Characteristically and consistently, he spoke of the provincial space of Assam as an 'economic geography': an empty, diagrammatic space indifferent to affect, and eminently available to governmental planning and judicious investment of capital.[34] The belatedness of Assam in the imperial sequence was spatially translated

[30] 'Letter Dated Jorhat, February 10, 1904 from Rai Jagannath Barua, *Bahadur*, President, Jorhat Sarbajanik Sabha' (to Chief Commissioner), in Ibid.
[31] 'Note by *Srijut* Kanak Lal Barua, Extra Assistant Commissioner, Dated February 12, 1904' (to Chief Commissioner), in Ibid.

[32] Martin Heidegger, 1994, quoted in John van Buren, *The Young Heidegger: Rumor of the Hidden King*, Bloomington: Indiana University Press, p. 237.
[33] Jawaharlal Nehru, 1941, 'In the Valley of the Brahmaputra', *The Tribune*, 14 December 1937. Reprinted in Jawaharlal Nehru, *The Unity of India: Collected Writings, 1937–1940*, London: Lindsay Drummond, pp. 189–99.
[34] For a general discussion of the Nehruvian economic geographies, see Satish Deshpande, 2000, 'Hegemonic Spatial Strategies: The Nation-Space and Hindu Communalism in Twentieth-Century India', in Partha Chatterjee and Pradip Jeganathan (eds), *Subaltern Studies XI: Community, Gender and Violence*, New Delhi: Permanent Black, pp. 182–7.

in the Nehruvian register as its economic virginity: Assam was almost an undamaged outside of the colonial in which the new could be successfully forged.

Elsewhere in India I have seldom had this sense of latent power and resources which the jungles and unoccupied spaces of Assam have given me. The place cries aloud for the mind and the hand of man to develop it, but this can only be for the public good if it is organized and planned and deliberately aimed at the betterment of the masses.[35]

The rhetoric of exteriority, however, could not be stretched too far. Assam was capable of emerging as an organized theatre of the postcolonial only to the extent it shared the burden of colonial history with the rest of the Indian nation.

Indeed, Nehru was particularly disappointed by the fact that the 'Congress organisation in Assam is not as strong and as widespread as it should be'.[36] Assam could not be allowed to 'lag behind politically' any longer, he said in his speech at Dhubri. 'India must get Swaraj today or tomorrow. Assam is not outside India and she will also get it.'[37] Nehru claimed that he knew of the problems that the provincial middle class was evidently concerned about: 'Opium, the future of Sylhet, immigration and the Line System, the tea gardens, and more especially the labour employed there, and the excluded and partially excluded areas with the various tribal folk inhabiting them.'[38] But,

as he wrote to the president of the Assam Provincial Congress Committee, 'I want your committee and the Assam people to realise that we have far bigger problems ahead and big changes are coming in the course of the next fear years, and not to bother much about other matters which will inevitably be taken in hand as soon as we have greater power'.[39] The provincial was a technical problem, a managerial failure, a loose bolt in the national machine. The national, on the other hand, was the only authentic ground of contesting the colonial.

In his public statements too, Nehru emphasized the overriding importance of the two major national problems of India, namely, the attainment of independence and the eradication of poverty. 'I came up against particular problems affecting Assam and exercising the minds of the people of the province, and yet they were secondary before the major problem of India,' Nehru wrote in *The Tribune*. 'It is this problem of poverty and that of Swaraj and national freedom that overshadow all local problems and we must always remember this if we are to retain a proper perspective and work effectively.'[40] In his address at Silchar, he linked the question with that of modernity. '[T]here is nothing as magic in this world,' he said. Hard work, criticality, and democracy would 'build up a nation which had become denationalised through long years of foreign domination'. Provincial parochialisms had no place in this world: 'What really is [sic] important today is not the local problems but the problems of India. I, therefore, urge you to think in terms

---

[35] Nehru, 'In the Valley of the Brahmaputra'.
[36] Jawaharlal Nehru to Bishnu Ram Medhi, Camp Jorhat, dated 1 December 1937, in AICC File No. P-4/1937–38, New Delhi: Nehru Memorial Museum and Library.
[37] *Amrita Bazar Patrika*, 28 November 1937.
[38] Nehru, 'In the Valley of the Brahmaputra'.

[39] Jawaharlal Nehru to Bishnu Ram Medhi.
[40] Nehru, 'In the Valley of the Brahmaputra'.

of India and to some extent in terms of the world.'[41]

Jnananath Bora, a political commentator and activist from Assam, published an impassioned response to Nehru's speech in the popular periodical, *Āvāhan*. In a certain sense, this response was a continuation of his earlier and lengthier piece in the same periodical, 'Kāmarūpa and India'. In that piece, Bora had entered into a detailed discussion of the relationship between a *deś* (country/nation) and a *pradeś* (region/ province). It was only after the arrival of the British, said Bora, that 'our ever-free country became a province'.

From then on, Kāmarūpa or Assam is not a *deś* anymore—it is a mere *pradeś*. In the beginning, our people could not understand it. For a long period of time our people continued to consider Assam as a different *deś* from India [Bhāratvarsha], and did not participate in any of its programs. This was only natural. For two thousand years our people have regarded their *deś* as an independent *deś* in the world…For the last thirty years or so, there have been signs of a change. Some of our people have started to think of our *deś* as a *pradeś* of India; but this is not a feeling common to all. Our people still cannot think of the people of Punjab or Madras as our own countrymen. They are as distant as the people of China or Afghanistan.

Turning the long nineteenth-century history of distance upside down, Bora argued that what had been condemned in the official accounts as isolation and remoteness of the province was actually indicative of Assam's refusal to accept a provincial status. According to him, provincialization of Assam had the most damaging effects on its people.

Only a century has passed under the British rule in Assam. Since Assam has been administered as a part of India over this century, our educated class has come to view its own *deś* as a *pradeś* of India. There cannot be any doubt that this change has narrowed the ideas of our people. Our ancestors, while having been based in Kāmarūpa, could look at the whole world and adopt different models of other *deśes* to improve the condition of their *deś*. But now our downfall is so complete that we can only look within the confines of India and not even the adjacent *deśes*. Today the *pradeśes* of India are our sole models. Our people are following the other *pradeśes* of India on every account. Forgetting our distinctiveness, our particularity, our originality, they are blindly imitating the *pradeśes* of Bengal or Punjab. This is the present condition of the ever-free *deś* of Kāmarūpa.[42]

Bora's own models therefore came from Europe. In a detailed chart, he compared the respective population figures and area measurements of Albania, Austria, Belgium, Bulgaria, Czechoslovakia, Denmark, Greece, the Irish Free State, and Switzerland with those of his proposed 'Kāmarūpa' (the British province of Assam in 1936 without the district of Sylhet but inclusive of the division of Jalpaiguri), and concluded that Assam suited almost every criterion of a modern nation-state, a *deś*.[43] In his response to Nehru a few months later, Bora criticized Nehru for not having recognized the true nature or intensity of the problems of Assam. If Assam's problems were secondary in priority because they were 'provincial problems' and not national, then—according to Bora—the best way to put these problems on top of the list was to make Assam an

[41] *Amrita Bazar Patrika*, 7 December 1937.

[42] Jnananath Bora, 1936, 'Kāmrūp āru Bhāratvarsha', *Āvāhan*, vol. 8, no. 3, p. 255.
[43] Ibid., pp. 260–1.

independent nation, a deś rather than a prádeś: 'If we cannot achieve our objectives in staying as a pradeś within India, then we should not hesitate to secede from India and form an independent deś.'[44]

It is not my purpose here to deal with the details of Bora's 'objectives' or his strong and complex rhetoric of anti-immigration; rather, I wish to call the reader's attention to his logic of deś and pradeś, which is of continuing interest to many political activists in the present-day Indian northeast.[45] In Bora's understanding, deś was the cancellation of pradeś: the dignity of the national was the best antidote to the disgrace of the provincial. In an article titled, 'Why Will the Assam *Deś* Stay within India', Bora, more explicitly, linked the understanding of a lived space as a provincial space to the fact of colonial occupation. The Indian National Congress, he said, actually continued and strengthened the imperial politics of provincialization as it entered Assam in the 1920s.

It was injected into the mind of the Assamese public that Assam was not a different *deś* but a *pradeś* of India...[It was taught that] We are Indians first and Assamese later. Every matter of Assam, each of its problems is provincial [*pradeśik*], and hence can in no way be given primary attention...As a result of these lessons, the problems of Assam were pushed out of purview. However deep our problems are, they are considered provincial and therefore unworthy

of attention...Now the situation has become such that our people feel embarrassed and ashamed if one mentions the interests of the Assamese nation. The educated people are always scared lest they are called insular and narrow-minded.[46]

For Bora, only nationalism, as a full-blooded politics of legitimation and authentication, could offer a promise of the fullness of presence, an answer to the self-denigration and ignominy of the provincial. The independent nation-state of Assam would not have to imagine itself as a bad copy of the other provinces of India; as a deś, it would preserve 'our distinctiveness, our particularity, our originality'. Needless to say, Bora did not wish to see the constant reproduction of the provincial within Assam—the domination and denigration of the Hills, the delegitimation and chastisement of *Bhāti*, the inauthentication and vilification of the 'settlers'.[47] Nor was he open to the possibility that the very desire for distinctiveness, particularity, and originality was the missing twin of what he criticized as embarrassment, shame, and self-doubt among the provincial middle class.[48] But there is a less obvious point too. The point concerns the putative autonomy and self-presence of a deś.

---

[44] Bora, 'Kāmrūp āru Bhāratvarsha', p. 120.

[45] In his controversial *Swādhīnatār Prastāb* (Proposition of Independence), the independentist activist, Parag Kumar Das, categorically reclaimed the legacy of Jnananath Bora while making a case for secession of Assam from India. See Parag Kumar Das, 1993, *Swādhīnatār Prastāb*, Guwahati: Author, pp. 36–40.

[46] Jnananath Bora, 1938, 'Asam Deś Bharatvarshar Bhitarat Thakiba Kiya (Asamiyā Jāti Āru Congress)', *Āvāhan*, vol. 10, no. 3, pp. 261–74.

[47] For a related discussion, see Bodhisattva Kar, 2008, '"Tongue Has No Bone": Fixing the Assamese Language, c. 1800–c. 1930', *Studies in History*, vol. 24, no. 1, pp. 27–76.

[48] Cf. Julia Kristeva 1993, *Nations without Nationalism*, trans. Leon S. Roudiez, New York: Columbia University Press, pp. 3–4. Of course, Kristeva's valorization of 'the French national idea' is disturbing, to say the least.

Provincialization, for Bora, is the effect of an exogenous force, an invasion, an assault that comes from an ever-present outside. The force confiscates a deś and turns it into a pradeś. Therefore, the project of turning a pradeś back into a deś necessarily involves a gesture of return: to the original place, to an etymological beginning, to Kāmarūpa.[49] Bora's repeated invocations of the history of 'two thousand years' of an 'ever-free deś of Kāmarūpa' are hardly incidental. Nationalism, as Derrida points out, has to 'indissociably' connect 'the ontological value of present-being to its situation, to the stable and presentable determination of a locality, the *topos* of territory, native soil, city, body in general'. He calls it the axiomatics of ontopology.[50] At the heart of the ontopology of Bora's political nationalism, however, is active the heterotopia of historicist pedagogy. The original place is always elsewhere, another space, 'outside of the time and inaccessible to its ravages'.[51] The nation-space (deś) becomes conceivable only as a misplaced space, the nation (*jāti*) as a displaced people. Sense of loss and proprietorial logic reinforce each other in the form of an unforgiving circularity. Without this spectral centrality of *elsewhere*, there is no 'here and now' of the nation.

Coming back from the ruthless expedition against the Abors in Assam in 1911, a young British soldier lamented in his journal that '[t]he frontier tribesman…always sees us at our weakest'. He mentioned the 'gigantic difficulties of road-making, transport, and supply' which had to be necessarily overcome 'before we can throw out the smallest feeler into his territory, and our subsequent victory over him is sometimes therefore not of the most signal kind'.

But when a little of what one might call 'punitive globe-trotting,' imposed as one of the terms of peace, might have a great effect upon our future relations. Imagine a band of hostages handed over to us at the close of hostilities for a couple of years, and the chance thus afforded of enlarging their political outlook. A dozen Abor *gāms* would, for instance, make excellent subjects for 'punitive globe-trotting.' We would start by a little general education of an elementary kind. Having thus rendered them receptive of larger notions, we would proceed to 'trot' them round the British Empire, expound to them the big physical facts upon which our empire is founded, and then send them back to their corner in the mountains to give a salutary account of what they had learnt to their fellow-tribesmen.[52]

Millington's fantasies are remarkable for too many reasons. But what matters most for the present discussion is his allusion to the enormous power of *elsewhere*. Even the severest conquest of a place is unfinished until the conquered is exposed to other places and forced to trot the globe at the heels of

---

[49] For an elaboration of the Kāmarūpa question, see Bodhisattva Kar, 2004, *What Is In a Name? Politics of Spatial Imagination in Colonial Assam*, Guwahati: Centre for Northeast India, South and Southeast Asia Studies, Omeo Kumar Das Institute for Social Change and Development.

[50] Jacques Derrida, 1994, *Specters of Marx: The State of the Debt, the Work of Mourning, and the New International*, trans. Peggy Kamuf, New York: Routledge, p. 82.

[51] Michel Foucault, 1986, 'Of Other Spaces', *Diacritics*, trans. Jay Miskowiec, vol. 16, no. 1, p. 26. See also, Kar, *What Is In a Name?*

[52] Powell Millington, 1912, *On the Track of the Abor*, London: Smith, Elder & Co., pp. 67–8.

the masters.[53] It is from one's place in a sequence that one must know the meaning of one's own place, and there is no sequence without other places. The obscene pride of the empire in the length and variety of its territorial sequence formally contrasts with the modest 'desire and designs' of the nation for its supposed homogeneity.[54] But, as Benedict Anderson points out, it is only in the 'new, restless double-consciousness' of comparison lies 'the origin of nationalism'.[55] What would Bora's 'Kāmarūpa' do in a world without the corresponding European exemplars? In a brilliant gloss on Anderson, Pheng Cheah writes that '[c]omparison is a specter precisely because it is a form of inhuman automatism conjured up by capitalism's eternal restlessness'.[56] In other words, the comparative moment can occur only in the series of autobiographical time of capital.

As the condition of comparison, *elsewhere* is intrinsic to the discourse of the nation. The deferral of the authentic is the only manner in which the power of authentication can continue to hold sway. What matters about this labyrinth is not that the nation never reaches the authentic, but that such a notion of the authentic cannot cease to govern the national imaginary. This ostensible ineffaceability of the provincial does not, however, make the work of deprovincialization utopian. On the contrary, it saves such work from being reduced to an exorcist gesture. The work of deprovincialization, explain Mbembe and Nuttall, involves reading the minor place of the provincial 'in the same terms as we read everywhere else'.[57] This activates a brilliant displacement: the cheery promise of familiarization ('the same terms as... everywhere else') develops into a scary project of defamiliarization. The nation begins to resemble the empire, and the province, in its turn, confirms the infinite replicability of the nation form with relentless capacities for further provincializations. Anderson's thesis of 'serialization' takes a wicked turn.[58] The novel of comparison becomes infinite histories of co-constitution.

It is at this point of the discussion that the specificity of the colonial again appears as a riddle. Amalendu Guha tells us that there were not too many takers for Jnananath Bora's 'secessionist' ideas in the 1930s, and that even Ambikagiri Raychaudhury's model

[53] See Robert Reid, 1942, *History of the Frontier Areas Bordering on Assam, from 1883 to 1941*, Shillong: Assam Government Press, p. 230 for a brief description of crop burning, village burning, 'rapid fire', and forcible displacements of the target population during the 1911 expedition.

[54] Roger Chartier, 1988, *Cultural History: Between Practices and Representations*, trans. Lydia G. Cochrane, Cambridge: Polity Press, p. 195.

[55] Benedict Anderson, 1998, *The Specter of Comparisons: Nationalism, Southeast Asia and the World*, London and New York: Verso, p. 229.

[56] Pheng Cheah, 1999, 'Grounds of Comparison', *Diacritics*, vol. 29, no. 4, p. 12. In such a description there is, however, an unmistakable shadow of Pheng Cheah's own neo-vitalist defence of the nation form as 'the last effective bearer of the idea of transcendental freedom for the majority of the world's masses'. Cf. Pheng Cheah, 2003, *Spectral Nationality: Passages of Freedom from Kant to Postcolonial Literatures of Liberation*, New York: Columbia University Press, p. 197.

[57] Achille Mbembe and Sarah Nuttall, 2004, 'Writing the World from an African Metropolis', *Public Culture*, vol. 16, no. 3, p. 351.

[58] Cf. Benedict Anderson, 1991, *Imagined Communities: Reflections on the Origin and Spread of Nationalism*, London and New York: Verso, pp. 184–5.

of dual citizenship did not have 'any general acceptance among the Assamese people'.[59] Within half a century, however, Bora became common sense for many. 'The struggle for national liberation of Assam never is a separatist or secessionist movement', declares the website of the United Liberation Front of Asom (ULFA), the particular insurgent organization around which the contemporary discourse of 'independent Assam' has consolidated since its inception in 1979. According to ULFA, the question of 'secession' is a mistaken one since 'historically', Assam has never been a part of the Indian nation and its location within the political map of India has to be explained simply as a fact of 'colonial occupation'.[60]

While the Indian state is too eager to assure its metropolitan citizens that ULFA's call for independence ('secession') is the voice of a few isolated youths in the province propped up by the bad neighbours, most of the perceptive commentators point at the facile naivety of such descriptions. Contending that 'the ideas that inspire ULFA are located in the mainstream of Assamese social, political and cultural life',

Sanjib Baruah offers informed accounts of critical complicities between 'mainstream' institutions and 'marginal' outfits.[61] The ULFA's description of the Indian nation-state as a colonial empire is, of course, neither original nor unusual. Scores of other guerrilla organizations in the northeastern frontier (and elsewhere) continue to challenge the postcolonial credentials of the Indian state, while the government statements routinely refer to the difficulties of '*regional* inequalities' in the northeast as an obstruction to 'nation building'. It is not my purpose to judge the verities of these contending constructs. What the continuing career of the idioms of deś and pradeś indicates is a larger paradox: consigned to the relentless reproduction of the provincial under the sign of modernization, territorial nationalism can never abolish its mythical other—colonialism—which always threatens to lodge itself within the very claims of nationalism.[62]

To ask if the postcolonial can begin, therefore, is to begin questioning the very

---

[59] Amalendu Guha, 1977, *Planter-Raj to Swaraj: Freedom Struggle and Electoral Politics in Assam, 1826–1947*, New Delhi: Indian Council of Historical Research, p. 316.

[60] Available at http://www.geocities.com/ CapitolHill/Congress/7434/ulfa.htm (Last accessed on 15 June 2004). See also, ULFA Chairman Arvind Rajkhowa's assertion that 'history does not sustain the argument that Asom and Asom's identity is part of India and the Indian identity…Asom was never a part of India. Indian history provides no instance of any Indian ruler ever ruling Asom', quoted in 'Assam Conflict: Chronology of Events'. Available at http://www.safhr.org/index.php?option=com_ docman&task=cat_view&gid=204&Itemid=647 (Last accessed on 27 December 2010).

[61] Sanjib Baruah, 2005, *Durable Disorder: Understanding the Politics of Northeast India*, New Delhi: Oxford University Press, p. 168. See also Udayon Misra, 2000, *The Periphery Strikes Back: Challenges to the Nation-State in Assam and Nagaland*, Shimla: Indian Institute of Advanced Study, p. 143.

[62] It must be added here that nothing is to be gained from sanitizing this paradox as 'internal colonialism', because the jargons and forms of interiority and exteriority are complicit in the project and cannot be deployed to comprehend it. Cf. Michael Hechter, 1975, *Internal Colonialism: The Celtic Fringe in British National Development, 1536–1966*, London: Routledge and Kegan Paul. See also Tilottama Misra, 1980, 'Assam: A Colonial Hinterland', *Economic and Political Weekly*, vol. 15, no. 32, 9 August, pp. 1357–65; and Apurba Kumar Baruah, 1991, *Social Tensions in Assam: Middle Class Politics*, Guwahati: Purbanchal Prakash.

idea of beginning, at least the epistemic–ontological privilege conventionally attached to it. In the delirious recurrence of capitalist modernity, in the endless repetitions of the difference we code as colonial, the trope of an epochal beginning makes as little sense as the fullness of the futural. '[F]orever promised in an imminence always nearer yet never accomplished', Foucault notices, the beginning necessarily recedes into the future.[63] It is this elusiveness of the postcolonial, guaranteed by the structural dynamic of the provincial in modernization regimes, which makes its inaugural gesture possible. The challenge may be somewhat different: if the capacity we call the postcolonial is a new realm of its negation, can we continue to hold on to 'our historical moment [as] that of the preparation for the other beginning?'[64] One of the distinctive challenges of modernity, after all, is the production of the new in an establishment which itself is premised on inexorable demand and fabrication of novelties.

[63] Michel Foucault, 1971, *The Order of Things: An Archaeology of the Human Sciences*, New York: Pantheon Books, p. 332.

[64] Cf. Martin Heidegger, 1994, *Basic Questions of Philosophy: Selected 'Problems' of 'Logic'*, trans. Richard Rojcewicz and André Schuwer, Bloomington: Indiana University Press, p. 172.

3

Maladies of Modernity
Malaria and the Making of Burdwan Fever*

Rohan Deb Roy[†]

The terms 'epidemic', 'time' and 'space' are the most general abstractions which we can form and if we bring them together the result must be something vague and visionary...An abstract term 'epidemic influence' is invented or utilized, and made to do as a substantive 'theory' of a more occult or quasi learned description...The whole process is a melancholy exhibition of false generalising.[1]

It is curious to note how mankind is led by watchwords. Be it religion, politics, or popular science, the commanding officer of the hour issues the countersign, and the sect, party, or society catches it up, and it is repeated, and echoed and re-echoed until the sound becomes faint, or the voice is deadened by the higher tone of new utterance. It is a strange phase of human life, this system of watchwords...[2]

This chapter explores the making of Burdwan fever. In various official registers, the Burdwan fever featured as a malarial epidemic that hit the Burdwan division of the Bengal Presidency in British India in the 1870s. Burdwan fever and 'the

* A shorter earlier version of this chapter was published in 2008 as '"An Unseen, Awful Visitant": The Return of Burdwan Fever', in *Economic and Political Weekly*, vol. 43, no. 12, March, pp. 62–70.

† I thank Saurabh Dube, Partha Chatterjee, David Arnold, Mark Harrison, Peter Robb, Gautam Bhadra, Sanjoy Bhattacharya, Anne Hardy, Ishita Banerjee–Dube, Guy Attewell, Projit Mukharji, Atig Ghosh, Bodhisattva Kar, Upal Chakrabarti, Shinjini Das, and the anonymous readers for their encouraging suggestions and invaluable criticisms.

1 'Editorial: Prominent Fallacies in Epidemiology',

Indian Medical Gazette (henceforth *IMG*), vol. 8, 1 July 1873, pp. 188–89, 217.

2 'Editorial: Draining Bengal', *IMG*, vol. 7, September 1872, p. 209.

malarial epidemic in Bengal' tended to figure interchangeably as almost identical categories. Unlike previous narrations of Burdwan fever, this chapter does not understand this 'malarial epidemic' as an event, which constituted the simultaneous replication of a single homogenous, monolithic malady in a million bodies. Instead, it shows how Burdwan fever and the 'malarial epidemic' could signify historically produced labels: shorthand expressions that provided convenient points of reference to a dispersed set of officials. In numerous acts of bureaucratic reporting in the second half of the nineteenth century in Bengal, 'the malarial epidemic' presented itself as a flexible medical metaphor, which could be invoked to explain myriad expressions of physical unease, varying over time and across space.[3]

This chapter, then, refrains from probing into *why* there had been a malarial epidemic in Bengal in the nineteenth century. Nor is it exclusively a study of the inadequate responses of the colonial government or the reactions of the local landed proprietors. Instead, it asks *how* a series of dispersed and dissimilar debilities could be put together as a single, continuous epidemic of malaria in Bengal and beyond over much of the nineteenth century.

Historians have frequently defined 'epidemics' as ontologically accessible phases of countless deaths and ceaseless sufferings. Critiques of colonial medicine have justifiably appropriated the 'reality of epidemics' as excuses to narrate a range of meaningful stories varying from governmental exploitation to mismanagement.[4] In the process, the category 'epidemic' itself has often been inherited from the colonial archive at face value. Such histories, I argue, are necessary but incomplete. Existing critiques of colonial medicine have often been inadequately sceptical about the foundational categories of medical knowledge. This chapter suggests that critiques of colonial medicine can be reinforced by interrogating its epistemological bases.

It considers 'epidemics', to begin with, as complex configurations of scientific knowledge. Such knowledge, this chapter argues, were framed and sustained through overlapping networks of interest and authority. It then resists the temptation of engaging into yet another hackneyed attempt of probing the causes or effects of Burdwan fever. Instead, it hints at the symbiotic world of investments and assumptions, which enabled the constitution and sustenance of Burdwan fever as an enduring phase in the history of colonial Bengal.

This chapter examines simultaneously the making of a locality. It argues that there was no 'local' that always and already existed as a natural geographical entity on the map of the British Empire. Locations like Burdwan were defined as the 'local' through conscious strategies of knowledge gathering initiated by the colonial state. Such strategies ended up circulating enduring impressions about land, landscape, and people.

---

[3] For a study of the different meanings associated with 'malaria' in nineteenth-century British India and beyond, see Rohan Deb Roy, 2007, 'Mal-areas of Health: Dispersed Histories of a Diagnostic Category', *Economic and Political Weekly*, vol. 42, no. 2, 13 January, pp. 13–19.

[4] For instance, see Arabinda Samanta, 2002, *Malarial Fever in Colonial Bengal, 1820–1939, Social History of an Epidemic*, Kolkata: Firma KLM.

Cinchona Disease

Surgeon Major Albert M. Vercherie left a tour diary narrating his visits to inspect cases reported as 'malarial' in different parts of the Burdwan town in September 1873. He referred to the case of a *dhobi*'s daughter who lived in the bazaar region. She was registered as a patient of one Dina Bondhu Dutt, a local physician, and was recorded as a case of 'malaria'. In the fourteen days Vercherie kept track of her, it was found that she was gradually diagnosed with the following maladies successively: typhus, enteric fever, cholera, and relapsing fever. 'I heard from Dr French that the case became complicated by pleuro-pneumonia about thirteenth or fourteenth day of disease.'[17] Thus, detailed individual case histories reveal that those who were labelled as suffering from 'malaria' could be diagnosed with different diseases in different phases in the same continuous course of illness. The given example also specifies some of the other jargons besides 'malaria' that could be invoked to explain a similar set of symptoms.

How could such confusion, marked by an overabundance of closely simulating diagnostic tropes, be resolved? Yadunath Mukhopadhyaya narrated a similar experience of attending to a little girl 8–10 years of age. She was initially diagnosed as suffering from cholera. When the relevant fever mixtures and stimulants failed, and the physician was about to give up the 'case', he decided to gamble with quinine. Subsequently, the girl gradually recovered. Mukhopadhyaya narrated this experience to suggest how the malarial identity of a particular form of physical unease could be determined from how a body reacted to quinine.[18] A careful study of individual case histories recorded during the 'epidemic' reveals that such examples could be multiplied. The figure of quinine was frequently invoked as a diagnostic tool. Cases labelled as 'malarial' well into the third quarter of the nineteenth century owed their identities not to laboratory tests, but to the experience and expertise of individual physicians. When both failed, such quick-fix pharmacological tests determined the fate of the patient.

In many more ways, the 'malarial epidemic' owed itself to quinine. Decades before dispersed expressions of little debilities in various parts of Bengal began to be written about as diverse articulations of single, continuous malarial epidemic, quinine had already been convincingly advertised as the quintessential remedy of every form of malarial disease. Such advertisements were vigorously reiterated in the official registers in various moments in the 1850s.[19] Quinine was confidently

[17] Albert M. Vercherie, 1873, 'Extracts from a Diary Kept during a Visit to Burdwan in September 1873', *IMG*, vol. 8, 1 November, pp. 287–9.

[18] Mukhopadhyaya, *Saral Jvara Chikitsa*, pp. 103–6.

[19] For instance, A. Bryson, 1854, 'Navy Medical Report Number XV on the Prophylactic Influence of Quinine', *Medical Times and Gazette*, vol. viii (new series), no. 1, London, pp. 6–7; A. Bryson (ed.), 1859, 'The Practice of Giving Quinine or Quinine Wine on Distant Expeditions on the West Coast of Africa', *Statistical Report of the Health of the Royal Navy for the Year 1857*, London: House of Commons, pp. 82–5; D. Blair, 1848, 'On the Employment of Quinine on West India Fevers', *Lancet*, vol. 52, no. 1308, p. 344; S. Rogers, 1862, 'The Protective or Prophylactic Preventive, and Some Points in the Curative Uses of

acknowledged not merely as a febrifuge but also as a prophylactic. This appeared firmly entrenched in the military files of the government. In certain regiments in British India, consuming regular doses of quinine formed a part of the mandatory breakfast.[20] Travelling officials like Lieutenant G.S. Hills who doubted the labelling of the epidemic as 'malarial' were nonetheless found to take daily preventive doses of quinine.

The more I saw of the District the less competent did I feel to determine upon any one particular cause for this dreadful scourge...I noticed in villages recently attacked, that a hot steamy atmosphere seemed to pervade the village, the nauseating and depressing effects of which were almost intolerable. I also experienced a cold chilly feeling creep over me in spite of the hot close atmosphere in the village...This sensation in my case was never followed by any pernicious effects, which may be attributed to taking quinine daily...[21]

As late as 1874, a considerable range of colonial officials sounded unsure about the malarial character of the malady. For instance, Dr Albert Vercherie, a member of the Indian Medical Service, was convinced that it was typhus.[22] Lieutenant Governor Sir Richard Temple, writing a decade after

Lieutenant G.S. Hills, seemed equally hesitant to attribute the series of maladies in contemporary Bengal to 'any particular cause'.[23]

However, there seemed to circulate a consensus that quinine could be its unquestionable remedy. Years before doubts involving the 'malarial' character of the epidemic could be conclusively resolved, quinine had made its way into the interiors of Bengal.[24] The indiscriminate use of quinine had been condemned even in certain governmental correspondence.[25] Through most of the 1860s and the early years of the 1870s, government files in Bengal revealed organized efforts to procure additional quinine from Madras and Bombay Presidencies to combat the 'outbreak'.[26] They also reveal obsessive efforts in indenting quinine from England[27] while, at the same time, tracking the details of its journey from England,[28] in frequently measuring its stock in the rapidly exhausting medical stores,[29] and in requesting the military department to spare some quinine in favour of the civil departments.[30] It is very difficult to miss the enormous correspondence between officials placed in different levels—the subdivision, districts, and divisions—supervising and instructing the distribution of quinine in the villages through the panchayats and in

Quinine, Applicable to Miasmatic Localities and in Miasmatic Diseases', *Transaction of the Medical Society of the State of New York,* Albany, pp. 181–202.

[20] Home, Medical Board, 21 October 1858, file no. 14; 28 October 1858, file no. 52; 2 December 1858, file no. 58, NAI.

[21] Lieutenant G.S. Hills, Executive Engineer, Shillong Division, on Special Duty, to H.L. Dampier, Commissioner of the Nuddea Division, 31 December 1864, Home, Public, 7 March 1868, 140–3A, NAI.

[22] Albert M. Vercherie, 1874, 'Extracts from a Diary Kept during a Visit to Burdwan in September 1873', IMG, vol. 9, 1 January, pp. 8–12.

[23] Richard Temple, 1875, 'The Causes of, and Remedies for the Burdwan Fever, Minute by the Lieutenant Governor of Bengal', dated 25 August 1875, Home, Medical, November, 53–5A, NAI.

[24] Home, Public, April 1872, 508A, NAI.

[25] General, Medical, May 1872, 92–3B, NAI.

[26] Home, Public, September 1872, 441–4A, NAI.

[27] Home, Public, December 1872, 344–53A, NAI.

[28] Home, Public, Septemebr 1872, 441–4A, NAI.

[29] Home, Public, August 1872, 574–7A, NAI.

[30] Home, Public, December 1872, 344–53A, NAI.

the circles through the dispensaries. Such correspondence suggests how the units of revenue extraction began to be projected as units of affording relief.

Since the 1850s, the careers of malarial diseases and quinine were repeatedly written about as inseparable parts of a single, shared history. Widely circulating publications in medical journals,[31] stories narrating past glories of the Jesuit Bark,[32] reports on adventures into the interiors of the Peruvian forests,[33] and the foundational programmatic statements from the early managers of cinchona plantations in India[34] informed official understandings. This resulted in impressions that quinine and malarial diseases were invariably associated. The presence of one seemed to imply the presence of another. At a time when official characterization of dispersed debilities and deaths in Bengal suffered from imprecision, governmental alacrity in distributing quinine contributed to the reinforcement of the malarial identity of the epidemic.

An understanding that the introduction of the drug in Bengal immediately preceded the outbreak of the epidemic was reflected in certain publications in late nineteenth century. In an editorial of the Homoeopathic journal titled, *The Calcutta Journal of Medicine*, the epidemic figured as a consequence of the introduction of quinine in Bengal. The editorial characterized the epidemic as a *Cinchona disease* that resulted from the side effects of consuming regular doses of quinine. It argued that while quinine relieved the body from milder and temporary forms of illness, it plagued the body with a worse and enduring form of disease: Cinchona disease.[35] Such impressions survived well into the last decade of the nineteenth century. Fuelled by revivalist flames, the Bengali medical journal, *Chikitsa Sammilani*, blasted the government policy of distributing quinine at cheap rates from the post offices for causing general sickness and fever in rural Bengal since 1893.[36]

Opportunity of the Epidemic

The careers of malarial epidemic and quinine in nineteenth-century Bengal were caught up in a symbiotic relation. It has been indicated how the figure of quinine had been invoked to add precision to the malarial identity of the epidemic. The epidemic as well proved to be an occasion when the usefulness of

---

[31] For instance, Bryson, 'Navy Medical Report Number XV on the Prophylactic Influence of Quinine'; Blair, 'On the Employment of Quinine on West India Fevers'.

[32] For instance, C.R. Markham, 1874, *A Memoir of the Lady Ana de Osorio, Countess of Cinchon and Vice-Queen of Peru (AD 1629–39) with a Plea for the Correct Spelling of the Cinchona Genus*, London: Trübner & Co.

[33] C.R. Markham, 1862, *Travels in Peru and India*, London: John Murray.

[34] For instance, the extensive range of official correspondences (Home Department, Medical Branch) involving the introduction of Cinchona plantations in India since the early 1860s preserved in the NAI.

[35] 'Editorial', *Calcutta Journal of Medicine*, vol. 6, no. 6, June 1873, p. 198.

[36] Anonymous, 1893, 'Quinine i malaria' (Quinine Is Malaria), *Chikitsa Sammilani*, vol. 9, no. 1, p. 402. Such attributions of malarial fever to the consumption of quinine have been witnessed in other contexts. For instance, see, W.B. Cohen, 1983, 'Malaria and French Imperialism', *Journal of African History*, vol. 24, no. 1, p. 29; Aran S. Mackinnon, 2001, 'Of Oxford Bags and Twirling Canes: The State, Popular Responses, and Zulu Antimalaria Assistants in the Early-Twentieth Century Zululand Malaria Campaigns', *Radical History Review*, vol. 80, Spring, pp. 76–100.

quinine could be tested once again. It was a moment when contemporary records within and beyond the fold of state medicine had begun doubting its potentials as either a febrifuge or a prophylactic.[37] The distribution of quinine, it was alleged, fell into the hands of 'unqualified imposters' and 'mischievous quacks' who frequently tampered with its purity producing adulterated versions. Quinine gave them access to quick, easy money despite its lukewarm curative functions. In a letter written in June 1869, the Sanitary Commissioner of Bengal himself expressed concern about the rapidly depleting faith in quinine in a context when different corrupt versions circulated in the market under the same name.[38]

How could distribution of 'pure quinine' be ensured? It was suggested that the government could depend on 'reliable agents' at the village level, for example, the schoolmasters and the 'pathsala' gurus.[39]

What was this 'quinine' that the state in India was keen on marketing as 'pure'? Government factories had repeatedly failed to produce 'pure quinine' in India till then. The factories managed to yield several substitutes of quinine: quinovium,

quinidine, cinchonidine, cinchonine, etc. The government was keen on endorsing these 'substitutes' as acceptable variations of 'pure quinine'. These substitutes were often regarded as 'adulterated quinine', while the state contested such allegations. Quinine continued to be advertised as a distant drug, which was very difficult to produce, but its virtue could only be sensed from the healing qualities of its substitutes.

... I had frequently been told that sulphate of quinine sold by native druggists in Calcutta and mofussil was largely adulterated by mixing it with flour, magnesia, arrowroot and other articles. I was therefore agreeably surprised to find that after analysis…were not adulterated by any foreign substances; but were either pure Cinchonidine, or contained Cinchonine, which are alkaloids found in the Cinchona bark, and which cannot be distinguished from quinine by the naked eye or unless by analysis…[40]

The epidemic confirmed supply of bodies affected with malaria. The epidemic provided an 'opportunity' to verify the 'purities' of different drugs circulating as quinine in the medical market. These tests also aimed to enquire whether the raw unprocessed Cinchona bark or the 'substitutes' could cure malarial patients. If confirmed, the government could give up its attempts towards manufacturing 'pure quinine' in

[37] For instance, see J. Elliot, 1863, *Report on Epidemic Remittent and Intermittent Fever Occurring in Parts of Burdwan and Nuddea Divisions*, Calcutta: Bengal Secretariat Office. Similar impressions were subsequently elaborated in Bengali medical texts. For instance, see the 1875 article by an anonymous author titled 'Bhati', *Anubikkhan*, vol. 1, no. 6, Calcutta, pp. 185–8.

[38] D.B. Smith, Sanitary Commissioner of Bengal, to A. Mackenzie, Officiating Junior Secretary to the Government of Bengal, Darjeeling, dated 5 June 1869, Home, Public, January 1870, 15–29A, NAI.

[39] General, Medical, File 192, Progs 1–4, July 1873, WBSA.

[40] No. 1238, dated Calcutta, 16 October 1872, S. Wauchope, Officiating Commissioner of Police, Calcutta, to the Officiating Secretary to the Government of Bengal, Judicial Department, General, Medical, Progs 6–8, October 1872, WBSA. There were considerable publications in the medical journals on adulterated versions of quinine and other abuses associated with it. For instance, see 1872, 'Editorial: Adulterated Sulphate of Quinine', *IMG*, vol. 7, 1 August, p. 187; T. Skinner, 1870, 'Toxic Action of Quinine', *British Medical Journal*, vol. 1, no. 474, p. 103.

India. In a correspondence drafted in July 1872, the Lieutenant Governor instructed the Inspector General of Civil Hospitals to take '*opportunity of the epidemic*' to test the capabilities of the Cinchona bark:

The Lieutenant Governor desires that opportunity may be taken of the epidemic fever in Burdwan to test the use there of the Cinchona bark which has already been ordered to be sent, in order to ascertain the capabilities of the bark when used as a simple infusion with boiling water. His Honor would like to find out whether a simple infusion of the bark is a really reliable febrifuge...[41]

We have noted in the earlier section how quinine acted as a diagnostic tool in determining the malarial identity of various maladies. Here, it appears that bodies identified as malarial were, in turn, employed to ascertain the 'purity' of quinine in circulation.

Local

The configuration and ordering of myriad sensations of physical unease into a particular epidemic in nineteenth-century Bengal was conditioned by the prior presence of the colonial medical bureaucracy and the intricate network of correspondences sustained by it. The bureaucratic correspondences revealed an intimate, detailed engagement with the geography of interior localities. Almost coinciding with the first census report presented in 1871, the demand for a coherent aetiology of the

epidemic converged with an aggravated desire for knowledge of the locality. The causes of the epidemic, it was argued, were inherent in 'the numbers and the classes of the population, of tenures and rents, rates of wages and prices of food'. A series of twelve questions was circulated from the Office of the Governor General in Council and the 'local officers' were 'specially desired to give in their periodical reports all they know...'[42]

These questions and the responses they generated were often shaped by various exigencies of colonial capital. Search for an aetiology of the epidemic led to a series of questions involving land and land tenures. 'Are there any symptoms of pressure upon the land? Are rents rising, and are there many applicants for any vacant lands?'[43] Summarizing the responses from local officers, the Lieutenant Governor of Bengal, Sir George Campbell, pointed out that the mass of figures received were 'very wide and vague'.[44] The answers supplied from Howrah, Burdwan, Midnapore, Hooghly, Chotanagpore, Chittagong, and Orissa often differed from each other. However, this wide range of responses revealed certain strategic options that the state could adopt in relation to governance of land. In areas marked by increasing pressure on land and rise in rent, the government advocated rack-renting. Campbell argued that if the

[41] Dated Calcutta, 6 July 1872, J. Ware Edgage, Officiating Junior Secretary to the Government of Bengal to Inspector General of Hospitals, Lower Provinces. General, Industry and Science, 5 July 1872, WBSA.

[42] Temple, 'The Causes of, and Remedies for the Burdwan Fever'.

[43] H.S. Cotton, Officiating Junior Secretary to the Government of Bengal to the Secretary, Government of India, Department of Revenue, Agriculture and Commerce. Home, Medical, November 1875, 53–5A, NAI.

[44] G. Campbell, 1875, 'Minute: Hooghly Fever and Conditions of the Ryots', in Home, Medical, November, 53–5A, NAI.

*ryot*s had fixity of rent as the zamindars had fixity of revenue, then the condition of ryots in Bengal would have been comfortable. Campbell believed that these concerns underlay 'the theory of the regulations of 1793'. However, he added that 'the practical working of the Permanent Settlement' failed to live up to the originally intended visions. The districts that had been hit by the epidemic 'do not imply that rents are more racked there than elsewhere, but that the people have not yet submitted to rack-renting to the same extent as elsewhere… the degree to which rent have been racked in different districts is a great degree the measure of the comfort or discomfort of the people'.[45] On the other hand, localities characterized by considerable margin of wasteland were earmarked for reclamation. Once reclaimed, such areas could be made available to the land market.

The official responses often tended to associate the epidemic with immobile labour. 'Would the people be willing to emigrate to other parts of India, or to Burmah, or Assam, if assisted by the government to do so?… Whether the people of the fever-stricken tracts go largely to Calcutta and Howrah for work?'[46] These reports celebrated mobile labour by characterizing it as more healthy. Chotanagpore supplied cheapest labour available from India. They were recruited in the industrial regions around Calcutta and Howrah, or in the plantations as far as Burmah, Assam, Mauritius, and Trinidad. George Campbell detailed in his minute how Chotanagpore as the home of cheap, mobile, tribal labour escaped the ravages

of the fever–epidemic. 'This facility of emigrating or going out for labor extends wherever *the aboriginal blood* predominates; e.g. into the Raneegunge portion of Burdwan, Bancoorah, Beerbhoom and upper Midnapore. But the fever tract is to the *east of this in an Aryan country*.'[47] This he contrasted with localities in Bengal affected by the epidemic. Such localities were marked by sedentary labour. 'People of this part of Bengal do not emigrate…so long as they are not killed down by disease they go on increasing at home…they won't go out and work and prefer to stay at home on their patches of ground and starve.'[48]

Desire for knowledge of the locality soon went beyond the living conditions of the 'people', and extended over to the landscape and the vegetation it bred. Mr C. Ducas, a Special Engineer entrusted with the job of locating the causes and remedies of the 'epidemic' in September 1864 in the Burdwan division, reported after having visited villages Balagore, Kanchrapara, Goopteepara, Jerat, Tribeni, and Magrah:

The *Kutchoo* and *ole*, both bulbous plants, thickly cover the village land, so much so that village roads have disappeared under them, and the ditches have been choked with them. The slopes of tanks are also covered with the *Kutchoo*. The bulbs of these plants are much used by the natives in daily food. The *Kutchoo* is used in place of potatoes and the *Ole* makes nice *chutney*, which is prepared in mustard oil, much in the same way a mango chutney is prepared in the United Provinces…[49]

---

[45] Campbell, 'Minute'.
[46] Ibid.

[47] Ibid.
[48] Ibid.
[49] Home, Public, 7 March 1868, 140–3A, NAI.

How could 'improvement' be guaranteed? Ducas's recommendation was simple: construction of roads; denudation of excess, rank vegetation; and cultivation of those lands. Babu Sunjeeb Chandra Chatterjee provided a list of thirty-three shrubs, creepers, and plants, out of which twenty-seven required to be burnt and completely destroyed as a preventive against malaria; six of them had to be uprooted. Among them, plants like *Kuchoo, Mankuchoo, Laoo, Shim,* and *Koomra,* when methodically cultivated in the fields could be spared, while *Monsha* had to be preserved for worship.[50]

Thus, a detailed engagement with certain aspects of local vegetation acquired central relevance in Ducas's narration of the causes behind the epidemic. Such details, otherwise quotidian and mundane, emerged as credible inputs informing the engineer's analysis of the 'locality'. Similarly, perceived shifts in subtle aspects within an elaborate landscape—the drying up of many rivers; the excessive deposition of silt; shifting levels in the adjacent subsoil; inconsistent rainfall; state initiatives at the subdivisional level that had backfired;[51] and gossips circulating out of rural gatherings—converged in government reports as reliable causes behind another malarial outbreak.[52] These various explanations could speak to one another in a shared vocabulary as the authors of these reports rearranged these stories by invoking some branch of science. These local tales were rewritten as physical changes in the landscape,[53] engineering debacles,[54] meteorological inconsistencies,[55] debates concerning contagion,[56] etc. The 'truth' of the epidemic was underscored in these reliable and credible ways.[57]

Draining Bengal

Even if inhabitants of the villages considered them as cheapest possible sources of food, vegetations which failed to circulate as profitable commodities in distant markets were discredited as uncombed, unwanted, rank, and malarial by the 'local' officials. Lack of tolerance towards such 'rural, unkempt vegetation' was paralleled by encouragement of agricultural cultivation. It was believed that certain undergrowths that were otherwise considered malarial became harmless when carefully cultivated in an agricultural land. 'The germination of malaria lessened, if not prevented, by cultivating the soil…'[58] Through much of the 1860s and the early 1870s, English newspapers like the *Englishman* kept asking

---

[50] Sunjeeb Chandra Chatterjee, to A. Eden, Secretary to the Government of Bengal, dated 1 May 1863, Home, Public, 7 May 1870, 65–71A NAI.

[51] Rogers, 'The Lower Bengal (Burdwan) Epidemic Fever', pp. 401–8.

[52] Romeshchunder Mookherjee, Deputy Magistrate of Kishaghur, to E. Grey, Magistrate of Nuddea, dated 30 November 1863, Home, Public, 7 May 1870, 65–71A, p. xlvi, NAI.

[53] Rogers, 'The Lower Bengal (Burdwan) Epidemic Fever', p. 407.

[54] Home, Public, 7 March 1868, 140–3A NAI.

[55] Mookherjee, to E. Grey.

[56] Ibid.

[57] The above-mentioned trends in medical reporting were elaborately witnessed in contemporary Mauritius. See, Charles Meldrum, 1881, *Weather, Health, and Forests,* Port Louis: Mercantile Record Co. Printing Establishment, prepared for the Sanitary Commission of Mauritius.

[58] John C. Snow, Civil Assistant Surgeon of Jessore, to the Magistrate of Jessore, No. 5, dated 15 January 1864, General, General, Prog. 84–5, March 1864, WBSA.

whether the epidemic could adversely affect the stability of agricultural prices. Contemporary bureaucratic correspondences conveyed similar mood.[59]

At the same time, it might seem simplistic to explain the projected geography of Burdwan fever in terms of the exigencies of colonial capital. Possibilities that malaria could have its origin in planting bamboo trees,[60] or rice cultivation,[61] or in the process of maceration of jute were seriously considered. However, unlike an extensive range of rural vegetations, local officers could hardly afford to instruct the uprooting of such practices. These practices were intimately tied to the enduring proliferation of the colonial economy. The harshness and alacrity of anti-malarial measures were deliberately relaxed to enable the sustenance of these practices.[62]

Official efforts towards dealing with the epidemic, in turn, sustained and reinforced the identity of Burdwan division as a 'malarial locality'. C.C. Adley, Executive Engineer on Special Duty since June 1869, appeared convinced that Burdwan fever had resulted from filth generating around

declining rivers, stagnating channels, and proliferating swamps. He proposed elaborate projects of improvement and drainage. Such public projects of improvement allowed the government considerable intervention into lands held by numerous proprietors. Adley began negotiations with the influential landed proprietors in the region. These included the Seorapooly rajas and their co-heirs, Joykrishna Mookerjee and Bamapada Chaudhari. Such negotiations were characterized by promises, assurances, and compromises. The principal landed proprietors were seduced in a language they could appreciate best. In course of their conversations with the principal proprietors, the government revealed that as a consequence of reclamation of land by drainage, landholders would reap an 'additional profit' of Rs 47,500 from cultivated land and Rs 72,000 from uncultivated land, that is, a total additional profit of Rs 119,500. Besides, it was pointed out, that drainage would inevitably promote navigation and irrigation. Apart from befitting the cultivation of sugarcane, rice, and vegetables, it was expected to guarantee easier access to the Calcutta market. The projected economics of profit seemed to have convinced Babu Joykrishna Mookerjee as well as Raja Poorno Chunder Roy of Seorapooly. Mukherjee proposed that the initial financial burden of the project should be borne by the government. The cost was to be repaid by the landowners in instalments, spread over several years.[63]

[59] C.F. Montresor, Commissioner of the Burdwan Divison, to the Officiating Secretary to the Government of Bengal, No. 148, dated Burdwan, 23 October 1867, General, General, Prog. 6, December 1867, WBSA.
[60] M.J. Shaw Stewart, Collector of Canara, to Mr W. Hart, Revenue Commissioner, Southern Division, No. 874, dated 16 April 1864, General, General, Prog. 25–8, August 1864, WBSA.
[61] General, Medical, Prog. 75–6, March 1869, WBSA.
[62] S.C. Bayley, Junior Secretary to the Government of Bengal, to the Commissioner of the Nuddea Division, No. 6064, dated 28 December 1864, General, General, Prog. 53–4, File 1–3, December 1864, WBSA.
[63] C.C. Adley, Executive Engineer on Special Duty, to Major J.J. Hume, Officiating Superintending Engineer, Western Circle, No. 109, dated 25 June 1869, Home, Public, 12 March 1870, 167–70A, NAI.

These led to the document that made up the 'Hooghly and Burdwan Drainage Bill'. This bill was eventually endorsed by the Lieutenant Governor and passed into an act on 18 March 1871.[64] Passed with the intention of facilitating drainage in the concerned districts, the bill opened up questions involving who owned the land and to what extent. For the execution of this act, the Lieutenant Governor had to appoint drainage commissioners. If half of the proprietors relevant to the *bheels* and swamps to be drained assented to the proposed scheme, the commissioners could proceed with it irrespective of what the other proprietors thought. The commissioners were thus empowered to override the objections raised by the proprietors to the schemes they proposed. Once the Lieutenant Governor had sanctioned any scheme, he could acquire the relevant pieces of land for public purpose. Within one month after any scheme had been completed, the commissioners had to determine the sums payable by each of the proprietors of land reclaimed or improved. If the proprietor had failed to pay up within one month from the day the sum was payable, the commissioners could recover that sum by sale of such lands. In case the proprietor of a piece of land was in dispute or if there was more than one claimant to proprietorship over a piece of land, the commissioners were given powers to determine the proprietor as it applied to this act.[65]

Unsurprisingly, such provisions could not leave every landholder elated. The British Indian Association—a voluntary association of Calcutta-based absentee landlords—described the legislation as a considerable infringement on private property.[66] Indeed, responses from unhappy landholders often revealed shades of enmity between proprietors. The following case hints at tensions among different layers of proprietors. In a petition addressed to C.C. Adley, a 'petty zemindar' of village Gobra, Showdaminy Debi, wrote:

…the people who applied for cutting a canal are my enemies, and thinking me to be a helpless woman, they are merely trying to injure me by cutting a canal through the fertile grounds of my zemindary and the rent-free lands of other holders; their principal object is not to make general good, but to put their enemies into trouble…[67]

Alliances struck with influential zamindars over the issue of drainage and improvement enabled the colonial state to explore newer opportunities of trade. C.T. Buckland, the Commissioner of Burdwan in April 1872, proposed the cultivation of sunflower in Burdwan and Hooghly. He referred to cases in Sonmaar, Belgium, France, and Northern America where sunflower had been cultivated to neutralize the deleterious effects of marshy exhalations. The Belgian government had apparently successfully planted sunflower after the drainage of the lake of Haarlem with a view to neutralize malaria. Buckland's message bore a detailed report from R.T. Thompson, the Civil Surgeon of Hooghly.

[64] Home, Public, 22 April 1871, 57–9A, NAI.
[65] Ibid.
[66] Joteendro Mohun Tagore, Honorary Secretary to the British Indian Association, to S.C. Bayley, Junior Secretary to then Government of Bengal, dated 16 July 1863, General, General, Prog. 92, October 1863, WBSA.
[67] Appendix D. Home, Public, 12 March 1870, 167–70A.

Thompson wrote about the remunerative aspects of the cultivation of sunflower on account of the valuable oil it produced. He suggested that sunflower yielded 'a beautiful clear oil' that could be cultivated all the year round in Bengal and North Western Provinces. He believed that sunflower oil tasted sweet, was nearly inodorous, and that the seeds yielded 50 per cent of oil. Although sunflower oil was well adapted for machinery soaps, cerates, liniments, and plasters, its chief use was thought to be as an aliment suited for culinary purposes. As an ingredient in cooking, Thomson thought that it was better than the costly olive oil. He hoped that sunflower oil, once produced in Bengal, could compete with the costly imported Spanish olive oil, if not throw it quite out of the market.

Once again, enticements of commerce converged with the obligation to deal with the epidemic. Buckland promised that the preliminary cost of procuring the seed from Agra may be charged against the epidemic fever fund. Babu Joykrishna Mookerjee was again requested for help, who along with Mr Pellew, the Magistrate of Hooghly, arranged for these experiments in four different villages: Kolora, Kinkurbutty, Madhabpur, and Ooterparah. Buckland mentioned that all these villages lay on the edge of the Dancoonee, Kathlia, and Roypore swamps that formed the core of the drainage scheme in the Hooghly district. Mookerjee found it very difficult to induce the ryots to displace a known cultivation for an experimental one. Sources suddenly go silent on what happened next.[68]

Proposals for agricultural improvement and drainage in Bengal in the 1870s stoked a series of discussions. Such discussions, quite predictably, revealed the colonial state, the influential zamindars, absentee landlords, and the petty zamindars as overlapping and conflicting layers of propertied authority in the interiors of Hooghly and Burdwan districts in Bengal. At the same time, in different medical narratives, Burdwan and its vicinities began to appear as one of the many malarial localities in the world. Burdwan figured as one of the many regions in the world that was desperately in need of improving its channels of drainage. It was suggested how the British bureaucrats in Burdwan could take lessons from the French in Algeria,[69] or medics in Massachusetts, or their counterparts in Natal.[70] The experience of drainage initiated in the Burdwan division could then be compared with other similar, distantly dispersed regions.

Travelling Epidemic

'Localities' in Burdwan found themselves connected with the wider world in other ways as well. Bureaucratic reports on the epidemic understood it as a mobile phenomenon.

That the fever did travel is no matter for doubt. Like the *waves* of a flowing tide it touched a place

---

[68] Memorandum by C.T. Buckland, Commissioner of the Burdwan Division, No. 178, dated Burdwan, the 8 April 1872, Municipal, Sanitation, Prog. 16–23, File 7, March 1873, WBSA.

[69] John Sutherland, R.S. Ellis, Joshua Paynter, and C.B. Ewart, 1873, 'Report on the Causes of Reduced Mortality in the French Army Serving in Algeria', *IMG*, vol. 8, 1 May, p. 139.

[70] 'Editorial: Marsh Fever Produced by Obstruction of the Outlets of Subsoil Water', *IMG*, vol. 8, 1 October 1873, p. 279.

one year and receded, reached it again next year with greater force and again receded, repeating this process until the country was wholly submerged and tide passed further on…[71]

It main feature is, as we have shown already, that it is travelling, slowly indeed, but, as some have remarked, yet travelling.[72]

Such widely circulating stories on travel fed into the idea of malaria as an ordering principle. These imaginings bound diverse symptoms of physical unease dispersed across time and space into the radar of a coherent, continuous, single malarial epidemic. This explains how, as late as 1899, Leonard Rogers could suggest a biography of 'Burdwan fever' that boasted a lifeline spanning half a century. He extended the life of Burdwan fever back and forth and wove 'outbreaks' in Jessore in 1824, Nuddea in 1862, Mauritius in 1869, Burdwan around 1870s, and Assam and Rangpur in the late 1890s as different expressions of the same unending epidemic.[73]

A close reading of contemporary bureaucratic correspondences reveals how the distances covered by the epidemic were represented in quantifiable terms. 'We have found it in our time to have travelled in thirteen years from Nuddea to Hughly.'[74] 'From Jessore it spread slowly (from 5 to 10 miles per year) from one district to another for a period of over 20 years.'[75] The Sanitary Commissioner for Burdwan in 1874

suggested that the epidemic followed this repetitive pattern until it left one locality for another: 'During the fourth, fifth and sixth years—six years being the average duration of the fever in any place,—there was a general and slow recovery, the fever in each successive year attacked fewer persons, was of a less fatal type, and prevailed for a shorter period, finally disappearing altogether in the seventh year.'[76]

At the End

A patient gleaning of contemporary advertisements and medical manuals in Bengali enables us to locate, quite conveniently, 'others' operating in the medical marketplace besides those who were configuring diverse expressions of physical unease into a continuous epidemic. This alternative, 'other' archive suggests how dissimilar ordering principles could be employed to frame quotidian little debilities that were being explained and expressed through the metaphor of malaria in certain other contexts. Practitioners who were contributing to this 'other' archive were often, with some exceptions, subjected to vigorous condescension. G.C. Roy, for example, spoke of 'a band of lawless resolute…whose prototypes we observe in quacks and empirics. These infest the country like locusts, and cause more devastation amongst humanity than the diseases which they pretend to combat.'[77]

Karal Chandra Chattopadhyaya, for instance, attributed his healing skills to

[71] Rogers, 'The Lower Bengal (Burdwan) Epidemic Fever', p. 402.

[72] Vercherie, 'Extracts from a Diary Kept during a Visit to Burdwan in September 1873', p. 287.

[73] Rogers, 'The Lower Bengal (Burdwan) Epidemic Fever', pp. 401–8.

[74] Roy, *The Causes, Symptoms and Treatment of Burdwan Fever*, pp. 57–8.

[75] Rogers, 'The Lower Bengal (Burdwan) Epidemic Fever', p. 404.

[76] Ibid., p. 402.

[77] Roy, *The Causes, Symptoms and Treatment of Burdwan Fever*, pp. 151–2.

divine benevolence, and his collection of medical recipes to his extensive travels across a geographical space he identified as 'Bharatbarssha'. In a booklet entitled *Vividho Mohaushodh*, he does not acknowledge his debt to any other individual or medical tradition. He barely met his patients in person, but interacted with them through the post, rarely finding the scope for diagnosing his patients. His patients wrote to him about their precise complaints: expressions of pain, unease from bleeding from the rectum, impotency, physical infirmity, gonorrhoea, ulcers, myriad expressions of fever, mercurial disorders, etc. Such 'complaints', as we have already noted, were co-opted otherwise within the 'vortex' of the epidemic: as preconditions, sequels, or simulations of a single malarial malady. Chattopadhyaya, in turn, responded by writing back to his patients, packing the required medicines in an envelope without forgetting to mention the exact dosage, and, of course, the price with postage that varied with every ailment. Through the agency of his advertisements in the Calcutta and Bombay newspapers, his patients came to know of him and wrote testimonials acknowledging his abilities in local newspapers published from places as distant as Dinajpur, Benaras, and Lahore.[78]

A detailed study of advertisements published in Bengali newspapers towards the end of the 1870s suggests that Chattopadhyaya was not alone in the medical market in his silence on the 'malarial epidemic'. Nor was he the only self-proclaimed healer in Bengal to prescribe generic medicines other than quinine, or to exploit the emergent networks of postal communication to extend his trade.[79]

This chapter has tried to read the Burdwan fever malarial epidemic in the 1870s as an epistemological configuration. It is obvious to locate medical actors, predominantly 'indigenous' and 'native' and definitely 'exotic', who represented other modes of framing diseases, alternate cosmologies, and patterns of cure, and did not seem to bother or have any clue whether an 'epidemic' had unleashed itself.

Such indifference to and disinterest in the language of the malarial epidemic, its aetiology, and its management, were paralleled by sustained contemporary critiques on the idea of epidemics from within 'medical science' itself. The *IMG* published a series of editorials in instalments in different volumes through the course of 1873 on a common topic entitled, 'Prominent Fallacies in Epidemiology', which challenged the idea of 'general' epidemics.

Another usage of epidemiologists, which leads to most unfounded conception, and encourages wild and unprofitable speculation, consists in the mixture of the term 'general' as applied to epidemics…An abstract term 'epidemic influence' is invented or utilized, and made to do as a substantive 'theory' of a more occult or quasi learned description…The whole process is a melancholy exhibition of false generalising.[80]

---

[78] K.C. Chattopadhyaya, 1876, *Vividho Mohaushodh* (Specifics discovered and experimented by K.C. Chatterjee), Calcutta: Iswar Chandra Basu and Company and K.C. Chattopadhyaya.

[79] For instance, see the advertisements on 'Morrison's tonic', *Sambad Purnochandrodoy*, 30 August 1862, pp. 1–2; 'New Apothecaries' Hall', *Somprakasha*, 15 April 1867. Available at Centre for Studies in Social Sciences, Calcutta Library.

[80] 'Editorial: Prominent Fallacies in Epidemiology', p. 217.

Such questioning of the projection of epidemics as a general, widely dispersed, homogenous phenomenon converged with considerable scepticism articulated in some of contemporary medical texts about the existence of 'malaria' itself. Surgeon Major Moore of the Indian Medical Service had summarized such trends of thinking in an official letter in January 1877.

…it is probably the uncertainty and difficulty in accepting seemingly opposed facts which have caused a minority among eminent medical observers both in this country and in other parts of the world, to doubt, or altogether deny the existence of any such poisonous agent as malaria. In France and Algeria Dr Burdel regards marsh poison as 'a myth'; Armam entirely rejects it as a figment of the brain. Among Anglo-Indian officers, Renine writing of China says: 'Let mud and malaria alone, it will give no one the ague'…Hutchinson thinks malaria will be 'only an old friend: Carbonic acid'; Dr Knapp, the President of the Iowa University, regards malaria as a 'hypothetical cause' that could never be empirically verified, which some practitioners were using as 'cloaks for ignorance' that would eventually 'hinder the progress of medical science'.[81]

It was in such an overall context of suspicion and doubt about the integrity of both epistemological categories 'malaria' and 'epidemic' that the Burdwan fever in predominant bureaucratic records was identified as a malarial epidemic—a credibly describable and sustained phase in the history of Bengal.

At the same time, the making of Burdwan fever epidemic can hardly be ascribed to conveniently locatable intentions or a straightforward series of causes. The history of unfolding of the epidemic hints at a 'game of relationships': between diagnostic protocols and pharmaceutical interests; codes of bureaucratic reporting and information gathering; medical relief, land control, and commercial opportunities; indenture labour market and medical geography; and between the colonial government and different layers of landed proprietors. Knowledge of the locality and the epidemic converged to stereotype the Burdwan division as a malarial landscape. Once identified as such, Burdwan began to be written about as one among many dispersed malarial localities within the British Empire and indeed on the world map.

[81] Home, Medical, January 1877, 47–8, NAI.

4

The *Mofussil* and the Modern
The Discrete Charms of Kangal Harinath

Atig Ghosh

In nineteenth-century Bengal, Harinath Majumdar (1833–96) was a literary figure and a man of many parts. On the stage of history at large, he embodies a twin tragedy. Precisely for this reason, his persona and its posterity underscore the importance of thinking through issues of the metropolis and the margin, or questions of *mofussil*s and modernities. These are tasks that I wish to take up in this chapter, beginning, of course, with the twin tragedy that Harinath embodies.

On the one hand, Harinath cuts a principally obscure literary figure within the formidable pantheon of the 'Renaissance' giants of nineteenth-century Bengal. This has much to do with his non-urban life/style. It is not only that Harinath was a mofussil figure, often self-consciously so. It is also that compounding this non-metropolitan,

non-'Renaissance' being was his acerbic criticism of the much-venerated, Calcutta-based luminaries of his time, including (Maharshi) Debendranath Tagore. Surely, then, these facts explain his obscurity in the annals of history and the chronicles of culture.

On the other hand, recent years have seen a sort of revival of interest in this maverick character, especially at the hands of Abul Ahsan Chowdhury. A number of books on Harinath—alongside several collections of his writings—have rapidly appeared in print.[1] Now, in my view, most (though not

[1] A sample of such publications would include: Ashok Chattopadhyay, 1995, *Unish Shataker Shamajik Andolon o Kangal Harinath*, Kolkata: Ubudash; Abul Ahsan Chowdhury, 1996, *Kangal Harinath Majumdar, 1833–1896*, Dhaka: Bangla Academy; Abul Ahsan Chowdhury (ed.), 1998, *Kangal Harinath Majumdar:*

all) of such endeavours have the intent of salvation in mind. Not that I am opposed to such an orientation: in fact, I confess to a certain feeling of vindication. But, at the same time, these near adulatory texts institute the second tragedy I have already alluded to. In loving hands, Harinath's figure is almost compartmentalized into two persons, so to speak: Harinath, the fearless journalist; and Harinath, the mystic. For Sudhir Chakrabarti, to take one very influential example, the '*baul*' songster Harinath was the 'complete opposite' of the journalist Harinath.[2]

I will argue that such a separation generates analytic difficulties in making sense of Harinath's life and career. Let me also jump the gun and suggest, the bifurcation, once rehabilitated, provides a different—if not new—way of considering the already-embattled idea of 'colonial modernity'. Actually, the bifurcation is not something the scholars thought up. Indeed, Harinath's life (and career) unfolded in a manner that permits such a division. The first part of his life was dedicated to journalism and the publication of his *Grambartaprokashika*, and then came the *volta*—to use a loaded literary term—and Harinath dedicated himself to a life of 'baul' mysticism and writing songs. The two phases informed each other. But, of course, that will be the knee-jerk academic

reflex. The further point to make here is that as soon as their complicity is revealed, they illuminate each other in a different light, so to speak, and open up new trajectories of understanding and analysis that, in its purport, supersedes mere considerations of the figure of Harinath and links up with broader (theoretical?) considerations.

At the same time, to begin with (and for the sake of clarity), I will toe the conventional line and discuss the two phases in sequence. There is an ulterior motive behind such a sequential narrative which I will clarify in due course.

Vita Activa

Harinath Majumdar was born and grew up in the mofussil. Poverty dogged his steps from childhood. It was a classic life of the struggling autodidact who stuck to his natal village, Kumarkhali, in Nadia, a district of Bengal, and ultimately, managed to get a job as a reporter for Ishwar Gupta's *Sangbad Probhakar*. Satish Chandra Majumdar writes about Harinath's motivation: 'He (Harinath) started writing articles in *Sangbad Probhakar* to make the readership aware of the sorrow and poverty of the people of his village.'[3]

However, Harinath soon felt the need to strike out on his own and started publishing his newspaper, *Grambartaprokashika* (Revealer of the Village Truth), from 1863. Probably, he felt the need for a newspaper that was entirely dedicated to the promotion of the cause of the village poor. That necessity could only be served

---

Nirbachito Rachona, Dhaka: Bangla Academy; Abul Ahsan Chowdhury (ed.), 1998, *Kangal Harinath Majumdar: Smarok Grantho*, Dhaka: Bangla Academy; Parijat Majumdar (ed.), 1999, *Kangal Harinath Smarok Grantho*, Calcutta: Jagari; and Dhananjay Ghoshal (ed.), 2006–2007, *Balaka* (Kangal Harinath Majumdar Sankhya), vol. 16, no. 25, 6 December–7 January.

[2] Sudhir Chakrabarti, 1992, *Bratyo Lokayato Lalon*, Calcutta: Pustak Bipani, p. 20.

[3] Satish Chandra Majumdar, 1901 (1308 Bengali Calendar [henceforth Ben.]), 'Kangal Harinather Jibani', in *Harinath Gronthaboli*, Part I, Calcutta, p. 5.

by a newspaper which was published from the village. Though for a decade *Grambarta* was printed in a Calcutta-based press, in 1873, Harinath established his own press in Kumarkhali, the *Mathuranath Jantro*.

Variously described as a fearless journalist, a friend of the poor, and a saint, Harinath's principal agenda was to expose the atrocities of the zamindars (the landlords) in the mofussil. Though his newspaper was called the revealer of *village* truth, the long expository pieces Harinath penned and published were often titled *mufassaley prajadiger durdasha* (that is, the misery of subjects in the mofussil), etc. Harinath had complete confidence in the innate goodness of colonial law and administration. His enemies were clearly the local, absentee zamindars, among who he counted the house of Tagores, the Corleones of Calcutta culture.[4] He eventually established his own press in Kumarkhali and continued writing against the zamindars. Maharshi Debendranath Tagore, the founder of the Brahmo movement and the father of Rabindranath Tagore, first tried to bribe him into silence. When that did not work, he sent Punjabi strongmen (*gunda*) to teach Harinath a lesson. It was only due to the intervention of Lalon Fakir that his life was saved. Well, it was not any spiritual intervention by the saint. Lalon had more strongmen it seems to fight the army of the

Tagores back.[5] In Biswanath Majumdar's opinion, this was no stray incident. In fact, the disciples of Lalon were always there to protect Harinath's life.[6]

Printing a newspaper was a matter of quite some expense. In Calcutta, the presses ran smoothly because they had solid economic backing of the landholding class, and this is well documented.[7] Harinath could not of course expect such support. Advertisement had yet to become a sufficient source of funds for the vernacular newspapers in general, but more so in the case of those from the mofussil.[8] Harinath was further hamstrung by the fact that most of his subscribers did not pay up in time or at all. He has left record of his dismay at this 'only-take, never-give' (*nebo debo na*) attitude of his subscribers.[9]

The resolve to continue with the publication was however strong. He tried for a while to sustain his newspaper by setting up a bookshop. This enterprise failed miserably. As threats to his life mounted, Harinath ultimately had to abandon the publication and turned to writing songs and

[4] Harinath 'wrote a series of articles against Babu Deebendranath Tagore who possesses a large zemindary [land-holding] in Pubna and neighboring districts', quoted from 'The National Magazine, April 1896', 1974, in Alok Roy (ed.), *Nineteenth Century Studies*, Calcutta: Biographical Research Center, p. 311.

[5] Hemanga Biswas, 1385 Ben., *Loksangeet Samikkha: Bangla o Assam*, Calcutta: A. Mukherjee & Co., pp. 67–8. Also see, Jaladhar Sen, 1931 (1338 Ben.), 'Kangal Harinath', *Bharatbarsho*, p. 783.

[6] Abul Ahsan Chowdhury, 2006–2007, 'Lalon Sain o Kangal Harinath: Samparker Khatiyan', in Dhanajay Ghoshal (ed.), *Balaka* (Kangal Harinath Majumdar Sankhya), vol. 16, no. 25, 6 December–7 January, p. 60.

[7] See, for instance, Muntashir Mamun, 2005, 'Unish-shatokey Sangbad-Shamoyikpotrer Kathamo, Sthayitto, Prochar o Bipanon', in Swapan Basu and Muntashir Mamun (eds), *Dui Shatoker Bangla Sangbad-Shamoyikpatro*, Calcutta: Pustak Bipani, pp. 13–25.

[8] Ibid., p. 17.

[9] *Grambartaprokashika*, 1873.

to peripatetic singing. He started calling himself Kangal Harinath and/or Baul Phikirchand.

Vita Contemplativa

Religiosity was not something that dawned on Harinath overnight. His intimacy with Lalon Shah has already been discussed. Additionally, for many years, Harinath was also a close associate of the Brahmo Samaj at Kumarkhali. However, towards the end of his life, Harinath turned against Brahmoism (perhaps owing to his disenchantment with the Tagores), publishing tracts titled '*markat brahmo*' (literally, the 'monkey brahmo'), and opted for the life Lalon Shah exemplified. In dubbing himself a 'baul', Harinath was doing more than just turning away from Brahmoism, which was popularly perceived as an urban religious orientation.[10] He was simultaneously falling out—and more vigorously—with that urban 'Hindu' sensibility which considered bauls as low class and deliberately dirty, part of the 'disreputable Chaitanyite sects of Bengal', of 'deplorable moral condition', and untrammeled sexual licence. For J.N. Bhattacharya, *bhadralok* and the President of the Brahmin Sabha of Bengal, these were reasons enough to justify the exclusion of the bauls from the pale of humanity by Brahmanism. Bhattacharya's bhadralok

sensibilities were revolted by the fact that the bauls were given to drinking solutions made from bodily excretions and exudations as a part of religious exercise (the 'Four Moons' practice or the *Chari-chandra bhed*[11])! He so much as contests the validity of granting the bauls the status of a Vaishnavite sect (that, in his opinion, being disgraceful already), for they are a 'godless sect'.[12] And we should keep in mind that Bhattacharya's is but only one such example.[13] In a way, J.N. Bhattacharya and others may be seen as confirming H.H. Risley's impression of the 'Baolas'. Risley had maintained that the 'Baolas' are 'separated from the main body of the Vaishnavas'. They 'never shave or cut their hair and filthiness of person ranks as a virtue among them'. They take their followers from the lower castes and belong to the rank of 'disreputable mendicant orders'. Grossly immoral, they are 'held in very low estimation by respectable Hindus'.[14]

From Jaladhar Sen's account, it seems that the 'baul' group of Phikirchand was formed suddenly one day and rather impulsively.

---

[10] In fact, in 1872, a resemblance between Brahmos and Lalon had been attempted in Harinath's *Grambarta* on the basis of the contention that both are dedicated to the worship of the aniconic, formless (*nirakar*) god, a 'charge' which was consistently refuted by Lalon himself. Indeed, the comparison is somewhat fanciful for a number of reasons but such a discussion is outside the scope of this chapter.

[11] For an elaboration of the practice, see Sakti Nath Jha, 1995, 'Cāri-candra bhed: Use of the Four Moons', in Rajat Kanta Ray (ed.), *Mind, Body and Society: Life and Mentality in Colonial Bengal*, New Delhi: Oxford University Press, pp. 65–108.

[12] Jogendra Nath Bhattacharya, 1896, *Hindu Castes and Sects: An Exposition of the Origin of the Hindu Caste System and the Bearing of the Sects towards Each Other and towards Other Religious Systems*, Calcutta: Thacker, Spink & Co., pp. 482–3.

[13] For a similar take, see Akshay Kumar Datta, 1969, *Bharatbarshiya Upashok Shamproday*, abridged version excluding the introduction to the first volume, ed. Benoy Ghosh, Calcutta: Karuna Prakashani (originally published in two volumes, Calcutta, 1870 and 1883), especially pp. 110–50.

[14] H.H. Risley, 1891, *Tribes and Castes of Bengal*, Vol. II, Calcutta: Bengal Secretariat Press, p. 347.

Lalon Fakir, the mystic who had his *akhra* in the neighbouring village of Chheuriya, had one morning come over to Harinath's house and sung a song for him. Harinath and the others present were overwhelmed. The impact was so great that, by the afternoon, Akshay Kumar Maitreya came up with the idea of forming a group of bauls. 'Can we not form a band of Bauls?' he asked. And everybody agreed. Pandit Prashonno Kumar said, 'We must compose songs in a new manner. But, there's no task that *Sriman Akshay* cannot perform.' Akshay Kumar said: 'There's nothing to worry about. *Jolda* (Jaladhar Sen), grab a piece of paper; let's write baul songs.'[15] And the group came into being in 1880.

No matter how serendipitous the formation of the group of Phikirchand may seem, it was in no way a novel event. At the time, the songs of at least three folk singers—Lalon Fakir (1778–1890), Pagla Kanai (1809–89), and Kubir Gosain (1787–1879)—were, by all accounts, extremely popular in the region.[16] It was not, as such, an absurd idea to band together as a group of baul songsters. Strains of Lalon's influence are often perceptible in the songs of Phikirchand. In fact, Jaladhar Sen writes about an overlap with yet another mystic singer of the time. He mentions one occasion when Harinath was supposed to sing his songs at Faridpur after a public performance by Pagla Kanai. Thirty or forty thousand people were enthralled by the songs of Pagla Kanai, he tells us.[17] If the group of Phikirchand was to perform after Pagla Kanai, evidently then, it had found an accepting audience in the region as well.

The group of Phikirchand composed songs and went around the region singing them. The peripatetic dissemination of songs may account for the group's rapid popularity. In this too, however, they were following a set pattern. Indeed, composition of songs and itinerancy may be considered the only two attributes that unite the otherwise diverse and conceptually fuzzy idea of the 'bauls of Bengal'.

Further, the group was organized around the figure of Harinath who functioned as the guru or *murshid* (preceptor)—an important figure for any group of bauls. Given the conceptual indeterminacy of the term 'baul', those who wish to sustain a conviction in a continuing essence or entity of the bauls (that is to say, those who wish to sustain the category 'baul' as an internally coherent sect or tradition, *samproday*), it is around the figure of the guru or murshid and the doctrine of the primacy of the guru, *guru-*

[15] Jaladhar Sen, 1913 (15 of Ashwin, 1320 Ben.), *Kangal Harinath, Part I*, Calcutta: Bengal Medical Library, pp. 23–4.

[16] For Pagla Kanai, see Majharul Islam, 1997 [1959] (1366 Ben.), *Kabi Pagla Kanai*, Dhaka: Agami Prakashani. For Kubir Gosain, see Sudhir Chakrabarti, 1985, *Shahebdhani Sampraday: Tader Gan*, Calcutta: Pustak Bipani; and his 2003, *Banglar Gounodharma: Shahebdhani o Balahari*, Calcutta: Pustak Bipani. On Lalon, the publications are virtually numberless. Yet, apart from Sudhir Chakrabarti's text already mentioned, one could see: Basanta Kumar Pal, 1955 (1362 Ben.), *Mahatma Lalon Fakir*, Shantipur, Nadia: Rahmaniya Library; S.M. Lutphar Rahman, 1983, *Lalonshah: Jiban o Gan*, Dhaka: Bangladesh Shilpakala Academy; Abul Ahsan Chowdhury, 1990, *Lalon Shah: 1774–1890*, Dhaka: Bangla Academy; and Sakti Nath Jha, 1995, *Fakir Lalan Sain: Desh, Kal ebong Shilpo*, Calcutta: Sanbad Prakashak.

[17] Jaladhar Sen, 1913 (15th of Ashwin, 1320 Ben.), *Kangal Harinath, Part I*, Calcutta: Bengal Medical Library, p. 24.

vad, that they construct the idea of what is essentially 'baul'.

The group of Phikirchand, however, was more a group of 'bauls through fancy or inspiration' or 'amateur bauls' (*shakher baul*) than one formed according to the tenets of baul philosophy and practice.[18] Though the event of Kangal's group performing alongside Pagla Kanai has been mentioned by Jaladhar Sen, it is doubtful whether the 'bauls' of the time considered Harinath's group as one of their own. Harinath once sang a few of his songs to Lalon Fakir—the figure whose songs had inspired the very conception of Harinath's group—and asked for the *fakir*'s opinion. Lalon's response cannot be considered enthusiastic. He said: 'The curry that you have cooked is rather good; only, it lacks a bit in salt.'[19]

This did not however affect the immense popularity of Harinath and his songs. In 1887, that is only seven years after Harinath's group had been formed,

Mir Mosharaph Hosen, a close associate of Harinath, sarcastically notes in a song that the popularity of such 'new' bauls as Phikirchand (that is, Harinath Majumdar), Ajobchand, and Rasikchand has practically eclipsed the more traditional and authentic exponents, such as Lalon and Pagla Kanai.[20] At one level, this is a laudable self-critical attitude. At another, however, it points at a more complicated historical process that was unfolding over the last half of the nineteenth century with regard to the idea of the 'real baul'. We will have the opportunity to briefly—and, I am afraid, in a rather hurried way—discuss the process in the last part of this chapter.

The Discrete Lives of Harinath Majumdar

The condensed biography serves the obvious purpose of introducing the unfamiliar life of Harinath. However, in introducing Harinath, it simultaneously introduces certain terms of discussion whose conceptual cachet may not be all that obvious: terms such as the mofussil. Then there are the Latinate subtitles for the two phases of Harinath's life which may strike some—and justifiably—as unnecessary posturing. I wish to take these issues up, one by one, but not necessarily in that order.

Through the deployment of the phrases *vita activa* and *vita contemplativa*, I was not merely pulling a silly stunt to camouflage my embarrassment for having to recount a straightforward report of Harinath's life. I was, on the contrary, trying to indicate that

[18] I am aware that the criterion for classification as 'baul' is a red herring. That is, the term baul, and the religious philosophy and practice implied by it, has been a highly contended academic issue. We have already spoken about the conceptually indeterminate nature of the term 'baul' and that it does not lend itself easily to any singular doctrinal definition nor to a uniformity of practice. Jeanne Openshaw deals with the matter at great length in her 2002, *Seeking Bauls of Bengal*, Cambridge: Cambridge University Press. If the doctrine of the primacy of the male preceptor is to be considered the continuing and unifying essence of being a baul, then even within guru-vad, Openshaw has uncovered contrary tendencies: 'including the multiplicity of gurus, the internalization of the gurus, and the fact that esoteric practice of necessity involves a male–female pair' (see Ibid.: chapter 6, pp. 140–65). In the present context, however, my effort is simply to demonstrate a historical point regarding the self-perception of Harinath's group.

[19] Pal, *Mahatma Lalon Fakir*, p. 104.

[20] The song by Mir Mosharaph Hosen (taken from his *Sangeet Lahari*) has been quoted in Sudhir Chakrabarti, *Bratyo Lokayato Lalon*, p. 154.

much of what has been written on Harinath chooses to make this distinction (though, it must be said, the writers do not always take a side with one phase to criticize the other). I was also staking out the ground for taking my argument to a next level. Like Charles Baudelaire, I think that the opposition between vita activa and vita contemplativa needs to be questioned: neither poles take into consideration the pleasures and struggles of everyday life. Harinath, the person, has been totally obfuscated by hagiographic renderings of the fearlessness and strident social commitment of Harinath, the journalist, or the spirituality and popularity of Harinath, the mystic. Let me provisionally suggest, following Baudelaire, that the heroism and beauty of modern life lies elsewhere—in private subjects.[21] Harinath's life was guided—and animated—by personal choices born out of private, practical pressures.

Let us begin by demystifying the figure and its achievements. The *Grambartaprokashika* was not the only newspaper that was published exclusively from a mofussil location, neither was it the first. The *Rangapur Bartabaho* (1847, Rangpur), the *Uttarpara Pakkhik Patrika* (1856, Uttarpara), and the *Rangapur Dikprakash* (1860, Rangpur)—at least these three had preceded the *Grambarta* which started in 1863. Many more quickly followed: *Pallibigyan* (1864, Bikrampur, Dhaka), *Amritabajar Patrika* (1868, Jessore),

Palligram Bartabaho (1868, Baidyabati, Hugli), and the list is virtually inexhaustible.

The *Grambarta* was not the unmediated voice of the oppressed and poor villagers either; it claimed to *represent* the plight of the village poor. Here is the fine difference. It was Harinath who took it upon himself to make the plight of these people known to the British government. He *assumed*, of his own accord, the role of the true representative of the downtrodden villagers. Harinath, in his diary, wrote as much:

I had already worked with the indigo planters and the moneylenders; I had already seen the district offices of the zamindars; and had probed into the conditions of the country/Bengal (*desh*). The oppression that was rife everywhere had left a deep imprint on my heart. When Mr. Robinson, the translator of vernacular newspapers, opened his office, I started the publication of *Grambarta* as well.[22]

He further declared:

I heard the government has decided to translate Bengali newspapers to gain knowledge about what is being written in them, and that an office has been established to that end. I felt that if I could start a newspaper to let the government know of how the subjects in the villages are being oppressed, then surely the government would alleviate their plight and adopt measures to improve their conditions.[23]

Let it be said that the good intention of Harinath is not in doubt. But, that apart, Harinath was limited by his

[21] Charles Pierre Baudelaire, 1972, 'Of the Heroism of Modern Life', in *Selected Writings on Art and Literature*, introduced and translated by Patrice Edouard Charvet, New York: Penguin Books, pp. 104–7.

[22] Jaladhar Sen, 1896, 'Harinath Majumdar', *Dashi*, June, p. 310. John Robinson was the government Bengali translator of 'Native Papers'.
[23] Brajendranath Bandyopadhyay, 1961 (1368 Ben.), 'Kangal Harinath', in *Sahitya-Sadhak-Charitmala*, vol. 3, Calcutta: Bangiya Sahitya Parishad, p. 13.

mofussil identity. The scope of the present discussion does not allow me to delve deep into the matter of the mofussil. Suffice it to say that—in my understanding—the mofussil is not a real geographical space. It is, on the other hand, a psychosocial self-understanding that developed in the nineteenth century and defined itself in contradistinction to the city, Calcutta. It was the stuff of educated (and, therefore, *mostly* male upper- and middle-caste–class Hindu Bengali) imagination which could not come to terms with Calcutta. The city, with its 'non-traditional' social and cultural markers was viewed as morally solvent and undesirable. The village was perceived as the repository of tradition and morally upright life. The mofussil, therefore, persevered to prove itself the true representative of rural purity as opposed to urban immorality. Against the city, the mofussil thereby could claim a rural authenticity.

The mofussil was the collective articulation of a regional identity, though the collectivity in question was relatively small. The exigencies of colonial rule had drawn the *men* who formed this collectivity out of their ritual homes (*bari*) in the village. They had gone to the city, Calcutta, in search of education and employment and set up their temporary residence (*basha*) there.[24] Yet, jobs often meant that these men were sent to distant parts of Bengal to man posts of teachers, doctors, postmasters, deputy magistrates, and so on. They were condemned, so to speak, to an unanchored life of eternal passage from one basha to another, to an identitary limbo. The deepening sense of deracination and loss of ancestral moorings led them to conceive of and knit together a regional (national?) meta-home: the mofussil. The legitimacy and tangibility of the mofussil could be established and sustained only if it could be given an incontestable anchor. Such an anchor was found in the village. The idea of the village was rarefied and presented as the eternal and uncontaminated repository of (Hindu) Bengali 'values' and 'tradition', and the mofussil now posed as its defender against the onslaught of the dissolute urban. The mofussil jealously strove to become the sole spokesman of the village.[25]

Such a desire to be the mouthpiece of the village runs through Harinath's rhetoric

---

[24] The bari–basha distinction is made very usefully by Dipesh Chakrabarty, 2002, 'Remembered Villages: Representations of Hindu–Bengali Memories in the Aftermath of the Partition', in Mushirul Hasan (ed.), *Inventing Boundaries: Gender, Politics and the Partition of India*, New Delhi: Oxford University Press, pp. 318–37. He writes,

The Bengali language has preserved this sense of distinction between a temporary place of residence and one's foundational home, as it were, by using two different words for a house: *basha* and *bari*. *Basha*, no matter how long one spends in the place, is always a temporary place of residence; one's sense of belonging there is transient. *Bari*, on the other hand, is where one's ancestors have lived for generations…*Bari* would also be exchangeable with the word *desh*, signifying one's native land. (Ibid.: 323)

In the present context, I am extending his argument and also using it in a different temporal context.

[25] The brief discussion does not do justice to the checkered and often counterintuitive history of the mofussil. Also, the complex and conjoint history of the city and the mofussil is not reducible to a simple *doppelganger* effect. There were overlaps and undertows, contradictions and connivance. For a detailed engagement with the mofussil, see Atig Ghosh, 2009, 'Construcción Colonial del *Mofussil*: La Economía Política y la Cultura en la Bengala del Siglo XIX', Unpublished Doctoral Dissertation, Centro de Estudios de Asia y África, El Colegio de México, Mexico City.

as well. He not only claims to be the mouthpiece of the village folk but also, at times, appropriates and conflates the rural with the mofussil. He writes:

The newspapers that have been published so far are full of news about the main cities and that from abroad. The conditions of *the village, that is the mofussil*, have not been given attention at all. That is why no good is happening to the villagers…The main purpose of the newspaper (*Grambarta*) is to publicize the condition of the villagers…civilization, history of the villages, the rule of the government officials in the *mofussil*, and sundry amusing events…[26]

The village folk, however, could not care less. I mean, the suffering and exploitation was real and, let me repeat, the good intention of Harinath is not in doubt. But the lowest rung of the village population did not see the messiah in Harinath, the journalist. They could not. The people for whom, in whose defence, Harinath was writing—the peasants, the indigo cultivators, the fishermen, and so on—were mostly uneducated with little or no access to his newspaper.

The class he lashed out against—the absentee zamindar, the moneylender, and the indigo planter—however, could read the *Grambarta* or at least have it read out. They had no patience, even less sympathy, for him. We have already seen the confrontation that Harinath had with the Tagores. Often enough, these zamindars had a social standing to preserve in Calcutta and they were in no mood to brook such defamation, true or not.

As the screws of the zamindars tightened on Harinath, he turned to what he had fondly believed to be his constituency: the villagers. The villagers however sprang a nasty surprise on him. Harinath wrote:

When the zamindars oppress me, and lodge false cases against me in the court, then I call all the villagers and let them know of my situation. If a village mutt is tyrannized in any way, the villagers do something for it. But such is my misfortune that nobody offered me their assurance or expressed the slightest willingness to do something for me. Such is the attitude of those for whom I cried, whose problems I took up as my own responsibility![27]

I am speculating that Harinath painfully realized the limits of his reach among the villagers and this caused a change of heart. He wanted to reach out to the village folk, and this time for real. The unforeseen, almost accidental, formation of the 'baul' group around him in 1880 provided the means. Harinath Majumdar turned Baul Phikirchand or Kangal Harinath. The change of heart coincided with a financially difficult phase of *Grambartaprokashika*. I am not suggesting that the disenchantment with journalism as the means to be the authentic voice of the rural people triggered the final discontinuation of *Grambarta*. It had indeed become financially unsustainable. So, it had to fold in 1885. However, the new avatar of the Kangal had already emerged and run parallel to that of the journalist for five years. Once the *Grambarta* disappeared, Harinath could now endeavour to become the voice of the people by that other means. Absolute judgements are impossible to pass. However, it is safe to say that Kangal

---

[26] *Grambartaprokashika*, 1863 (the month of Boishakh, 1270 Ben.)

[27] Bandyopadhyay, 'Kangal Harinath', p. 21.

Harinath, in his times, received greater admiration and devotion from the villagers than the journalist Harinath who had to wait for a later time—almost a century—for the well-deserved appreciation of academics. Harinath *did*, after all, achieve what he had so assiduously striven for all his life.

Colonial Modernity and Harinath Majumdar

No matter whom he chose to represent and whom to oppose, there is one aspect of Harinath's journalistic enterprise that remains incontrovertible. Harinath had chosen his audience: the British government. However limited in extent, he did even manage to reach out to this desired audience. To give but one example: a report from *Grambartaprokashika*, dated 6 November 1875, was translated and brought to the notice of the government.

A correspondent of the same paper (that is, *Grambarta*) notices with regret that on emigration vessels, collies, proceeding to the tea districts suffer great inconvenience from want of proper accommodation, medicines when sick and supervision. In the tea plantations they live apart from each other, and are compelled to do an excessive amount of work. It seems to be the general impression that there is none to care for them. It would be better if Government were to make enquiries into the subject.[28]

Harinath clearly had great faith in the colonial rule and its benevolence. For him, the plight of the village poor was a clear case of administrative oversight. If the suffering could be brought to official view, remedies would follow immediately. Apart from his supplications to the British government to take note, Harinath also left no opportunity to laud the British rule. When Victoria assumed the title of 'Bharateshwari' (literally, the 'Goddess of India'), we find an anonymous writer narrating the celebration that took place in Kumarkhali. In assuming such a title, the queen had apparently expressed her 'great affection for India'. A speaker exhorted the assembled crowd to wish for the queen's long life, and also sang a song in her honour which described her as the Protector of India (*Bharater Rokkhakortri*). From the language of the speech and the song, it can be surely deduced that the speaker was none other than Harinath himself.[29]

But if this does not suffice, then there is the other long poem (with an introduction) that came out in *Grambarta* in honour of the Duke of Wellington's visit to India. This poem, however, serves not only as a simple eulogy but is laced with complaints. The Duke had not visited the villages; if he had, then he would have witnessed for himself the deplorable condition of his rural subjects and that would have resulted in great benefit and improvement for the rural lot. Such is the hope expressed by Harinath. However, the Duke is not to be blamed. It is not his fault. It is the dismal *kismet* of the village people that is to be blamed.[30]

Harinath Majumdar was not alone in having faith in the beneficial nature of the colonial government. Among other contemporaries, Dinabandhu Mitra, who

[28] *Report on Native Papers*. John Robinson, Government Bengali Translator, 13 November 1875, Confidential No. 46 of 1875.

[29] *Grambartaprokashika*, 20 January 1877.
[30] Ibid., January 1870.

vociferated against the atrocities of the indigo planters in his play, *Neel-Darpan*, had, at the same time, such confidence in the beneficial, do-gooder nature of the British rule. Ranajit Guha pronounces an excoriating damnation of such attitudes. He is speaking of Dinabandhu Mitra, but the statement, I am confident, neatly applies to the case of Harinath. '[O]ur nationalism has in it an ideological element with a fairly low anti-imperialist content. This element represents the contribution of that section of our bourgeoisie who are interested in opposing imperialism but cannot do so firmly and consistently owing to the historical conditions of their development.'[31]

We may take a less acerbic view. Perhaps, it is in the logic of colonial governmentality that it produces docile bodies that, even in protest, cannot phrase an anti-colonial vocabulary. 'In the colonial world,' writes David Scott, 'the problem of *modern* power turned on the politico-ethical project of producing subjects and governing their conduct'. The 'formation of colonial modernity' represented a 'discontinuity in the organization of colonial rule characterized by the emergence of a distinctive political rationality—a colonial governmentality—in which power comes to be directed at the destruction and reconstruction of colonial space so as to produce not so much extractive-effects on colonial bodies as governing-effects on colonial conduct'.[32]

The agency-less fatalistic grimness of such a formulation may be abated if we consider the argument of Dipesh Chakrabarty. Over the years, Chakrabarty has emphasized the depth of the critical engagement of Bengali intellectuals with British modernizers and has adumbrated a particular Bengali-modern position. In his discussions, Chakrabarty has brought forth a series of Bengali intellectuals of late nineteenth century who creatively engaged and negotiated the British claims of being the sole representative of progress as also the British condemnations of certain aspects of Hindu culture. These intellectuals endeavoured to project a model of progressive Hinduism that made good use of aspects of British technology, law, and social practices. At the same time, this selective appropriation did not amount to a wholesale indictment of Hindu 'civilization' as something static and to be superseded. In their view, there were elements of Hinduism that could be retained in order to build a more prosperous, not to say progressive, India which was still true to its cultural moorings.[33] On the plane of argument, such an elucidation of the Bengali-modern position makes a reference to a philosophy of 'difference' and 'non-commensurability'— that there exist worlds that force upon us the recognition of the limits of rational analysis. Such worlds are not amenable to cold classification and enumeration; such worlds are teeming with cultural practices

[31] Ranajit Guha, 1993, 'Neel-Darpan: The Image of a Peasant Revolt in a Liberal Mirror', in David Hardiman (ed.), *Peasant Resistance in India, 1858–1914*, New Delhi: Oxford University Press, p. 78.

[32] David Scott, 1999, *Refashioning Futures: Criticism after Postcoloniality*, Princeton, NJ: Princeton University Press, pp. 52, 40.

[33] Dipesh Chakrabarty, 2000, *Provincializing Europe: Postcolonial Thought and Historical Difference*, Princeton, NJ: Princeton University Press; and Dipesh Chakrabarty, 2002, *Habitations of Modernity: Essays in the Wake of Subaltern Studies*, Chicago: University of Chicago Press.

which are irreducible to either irrationality or rational calculation. Chakrabarty's analysis explodes the zygomorphism of *a* modernity of enlightenment and secularism and *a* tradition of irrationality and superstition.[34]

Chakrabarty's explanation fits celebrated figures such as Ishwarchandra Vidyasagar, and also my less-celebrated figure of Harinath Majumdar, the journalist. Consider the two passages Harinath wrote in the *Grambarta*: '*Madya ki Bhoyanok Ripu*' (1866; What a Deadly Vice Is Alcohol!) and 'Babu' (1874). The colonial rule has created this class of pleasure-loving, worthless, effeminate *babus*; yet, it is Sir George Campbell's decision to make physical education mandatory for civil services that gives Harinath the hope that Bengalis would now have the chance to uplift themselves to becoming masculinity.[35] Alcoholism, Harinath hints, has been a colonial import. He advises Bengalis, and also the Europeans, to desist from this 'deadly vice'.[36]

A critical engagement with British claims of representing progress is evident. Harinath's acceptance of certain elements of colonial rule (justice, for instance, as discussed earlier, and education) even while remaining true to Hindu cultural values is also evident. Following Dipesh Chakrabarty, this makes a strong case for the colonial modern self of Harinath, the journalist. But, staying with Chakrabarty's model a little longer, what do we make of Harinath, the baul?

Disillusionment and financial difficulties along with a desire to be among the village people, to be one with them rather than merely represent them, led Harinath to change his spots, so to speak. He stepped out of the colonial modern self and into 'tradition'. This is a story we have already gone through.

Tradition is what is produced when some come to imagine themselves as modern. Tradition and modernity are co-constitutive. That is not in doubt. And that is why it is not a simple story of return to tradition, a 'traditionalization'. Perhaps, what I am trying to say comes very close to what James C. Scott has called *mētis*: practical, locally rooted knowledge, the mixture of ideals of change with the acceptance of the messiness of life, a more personal sense of human relations.[37] It is, in my view, a reaffirmation of faith in mētis (which is now perceived as a 'traditional' way of being in the world, connecting to it—a *re*traditionalization) that Harinath worked out for himself in his later life. It is a manoeuvre that is guided by private—moral and material—exigencies. It is a strategy of self-preservation for Harinath in the face of disillusionment and bankruptcy.

If 'the problem of *modern* power turned on the politico-ethical project of producing subjects and governing their conduct',[38] then the project of modern, colonial power had surely suffered a setback in the Kangal. If retention of certain traditional values

[34] Dipesh Chakrabarty, 1995, 'Radical Histories and Question of Enlightenment Rationalism', *Economic and Political Weekly*, vol. 30, no. 14, 8 April, pp. 751–9.

[35] 'Babu', in *Grambartaprokashika*, June–July 1874.

[36] 'Madya ki Bhoyanok Ripu', in *Grambarta-prokashika*, August 1866.

[37] James C. Scott, 1998, *Seeing Like the State: How Certain Schemes to Improve the Human Condition Have Failed*, New Haven: Yale University Press.

[38] David Scott, 1999, *Refashioning Futures: Criticism after Postcoloniality*, Princeton, NJ: Princeton University Press, p. 52.

combined with a selective appropriation and reconfiguration of aspects of colonial rule is the defining feature of the Bengali modern, then one can still make a case of colonial modernity for the Kangal. As Jeanne Openshaw writes, 'when those alienated by the processes and effects of imperial domination searched for their roots, they found, among other iconic figures, "Bāuls"'.[39] Openshaw, however, is not making an explicit case here for the Bengali modern, though at the heart of her concerns lie the matter of colonized self-reckoning. So she writes, 'Questions of identity were crucial to the colonized elite, and,...Bāuls were variously co-opted in this cause as Other to the Self, as a lost Self, or as a true Self.'[40]

Yet, one wonders as to how far we are willing to expand the idea of 'colonial modernity' in so far as to accommodate a strategy of retraditionalization, or a mind-numbing array of complex configurations of the other and the self within a singular analytic.[41] Would it not lose its analytic purchase? Wouldn't 'modernity' then become an empty term that each can pack according to her own predilection?[42]

[39] Openshaw, *Seeking Bauls of Bengal*, p. 21.
[40] Ibid., p. 22.
[41] I am aware that the idea of retraditionalization has been employed in studies such as Alice Conklin's 1997, *A Mission to Civilize: The Republican Idea of Empire in France and West Africa, 1895–1930*, Stanford, California: Stanford University Press. I am merely borrowing the term and not the idea as such for my own purposes.
[42] For an argument about the 'emptiness' of modernity, see Benjamin M. Zachariah, 2007, 'Modernity and Its Emptiness: Some Indian Discussions', Presented at the International Colloquium, 'An Indian Modern: Politics, Culture, Political Cultures', *El Colegio de México*, 19 April.

Admittedly, Kangal's is a strange case—something that we do not run into every day. For Harinath did not merely—discursively—'find' a lost self or a true self in the 'bauls'. He actually became one. Dipesh Chakrabarty's elucidation of the Bengali modern may be applicable to a vast majority of the nineteenth-century figures. Yet, at least in the solitary and specific case of the Kangal, its purchase is doubtful. I am not suggesting—even for a moment—that Harinath made a conscious choice of trashing his 'colonial modern' self. He had resources (options?) to choose from and, driven by personal anxieties, he opted for one. In fact, I am not even making a case for a clear-cut transition, a break. The prefix in *re*traditionalization not only pushes the conceptual frontiers of any or all traditionalizations, but also presupposes a perceived return, and returns we know are always messy. Residues of past life stuck on and often resurfaced. A conservative reader could even call the Phikirchand group a band of *ersatz* bauls who wore false beards and wigs during performances, and more than most of whom went on in life to become classic exemplars of Chakrabarty's Bengali modern: Akshay Kumar Maitreya or Jaladhar Sen. But, for Kangal himself, such *modern* survivals, paradoxically, were residues of the *past*.

In a short digression, let me try and lull doubts: I am not positing the category of 'ersatz' or, to use the more popular gloss, 'amateur' bauls to hint at the prior existence of some 'real, authentic' bauls. As Jeanne Openshaw and Hugh B. Urban have separately argued, the category of 'bauls' was probably substantialized over the last half of the nineteenth century.[43] This was largely due to a 'romantic' search for an authentic, uncolonized, and uncontaminated self by the urban bhadralok, specifically Rabindranath Tagore and Ksitimohan Sen. The figure of the 'baul' as this self-absorbed, solitary, male renouncer (*udasin*) wandering in search of the *maner manush* (the 'Man' of the heart and mind), once forged, was imposed retrospectively on a (roughly similar but) wide spectrum of persuasions and practices. 'The baul' was born. It is tempting to extend Openshaw's argument, to suggest that the so-called 'amateur bauls', in fact, were the only 'real bauls' who, in the course of time, helped the articulation of the romanticized, Tagorean 'baul'—a category which from its inception has fostered immense analytical hazards for researchers.[44] Before that, 'baul' was just a word, an adjective perhaps, analogous to *batul*, *khyapa*, or 'mad', applied to a whole range of antinomian— and, therefore, socially radical—rural practitioners.[45]

To return to the principal argument and recapitulate, Harinath's was a choice made, albeit forced to some extent and definitely with no conscious project of repudiating the modern self in mind. It is this very unwitting aspect of the choice which gives me food for thought and fodder for argument.

Modernity was at the heart of colonialism (and capital) no matter how checkered and counterintuitive its articulation might have been in Europe. So, an academic 'shoo' delivered via the case of Harinath would not send modernity packing and forever. Modernity for all practical purposes is in our kitchen garden: it is tangible not merely in the sense that a vast number of people have made and still make sense of their lives 'passively' in terms of modernity but also that we have encountered modernity, and repeatedly, as a powerful 'active' claim-making device. Given that, I am merely speculating here as to how useful it is to subsume all strategies of self-articulation under the sign of modernity—that all-encompassing meta category of analysis. Do we not need to think at times in other terms, without the guarantee of modernity? 'Engaging a history without warranty,' writes Saurabh Dube, 'is a possible means of calling into question the guarantees of progress under regimes of modernity and thinking through the projections, presuppositions,

---

[43] The historical process is infinitely more complicated and nuanced than the reductive account that will be outlined here. For details, see Hugh B. Urban, 1999, 'The Politics of Madness: The Construction and Manipulation of the "Baul" Image in Modern Bengal', *South Asia*, vol. 22, no. 1, pp. 13–46; and Openshaw, *Seeking Bauls of Bengal*, especially pp. 19–72.

[44] '[I]t was Western-educated *bhadralok*—aided and abetted by imperial officials and scholars—who substantialised *bāuls* into a fixed and exclusive identity for certain kinds of rural practitioner, and even into a *sampradāy*. To say that the "amateur" or other *bhadralok* Bāuls precipitated the "real" Bāuls, rather than the other way round, constitutes only a slight distortion' (Ibid., p. 112).

[45] 'Clearly the use of the word *bāul*—or related words, such as *bātul*—to denote certain qualities

---

and loosely, by extension, persons possessing such qualities, has a long history in rural as well as urban Bengal. However, my argument would be that its transformation into a proper noun probably does not predate the middle of the nineteenth century, and that its substantialised use to denote specific groups or communities occurred even later than this' (Ibid., p. 111).

schemes, and scandals that it produces and sustains'.[46]

I am pushing the envelope further: what if we were to think without the guarantee of modernity altogether, without the entire package of the projections and presuppositions, schemes and scandals? I am not trying to stake out an uncontaminated outside of the modern (and by extension, the colonial and capital). That is a utopian space some fancy still. I am making a case for the setting aside of the guarantee of modernity which would enable other arguments and positions to emerge and practice their distinctive responsibility.

The case of Harinath Majumdar, the journalist–mystic, is tiny but not inconsequential. It has the potential of halting the single-note symphony of modernity and opening up possibilities for a radical history without warranty.

[46] Saurabh Dube, 2004, *Stitches on Time: Colonial Textures and Postcolonial Tangles*, Durham and London: Duke University Press, p. 20.

II

Probing Politics

5

Minority and Modernity
B.R. Ambedkar and Dalit Politics*

Anupama Rao

Bhimrao Ramji Ambedkar (1891–1956) or 'Babasaheb' Ambedkar is a ubiquitous name in contemporary India. Celebrated for his centrality to the project of Dalit emancipation, and for winning dignity and self-respect for a stigmatized community, Ambedkar's legacy is today materialized through acts of political commemoration. Ambedkar statues are now commonplace not only in Maharashtra, but across the country, attesting to the enhanced visibility of Dalit politics and to Ambedkar's iconic significance in contemporary Indian politics. In 1997 alone, 15,000 statues of Ambedkar were installed across Uttar Pradesh, which

has seen a most remarkable rise of Dalit and Backward Class (BC) politics in recent decades. This provoked widespread conflict with caste Hindus who (rightfully) perceived this as a challenge to upper-caste power and the representational economy of caste Hinduism. Indeed the renowned journalist P. Sainath notes, 'Currently, there are more Ambedkar statues in India's villages than any other leader. His statues are not government installed—unlike those of the others. The poor put them up at their own expense.'[1] As the production (and circulation) of visible signs of Dalit militancy has increased, so too has the power of Ambedkar's name, which has accumulated fetish value through

* This chapter condenses arguments that are developed in detail in Anupama Rao, 2009, *The Caste Question: Dalits and the Politics of Modern India*, Berkeley: University of California Press (2010, New Delhi: Permanent Black).

[1] P. Sainath, 'The Fear of Democracy of the Privileged', *The Hindu*, 8 December 2008.

repeated association with Dalit self, community, and the Dalit future.

This chapter does not address contemporary Dalit politics. Nor does it address Ambedkar as a movement leader and identitarian symbol, for these positions that run the risk of scanting Ambedkar's important contributions to social and political thought. Rather, my aim is to place Dalit politics in longer-term perspective, and to examine how Ambedkar's response to historical stigma developed through creative engagements with, and significant emendations of political liberalism (and its animating fiction of the individual rights-bearing subject as the elemental unit of politics). Unlike Euro-American traditions of political thinking that privilege the universality of the political subject—even when the idea of universality contradicts the historical experience of embodied particularism and political unfreedom— Ambedkar conceived the Dalit as a minority whose identity derived from historically specific forms of suffering and exclusion that required political redress. Thus, Ambedkar's effort to articulate a specific political subjectivity for Dalits was predicated on their identity as subjects constituted in antagonism to Hinduism: history from the perspective of the Dalit subaltern was defined by struggles to convert the Dalit's structural negativity within the caste order into positive political content, and to make historic suffering and humiliation—the experience of being 'ground down' and 'broken'—central to the Dalit's identity as both a non-Hindu minority and an inaugural political subject.

Ambedkar's thinking on Dalit minority coincided with a key rearticulation of the colonial state in the interwar period, and took shape against the backdrop of a series of eventful events: Ambedkar's transformation from leading a regional struggle for civic rights and social recognition, to his emergence as a national figure through a spectacular conflict with M.K. Gandhi in 1932 over the demand for separate Depressed Class representation, followed by his important role in crafting a constitutional 'resolution' to historic discrimination and caste inequality through civil rights law. I will use these transformative moments only in so far as they help us answer a broader set of questions: Who was the Dalit? How and at what point did Dalit suffering become consequential to demands for political recognition?

Community as Constituency

In his discussion of the relationship between democracy and political equality, Ernesto Laclau notes, 'To say that two things are equal—i.e., equivalent to each other in some respects—presupposes that they are different from each other in some other respects (otherwise there would be no equality but identity). *In the political field equality is a type of discourse that tries to deal with differences…*'[2] Laclau's discussion of democracy as a process of commensuration brings the distinctive terrain of colonial politics into sharper relief: colonial politics regulated 'the political' by retaining zones of exception, rather than of enabling the commensurability of putatively different political subjects.

[2] Judith Butler and Ernest Laclau, 1997, 'The Uses of Equality', *Diacritics*, vol. 27, no. 1, Spring, p. 5.

Scholars have argued that community was the generative ground for political identity in the post-Mutiny state.[3] Indeed community was a category that illuminated the reach (and the limits) of colonial modernity, even as it defined the peculiar culturalization of the colonial state and became a key conduit for the exercise of colonial power. As complex Old Regime associations between social status, political power, and ritual idioms were broken and replaced by an extractive, bureaucratic state whose sources of authority were external to Indian society, community, defined as a substitute for modern associational forms, increasingly played a mediating role between the colonial state and its subjects. Colonial intervention, now viewed as a necessary and improving tutelage, was posited against precolonial social forms even as some forms of collective life—caste, religion—were invested with political value. Thus, religious and political domains, though theoretically separate, were practically intertwined. This contradiction was constitutive of the colonial state form: religion was redefined as community, while community gained political salience as constituency. This was the route whereby religion was politicized. A paradox of political commensuration followed: religious communities were seen as *quantitatively incommensurable* but *qualitatively equivalent*.

In turn, colonial state intervention resolved the paradox, mediating between communities as neutral (external) arbiter.

We might thus extend Philip Abrams famous deconstruction of the political realism of state theory to examine what might be termed the *colonial state effect*.[4] Abrams argued that 'the state' was an enabling fiction for masking decentralized practices of power, and that the putative materiality of the state as a thing or a place was in fact an 'effect' of practices of power that produced the state as an autonomous whole. Misrecognition plays a critical role in Abrams' account of the state effect, as it does in our description of the colonial state. However, the colonial state effect is derived from an opposite set of moves to what is obtained in Abrams' account, for colonial power was repeatedly denied, dissimulated, and devolved onto native social and political forms. The bifurcation and racialization of the colonial state under diarchy is a perfect example of the peculiar culturalization of the state: with the Montford reforms of 1919, a native elite was given charge of provincial politics and infrastructural reforms, while the colonial state retreated from direct intervention even as it maintained control over key repressive apparatuses of state, for example, army and finance. The ensuing politics of community, or communalism, was the result of the ideological alignment of (religious) community with constituency, followed by the effort to balance

[3] See, for example, Michel Foucault, 1991, 'Governmentality', in Graham Burchell, Colin Gordin, and Peter Miller (eds), *The Foucault Effect: Studies in Governmentality*, Chicago: University of Chicago Press, pp. 87–105; David Scott, 1995, 'Colonial Governmentality', *Social Text*, vol. 43, Autumn, pp. 191–220; and Partha Chatterjee, 1993, *The Nation and Its Fragments: Colonial and Post-Colonial Histories*, Princeton: Princeton University Press.

[4] Philip Abrams, 1988, 'Notes on the Difficulty of Studying the State', *Journal of Historical Sociology*, vol. 1, no. 1, pp. 58–89. See also, Timothy Mitchell, 1999, 'Economy and the State Effect', in George Steinmetz (ed.), *State/Culture*, Ithaca: Cornell University Press, pp. 76–97.

communities (rather then individuals) against each other to produce something resembling 'representative government'. This is the background against which demands for political representation from minorities—Muslims, Dalits, and women—emerged. Muslims were regional majorities, while the number of women was equal to (if not greater than) the number of men. The identity of Dalits—or Depressed Classes according to governmental classification—was clarified in the course of Dalit struggles for separate recognition.

I argue that colonial liberalism presents us with an alternative narrative of subject formation to the genealogy of liberal secularism, whose constitutive limits were explored by Karl Marx in his essay, 'On the Jewish Question'.[5] Marx's text examines the normative (and normalizing) effects of political liberalism by examining a limit case, the problem of minority. It is a very

particular form of minority that Marx examines, however. By addressing the public effects—exclusion and inequality—that result from the private right to religion, Marx insists that the resolution of the Jewish question is dependent on the political emancipation of the Jew (from religion). That is, the universalization of citizenship also necessitates a political resolution to the problem of religious difference.

Marx argues that though the term 'Jewish minority' might appear oxymoronic, it is the product of the peculiar division between private (belief) and political rights that defines the liberal imaginary: liberalism produces the category of 'minority'. In the case of the Jew, it is experienced as incomplete universality, or a divided personhood, caught between religious particularism and the promise of universal citizenship. Minority is a mediating term between the domains of state and civil society, which converts religious distinction into a form of political lack. Thus, the problem of minority manifests when the Jew's religious identity becomes the grounds for the denial of universal rights, and for the granting of privileges. To accept privileges rather than rights, Marx argues, is to support the practice of prejudice. Indeed, so long as the possibility of *Jewish citizenship* remains, there can be no universal citizenship.

According to Marx, the founding moment in the paradox is the spurious separation of religion and state, and of state and civil society, with religion relegated to the latter domain. This separation is spurious, Marx argues, because the separation of the religious and the political is itself the effect of a prior secularization of religion. By asserting

---

[5] Karl Marx, 1978, 'On the Jewish Question', in Robert C. Tucker (ed.), *The Marx–Engels Reader*, 2nd edition, New York: Norton, pp. 26–52. The text was written between 1843–4. It will be obvious to the reader that this is a partial and interested reading of Marx's text, which neither addresses the more familiar criticisms of Marx's equation of the Jew with capital accumulation, nor Marx's arguments about the relationship between capital, the state form, and the ultimate aims of human emancipation. For one important analysis of the continued relevance of the text, see Wendy Brown, 1985, 'Rights and Identity in Late Modernity: Revisiting the "Jewish Question"', in A. Sarat and T. Kearns (eds), *Identities, Politics and Rights*, Ann Arbor: University of Michigan Press, pp. 85–130. For an innovative extension of Marx's argument to a consideration of Muslims minority existence on the subcontinent, see Amir Mufti, 2007, *Enlightenment in the Colony: The Jewish Question and the Crisis of Postcolonial Culture*, Princeton: Princeton University Press.

that minority is 'the political mode of emancipation from religion',[6] Marx describes this as a necessary stage in the passage from the particular to the universal, from privilege (and prejudice) into full political emancipation, so long as religion can be excised from public and private life.

Marx suggests that the problem of minority is coterminous with the history of liberalism because it is the problem of how liberalism is to incorporate, accommodate, and to recognize alterity.[7] The typical response of liberal states in the West has been to institute a set of rules and procedures by which salient forms of difference are brought within the field of commensuration, while political struggles have typically challenged the fact that certain forms of particularism—religion, gender, race, and caste—are considered ineligible for minority recognition. However, by exploring Dalit struggle, we can also understand an alternative model of political subject formation that works through particularism rather than universality as the governing logic of democratic recognition to elaborate.

Ambedkar's dual efforts to represent Dalits as an alternative ethical community and a political constituency acknowledged

the colonial transformation of community into constituency, but attempted to harness its logic to a different political purpose. Ambedkar's repeated efforts to theorize the complexity of caste dispossession can be examined chronologically as they were evolved and refined, but these were also strategic responses to the political conjunctures in which he found himself. This chapter reflects upon three dominant themes in Ambedkar's thought: *the political*, reflected in Ambedkar's effort to work within the framework of liberal democratic thought to generate the grounding principles for a new conception of minority; *the socio-legal*, evinced by the theorization of caste as a doubled structure of symbolic and material dispossession, that drew upon Marx's argument about the commodity form; and last, *the cultural–historical*, reflected in Ambedkar's genealogy of the Broken Men, or the Dalit Buddhist. In reclaiming the Dalit Buddhist as a non-Hindu ethical subject, Ambedkar, like his important predecessor, Jotirao Phule, transposed the dimension of political antagonism from the caste ordering of social space onto the plane of historical time. This was not a rewriting of history, a difficult task in any case given the highly speculative and polmic tenor of Ambedkar's genealogy. Rather, it was a claim to the act of (self) representation through the imagination of an alternate political and ethical community. Taken together, these multiple responses to the 'hydra-headed' problem of untouchability were characterized by immediate failure and their delayed (and partial) realization in the postcolonial period. They reflect the paradox of recognition for exceptional political subjects like Dalits, who

[6] Karl Marx, 1978, 'On the Jewish Question', in Robert C. Tucker (ed.), *The Marx–Engels Reader*, 2nd edition, New York: Norton, p. 36.

[7] The classic text is Charles Taylor, 1994, *Multiculturalism, Examining the Politics of Recognition*, edited and introduced by Amy Gutmann, Princeton, NJ: Princeton University Press. For an important critique of the limits of liberal models of recognition, see Elizabeth A. Povinelli, 2002, *The Cunning of Recognition: Indigenous Alterities and the Making of Australian Multiculturalism*, Durham, NC: Duke University Press.

had to think outside colonial and nationalist frames.

The Right to Representation as the Right to Politics

By 1920, Ambedkar had begun to argue that the Depressed Classes would remain powerless unless they were to use their political potential to threaten Hindu hegemony.[8] As an exceptional community, untouchables had to harness their latent political power to make Hindus realize that they were of greater significance than their mere numerical strength. 'Our untouchable brethren will recognize their own strength once they realize that Muslims cannot win without us and equally Hindus cannot win without us. They [untouchables] alone have the power to bring about a decisive shift one way or the other.'[9] The position of the untouchables as a third community, a distinctive though recessed (political) constituency, was precisely what Gandhi, Ambedkar's most instructive rival, contested.

At the Second Round Table Conference, Gandhi offered a powerful reason why the untouchables did not constitute a community with the right to special political representation. 'Sikhs may remain as such in perpetuity,' he pointed out, 'so may Muslims, so may Europeans. Would "untouchables" remain untouchables in perpetuity?'[10] Gandhi argued that it was both dangerous and self-defeating for untouchables to dwell upon their experiences

of abjection and servitude to claim separate political representation. Instead, what was required was to transcend the history of caste subjection. However, Gandhi firmly believed that it was the caste Hindu who was to perform this act of redemption by recognizing the untouchable as a *Harijan* (literally, people of god), an object of devotion whose historic suffering required the repayment of a debt in the form of ceaseless service. The caste Hindu could remake himself as an instrument of service through an economy of sacrifice.[11]

Gandhi's description of caste Hindus' relationship to untouchables is suffused with terms associated with indebtedness, debt, reparation, and repentance; it is a debt that in turn required the performance of

[8] *Muknayak*, February and March issues, 1920.

[9] 'Editorial', *Bahishkrit Bharat*, 20 May 1927.

[10] Pyarelal, 1932, *The Epic Fast*, Ahmedabad: Mohanlal Maganlal Bhatt, p. 7.

[11] For an important reading of Gandhi's critique of liberal politics, see Ajay Skaria, 2002, 'Gandhi's Politics: Liberalism and the Question of the Ashram', in Saurabh Dube (ed.), 'Enduring Enchantments', *South Atlantic Quarterly*, Special issue, vol. 101, no. 4, Fall, pp. 955–86. My focus is on Gandhian ethics as a sophisticated form of caste Hindu ethicality, which addressed the Harijan but as the figure *through whom* the caste Hindu might be redeemed. Indeed the category of the Harijan was anomalous, to be replaced by the category of the Shudra as the general figure who manifest a philosophy of service and sacrifice. See, for example, 'Varnadharma', in *Collected Works of Mahatma Gandhi* (hereafter *CWMG*), 19 March 1933, translated from the Gujarati *Harijanbandhu*. Service and sacrifice found articulation in Gandhi's discussion of Hindu hegemony as a form of indebtedness that placed the caste Hindu's relationship to the Harijan both within and without the logic of exchange, thereby short-circuiting the possibility of reciprocity between caste Hindu and Harijan. For critical readings of Gandhi's untouchability programme, see Dilip Menon, 1994, *Caste, Nationalism and Communism in South India*, Cambridge: Cambridge University Press; Vijay Prashad, 2000, *Untouchable Freedom: A Social History of Dalit Community*, New Delhi: Oxford University Press.

service, of ceaseless, unrequited labour as the apt modality of compensation. Indeed this penitential model of citizenship coalesced around the figure of the Harijan. For Gandhi, the Harijan stood outside history; he was a figure of pedagogical instruction for the caste Hindu *through* whom humanity was regained. The (feminized) forms of *bhakti*, or devotion, offered an apt model of emphatic identification. Bhakti was the quintessential form of submission: the devotee became abject by subjecting herself to the object of love, to god, and in the process obtained his *darshan* (divine sight) while in an ecstatic state.[12] Like becoming a woman or identifying with a feminized politics of patient overcoming, desires that Gandhi also articulated, becoming a Harijan indicated a desire for submission, and the experience of giving oneself over to the other through identity with (caste) stigma. Thus, we find Gandhi expressing a desire to become an untouchable, or claiming that he is already one. Often, he claimed to be a Hindu by birth, and an untouchable 'by choice'. Or else, he argued that repentance came only through complete identification with the untouchable.[13] Ambedkar chose to counter Gandhian ethics by developing a political ethics of his own,[14] and yet no

one knew better than him that the demand for separate recognition deepened the conundrum of Dalit identity: how to ground political struggle in a stigmatized identity?

Between 1918 and 1928, in a series of representations before the Southborough and Simon Commissions, established to consider the issues of franchise and the functioning of diarchy, Ambedkar argued that because the Depressed Classes constituted a third community alongside Hindus and Muslims, they required adequate representation.[15] Two broad arguments characterized Ambedkar's position on Depressed Class representation in the period between 1919 and 1928: (i) any demand for separate representation ought to be a fallback option in the absence of adult franchise plus reserved representation; and (ii) representation for the Depressed Classes was distinct from communal electorates for Muslims, as the entire Depressed Class community suffered civic and economic disabilities. Ambedkar drew on a generic theory of representative

---

[12] Dipesh Chakrabarty, 2000, 'Nation and Imagination', in *Provincializing Europe: Postcolonial Thought and Historical Difference*, Princeton: Princeton University Press, pp. 149–79.

[13] M.K. Gandhi, 1956, 'Letter to Rajbhoj, September 20 1932', in M.P. Mangudkar and G.B. Nirantar (eds), *Gandhi–Rajbhoj Correspondence, 1932–1946*, Poona: Bharat Dalit Sevak Sangh Prakashan.

[14] A most sensitive reading of the encounter between Gandhi and Ambedkar can be found in D.R. Nagaraj, 1993, 'Self Purification and Self Respect', in *The Flaming Feet: A Study of the Dalit Movement*,

Bangalore: South Forum Press, pp. 1–30. See also, Nicholas Dirks, 2001, 'The Reform of Caste: Periyar, Ambedkar, and Gandhi', in *Castes of Mind*, Princeton: Princeton University Press, pp. 255–74; and Eleanor Zelliot, 1988, 'Congress and Untouchables: 1917–1950', in Richard Sisson and Stanley Wolpert (eds), *Congress and Indian Nationalism: The Pre-Independence Phase*, Berkeley: University of California Press, pp. 182–97.

[15] For the first time in 1911, the census contained three subcategories under the denomination 'Hindu': Hindus; Animists and Tribals; and the Depressed Classes or Untouchables. At the First Round Table Conference in 1931, Ambedkar and Rao Bahadur Srinivasan argued that the term 'non-caste' or 'non-conformist Hindus', was more appropriate than the insulting term 'Depressed Classes'. However, the term was used until the current terminology of Scheduled Castes came into effect in 1935.

government based on adult franchise in order to make demands on behalf of an emergent political community, the Depressed Classes. The second was a pragmatic position that countered prevailing definitions of minority by drawing attention to the Depressed Classes' material exploitation and civic exclusion. The two positions, taken together, redefined the grounds of 'minority'. As we shall see, a community without political value could demand political power by claiming a universal right *to* politics.[16] That right to politics could be used to, in turn, redefine the meaning of a 'minority' community.

At the Southborough Commission, Ambedkar argued that Depressed Class representation was contingent on the extension of adult franchise. This was an important critique of colonial models of limited representation that articulated with, and reproduced, upper-caste hegemony. Instead, enfranchisement could be used proactively, to reveal potential constituencies or groups such as the Depressed Classes. Only then, Ambedkar suggested, could a subsequent lowering of the criteria of eligibility, that is, the property (and taxation) qualification for the Depressed Classes produce substantive results. Ambedkar argued that reserved or communal seats would enhance Depressed Class representation in the legislative council, but communal electorates had a better chance of ensuring the selection of candidates who

truly represented the community's interest.[17] For untouchables, 'communal representation and self-determination are but two different phrases which express the same notion'.[18]

Ten years later, Ambedkar's representation to the Simon Commission marked a refinement of these arguments through a sustained critique of the Muslim separate electorate.[19] Distinguishing the Depressed Classes from the Muslims, Ambedkar described the former as 'educationally backward, that it is economically very poor, socially enslaved'.[20] As for Muslims, Ambedkar had argued before the Southborough Commission that Hindus could represent 'the *material* interests of the Mohammedans and vice versa'.[21] Instead, material deprivation and social stratification was seen to unite the Depressed Classes. Indeed the Depressed Classes defined a particular *class interest*. They required protection due to their low social and economic status, and their small numbers required some form of compensation.

[16] Etienne Balibar, 1994, '"Rights of Man" and "Rights of the Citizen": The Modern Dialectic of Equality and Freedom', in James Swenson (trans.), *Masses, Classes, Ideas*, New York: Routledge, pp. 39–59.

[17] Supplementary written statement of B.R. Ambedkar, in *Babasaheb Ambedkar Writings and Speeches* (hereafter *BAWS*, ed. Vasant Moon, Mumbai: Education Department, Government of Maharashtra), vol. 1.

[18] Evidence before Southborough Committee, in Ibid., p. 270.

[19] Ambedkar was labelled a 'British stooge' for agreeing to be a member of the Bombay Committee of the Simon Commission, which was boycotted by the Congress and the Muslim League. He eventually submitted a book-length rejoinder criticizing the Simon Commission's recommendations. See 1930, Indian Statutory Commission, vol. III, Appendix D, pp. 87–156.

[20] Evidence of Dr Ambedkar before the Indian Statutory Commission on 23 October 1928, in *BAWS*, vol. 2, p. 465.

[21] Ibid.

Both issues could be addressed through the provision of reserved electorates.

The principle of weightage was first articulated in connection with the Muslim electorate. Ambedkar forefronted the socio-economic marginalization of the Depressed Classes to demand similar measures for them, however. Representing the Bahishkrit Hitakarini Sabha, Ambedkar noted that weighted representation was 'literally showered upon a community like the Mahomedans holding a stronger and better position in the county than can be predicated of the Depressed Classes. The Sabha protests against this grading of the citizens of a country on the basis of their political importance.'[22] When taken together with the considerable strength of Muslims as a demographic majority in Sind, Bengal, Punjab, and the Northwest Frontier Provinces, Ambedkar argued, Muslims could be said to represent the principle of nationality and not of political minority. Nationality rendered number unimportant; indeed, national affiliation was an affective bond and a feeling of commonality, whereas majority and minority were enumerated entities within the nation. The Muslim-majority provinces were an 'ingenious contrivance' that 'involved the maintenance of justice and peace by retaliation'.[23] Hindu and Muslim minorities would be ruled by fear and anxiety since they could be held hostage for the behaviour of their co-religionists in other parts of the country. 'For if the Hindu majority tyrannized the Muslim minority in the Hindu provinces the scheme provides a remedy whereby the Mohammedan majorities get a field to tyrannize the Hindu minorities in the five Mohammedan provinces. It is a system of protection by counterblast against blast; terror against terror and eventually tyranny against tyranny.'[24] This was a politically prescient argument, and it was reproduced in *Pakistan or the Partition of India*, published in 1940.[25] What distinguishes Ambedkar's efforts here, in this early conjuncture, is the effort to define an emergent, as yet unrecognized, community through such negative comparisons.

If the 'historic and political importance' of Muslims had led to their being guaranteed protection of their political interests and aspirations, then the late 1930s would see the discourse of minority transformed into a demand for the recognition of Muslims as a nationality located within a distinctive territory. On the other hand, representation for the Depressed Classes was necessary in order to redress their social and political invisibility. Characterizing the relationship between caste Hindus and untouchables as a 'fundamental and deadly antagonism,' Ambedkar argued:

---

[22] Statement concerning safeguards for the protection of interests of the Depressed Classes as a minority in the Bombay Presidency and the changes in the composition of and the guarantees from the Bombay Legislative Council necessary to ensure the same under Provincial Autonomy, submitted by B.R. Ambedkar on behalf of the Bahishkrit Hitakarini Sabha (Depressed Classes Institute) to the Indian Statutory Commission, 29 May 1928, in Ibid., pp. 438–9.

[23] A report on the Constitution of the Government of Bombay Presidency, presented to the Indian Statutory Commission, in Ibid., p. 320.

[24] Ibid., p. 319.

[25] *Pakistan or the Partition of India*, in *BAWS*, vol. 8.

The first thing I submit is that we [untouchables, Depressed Classes] claim that we must be treated as a distinct minority, separate from the Hindu community: a distinct and independent minority. Secondly I should like to submit that the Depressed Classes minority needs far greater political protection than any other minority in British India for the simple reason that it is educationally backward, that it is economically very poor, socially enslaved and suffers from certain grave political disabilities from which no other community suffers. Then I would submit that, as a matter of demand for our political protection, we claim representation on the same basis as the Mahomeddan minority. We claim reserved seats if accompanied by adult franchise.[26]

Let us extrapolate the immense significance of these efforts. If the Depressed Classes, Hindus, and Muslims could be said to constitute *three* distinct communities of interest, with the Depressed Classes forming 18–20 per cent of the population, then this third community disturbed the idea that only 'fixed permanent communities' existed in political space. The Depressed Classes were to be defind by a different principle of minority, that of socio-economic status and material deprivation, rather than the primordial differences of religion. As a third community produced by the practice of power and inequality, the very existence of this community challenged the colonial obsession with Hindu and Muslim communities as primordial political actors. As well, Hindu majoritarianism was compromised. Increasingly, the Depressed Classes came to be defined as a community

that Hinduism produced outside or apart from itself. Indeed Ambedkar had used the social fact of a fundamental contradiction between Hindus and the untouchables to subvert the colonial discourse of community as constituency.

I would argue that for Ambedkar, the idea of full franchise was important because it represented a right to politics. What do I mean? Etienne Balibar has argued, for instance, that the enduring legacy of the French Revolution lies in the equation that was assumed between 'man' and 'citizen', characterizing all subsequent political struggles as an effort to align the rights of man with those of the citizen.[27] Balibar's formulation of the primacy of the political, I suggest, also allows us to think about politics as the precondition for the recognition of 'the human'. Indeed this is also Marx's argument in 'On the Jewish Question'. We might draw on these insights to examine the strategic role played by Ambedkar's demand for universal franchise, for what such a demand accomplished was to draw attention to a hitherto unrecognized political constituency that possessed no distinguishing qualities but for the mere fact of its humanity. The demand for universal franchise was a strategic manoeuvre to draw attention to a stigmatized and deprived community that had to be endowed with political *value*.

With this in mind, let us turn now to Ambedkar's theorization of caste society, a preoccupation that was simultaneous with the demand for Depressed Class representation, and which increasingly

[26] Evidence of Dr Ambedkar before the Indian Statutory Commission on 23 October 1928, in Ibid., p. 465. Ambedkar also submitted his own report to the (Simon) Indian Statutory Commission, Vol. III, Appendix D, pp. 87–156.

[27] Balibar, '"Rights of Man" and "Rights of the Citizen"'.

convinced him of the necessity of finding a political response to Hindu hegemony through the demand for separate electorate.

The Critique of Political Hinduism

Ambedkar had underscored the incommensurable position of the Depressed Classes and Muslims from the start. If the Depressed Classes were united in their experience of ritual segregation and material deprivation, Muslims were defined by their religious difference. Untouchables were a community without political worth; they were yet to find recognition as political subjects. In being placed outside the general (Hindu) electorate, Muslims had managed to parlay their religious distinction into a position of political strength. Increasingly however, it became apparent that the two communities were equivalent with respect to a hegemonic formation: political Hinduism.

In a paper presented at the Anthropology seminar at Columbia University in 1916, later published in the *Indian Antiquary* in 1917, and entitled 'Castes in India: Their Genesis, Mechanism, and Development',[28] Ambedkar portrayed caste society as an involuted class formation. He acknowledged the thematic continuities between this early essay and his later writings on caste, and appears to have understood this essay as the effort to articulate a theory of social reproduction.[29] The main components

of that theory can be characterized as follows. Caste society was an involuted class formation which was reproduced on a daily basis through the imitation of the Brahmin by the lower castes, and secured by the textual justification for Brahminical hegemony found in the *Manusmriti*, which instantiated Hinduism's 'illegal laws'. Sexual regulation was the interior of caste society, since it was the ban on inter-caste marriage and mechanisms for the removal of excess or 'surplus' women that characterized the economy of caste. Ambedkar argued that caste society did not merely justify material deprivation, but also ritual, psychic, and even physical segregation. Organized along 'an ascending scale of reverence and a descending scale of contempt', caste society was the perverse ordering of persons along a hierarchy of dignities.[30] Untouchability was 'an aspect of social psychology: it [was] a sort of social nausea of one group against the other'.[31]

In contrast to dominant ethno-historical characterizations of the caste order that privileged the Brahmin as the fulcrum of the system, Ambedkar argued for the centrality of untouchability to the very coherence of 'caste'. Ambedkar argued that untouchability formed the glue of the Hindu order, while the untouchables, though despised and marginalized, possessed a latent political power. The principle of untouchability provided the single point of unification for the touchable but otherwise fragmented Hindu castes. In every other respect, differences of belief and practice

---

[28] *Castes in India: Their Genesis, Mechanism, and Development*, in *BAWS*, vols 1 and 9.

[29] Ambedkar regretted that he could not incorporate *Castes in India* in the third edition of *The Annihilation of Caste*. The posthumously published text *Revolution and Counter-Revolution* (*BAWS*, vol. 3, pp. 296–302) also cites *Castes in India*.

[30] B.R. Ambedkar, 1946 [rpt 1970], *Who Were the Shudras?* Bombay: Thackers.

[31] Ibid., p. 370.

fractured Hinduism irretrievably. To locate untouchability, that which was extraneous or supplementary to caste Hinduism as caste's secret, was perhaps the most powerful attempt yet by anyone to provide a systemic theory of caste.

As early efforts to analyse the caste system increasingly gave way to efforts to change caste relations, the *bahishkar*, or the caste boycott, was elaborated as the generic form of caste antagonism. Bahishkar worked at all levels, physical, economic, and psycho-religious; it was a disciplinary tool that caste Hindus used to temporarily separate or to excise an errant member of the body politic.[32] In the 1920s, at the height of popular mobilization and Dalits' demands for civic access, Ambedkar began to focus on bahishkar as a principle of both structural and transacted violence. As transacted violence, bahishkar could be used as a penal mechanism against erring members of a caste, or against an entire community. The exclusion of the untouchables was a structuring violence, however, it was a segregation principle. Indeed bahishkar could only be defined as a form of violence by drawing upon the discourse of modern legality. Importantly, bahishkar was translated into the judicial language of 'civic exclusion' and of 'civic disabilities'. The Starte Committee, which conducted one of the most thoroughgoing inquiries into the status of the Depressed Classes in Bombay,

declared: 'We do not know of any weapon more effective than this social boycott…The method of open violence pales before it, for it has the most far reaching and deadening effects. It is the more dangerous *because it passes as a lawful method consistent with the theory of freedom of contract.*'[33]

Ambedkar uses the phrase the 'illegal laws of the Hindus' to describe not merely bahishkar, but the justification for caste society *in toto*. Indeed, for Ambedkar, the possibility of a direct confrontation between caste Hindus and untouchables was sublated through the structure of *chaturvarna*, an expansive system of graded inequality that distributed conflict across the caste order. Violent conflict was avoided, yet violence haunted the caste structure as a threat to full personhood. Bahishkar, a traditional penal sanction, played a particularly important role in muting the contradictions of caste society. The untouchables had internalized bahishkar as a form of physical vulnerability, and experienced it as a principle that structured their permanent socio-political segregation.

Ambedkar repeatedly drew upon the metaphor of failed exchange to characterize the caste order as a doubled structure, governed both by material dispossession and the denial, or withholding, of sociality. By adopting a worm's eye view, so to speak, Ambedkar began to insist that the withholding of sociality was the coercive force keeping the caste system together. In a sense, this was the counter to a Dumontian perspective *avant la lettre*. It was not the principle of hierarchy or the aspiration for purity against pollution that organized

[32] Ranajit Guha has written eloquently about the violence of the boycott and its transformation into a tool of Gandhian discipline. See Ranajit Guha, 1997, 'Discipline and Mobilize: Hegemony and Elite Control in Nationalist Campaigns', in *Dominance without Hegemony: History and Power in Colonial India*, Cambridge: Harvard University Press, pp. 100–51.

[33] *What Congress and Gandhi Have Done to the Untouchables*, in *BAWS*, vol. 10.

castes as a system. The latter view assumes a positive sense of sociality in which violence is used mainly against threats to the maintenance of hierarchy, while hierarchy can be understood as a purely consensual social form. As opposed to this, Ambedkar argued that structural violence was integral to the molecular structure of caste.

Violence was rarely apprehended as sheer force, however. Rather, violence structured the social relations between untouchables and caste Hindus, and justified their degradation as well as their separation from the other castes. Unlike capitalist relations of production to which labour was central, however, caste society was organized not on the model of bourgeois accumulation, but on ritual action as a form of symbolic expenditure, to which the untouchables' labour (and being) were rendered extraneous because impure. Untouchability was central to the caste order as a negative principle.[34] How could this negative principle become manifest, when it was precisely its misrecognition that reproduced the caste order? How to make the Depressed Classes visible as a 'separate element' whose interests were orthogonal to the Hindu community?

Are Dalits Minorities?

Prime Minister Ramsey Macdonald's Communal Award of 16 August 1932 allowed the Depressed Classes a double vote. They could vote for Depressed Class candidates through a separate electorate

in areas where Depressed Class voters predominated, and they could also cast a vote in the general (Hindu) electorate. The award thus marked the anomalous status of the Depressed Classes as a degraded Hindu minority, within and without the Hindu community. Ambedkar had demanded a separate electorate for the Depressed Classes even while other Depressed Class leaders shifted away from earlier demand for separate representation. To understand his dependence on this political mechanism thus requires clarifying Ambedkar's understanding of how the separate electorate worked.

I have argued that Ambedkar understood Hindu ideology as justifying a complex form of inequality, characterized by secular and religio-ritual forms of exclusion. Thus, if Gandhi (and Congress nationalists) characterized untouchability as a problem of religious inclusion, Ambedkar politicized the putative split between these two domains, and simultaneously questioned the terms of religious and political inclusion, to argue that the horizon of emancipation could not be contained within existing social relations. But how was this sophisticated theorization of caste society to be operationalized? The separate electorate appeared to be a procedural mechanism that could enable 'thick' results. By this I mean to suggest that because there was no single procedural mechanism or political form that could respond to the complexity of caste inequality, the separate electorate was an overdetermined political option from the start. By drawing attention to the Depressed Classes as a politically vulnerable non-Hindu community, the separate electorate would also position the Depressed Classes as politically consequential, since both Hindus

---

[34] I am grateful to Lee Schlesinger for pushing me to clarify the analogy between the commodity form and the caste order. Personal communication, 27 April 2005.

and Muslims would recognize that the Depressed Classes 'had the power to bring about a decisive shift one way or the other'.[35] The separate electorate suggested itself as a mechanism of (historical) redress because it endowed the Depressed Classes with political value by positioning them as an exceptional community on par with both Hindus and Muslims, but this could only be successful to the extent that the Depressed Classes could be defined as a non-Hindu religious minority! As Ambedkar had repeatedly argued, however, the Depressed Classes were distinguished by material deprivation, by their physical vulnerability, and by their stigmatized status within the caste order. They represented an altogether different principle of minority. This was indeed the political conundrum of Depressed Class identity, as Gandhi noted: theirs was an identity to be transcended, not reified. And Gandhi's fast-unto-death and the ensuing Poona Pact, by reaffirming the identity of the Depressed Classes as degraded Hindus, also made the problem of untouchability an internal problem for the Hindu community.

Mobilizing his power as an exemplary individual, Gandhi withdrew his consent to the entire theatre of politics, and thereby accrued moral capital and scored a political victory in the process. Ambedkar, in turn, described his capitulation as an act of humanitarianism: 'I responded to the call of humanity and saved the life of Mr. Gandhi by agreeing to alter the Communal Award in a manner satisfactory to Mr. Gandhi. This award is known as the Poona Pact.'[36] As the colonial state stepped back from interfering in what was now characterized as an internal problem for the Hindu community, it became obvious that the majority of caste Hindus would not tolerate any form of internal regulation. The separate electorate had offered the possibility of transcending community, but only to the extent that the Depressed Classes could mimic the form of religious community. (This was the pernicious constraint of colonial liberalism.) There was no mechanism to democratize the community from within, however, because the perpetrators, that is, the caste Hindu majority, were the ones who were being asked to adjudicate their behaviour. Gandhian reformism, with the focus on changing the hearts and minds of even the most orthodox Hindu, substituted penitence for procedure.[37]

The Postcolonial Transition

Ambedkar's efforts to resolve Dalits' political status through recourse to the logic of *equivalence and exception* had challenged the governing efficacy of democratic logic, but it

---

[35] 'Editorial', *Bahishkrit Bharat*, 20 May 1927.
[36] *What Congress and Gandhi Have Done to the Untouchables*, in *BAWS*, vol. 9, p. 88.

[37] I don't discuss the Indian Labour Party (ILP), formed in 1936, due to constraints of space. However, it is important to note that along with the decision to leave Hinduism in October 1935, Ambedkar's other important activity in the mid-1930s was to establish a party forged around a dual critique of caste and capitalism, *Brahmanshahi* and *bhandwalshahi*, that explored a possible alliance between landless peasants and the working classes, between Dalits and caste Hindus. Reflecting Ambedkar's receptivity to a Marxian critique of dispossession, the ILP's political platform demanded support for the state management and ownership of industry; support for credit and cooperative societies; tax reform to reduce the burden on agricultural and industrial labour, and free and compulsory education.

had also ended in failure. For a community that was stigmatized and territorially dispersed, self-representation was neither possible from within nor without the terrain of politics as constituted by the Hindu communal majority. In a vituperative attack on Ambedkar's text, *What Congress and Gandhi Have Done to the Untouchables*, C. Rajagopalachari argued that the Scheduled Castes had no claims upon a separate democracy. He argued:

The Scheduled Castes are evenly distributed all over India and are about ten per cent of the population...Thus distributed, they have to be part of the general population and cannot isolate themselves into a separate democracy. Nothing therefore follows from the argument even if conclusively proved that the Scheduled Castes do not stand behind the Congress and do not support its claim for political freedom.[38]

Swaraj was unabashedly majoritarian, and Ambedkar's critique of the non-representative character of the Congress was a moot point, since 'it may often be impossible to get minorities to agree to the claims for self-government which is majority rule even though the minorities be fully protected in their civil and political rights'.[39] Indeed by this point, demand for Scheduled Caste representation was represented as a 'short cut' to political power for Scheduled Caste leaders who benefited from the safeguards enjoyed by their community.[40]

Another text, *Ambedkar's Attack*, went even further and represented Ambedkar as a British stooge, as the colonial government wanted to 'magnify the difference in the Indian social structure as a justification for British domination'.[41] For Santhanam, as for Rajagopalachari, the status of the Scheduled Castes as a *territorially dispersed minority* was significant. 'Whether there are 50 or 60 millions, it is of minor importance. I may point out that they are distributed almost evenly in all the villages of India. In each village they constitute a minority.'[42] As a dispersed and fragmented community, the Scheduled Castes posed no political threat to Congress hegemony. It was Ambedkar who held on to untouchability as though it were a 'precious possession', resisting efforts at assimilation and integration. Increasingly, it appeared as if a new principle of Dalit personhood required elaboration.

The final and most powerful symbolic challenge to Hindu inclusiveness would come two decades after the Poona Pact compromise, with Ambedkar's 'conversion' to Buddhism on 14 October 1956, shortly before his death. Though he described it as Dalits' *return* to their Buddhist past, Ambedkar's actions were perceived as Dalits symbolic exit from the Hindu community; a final refusal to countenance Hinduism's historic degradation of the untouchable. For Ambedkar, Buddhism was significant to the extent that its demise was personified in the figure of the Dalit Buddhist. It is to this that Ambedkar turned in his later writings.

Ambedkar rewrote the history of caste subjection as a process of subject (de)formation by introducing Buddhism

[38] Chakravarti Rajagopalachari, 1946, *Ambedkar Refuted*, Bombay: Hind Kitabs, pp. 5–6.
[39] Ibid., pp. 8–9.
[40] Ibid., pp. 33–4.

[41] K. Santhanam, 1946, *Ambedkar's Attack: A Critical Examination of Dr. Ambedkar's Book: 'What Congress and Gandhi Have Done to the Untouchables'*, New Delhi: The Hindustan Times Press, p. 25.
[42] Ibid., p. 20.

as a (forgotten) agent of history, and persuasively argued that the epochal conflict between Buddhism and Brahmanism was a persistent religious and political antagonism borne on the untouchable's body. The untouchables were described as Buddhists and Broken Men hence Dalit, meaning 'ground down' or broken to pieces. (This was a term that Ambedkar had first used during the late 1920s, in his newspaper, *Bahishkrit Bharat*.) A destitute, territorially dispersed community of suffering, they were history's detritus. Because the Broken Men had resisted the movement of history, they symbolized obdurate social forms and practices that could not be subsumed by the mainstream. Contemporary caste society was thus characterized by the insufficient incorporation of ethnic or political others who were then rendered its most vulnerable (and violated) elements.

Ambedkar's genealogy of the Dalit Buddhist is indeed a highly speculative history, but its importance lies in his *transposition of the dimension of political antagonism from the caste ordering of social space onto the plane of historical time*. The reflexive appropriation of historicality thus became a potential mode of political redemption. Ambedkar altogether bypassed the necessity of asserting a high-caste status for the untouchables that they consequently lost through *their* actions, for example, the adoption of degrading practices such as scavenging and eating beef or carrion. Rather, Ambedkar argued that the untouchables were a distinct group of Buddhists, the Broken Men, who belonged to a group of wandering tribesmen defeated in battle(s) as nomadic society gave way to settled agriculture and as blood affiliation gave way to territorial affiliation; that is, as the principle of clan and tribe gave way to the principle of nationality. Living at the edge of villages, and guarding the village, as well as its mobile and landed wealth, the Broken Men were 'not of the blood of the Settled tribes'. The Broken Men had become dependent on eating dead cattle for sustenance, and they had refused to accept Brahmanism. Unlike the Shudras, with their militant Kshatriya past, the untouchables had always been Broken Men—degraded, homeless, and fated to inhabit the margins. They were vestiges from the past; living reminders of a society that once existed. Ambedkar's genealogy of the untouchables thus wove together *two* models of historical causality: the evolution of settled society from nomadic communities; and the religious–political conflict between Brahmanism and Buddhism.

Ambedkar had defined the Dalits as an exceptional, perhaps autochthonous community locked in an antagonistic relationship to Brahmanism. As victims, they were history's losers, yet they exemplified a crucial space of alterity. Ambedkar's efforts to hold in tension the injurious history of the Dalit Buddhist together with the political utopia of Buddhism meant, however, that the partial subjectivity of the Dalit was to be addressed through the positive discrimination of the state.

At the End

As Ambedkar made new demands for political rights, he also had to define whom the rights were being argued for. A group defined in negative terms was being constituted as a community in the making, or 'community' was part of a necessary passage of forms for untouchables in their quest for emancipation, but only insofar as it could be rendered into (political) constituency. If by way of summary we outline a stagiest model of growth of Dalit politics, we notice at least three. First of all we can distinguish Ambedkar's attempt to define untouchables as political minorities in the way that Muslims had been able to do, as a distinct community whose rights were certain to be diminished by the majority Hindu community. But since the logic of Muslim minoritarianism was predicated on absolute (religious) separation, he had to redefine the untouchable minority by exploring agonisms within Hindu community to render Dalits visible. If remaining within the given frame of liberal politics was a choice, it was a difficult one to say the least. The conditions by which a given realm came to be constituted as political itself had to be brought into debate, which meant that the boundaries of liberalism were themselves ruptured by events from a larger political field. If the first stage sought to incorporate Dalits as liberal political actors within a procedural logic of commensuration, in the second stage, Ambedkar had to challenge liberalism by arguing that untouchables were, by virtue of their past, incommensurable. History

became the means of bringing a hitherto excluded antagonism within the political field, as Ambedkar pointed to the hostility of the Brahmin towards the untouchable as the deep structure of Hindu society. To overcome this legacy of history, positive rather than procedural action was required. The culmination of this movement we can identify in the third stage, where in a sense, the former untouchable becomes the new lawgiver, and enunciates a new schema of jurisprudence.

B.R. Ambedkar posed the problem of Dalit emancipation not as an abstract thought experiment, but from the embodied space of stigmatized selfhood. In the process, two things became evident: (i) by questioning the terms of religious *and* political inclusion, Ambedkar revealed that the horizon of emancipation could not be contained within existing social relations; and by so doing, (ii) he suggested that the experiences of caste subalternity could never be fully encompassed by the enumerative logic of the political majority and minority, nor the ameliorative logic of a reformed Hinduism. If caste, and especially untouchability, is the deep structure of secular and religious configurations of community and nation, can we address India's political modernity without an account of the subject who inaugurates that modernity—the Dalit?

6

Gandhi's Religion

Ajay Skaria[†]

In his writings and speeches, Gandhi quite consistently drew on an opposition between *aadhunik sudhaara* or 'modern civilization' and *dharma* or 'religion.' His book *Hind Swaraj*,[1] for instance, is organized as a 'dialogue' between two figures—the Editor

---

† This chapter is the result of ongoing conversations with many of my colleagues and friends at the University of Minnesota, but especially of those with Vinay Gidwani, Qadri Ismail, and Simona Sawhney. I was also very fortunate to be able to discuss the arguments of the chapter with Saurabh Dube, Ishita Bannerjee–Dube, David Hardiman, and Vinay Lal. I am also deeply indebted to the students in my Spring 2008 course on Gandhi, especially Abir Bazaz and Aniruddha Datta, for their many searching questions. Writing this chapter has been an especially thought-provoking task for somebody like me, who has been brought up as an atheist, and who is not aware of experiencing a desire to give up on his atheism.

[1] In these notes, I first refer to the language in which Gandhi originally wrote, and where it has proved possible, provide a reference to the translation.

Where Gandhi originally wrote/spoke in Gujarati, I have, wherever possible, tried to adhere to the official translation. However, I have sometimes modified the official translation. In such cases, I have wherever necessary provided the official translation in parentheses. Where he originally wrote/spoke in Hindi, I have depended on the English translation. I draw on the *Gandhijino Akshardeha*, Gandhi's collected works in Gujarati and *Collected Works of Mahatma Gandhi*, Gandhi's collected works in English. When citing from *Hind Swaraj*, I have, given the number of editions available, tried to make things easier for the reader by indicating the chapter from which the citation is taken. Since these chapters are fairly short, it will presumably not be a problem to find the citation within the chapter. An electronic edition of *Hind Swaraj* is available at http://www.archive.org/details/hindswarajorindi00ganduoft. See also *Gandhijino Akshardeha* (hereafter *Akshardeha*), 81 vols, Ahmedabad: Navjivan Press, 1967–1992; *Collected Works of Mahatma Gandhi* (hereafter *CWMG*; Electronic Book), 98 vols, New Delhi: Publications

and the Reader. Both share a commitment to *swaraj*—independence or 'home rule'. But they differ quite radically on what swaraj means, or how it might be achieved. The Reader is a figure who makes the conventional nationalist arguments about why and how the British need to be driven out of India. For the Reader, swaraj involves India securing, as he puts it in Gandhi's English translation of chapter 4 (titled 'What is Swaraj?'), the same powers as England or Japan: 'We must own our navy, our army, and we must have our own splendour, and then will India's voice ring through the world.' And to achieve this goal, the Reader is willing to use any means possible. As he puts it in Gandhi's English translation of chapter 15: 'Why should we not obtain our goal, which is good, by any means whatsoever, even by using violence?'

But the Editor, ventriloquizing Gandhi's explicit positions, argues that such violence would not bring about swaraj or 'home rule', independence. For the Editor, the swaraj that the Reader seeks is only 'English rule without the Englishman'. He insists that swaraj in this sense is not only inappropriate for India, but that it has already reduced England to a 'pitiable' condition. For this pitiable condition, the Editor blames not the English themselves but 'modern civilization'.

That phrase is used for the first time towards the close of chapter 5 ('The Condition of England'), and is Gandhi's translation of the Gujarati phrase '*aajkaalna sudhaara*'. Leaving for another occasion the appropriateness of this translation, what I wish to stress for now is that while the

Editor attacks 'modern civilization' on several registers, its irreligiosity is an overwhelming concern. The stress on this irreligiosity is especially marked in chapter 6.

In it there is no thought for niti [ethics; 'morality'] or dharma ['religion']. The votaries of sudhaara ['modern civilization'] say quite clearly that it is not their job to teach people dharma. So many believe that religion is only a false pretense [*dhong*, 'superstitious growth']. Also, so many wear the mantle of *dharma*; they even talk of *niti*; nevertheless I tell you after twenty years of experience that *aniti* is taught in the name of *niti*…This sudhaaro is *adharma* ['irreligion'], and it has spread to such an extent in Europe that the people there ['the people who are in it'] appear half-mad.

The Editor again devotes much of chapter 8 (the first of five chapters named 'The Condition of India') to *dharma*.

Dharma is dear to me, and so my first reason for grief is this that Hindustan is becoming ever more corrupt in *dharma* [*dharmabhrasht*; 'irreligious']. By *dharma* I do not here mean Hindu or Mussalman or Zorastrian religion. But the religion which stays in all these religions has gone. [Here I am not thinking of the Hindu or the Mahomedan or the Zoroastrian religion but of that religion which underlies all religions.] We are turning our faces away from Ishwar [God].

In Gandhi's argument, then, 'modern civilization' is making India 'irreligious', much as it had made England 'irreligious'.

Religion was at the centre of Gandhi's politics in many other ways too. In his writings on politics, for instance, vows, promises, and pledges (or what Gandhi in his Gujarati writings describes as *yama*s and *vrat*s) are especially important. Dharma or religion involves the observance of vows or promises, or the making of the human into a

---

Division Government of India, 1999. Available online at http://www.gandhiserve.org/cwmg/cwmg.html.

promising animal, into a figure made distinct by repetition and return. This dimension of dharma was something that Gandhi stressed repeatedly. Thus, he insisted on the importance of the *yamaniyamas*, a phrase that the editors of the English *Collected Works* gloss suggestively: '*Yama* is a duty or observance enjoined by religion. *Niyama* is a voluntary acceptance of that discipline.'[2] During most of his civil disobedience campaigns, he called on Indians to observe vows—the vow of *swadeshi*, of *ahimsa*, of *satyagraha*, and so on. Civil disobedience, non-cooperation, etc., all these political strategies were for him religious strategies.

This inseparability for him of politics and religion was something that Gandhi alluded to on many occasions. In November 1924, for example, Gandhi wrote a piece in *Young India* announcing that he had '[a]fter much prayer, after much heart-searching, and not without fear and trembling' decided to accept the invitation to preside at the next session of the Indian National Congress. But, he added: 'I must not deceive the country. For me there is no politics without religion [*dharmathi bhinn raajniti*]—not the religion of the superstitious [*vahem*] and the blind [*andhshraddha*], religion that hates and fights, but the universal [*vishwavyaapi*] Religion of Toleration [*sahisnuta*]. Politics without morality [*niti*] is a thing to be avoided.'[3] After reviewing the considerable challenges he would face as president, he ended his piece by remarking: 'May God help us all'!

Nevertheless, at least by the 1940s (and perhaps earlier too), Gandhi affirmed a secular vision of the state over and again. In a conversation with a Christian missionary in 1946, Gandhi insisted:

If I were a dictator, religion and State would be separate. I swear by my religion. I will die for it. But it is my personal affair. The State has nothing to do with it. The State would look after your secular welfare, health, communications, foreign relations, currency and so on, but not your or my religion. That is everybody's personal concern![4]

And in a similar vein, he argued after independence:

After all, we have formed the Government for all. It is a 'secular' government, that is, it is not a theocratic government, rather, it does not belong to any particular religion. Hence it cannot spend money on the basis of communities. For it, the only thing that matters is that all are Indians. Individuals can follow their own religions. I have my religion and you have yours to follow.[5]

It is tempting to think that his formulations about secularism and about religion belong to different periods in his life, and that while he insisted till the 1930s or early 1940s that there could be 'no politics without religion', he came to affirm secularism as Hindu–Muslim violence spiraled upwards in the 1940s. There is certainly something to this argument, for it is only by the late 1940s that, as far as I can tell from his voluminous writings, he explicitly insists on separating religion and state.

---

[2] 'Letter to Manilal Gandhi before January 18, 1913', in *CWMG*, vol. 12, p. 377; original Gujarati.

[3] 'May God Help', *Young India*, 24 November 1924; *CWMG*, vol. 29, p. 373ff.; *Akshardeha*, vol. 25, p. 340.

[4] *Harijan*, 22 September 1946; *CWMG*, vol. 92, p. 190.

[5] 'Speech at a Prayer Meeting, 28 November 1947', in *CWMG*, vol. 97, p. 414.

Yet, it is not as though there is a significant change in his arguments on this subject. In his earlier writings too, he does, on occasion, warn against theocratic rule, and he never seems to have suggested that religion and state be melded. In the 1940s, he kept up his insistence on practicing a religious politics: one only has to recall the epic fasts that he undertook as a Hindu. So, while by the late 1940s there might have been a sharper emphasis on separating religion and the state, this is not so much a change of perspective as a more explicit elaboration of what had earlier been an implicit argument.

Secular

This affirmation of religious politics already raises intriguing questions, and the questions are only made all the more intriguing by his simultaneous affirmation of secularism. Our dominant traditions—and these are by no means only modern, Western, or secular—conceptualize religion in terms of a distinction between the transcendent and the immanent realms. Here, religion privileges the transcendent plane, or the plane of the godly and divine. This transcendent plane is assumed to ontologically and epistemologically ground the world—to constitute the truth of the world, and to constitute the ways the world can be known. This insistence on grounding can take various forms—the conviction that gods intervene in the immanent world, that the real purpose of immanent or worldly life is to serve the transcendent, and so on.

One powerful way of thinking of the European secular project is that it inverts and radically systematizes the distinction between the immanent and the transcendent. Insisting that the immanent world has its own logic, secularism grounds the ethics of everyday life in the immanent world. As a recent magisterial reiteration of secular humanism by Charles Taylor puts it:

…we have moved from a world in which the place of fullness was understood as unproblematically outside of or 'beyond' human life, to a conflicted age in which this construal is challenged by others which place it (in a wide range of different ways) 'within' human life… The great invention of the West was that of an immanent order in Nature, whose working could be systematically understood and explained on its own terms, leaving open the question whether this whole order had a deeper significance, and whether, if it did, we should infer a transcendent Creator beyond it. This notion of the 'immanent' involved denying—or at least isolating and problematizing—any form of interpenetration between the things of nature on one hand, and 'the supernatural' on the other, be this understood in terms of the one transcendent God, or of Gods or spirits, or magic forces, or whatever.[6]

Now the focus is on what Taylor calls 'human flourishing': 'a secular age is one in which the eclipse of all goals beyond human flourishing becomes conceivable; or better, it falls within the range of an imaginable life for masses of people'.[7] Central to this immanent ethics of human flourishing is an affirmation of the human as the figure who is uniquely free. Secular and liberal thought at its finest (and here at least there is little sense in dealing with anything else) seeks explicitly, albeit within its terms, to

[6] Charles Taylor, 2007, *A Secular Age*, Boston: Harvard University Press, p. 15ff.
[7] Ibid., p. 19ff.

affirm and sustain the freedom unique to the human as the rational being. The human is here understood as a figure marked by constative power—by the ability to produce and live by rational iterable truths, and to govern the world by these truths. And freedom is conceived as the sustenance of those conditions which enable the exercise of constative power.

Such a conception of a freedom unique to humans by virtue of their rationality leads inevitably to an emphatic affirmation of the equality of rational humans to each other. This equality is realized or made real by the criteria of constative power—by insisting that all humans are equal in terms of some abstract measure. Thus, equality takes the form of measurably equal rights enshrined in law, whether these rights be positive or negative.

This twinned emphasis on freedom and equality also provides the criteria for the secular delimitation of the realm of religion. In the secular understanding, while the specific teachings of some specific religions (usually Christianity) may encourage and promote freedom and equality, while freedom and equality may even be God-given, the practice of freedom and equality must nevertheless limit religion to certain spheres. Most of all, it must exclude religion from politics. From a secular perspective, the ontological and epistemological truths of religion are totalitarian, and do not allow for otherness. From a secular perspective, a religious politics cannot thus allow for equality to other religions, and it might create hierarchies even within its own religion. As such, for secular thought, religious rule will result in a theocracy and inequality rather than pluralism and equality.

As this suggests, religion can be legitimately affirmed within the secular tradition only after it has remade itself as a religion within the limits of reason alone. It now becomes a secularized religion that understands the distinction between the immanent and the transcendent, acknowledges the subordination of the latter to the former in the public sphere, and only in a private sphere affirms the primacy of the transcendent. For the secular tradition, a religion that does not recognize these limits is dangerous, for it intervenes in the immanent world without recognizing that it is not capable of recognizing difference. It can quite appropriately be called 'fundamentalist', for such religion returns to the insistence on its fundamental—the logic of transcendence.

It is partially to refer to this secular delimitation of religion that Ashis Nandy has on several occasions pointed out how secularism claims a monopoly on religious and ethnic tolerance and on political rationality. It insists that only it can practice a pluralism that defends religion from itself by guaranteeing the right to diverse religious practices. From the perspective that affirms this secular delimitation of religion, Gandhi's simultaneous insistence on a religious politics and secularism can be read several ways. It can be read, first, with aggressive impatience as a soft fundamentalism. On such a reading, commonsensical in the communist party to which I belonged in my teens and early twenties, and in many ways quite correct sociologically, Gandhi's personal commitment to an inclusive nation allowed him to affirm secularism. Nevertheless, by introducing religion into politics, Gandhi's interventions accelerated Indian politics down the path that heightened Hindu–Muslim conflict.

It can be read, second, with the more benevolent impatience of the sort that Nehru often displayed towards Gandhi's professions of religion. On such a reading, what Gandhi attacks as irreligiosity is only the modern concern with the pursuit of wealth and power at the cost of all other values. With such an attack, early twentieth-century Indian nationalists such as Nehru would have had little problem. They could have agreed with its broad contours, if not with what would seem to be its eccentric vehemence. While they desired and sought economic well-being for India, they sought to sustain 'Indian' spiritual and cultural values. Relatedly, on such a reading, what Gandhi calls religion is only ethics in the broadest and most inclusive sense. As such, when Gandhi talks of religious politics, he does not so much introduce religion into politics as insist on the ethical dimension of politics, on a politics that is driven by values.

When understood in this way, Gandhi's insistence on 'no politics without religion' was not only acceptable, but a powerful way of appropriating ethical values to ground politics. There is no doubt that Gandhi rarely himself explicitly distinguished his position from this second reading of his argument. Thus, for instance, his remarks quoted earlier: '[N]ot the religion of the superstitious [vahem] and the blind [andhshraddha], religion that hates and fights, but the universal [vishwavyaapi] Religion of Toleration [sahisnuta]. Politics

without morality [niti] is a thing to be avoided.'

Here, Gandhi's affirmation of religion and Nehru's affirmation of secularism seem to converge around what might be called a religious secularism. This religious secularism can be encountered in a most elaborate form in a book that he translated into Gujarati in 1908, William Salter's *Ethical Religion*. Salter argued that secular ethics should become religious. For Salter, religion 'defined from its objective side' 'is man's relation with what is ultimate and supreme in the world. The truest religion would be that one in which the supreme interest gathers about that which is really supreme and ultimate in the world.'[8]

Seeking to distil a morality from religion appropriate to modern times, the supreme interest, morality, or 'social ideal' that Salter affirms is that of equality, and the freedom proper to equality. Drawing perhaps on Kant (who he might have been familiar with, since he also wrote a book on Nietzsche), Salter suggested that the equality he wanted was

not indeed similarity of place and function for everyone; not that all should do the same work or get the same returns for their work; but simply that all should be in turn ends as well as means, that no one should dare make of another a mere instrument to his own satisfactions, but should regard him as having an independent worth and dignity of his own.[9]

He went on: 'I feel that if I do not honour another I do not honour myself, for I fundamentally am every other: it is one

[8] William Salter, 1905, *Ethical Religion*, 2nd edition, London: Watts and Co. (originally published Roberts Brothers, Boston, 1889), p. 15.
[9] Ibid., p. 61.

common nature, wherein we all share.'[10] Salter stresses that this is a distinctively secular and modern notion of equality: 'I need not point out that this principle has not been generally recognised in the past... The notion of the universal rights of man is a modern one. It is neither in the Old Testament nor in the New. I doubt if it be in the Scriptures of any of the religions of the world.'[11]

Salter's formulations are symptomatic of the inadequacy of presuming that in our secular societies 'you can fully engage in politics without ever encountering God'.[12] As indeed a considerable scholarship has by now suggested, even where secularism (and the modern forms of sovereignty it is inseparable from) thinks of itself as irreligious, it is grounded in an ontology and a political theology. The figure of god is never very far from the figure of the modern sovereign. What is presented thus as secular political government is always a government that has arrogated to its immanent sphere the power that it saw as earlier residing in the transcendent sphere. Rather than secularism being antithetical to religious politics, secularism is thus always a politics that tries to appropriate religiosity for itself. When Gandhi says 'no politics without religion', for benevolent interpreters like Nehru, it is a religious secularism that Gandhi affirms.

[10] Salter, *Ethical Religion*, p. 66ff.
[11] Ibid., p. 60.
[12] These words are taken from Taylor's *A Secular Age*, which is perhaps the best recent reiteration of secular common sense.

Exclusions

But things unfortunately are not so simple, even if Gandhi's secular admirers, and sometimes Gandhi himself would have preferred it to be so. In my book under preparation, *Immeasurable Equality: Secularism, Religion, and Gandhi's Politics*, I explore how when Gandhi translated Salter, the argument that emerged was (largely inadvertently, I would expect) quite different from the one that Salter ventured, and how this difference from Salter became even more acute by the time of *Hind Swaraj*. As I suggest there, Gandhi was, to begin with, vehemently critical of the kind of equality that was central to 'modern civilization' and its secular ethics.

In order to encounter this criticism, perhaps we can turn to an especially charged moment in chapter 12 of *Hind Swaraj*, where Gandhi draws a contrast between religion or dharma and 'modern civilization': 'European doctors are the worst of all. For the sake of a mistaken care of the human body, they kill annually thousands of animals. They practise vivisection. No religion sanctions this. All say that it is not necessary to take so many lives for the sake of our bodies.' For the Editor, 'modern civilization' is marked by a mastery of animals, a justification always of the killing of animals. Even where it affirms the equality and freedom of humans, this equality is itself premised on the inequality of humans and animals.

This inequality of animals is not incidental. It is inscribed in the very thinking of freedom and equality in terms of constative power: the animal is the figure who is necessarily deficient in constative power, and who is therefore not capable of exercising freedom, not capable of being equal to the human. This inequality between the figure who has and exercises reason (the human) and the one who does not (the animal) is constitutive of the conceptual and political complex that Gandhi identifies as 'modern civilization', even, and perhaps especially, where strands within that complex may call for a 'humane' or compassionate treatment of the animal.

The line between the human and the animal, moreover, cannot ever be stabilized in such a manner as to correspond to some biological distinction; that line must always pass through the human. For in this frame of thinking, there are always those humans who are lacking in constative power, or in the ability to produce and live by rational iterable truths. These humans (amongst whose historical names one must include women, the colonized, lower castes, 'tribes', and terrorists) cannot be granted equality in the same way; they must necessarily be dominated for the freedom and equality of 'modern civilization' to sustain itself. These humans are thus always foremost amongst those that 'modern civilization' animalizes as dispensable.

Salter's affirmation of secular equality, for example, includes this attack on the American treatment of Native Americans:

And though I grant that civilisation has a perfect right to dispossess barbarism of an exclusive and profitless occupation of the soil, it is nonetheless a crime, and a heinous crime, to do as our country has done—treat the dispossessed barbarians as if they had no claims whatever upon us. The Indians are human beings, they have the rights of human beings; and if they cannot defend those rights, all the more shame on that Government which will wantonly trample upon them.[13]

Salter's commitment to secular equality is evident in his insistence that 'the Indians are human beings, they have the rights of human beings'. But that radicalism nevertheless occurs within a distinctive hierarchy, where it is, in principle, acceptable to Salter (as it was to Locke earlier) to dispossess the Indians of their land for a more rational good, as it would, in principle, be acceptable to the Indian government today to displace tribal groups in order to construct a new dam.

Salter's formulation is in other words exemplary of the working of the secular concept of human. Even where secular traditions extend an abstract equality to the other, this abstract equality is always undercut by the insistence that full equality requires the exercise of reason. Thus, it is that 'modern civilization' can, without contradicting itself in the slightest, always justify colonialism, or the expropriation of land from Native Americans, or the treatment of some religions or peoples as inferior, or some 'just war'.

Secular tolerance, with its distinction between private and public spheres, is again exemplary of the domination and inequality that underwrites abstract equality. The equality that secularism privileges is the equality of the public sphere. But only that can be part of the public sphere which claims to be ontologically and epistemologically grounded in constative reason. That which cannot be grounded by such reason must either be extirpated (as with fundamentalism) or confined to the

[13] Salter, *Ethical Religion*, p. 62.

private sphere. And though the equal right to a private sphere is perhaps constitutive of secularism from its very origins, the private sphere is subordinate to the public sphere. It is at best tolerated, and is constantly under siege, being remade in the image of public reason.

Immeasurable

If Gandhi attacks secularism and 'modern civilization' over and again, then, it is for the domination and inequality that organizes its very practice of equality. He tries instead to think another equality, and it is to the category religion that he turns in order to do so. His argument was not that some practices associated with some religions instituted social equality. True, he did point to such practices. In this vein, he often referred to Islam as a radically egalitarian religion, one that succeeded in India because of its doctrine of equality, that 'allows equality' more than either Hinduism or Christianity. But that was accompanied by an acknowledgement of the way other practices associated with religions, for instance, untouchability, instituted inequality.

More importantly, for Gandhi, the very concept of religion was inseparable from equality. Thus, he suggested that 'we have been taught in the Gita to treat all [badhane] as equals'.[14] In an interview with the Dalit leader M.C. Rajah in 1936, Gandhi argued:

In the purest type of Hinduism a Brahmin, an ant, an elephant and a dog-eater (shvapaka) are of the same status. And because our philosophy is so high, and we have failed to live up to it, that very philosophy today stinks in our nostrils. Hinduism insists on the brotherhood not only of all mankind but of all that lives. It is a conception which makes one giddy, but we have to work up to it. The moment we have restored real living equality between man and man, we shall be able to establish equality between man and the whole creation. When that day comes we shall have peace on earth and goodwill to men.[15]

Furthermore, while Gandhi discussed this equality most often with reference to Hinduism, it was by no means for him a teaching specific to Hinduism. Rather, running through his various arguments is the presumption that equality is constitutive of the very concept of religion or, even more daringly, that it is only religiously that equality can be properly conceptualized. Suggestively, when Gandhi conceptualizes his famous vow of *sarva dharma sambhaav* in almost direct opposition to the secular concept of tolerance, it is again a religious equality—both an equality of religions and an equality internal to the concept of religion—that he struggles to articulate.

This [sarva dharma sambhaav] is the new name we have given to the Ashram observance which we know as *sahisnuta*. 'Sahishnuta' is a translation of the English word 'tolerance'. I did not like that word. But I could not think of another ['a better'] one. Kakasaheb [Kalelkar], too, did not like that word. He suggested 'Respect for all religions' [*sarva dharma aadar*]. I didn't like that either. In tolerating other religions, they are considered deficient [*unap*]. In respect there always enters a sense [*bhav*] of patronage [*maherbaani*; tolerance may imply a gratuitous assumption of the inferiority of other faiths to one's own and respect

---

[14] 'Speech at Women's Meeting, Dakor, October 17, 1920', in *Akshardeha*, vol. 18, p. 364; *CWMG*, vol. 21, p. 405.

[15] Interview with M.C. Rajah, 22 March 1936, *CWMG*, vol. 68, p. 320.

suggests a sense of patronizing…]. Ahimsa teaches us *sambhaav* for other religions [to entertain the same respect for the religious faiths of others as we accord to our own]. Tolerance and respect is not enough from the perspective of *ahimsa*. In the fundamental principle [*moolma*] of keeping *sambhaav* towards other religions, there is also an acceptance [*swikaar*] of the incompleteness [*apoornata*] of one's own religion.[16]

Limit

An argument such as this simply does not make sense if we understand religion in terms of the immanent–transcendent distinction. Within its terms, a secular delimitation of religion is required in order to think the equality of the other, and secularism remains the only way that equality can be thought, even where equality is presumed to be God-given.

How then do we think of Gandhi's religious equality? What makes it more radically equal than secular equality? Why is it in an antagonistic relation to secular equality? These questions cannot be adequately addressed here, but in order to prepare for them, I would here like to argue that what Gandhi ventures in *Hind Swaraj* and elsewhere, is nothing less than another concept of religion itself, where religion names the practice of finitude. This finitude enables a very different equality, what might be called an immeasurable equality.

But what is meant by finitude? To address this question, we might begin with his obsessive insistence on the observance of limits. For him, such an observance of limits

was not a given trait of Indian civilization to be harnessed to create a distinctive Indian modernity. Rather, it was itself a politics, and one with very distinctive entailments. (Indeed, this was the sense in which he was never quite part of the nationalist problematic despite being the most prominent leader of the Indian nationalist movement.) The centrality of limits emerges in his remarks about swadeshi, which for him was necessary if swaraj or self-rule was not to produce an English rule without the Englishman:

After much thinking, I have arrived at a definition [*lakshan*] of swadeshi that perhaps best illustrates my meaning. Swadeshi is that spirit [*bhavana*] in us which restricts us to the use and service of our immediate surroundings [*paaseyni paristhithi*] to the exclusion [*tyaag*, sacrifice or surrender] of the more remote. Thus, as for religion, in order to satisfy the requirements of the definition, I must restrict myself to [*vadgi rahevu*, adhere to] my ancestral religion. That is the use of my immediate religious surroundings. If I find it defective, I should serve it by purging it of its defects. In the domain of politics, I should make use of the indigenous institutions and serve them by curing them of their proved defects. In that of economics, I should use only things that are produced by my immediate neighbours [*maari paasey vasnaraoey*] and serve those industries by making them efficient and complete where they might be found wanting.[17]

Indeed, limits marked dharma itself. Consider Gandhi's contrast in chapter 8 of *Hind Swaraj* between dharma or religion and 'modern civilization.'

[16] 'Letter to Narandas Gandhi, September 21–23, 1930', in *Akshardeha*, vol. 44, p. 165; *CWMG*, vol. 50, p. 78.

[17] 'Speech on Swadeshi at Missionary Conference, Madras, February 14, 1916', in *CWMG*, vol. 15, p. 159; *Akshardeha*, vol. 13, p. 202ff.

Hinduism, Islam, Zoroastrianism, Christianity and all other religions teach that we should remain passive [*mand*] about worldly things [*dunyavi vastu*] and active about religious things [*dharmik vastu*], that we should set a limit [*hadh*] to our worldly ambition and that our religious ambition should be open [*mokda*; 'illimitable']. Our activity should be kept only to that ['latter channel'].

It is all too easy to read 'limit' or hadh in terms of the conventional immanent–transcendent understanding of religion. If we were to do so, we would understand 'limit' privatively, and presume that the call is to limit 'worldly ambition' in order to transcend the worldly and reach an illimitable religious ambition. Such a privative understanding presumes that the limit involves ascesis, where ascesis is understood as the practice of austerities in order to transcend the physical for something spiritual, infinite, larger. Here, the limit is not itself the concept of religion; it is merely the requirement for an absorption into the transcendent infinitude that is god. Such an understanding of Gandhi's argument seems all the more persuasive since Gandhi himself seems over and again to explicitly resort to it.

Superstition

But such an understanding of Gandhi's argument in privative terms misses out on its more far-reaching implications. More rigorously considered, Gandhi's finitude was not necessarily about privative limits, but about the singularity sustained by the limit, and the equality that such singularity made possible. To indicate what is meant, it might help to turn to a provocative and notorious occasion, where he described the 1934

earthquake in Bihar as a 'divine chastisement [*saja*] sent by God for our sins', specifically the sin of untouchability.[18]

From a secular perspective, such a remark reveals the dangers of a perspective that privileges the transcendent. For it, such anthropocentrism not only mixes up orders of causality, but implies an ethics that shifts responsibility away from humans to the divine. One might, for example, ask in the outraged secular vein (which I for one most certainly cannot not share) that marked many of the letters that Gandhi received: if earthquakes are divine chastisement for sins, why does god punish the innocent?

On the other hand, it is also perhaps worth tarrying with Gandhi's formulation:

I share the belief with the whole world—civilized and uncivilized—that calamities such as the Bihar one come to mankind as chastisement for their sins. When that conviction comes from the heart, people pray, repent [*pashtaap*] and purify themselves. I regard untouchability [*asprishyata*] as such a grave sin as to warrant divine chastisement. I am not affected by posers such as 'why punishment for an age-old sin' or 'why punishment to Bihar and not to the South' or 'why an earthquake and not some other form of punishment'. My answer is: I am not God. Therefore I have but a limited knowledge of His purpose. Such calamities are not a mere caprice of the Deity or Nature. They obey fixed laws as surely as the planets move in obedience to laws governing their movement. Only we do not know the laws governing these events and, therefore, call them calamities or disturbances. Whatever, therefore, may be said about them must be regarded as guess work. But guessing [*anumaan*] has its definite place in man's life. It is an ennobling thing for me to guess that the Bihar

18 *CWMG*, vol. 63, *Harijan*, 24 January 1934, Speech at Tinivelly; *Akshardeha*, vol. 57, p. 45.

disturbance is due to the sin of untouchability. It makes me humble [*namra*], it spurs me to greater effort towards its removal, it encourages me to purify myself, it brings me nearer to my Maker. That my guess may be wrong does not affect the results named by me. For what is guess to the critic or the sceptic is a living belief [*jeevtijaagti shraddha*] with me, and I base my future actions on that belief. Such guesses become superstitions [*vahem*] when they lead to no purification and may even lead to feuds. But such misuse of divine events cannot deter men of faith from interpreting them as a call to them for repentance for their sins.[19]

I have elsewhere provided[20] an extended reading of the several disconcerting and even uncomfortable moves involved in this passage. Here, I only wish to stress the guess that has its definite place in man's life, but that is religious where it leads to purification and superstitious where it leads to feuding. The guess properly observed 'makes me humble', and leads to faith, belief. There can be disagreement and conflict where there is humility, but there cannot be a feud.

Guess

But what is the nature of this anumaan (guess)? Gandhi's guess does not belong to the reasonable realm of that which is probable but unprovable; there is nothing reasonable about it. It is just that—a guess. As a guess, it does not have to and does not claim to answer several questions—why here,

why now, how? With the guess, one is in the realm of faith. The guess is centrally, thus, about a conviction and a belief that cannot be justified by the criteria of causal reason, that will not submit to reason, and will yet intervene in the domains of science and ethics and everyday life that Enlightenment traditions would consider reason's own.

This suggests why humility or *namrata* should be proper to the guess. Gandhi presents the matter sometimes in somewhat conventional terms, as in the passage earlier, where he says that he cannot know the workings of god. In such a formulation, the humility and finitude of the guess of faith is presented in a metaphysical manner—privatively, as an acknowledgement of the way that human agency is limited and can always be overcome by 'acts of God' (and it is surely not accidental that the agential understanding of the divine enshrined in this phrase is central to insurance law today), that the finitude of the human glance cannot take account of the infinitude of god. And the infinitude of god is also thought metaphysically here—as that which is too large and too huge for comprehension by the finite human being.

But the guess of faith is also humble in another quite non-metaphysical way here: even where it is absolute (as it must be where it becomes a 'living belief' or faith), such a guess must acknowledge its singular limit—that it is constituted by and constitutes only its own singular relation to god, that it must be both absolute and yet not make any ontological or epistemological claims. This is the other finitude and limit that is constitutive of the guess of faith. In order to be faithful, it must practice this singularity. In this very observing of finitude, the 'living

[19] 'Bihar and Untouchability', in *CWMG*, vol. 63, *Harijan*, 2 February 1934; *Akshardeha*, vol. 57, p. 90.
[20] Ajay Skaria, 2009, 'No Politics without Religion: Of Secularism and Gandhi', in Vinay Lal (ed.), *Political Hinduism: The Religious Imagination in Public Spheres*, Delhi: Oxford University Press, pp. 173–210.

belief' is always already open to the other: even though Gandhi's faith can never be proven wrong, it remains only his living belief.[21] As such, the rightness or wrongness of either Gandhi's or the other's guesses becomes completely unimportant ('that my guess may be wrong does not affect the results named by me').

The finitude that Gandhi ventures to think can thus perhaps be described as one where there is a claim to absolute faith, and where this faith nevertheless can neither claim an ontological or epistemological grounding. From its perspective, every guess that claims ontological and epistemological grounding (and of such a claim, perhaps secularism and its constative truths are exemplary) is superstition. A 'feud' is premised on a conviction in the rightness of one's guess, the conversion, in other words, of a guess into a matter of ontological and epistemological knowledge. Once a truth is ontological and epistemological, that which does not accord with it is false. The only way such a truth can be tolerant is by being weak. But it obviously cannot be too weak, for it will then no longer be a truth. It must continue to be defined and centred, however surreptitiously and unconsciously, by its truth (this surreptitious persistence of the centre is what many radical critiques of multiculturalism have pointed to). In other words, an ontological and epistemological truth can only feud with other claims to truth. The only equality it can grant to its other is what Gandhi describes, on occasion, as the equality established by the sword,

when it is opposed by a truth of equal ontological and epistemological power. Hierarchy and inequality, in other words, are central to ontological and epistemological truth, whether that truth takes the form of transcendental religion or, preferably, immanent and secular facts.

In contrast, because the guess of faith does not claim any such grounding, it is marked by a radical openness to the other. This openness to the other is the original equality that 'living belief' must always give to the other. In this openness, we receive an intimation of an equality that is not organized by the abstract epistemological criteria of knowledge.[22] This equality that is always involved in living belief—is this what Gandhi names in the previous passage as making him humble? If it is an ennobling thing for Gandhi to guess that the earthquake was because of untouchability, is this because the practice of untouchability denies the equality that the faithful guess gives to both itself and the other?

Province

It is this other equality that Gandhi struggles to articulate in his arguments for sarva dharma sambhaav. This other equality involves questioning truths that claim an ontological or epistemological grounding. But, that questioning itself can proceed only in the spirit of this other equality—by provincializing both itself and that which it encounters. But to provincialize is never

---

[21] On another occasion, I will explore a related theme—that of how this living belief also conceptualizes one's equality with oneself.

[22] Despite evident differences, my discussion here clearly owes a great deal to Akeel Bilgrami's article, 2002, 'Gandhi's Integrity: The Philosophy behind the Politics', *Postcolonial Studies*, vol. 5, no. 1, pp. 79–93.

to reject. The move of provincializing operates here on two registers. First, reason is affirmed. Both here and even more emphatically in the years around and after the *Mangalprabhat* letters, there is the insistence that 'on matters which can be reasoned out, that which conflicts with Reason must also be rejected'.[23] That which is 'amenable to rational enquiry' must be submitted to it.[24] He stressed the centrality of reason even in conversations between faiths. Thus, when asked in a discussion with a missionary, Dr Crane, what he would do with 'a man who says he is commanded by God to do violence', Gandhi insisted: 'There you would not put another God before him. You need not disturb his religion, but you will disturb his reason...You will not pit one word of God against another word of God. But you will have to bear down his reason.'[25]

Second, the relation between faith and reason is refigured. That faith is not opposed to reason is, for Gandhi, already given in the Gujarati words he uses for faith and superstition—*shraddha* and andhshraddha. Shraddha, in other words, is by its very nature not blind or unreasonable; when it becomes andhshraddha or 'blind faith', it is no longer faith but superstition. He translates this word often as superstition, but he contrasts it not with reason, but with shraddha or faith. For Gandhi, 'faith begins where reason fails. That is to say, faith is beyond reason'.[26] But it is not beyond reason in the sense that it transcends reason (though he says precisely that it does in the English interview with Dr Crane). The relation is rather originary, but originary in the only way that radical finitude can be originary: as a supplementary move—faith is 'that in us which sanctifies reason'. The word 'sanctify' is suggestive, as is its translation by the powerful word *paavan*. To sanctify is to make holy. In other words, reason itself is marked by a sanctity, but that sanctity comes from faith, and from the work of faith as *daya* and *prem*. To sustain a reason in accordance with this sanctity is one of the tasks that a religious politics sets itself.

This other way of sustaining reason is what leads Gandhi, I would like to suggest, to an affirmation of secularism. When he affirms secularism, he does so no longer from the perspective of a secularist. Rather, it is symptomatic of an external relation with secularism. What this external relationship involves, how it was to be sustained—these are questions to which we will have to turn on another occasion.

[23] 'Interview to Dr. Crane, February 25, 1937', *CWMG*, vol. 71, p. 2; *Akshardeha*, vol. 64, p. 426.
[24] 'Reason vs. Faith', *Hindi Navajivan*, 19 September 1929, *CWMG*, vol. 47, p. 108; *Akshardeha*, vol. 41, p. 427.
[25] 'Interview to Dr. Crane', *CWMG*, vol. 71, p. 2; *Akshardeha*, vol. 64, p. 426.

[26] 'Reason vs. Faith', *Hindi Navajivan*, 19 September 1929, *CWMG*, vol. 47, p. 108; *Akshardeha*, vol. 41, p. 427.

7

Apocalyptic Effects
Questions of Globalization and Islam

Faisal Devji

Despite its current celebrity, globalization remains curiously undefined as an analytical or historical category. On the one hand, it seems to evoke the primacy of movement, whether of people, goods, ideas, or money, that has supposedly increased to an unprecedented level both in rapidity and in extent. On the other hand, globalization evokes a theory of capitalism that would enclose all the social possibilities and experiential implications of such movement in a singular history of economic reach. In either case, this movement is supposed to be made possible in large part by new technologies, which thus mediate it as a kind of ever-renewed present, globalization as the newest of the new.

But the problem with conceiving of globalization as a movement mediated by technology into some ever-renewed present is that it ceases to have a past, properly speaking. And this is because the difference between its form of movement and any other is one of degree rather than of kind. For instance, how is the Internet more illustrative of globalization than the telegraph? Or, how is today's virtual economy more global than yesterday's finance capitalism? No matter how radical their repercussions, do the new technologies mark new beginnings, or do they simply exist in the wake of older ones? This problem of historical and analytical regress exists only because accounts of globalization tend to be seduced both by the narcissism of the present, and by the glamorous novelty of objects or experiences, in the process quite dispensing with the term's intellectual genealogy. Such narcissism of the present and glamorization of experience might well bear witness to globalization, but they do little to interpret it.

Let us take ideas seriously by asking when it was that the globe (and therefore, the possibility of globalization) ceased to be a classroom model or a geographical abstraction and became real. This is to ask: at what point did the globe part company with the notion of world, itself connected to a particular religious history in terms like worldliness, to become a new beginning? Languages like French, of course, continue to derive globalization (*mondialisation*) from the older notion of world (*monde*), thus linking it back to another kind of history. Nevertheless, there is a point when we can say that the globe becomes, as it were, global, a point which for our purposes we can locate during the Cold War. This is illustrated by the two great technological events of that time: the atom bomb and the moon landing, both of which literally permitted us not only to grasp and see the globe as such, but also and in the same moment to destroy and abandon it. The globe, then, like the commodity of earlier times, is known only in the moment of its consumption as something destroyed or abandoned. And this apocalyptic manner of knowing the globe allows thought in general, and religious thought in particular, to emerge from a world divided in terms of public and private, secular and sacred, to contemplate as real something that had been denied legitimacy for two centuries: the end of the world. It is in the rapture of apocalypse that the world is destroyed and the globe is born, even if only as the ghost of this world.

The birth of the globe during the Cold War did not go unnoticed, its implications being noted by Hannah Arendt among others. In an essay on Karl Jaspers, who had himself expounded the phenomenology of a nuclear apocalypse, Arendt wrote about the ironic unity of the globe that the atom bomb had made possible:

It is true, for the first time in history all peoples on earth have a common present: no event of any importance in the history of one country can remain a marginal accident in the history of any other. Every country has become the almost immediate neighbor of every other country, and every man feels the shock of events which take place at the other side of the globe. But this common factual present is not based on a common past and does not in the least guarantee a common future. Technology, having provided the unity of the world, can just as easily destroy it and the means of global communication were designed side by side with means of possible global destruction.[1]

The question Arendt tackles in her essay is not the practical one of how to prevent an apocalypse, but rather a question about the new experience that such an apocalypse brings into being. Here, apocalypse itself being not the brute fact of nuclear destruction (or the biological and ecological holocausts that are its heirs) so much as the general thinking and experience of the globe that this destruction makes possible. For instance, according to Arendt, the unity of the globe that technology produces is purely negative because it is based neither on a common past or future, relying instead on an evacuated present as a kind of apocalyptic effect. One of the issues I want to explore in this chapter is how such an effect allows religion to situate itself at the heart of the

---

[1] Hannah Arendt, 1995, 'Karl Jaspers: Citizen of the World?' in *Men in Dark Times*, San Diego, New York, and London: Harcourt Brace Jovanovich, p. 83.

global on the basis of what has always been its own stock in trade, annihilation.

The globe becomes real at the same time as humanity, which serves both as the agent and the victim of its possible destruction. For, mankind is now no longer an ideal or an abstraction, but a reality too insofar as it is capable of being destroyed.[2] Indeed the technology of destruction and abandonment itself, in its sheer instrumentality, undoes the particularity of origins and ownership, so that in a certain sense it is mankind, and not America, which becomes the true agent of global events like the atom bomb or moon landing. Therefore, it was entirely appropriate that Neil Armstrong, when first stepping upon the surface of the moon, should speak of taking a small step for man and a giant leap for mankind. After all, in the face of global destruction or abandonment, the particular ownership of that act is also destroyed, leaving behind only humanity as its combined agent and victim. Arendt, remarking upon the new reality of mankind, has this to say: 'Our political concepts, according to which we have to assume responsibility for all public affairs within our reach regardless of personal "guilt," because we are held responsible as citizens for everything that our government does in the name of the country, may lead us into an intolerable situation of global responsibility.'[3]

Again, the form globalization takes in this interpretation allows religion to return to its old theme of moral responsibility by raising the question of what it means to act in such a situation, and indeed how action is at all

possible. Here is another issue that I want to explore in this chapter. Both issues, that of apocalyptic effect and human responsibility, situate religion at the heart of the global because they have suddenly ceased to be the arcane speculations of private conscience to become matters of public attention and welfare. And this only became possible once the old order, which was based upon managing an economy of living needs and interests that were bifurcated into public and private, secular and sacred, found itself upstaged by totalities like apocalypse and humanity, which destroyed the particularities of life and economy both.

I have been arguing so far that the Cold War provided the origins of globalization as this term is used today. It did so by replacing the world with the globe and man by mankind, all within the horizon demarcated by an apocalyptic technology, whose power subordinated all links with the past to the false unity of a global present. Globalization itself came to replace internationalism, which had been the ideology both of the European empires and of the Communist bloc. These orders were international because they were based on the expansion of a substance (civilization, justice, power, democratic institutions, and the like) in territories that were connected either by contiguity or by historical and political intention. Globalization, on the other hand, depends neither on the expansion of a substance nor upon links of intention, but precisely on the unintended effects and consequences that make up its universal present. Arendt, referring to the false unity of this global present, puts it like this: 'It is difficult to deny that at this moment the most potent symbol of the unity of mankind is the

[2] Arendt, 'Karl Jaspers', p. 82.
[3] Ibid., p. 83.

remote possibility that atomic weapons used by one country according to the political wisdom of a few might ultimately come to be the end of all human life on earth.'[4]

Now the apocalyptic tone of Cold War thinking might have dissipated today, but it is best to remember that globalization came to be only with the 'remote possibility' of a nuclear holocaust (and its biological and ecological twins), which thus continues to inform contemporary notions of the global. Media, for example, continually ape the apocalyptic effect that Arendt describes in the given quotation, because they bring together widely scattered constituencies in the contemplation of an event with which they have no real connection, and which is not even a substance spread by connections of contiguity or intention. The rupture with internationalism here is absolute because the global effect of media is not due to consequences that go beyond particular intentions (as in all previous theories of structural agency). It is rather due to the false unity of a present made possible by events that can only function randomly once separated from local contexts.

Having described the Cold War emergence of what is today called globalization, Arendt raises the problem of what it might mean to belong in such a universe. She seems to advocate the theory of pluralism and universal communication propounded by Karl Jaspers, but writes about this in an almost elegiac way, as if recognizing it as a good idea whose time has passed. So the subtitle of her essay on Jaspers ends with a question mark: citizen of the world? Jaspers' theory, after all, remains

internationalist, while Arendt was concerned precisely with the end of internationalism in the eternally present and forgetful nature of technological globalization, which puts man and all his acts, especially his political acts, into question.

I want to argue that religion today is capable of addressing precisely this putting into question of man and his acts in an interesting way. And this is because globalization has subordinated the world and its distinctions of public and private, secular and sacred, to the awful reality of apocalypse, whether this is atomic, biological, or ecological. With the emergence of the globe and of mankind, in other words, such worldly distinctions have been overshadowed, and religion allowed an approach to its traditional concerns in a reinvigorated way. How is it possible to be a citizen or political actor in the false unity of a globalization with no common past or future, where mankind has replaced man as the agent and victim of history? I want to look at the way in which Muslim thought recognizes the global as a condition, and reflects upon what it means to belong politically in such a universe, a reflection in which the Prophet Muhammad serves as a cipher for man as such.

Prophet Motive

The massive protests occasioned in 1989 by the publication of Salman Rushdie's novel, *The Satanic Verses*, arguably provided the non-Muslim world with its first demonstration of Islam's globalization. Something that differs from an international Islam in that more than any such incident in the past, the protests over Rushdie's novel

[4] Arendt, 'Karl Jaspers', p. 82.

referred neither to a particular interest being threatened nor to a particular cause being fought. Rather their apparently idealistic concern with the Prophet Muhammad's portrayal meant that these protests were defined in terms of equal relevance for Muslims everywhere. More than pilgrimage, holy war, or the kind of pan-Islamism that would mobilize Muslims internationally in support of Bosnians or Kashmiris, or Chechens, the Rushdie Affair was global because it concentrated Muslim attention on an issue completely detached from persons and places.

Of course, protests against *The Satanic Verses* did have particular meaning at every point in their trajectory, from Bradford to Srinagar, Islamabad to Tehran, and beyond. But what made these events global was their lack of fixed location, geographic and political, a phenomenon rendered possible in large part by the unprecedented media exposure within which they occurred, such events being made available instantaneously and repeatedly in the virtual space of television. Given the much publicized Muslim refusal to read *The Satanic Verses* or deal with issues like its author's freedom of expression and interpretation, it is even possible to say that Muhammad's portrayal became the site of a global debate for which Rushdie himself was incidental.

Early protests against the novel, for example, used it almost randomly as a kind of weapon at hand. One that allowed Muslims in Bradford to find a voice which could be heard outside the cloisters of state-funded race relations programmes, in this way ironically fulfilling the novel's attempt to give British Asians their own voice. Or that allowed Indian Muslims to agitate against the

bigotry of Hindu nationalists by asking for a ban on the book. In this pre-global phase of the Rushdie Affair, when *The Satanic Verses* represented British or Indian bigots in almost random fashion, the rest of the Muslim world remained unfazed. Even the Ayatollah Khomeini dismissed the novel as yet another petty irritant in the eye of Islam. But somehow, with the media blitz in Britain and riots in the Indian subcontinent, the Rushdie Affair catapulted, again randomly, into a global event. My point here is twofold: that the author and his novel were incidental to the Rushdie Affair; and that randomness, or even mystery, was essential to its globalization. So, attempts by certain Muslim groups to stage a repeat performance of this event, in concert with sections of the media in Europe and America, have not been successful. For instance, efforts to make the Bangladeshi author Taslima Nasreen into another Rushdie seem to have been believed only by her and Rushdie himself.

But then, for many Muslims, the real subject of the Rushdie Affair was not Salman Rushdie but the Prophet Muhammad. It was the interpretation of his life and work that constituted the stuff of their debate, one which I believe was so passionate because it radicalized the portrayal of Muhammad in a more thoroughgoing fashion than *The Satanic Verses* itself. The title of Rushdie's novel refers to an obscure event in the life of the Prophet, a case of satanic interpolation in the revelation he was vouchsafed, which ostensibly puts both Muhammad's integrity and that of this revelation in doubt. Yet, Muslim reaction to the novel, including the Ayatollah Khomeini's *fatwa* against it, did not deal with any of the theological issues raised by the book. It consisted instead of objections to Rushdie's unflattering portrayal of the Prophet as leader, friend, and family man, in the process putting aside a whole polemical tradition that would demonstrate Muhammad's veracity by textual interpretation and theological reasoning. Muslim reaction to the novel was not concerned with demonstrations of veracity, only those of offense and injury.[5] This is particularly true for the Shia branch of Islam, to which Khomeini belonged, since it refuses to acknowledge the occurrence, and so the theological status, of the satanic verses incident.

The Prophet was not a properly religious figure in this debate but rather a model of civic virtue, in keeping with long-standing efforts, part of a phenomenon known as political Islam, to conceive of a global order by rethinking the idea of citizenship on the model of Muhammad's Medina. The Prophet's properly religious position was even undermined by this debate, in which he no longer related to his followers by way of miracles, saintly figures, sacred texts, or even theological reasoning, but simply by representing a civic ideal. And Muhammad as the model citizen of a virtual state becomes the sign of a global order, in part, because he is deprived of any real particularity, having been transformed simply into the ideal of this order. Here is to be found a virtual order that is both everywhere and nowhere, like an afterimage of the historical state. Naturally, I am exaggerating the distinction between the old Prophet

and the new, but only so as to point out the implications of liberating Muhammad from the chains of theological reasoning and mystical emanation that had once bound him to believers. The chief such implication being that the Prophet comes to represent a certain kind of civic ideal calling for a very different sort of allegiance from his followers.

The Mystery of Citizenship

What manner of relationship can Muslims have with the Prophet as model citizen? One of identification presumably, which is what political Islam's adoration of the Prophet's example is about. But what does identifying with Muhammad mean exactly? This question lies at the heart of the passions evoked by the Rushdie Affair. After all, what remained most obscure about the Affair was precisely the nature of this identification, which the incoherence of Muslim discourse rendered ever more mysterious. It is this mystery at the heart of Muslim identification that I want to look at, because I believe it constitutes a reflection on the globalization of Islam represented by the ideal of the Prophet as citizen. Regretfully, I must do so by abandoning my freewheeling interpretation of the Rushdie Affair and moving to the somewhat more disciplined interpretation of a text.

Khomeini is the only writer to have grasped the mystery of Muslim identifications with Muhammad in a theoretically sophisticated way. In fact, the Ayatollah's participation in the Rushdie Affair was just one episode in the genealogy of this theoretical enterprise, which goes back at least to his important pre-revolutionary work, the *Vilayat-e Faqih*, or Governance

[5] There were a few exceptions to this rule, among the most interesting being an analysis of *The Satanic Verses* by Iran's Minister of Culture. See Sayyid Ataullah Mohajerani, 1378, *Naqd-e Tuteyeh-e Ayat-e Shaytani*, Tehran: Entesharat-e Ettela'at.

of the Islamic Jurist. The Rushdie Affair is important in this trajectory only because it allowed Khomeini to speak as a global Muslim leader for the first time, and not accidentally, since his fatwa broke the rules of its form by exceeding recognized bounds of jurisdiction and judgement to become a verdict without borders. In this chapter, I shall be concentrating for the most part on Khomeini's political and spiritual testament, the *Wasiyyat Namah*, which was released after his death in 1989. It was here that the Ayatollah wrote most succinctly about Muhammadan citizenship, which he located in a world imagined in terms of a global exchange of goods and ideas.

Islam in the *Wasiyyat Namah* exists in a world of unequal exchanges, sometimes described in the familiar terms of Third World socialism, as in the following passage on First World capitalism: 'And sadder than this, they have kept the dictatorially oppressed peoples backward in everything and forcibly made them into consuming countries and by their progress and satanic powers have made us so frightened that we have not the courage to take any initiative and have submitted everything to them…'.[6] The familiarity of this ode upon production, however, fades once the reader realizes that Khomeini models Islam itself on this world of exchanges, since it is the chief commodity he wants to retail:

…the enlightened face of Islam should be revealed to the world's peoples, because if this face with that beautiful appearance which the Quran and Tradition in all their aspects have invited (us) to is allowed to appear from beneath the veil (cast over it by) the enemies of Islam and by its uninformed friends, Islam will be world-conquering and its proud flag will fly everywhere. How painful and saddening it is that Muslims, who possess a commodity which from the beginning of the world to its end has no equal, should not have been able to offer (to others) this valuable gem which the free nature of every human being is in search of, and indeed are themselves neglectful and ignorant (of its value), and sometimes (even) flee it.[7]

It might appear scandalous that this passage portrays Islam as a woman who must be unveiled and sold to the world. But Khomeini's imagery here is drawn from classical poetry, a genre in which he also wrote. Such poetry often praises scandalous objects like wine, women, and song not for their own sake, but in order to reflect critically upon the moral order that would proscribe them, and this in a way that might not itself bear any relation to objects so scandalous. In fact, Khomeini was openly critical of Islam's moral order as it was commonly understood, and sought to invest its sterile regulations with an inner life, described in the same scandalous terms he uses above.[8] So, the passage quoted could well be part of an effort to invest the common world of exchanges with an inner life of its own. For it is this world of exchanges that the moral order regulates in commercial, political, sexual, and other ways. At the very least, the terms of scandal employed here suggest a critical reflection

---

[6] Ruhollah al-Musavi Khomeini, 1361, *Akhirin Payam*, Tehran: Sazman-e Hajj-o Awqaf-o Umur-e Khayriyyat, p. 27.

[7] Ibid., pp. 42–3.
[8] See, for instance, Khomeini's mystical treatise, the *Rah-e Ishq*, 1368, Tehran: Sazman-e Chap-o Intisharat-e Vizarat-e Farhang-o Irshad-e Islami.

upon the order of exchanges they do so much to enliven.

The difference between a moral and an immoral world of exchanges is ambiguous enough for the Ayatollah to have made Islam into a commodity while criticizing the commodities of capitalism. And this ambiguity continues to make itself felt in his picture of an Islamic order, whose completely regulated character can easily become a mirror image of the unregulated capitalist order it is meant to resist, but by the same token, can also become a self-critical reflection on such an order. So, for Khomeini, the world of capitalist exchanges must be regulated because it destroys all productive human action. But the totality of this regulation again puts human agency in doubt, and particularly the agency of citizens, which is what the Ayatollah is primarily concerned with. The *Wasiyyat Namah* then imagines an ideal world of exchanges as a system regulated almost entirely by a structural rather than an individual causality, so that Muslims are robbed of the moral initiative Khomeini would win them from capitalism:

…and it is a school that, unlike non-monotheist schools, participates in and orders all individual, social, material, spiritual, cultural, political and economic aspects (of life) and has not overlooked anything, no matter how insignificant, which might play a role in the development of man and society and in material and spiritual progress, and has warned against the barriers and difficulties in the road towards the perfection of society and the individual, and has pointed out how these may be overcome.[9]

The totality of this order is such that it abrogates time itself, so that historical events become equivalent, each one exchangeable with the other, representing only some function in a system. A system here is an order in which historical acts are reduced to functions that can be performed by different people in different places. The following quotation compares very disparate struggles against oppression to the martyrdom of the Prophet's grandson in just this way:

And they should know that the injunctions of the Imams, peace be upon them, regarding the commemoration of this momentous event in the history of Islam, and the cursing and hating of those who oppressed the Prophet's household, are all (of a piece with) the protesting laments of communities (everywhere) against oppressors throughout history until eternity. And you know that the cursing and hating and lamenting against the unjust Umayyad dynasty, God's curse be upon them, although they have been destroyed and sent off to Hell, are cries against (all) the world's oppressors and keep alive these cries which break oppression. And it is necessary that in the dirges and elegies and panegyrics for the Imams of Truth, upon whom be the peace of God, the sufferings and oppressions brought about by oppressors at every time and place be recounted. And in this age, which is the age of the tyrannizing of the world of Islam at the hands of America, the Soviets, and the clients attached to them, including the House of Saud, these traitors to the Great Sanctuary of the Divine, upon whom be the curses of God, his angels and the prophets, their crimes must be energetically recounted, cursed and hated.[10]

If historical events simply fulfil functions in a system, then, of course, they can be replaced by other events, serving these latter only as ideals. Yet, the relationship between

---

[9] Khomeini, *Akhirin Payam*, p. 13.

[10] Ibid., p. 9.

two events of this kind remains troubling, because identifying with something and taking its place are not equivalent acts. Something unnamed is left over from the original event which can neither be subordinated to a function nor replaced by another event. This remainder is individual causality, which exists here as a ghost haunting the machine of structural causality that operates Khomeini's system. The ghost, we might say, of a citizenship whose sovereignty has become problematic in a world of global exchanges regulated entirely by a structural agency.

The Ayatollah made his first significant statement about system and function in the *Vilayat-e Faqih*.[11] There he justified the rule of the Islamic jurist by allowing him to take the place of the imams, who for the Shia are successors to Muhammad's authority. Instead of representing the authority of the last imam, who went into occultation in the ninth century, Khomeini's jurist actually adopts this authority. He can do this because the imam's role has been made into a function that can be assumed by the jurist. Of course, the jurist does not become the imam, who survives as the ghost of individual causality in Khomeini's system of functions, but he does radicalize his relationship to the imam in an unprecedented way. It is not the reduction of the imam to a function that is radical, but his ghost, which haunts this function with the desire for a sovereignty that has disappeared from Khomeini's world of exchanges.

Already we begin to see the lineaments of Khomeini's theory of identification, and those of a world of exchanges that makes it possible. We may gauge the character of this identification by comparing it to the mystical identification with god that had preceded it. This latter had been phrased in terms of the destruction of human selfhood in the divine self, a destruction that, at another move, allowed the mystic to claim this divine selfhood in an ironic reversal. The tenth century mystic, Mansur al-Hallaj, is the most celebrated claimant of such a divinity, whose statement, 'I am the Truth', and subsequent execution by religious authorities have served as literary cliches for a thousand years. The Ayatollah himself made use of this trope in his poetry:

Farigh az khud shudam-o kows-e anal haqq zadam
Hamchu mansur kharidar-e sar-e dar shudam

(Freed from myself I uttered the cry 'I am the Truth'
Like Mansur I accepted [my position at] the gallows' head)[12]

There is a play on the word head or *sar* here, which refers both to the head that Mansur lost and to the headship he gained. The phrase *sar-e dar*, which literally means head of the gallows, refers to the selfhood Mansur both lost and gained. This phrase, of course, can also be read as a combination of sar, head, and *dar*, gallows, which put together also make up the word *sardar* or headship. This false genealogy (since the word for headship bears no relationship to that for gallows) gives an even more lugubrious twist to Khomeini's conceit.

---

[11] Imam Khomeini, 1378, *Vilayat-e Faqih*, Tehran: Muasiseh-e Tanzim-o Nasr-e Asar-e Imam Khomeini.

[12] Ruhollah al-Musavi Khomeini, 1368, *Sabu-ye Ishq*, Tehran: Intisharat-e Sada-o Simai-e Jamhuri-e Islami-e Iran, p. 15.

By the time the *Wasiyyat Namah* came to be written, Khomeini had turned his attention from the specialized identifications of the jurist and mystic to the identifying practices of Muslims in general; an innovation made necessary by the Islamic Revolution, which required an elaboration of the Ayatollah's theory of rule in the terms of popular citizenship. And indeed, the Revolution is central to the *Wasiyyat Namah*, as in this extraordinary description of the masses who made it:

I claim with courage that the Iranian people and its masses of millions today are better than the people of the Hijaz during the time of the Prophet, peace be upon him and his descendants, and the people of Kufah and Iraq in the time of the Prince of Believers and Hassan bin Ali, upon whom be the peace of God.[13]

The boldness of Khomeini's rhetoric goes against all the usual descriptions of political Islam, which would make it into a mere adulation of origins. For Khomeini, origins are important because they no longer exist, having been transformed into ideals, which he regards as being far more powerful. So, his explanation of the Iranian people's superiority compared to those Muslims who lived in the founding period of Islam:

…and these result from their love, attachment and great faith in the exalted Lord and (in) Islam and life everlasting, even though they are neither in the auspicious presence of the gracious Prophet, peace be upon him and his descendants, nor in the presence of the infallible Imams, upon whom be peace. And their motivation is faith and trust in the unseen.[14]

With the destruction of those genealogical and Neoplatonic forms that had once linked believers to sacred figures and events, the Prophet became an ideal who could affect Muslims by his very absence. A figure not messianic so much as civic, since what he effects is a revolutionary mobilization. Indeed, Khomeini's speculations on the political effect of absence and ignorance are similar to the speculations of someone like Georges Sorel on the myth of the general strike. In either case, political action is explained not by what are known to be interests, or grievances, or oppression, but by what remains unknown.

Theorists of political consciousness and objective conditions cannot explain the contingency of events, why a popular uprising today rather than yesterday or tomorrow, for example, and so, they diminish the importance of such events, consigning them to the realm of the accidental. But Khomeini is concerned with this very contingency, this mystery in which he sees the religious nature of political action. And in truth, revolutionary mobilization can only be faithful because it depends upon what is absent, which is why it illustrates the mystery of Muslim identification in its grandest form.

We know that for Khomeini, individual causality exists only as a function in the world of exchanges conceived as a system. But the individual can become a citizen by identifying with Muhammad, the ghost of whose sovereign causality haunts this system of functions. What we have here is a theory of citizenship without the citizen. A citizenship founded upon absence and faith. Far from being seen as a lack, this absence is praised in Khomeini's writing, generally

[13] Khomeini, *Akhirin Payam*, p. 21.
[14] Ibid., p. 22.

in terms of a literary and mystical trope that would savour separation from the beloved as a kind of pleasure.[15] But Khomeini does envisage a future in which the Muslim joins the Prophet to become a sovereign subject:

The Prophet of God, peace be upon him and his descendants, said 'I leave two things with you, the Book of God and the descendants of my household; indeed they shall not be separated until they return to me at Heaven's lake...'

Perhaps the phrase 'they shall not be separated until they return to me at Heaven's lake' might be an indication of the fact that after the holy existence of the Prophet of God, peace be upon him and his descendants, whatever is suffered by one of these two is also suffered by the other, and the neglect of one is the neglect of the other, until these two neglected entities return to the Prophet of God at Heaven's lake. And whether this lake is the place that joins multiplicity to unity and droplets in the sea, or anything else, can it be grasped by the mind and soul of man? And it must be said that the cruelty which tyrants have done these two trusts left behind by the gracious Prophet, peace be upon him and his descendants, has also been inflicted upon the Muslim community, and indeed upon mankind, so (much so) that the pen cannot transcribe it.[16]

Two things are worthy of notice in this passage. First, the entire Muslim community is smuggled into the relationship between Quran and imams in the tradition Khomeini quotes. In good revolutionary style, the Muslim community has, in fact, taken the place of the imams and so of the Prophet as well in Khomeini's text. Second, the Ayatollah invokes a mystical destruction of selfhood to describe the final conciliation of man and citizen on the Day of Judgement, as if to suggest the mythical character of the sovereignty represented by Muhammad. For a citizenship of this kind can only be mythical in the world conceived as a totality or system. Perhaps this is why Khomeini leaves the apocalyptic unity of man and citizen a mystery. Mystery, after all, provides the key to his theory of citizenship, which invests the world of exchanges with an inner life that acts as the root of all political action.

Back to the Future

Sixteen years after the Rushdie Affair, Khomeini's fatwa, and the Ayatollah's political testament, Muhammad, once again, provided the cause for a grand manifestation of Islam's globalization. In September 2005, the Danish newspaper, *Jyllands-Posten*, published a number of caricatures on the subject of Islam, Muslims, and the Prophet Muhammad. It had solicited these as part of a competition in which cartoonists had been asked to address the supposed fear that Danes and other Europeans felt in depicting Islam critically. In response to the publication, Muslims in Denmark protested against some of the cartoons, such as that portraying Muhammad as a terrorist, with one group of protestors actively trying to gain the support of Muslim leaders in the Middle East. The series of diplomatic and other representations made by Muslims to the Danish government during this period all resulted in the latter invoking the liberal principle of freedom of expression in defence of *Jyllands-Posten*'s right to print such material.

---

[15] See especially the *Rah-e Ishq* for this.
[16] Khomeini, *Akhirin Payam*, pp. 1–2.

By the end of the year this obscure event had snowballed into a global controversy, with Muslims the world over protesting, often violently, against Danish and other Western interests in countries from Indonesia to Lebanon. In their non-violent aspect, these demonstrations included a widespread boycott of Danish goods that was unprecedented in its extent. Such events kept the cartoon controversy at the centre of global attention for many weeks, even pushing news from the war in Iraq off the front pages. But despite the extraordinary passions unleashed among the protestors as much as among their opponents, Muslim demonstrations had completely dissipated by March 2006, leaving in their wake a state of universal confusion about what the crisis had all been about.

Both controversies, of 1989 and of 2005, revolved around the portrayal of Islam's prophet, and both were discussed in the West as threats to freedom of expression. The debate on freedom of expression goes back to the origins of liberalism—or rather to the origins of the nation-state that is its political body. Sadly, the terms of this debate also go back to the beginnings of liberalism, and are unable to encompass the radical novelty of the challenge that confronts it. Unlike the weight of tradition that loads down such debate, the illiberal character of Muslim protest is astonishingly modern in form. After all, freedom of expression only has meaning within old-fashioned national states, because it protects the speech of one section of citizens against another, and even against the state itself. Muslim protests, on the other hand, have meaning in an absolutely new global context.

The cartoon protests were remarkably dispersed geographically, and unconcerned for the most part with the rights of states or the responsibilities of citizenship. If this unconcern were due only to ignorance or irrationality among them, such protesting Muslims might eventually be educated to become the good citizens of a liberal democracy. Unfortunately, this was not the case. Muslim protests, which moved so far beyond the bounds of state and citizenship, were informed by the new rationality of a global arena. Within this arena, freedom of expression's more restricted realm had been rendered irrelevant. For at the global level, there is no common citizenship and no government to make freedom of expression meaningful even as an expression. Liberalism was being challenged here not by its past but by its future.

Muslim protesters did not represent some religious tradition that needs to be schooled in the lessons of modern citizenship. Rather their protests brought into being a hyper-modern global community whose connections occur by way of mass media alone. From the Philippines to Niger, these men and women communicated with each other only indirectly, neither by plan nor organization, but through the media itself. And just as during the Rushdie Affair of 1989, most Muslims in 2006 were hurt not by the offending item, a book read, or an image seen, but by its global circulation as a media report. Yet, it was this very circulation of the offending item as news that also allowed Muslims to represent themselves as a global community in, through, and as the news. Moreover, they could only do so by way of English as a global language. It is no accident that the cartoon controversy took the Muslim world by storm only when it was reported on the BBC and the CNN. English not Arabic is the source language of global Islam.

In this hyper-modern community, traditional distinctions of belief and practice have ceased to be relevant, as indeed has religion itself in an old-fashioned sense. For, the generic Muslim protester who was displayed on television screens across the world could not be marked by any specifically theological concern. If in the Rushdie Affair the explicitly religious issue of the 'satanic verses' was never taken up as a cause for offence even in the Ayatollah Khomeini's fatwa, Muslims protesting nearly twenty years later also made nothing of Islam's supposed proscription of the Prophet's image. In any case, there is a long if contested history of Muslims depicting their prophet. Such images continue to proliferate among Shiites, for example, without in any way dampening the outcry over the cartoons in Baghdad or Tehran.

These theological concerns are, in fact, interesting only to the defenders of liberal democracy, who think of challenges to its freedoms in terms that are a few centuries out of date. That it should be a religious group demonstrating its globalization here was in any case consonant with liberalism's past. The nation-state, after all, was founded to subdue religion, seen as the only entity capable of providing an alternative foundation for political life. So, it is only natural if today Islam seems to confront the liberal state with its own founding myth, having become the Frankenstein's monster of its history. Liberal democracy appears doomed to repeat its own past by the way

in which it prefigures its enemies—always understood as offering politics alternative foundations like that of religion. If not religion, then anarchism, fascism, or some other historical rival of the liberal state comes to occupy this role in the long-running comedy of its founding. But this is not true of global Islam, which should be defined in terms of liberalism's future instead of its past.

As in the Rushdie Affair, the Prophet insulted by these Danish cartoons is not a religious figure of any traditional sort. In 1989, it was Muhammad as husband and family man who stood impugned in the eyes of protesters. Many protesters in the new century continued to express their hurt by comparing the Prophet to members of their 'family', hardly a religious role for him to play and one of dubious orthodoxy in any case. This is language that belongs more in the Christian than the Muslim tradition. In fact, Muhammad as father, husband, and family man has become a role model of the most modern kind, one representing the ideal Muslim not as the citizen or even the leader of a state, as he did for yesterday's fundamentalists, including even the Ayatollah, but as a properly global figure instead. And the Prophet as a global figure manifests himself in domestic rather than political ways. It is his very particularity as father, husband, and family man that has been universalized beyond the language of state and citizenship, giving Muhammad a global countenance as part of a mythic family.

Muslim protests over the caricatures of Muhammad published in the Danish newspaper, *Jyllands-Posten*, did not pose any threat to the freedom of expression in liberal democracies. They presented a challenge to liberal democracy itself as a political form that is being made parochial within a new global arena. And if this challenge by no means spells the doom of nation-states, it does force them into new shapes that put liberalism's premises and foundations into question. What could be more indicative of this than the erosion of civil liberties in such states as part of the global war on terror? Liberal democracies today are increasingly shot through with new global vectors, running the gamut from immigrants to multinational corporations. Islam provides only one, though perhaps the most interesting one, of these vectors.

While Islam is certainly not the only global movement around, or the only one to issue challenges to liberal democracy, its geopolitical situation has made this populous religion the most volatile phenomenon of our times. Islam's globalization is possible because it is anchored neither in an institutionalized religious authority like a church, nor in an institutionalized political authority like a state. Indeed, it is the continuing fragmentation and thus democratization of authority in the world of Islam that might account for the militancy of its globalization. What did the global protests over a few Danish cartoons demonstrate if not the splintering of Islamic authority, since these expressions of Muslim outrage were rarely organized by any seminary or political party? In the absence of any significant religious or political authority in the Muslim world today, it is precisely unseen figures like al-Qaeda or the Danish cartoons that have the ability to mobilize Muslims globally, though, of course, in different and even opposing ways. For example, the cartoon protests, by and large,

eschewed the rhetoric of holy war, though they did invoke the same themes of hurt and respect as al-Qaeda.

Islam no longer serves merely to voice reactions against neocolonialism or democracy, capitalism or modernity, but increasingly sets the terms for politics globally. So, the unexpected escalation of the cartoon controversy moved it well ahead of any demonstrations over Iraq, Afghanistan, or Guantanamo Bay. Of course these and other, more local issues certainly informed Muslim anger. But they did so by providing global Islam an opportunity to manifest itself in the most arcane and therefore autonomous way: through a set of caricatures. By chancing in seemingly arbitrary fashion upon the Danish cartoons as a cause, Muslim protesters were only proving global Islam to be relatively unhampered by the political traditions proper to liberalism. Like other global movements, from environmentalism to anti-globalization, the Muslim one we are looking at is free to map its own trajectory and will not follow the dictates of someone else's idea of political rationality.

It was left for liberal democrats to puzzle over the meaning of this movement, coming up with explanations for it like American imperialism, economic exploitation, or Third World dictatorship. Meanwhile, the protesters themselves, who must have been more than familiar with such shibboleths, were content to ignore them altogether. The Danish cartoons did not simply disguise the political or economic causes of Muslim anger in religious terms, for we have seen that their anger had little or no religious substance. Rather, they allowed Muslims to set the terms for global politics precisely by fixing on an issue that national states are unable to address. Yet, this very issue, of personal hurt, insult, and offence, illustrates the global nature of the protests, because it located Muslims outside the geographical boundaries and juridical categories of any state. As global subjects, these Muslims and their Prophet were so easily hurt because they had been denuded of the protection that states and citizenship have to offer. Their hurt was nakedly felt and nakedly expressed, existing outside the cosseted debate on freedom of expression.

It is because global Islam comes to us from the future that it exposes so clearly the limits of liberal democracy. Such limits are evident in the circular definition that has marked liberalism from its founding days: only those will be tolerated who are themselves tolerant. Such a definition deprives tolerance of any moral content by making it completely dependent on the behaviour of others. Tolerance, therefore, becomes a process of exclusion in which it is always the other person who is being judged. Even at its most agreeable, however, the definition is severely limited, because its circularity works only within the bounds of a national state. It is unable to deal with real differences at all and certainly not with difference at a global level. As important as it undoubtedly is, we should remember that liberal tolerance was never meant to replace every other ethic in civil society, but is instead a procedural and legalistic form specific to the functioning of the nation-state.

There are many other kinds of tolerance possible, including the Christian one called charity, which would convert others or foster good relations with them by forbearance and example. But ethical rather than legal definitions of tolerance, like the Christian

one, tended not to be invoked in this controversy, with commentators abandoning the claims of civil society altogether to become ventriloquists for the state. Yet, it is surely within civil society that the problem lies, and statesmen from Gandhi to Mandela have in the recent past mobilized precisely such non-legal conceptions of tolerance to effect great social transformations. One does not have to legislate this kind of respect, simply inculcate it as an ethical principle. And this is only possible by sinking below the negative universality of liberal tolerance, tied as it is to the state's neutrality and indifference, to grasp the positive if particular tolerance of Hindus, Christians, or indeed atheists. The paradox of this particularity is that it is far more expansive than the universality of liberal tolerance, because it cannot be confined within the borders of a nation-state.

It was this particularity of respect, and even the positive tolerance of Christian charity, that so many Muslim protesters had been demanding, in no matter how frightening a manner. Their fulsome expressions of hurt, after all, were not derived from the cartoons in any direct way, since these remained unseen for the most part, but from the absence of respect for Muslim feeling. Unlike the photographs of American soldiers abusing Iraqi prisoners at Abu Ghraib, these images had not been globally circulated to spur Muslim anger. Like Rushdie's novel before them, Muslims protesting against them did not, in fact, see the cartoons. That a few unseen caricatures should cause more offence globally than large numbers of photographs depicting torture in the most real way is an important fact, and one that has little to do with the outrage of any specifically religious feeling at their appearance. Given the invisibility of the cartoons in the Muslim world, there was no real outrage to religious feeling there but only the report of European disrespect. In other words, the materiality of the images themselves had nothing to do with the protests they inspired, only the apparent injury done to Muslim feeling by the report of their circulation. More than an offence experienced, or a reality recognized, Muslims were protesting the violation of an ethical principle. This was the naked because non-juridical principle of respect within a global civil society made possible by media, markets, and migration.

Yet, the initial demand by Danish Muslims to have their own prejudices protected did not threaten freedom of expression in any way. Nor did Muslims in Denmark or elsewhere in Europe and North America make their demands in a criminally violent manner. Such demands are, in fact, made all the time in liberal democracies, whose boundaries of free expression are therefore constantly shifting. From state secrets to racial discrimination, libel and copyright to sexual harassment, proscriptions on expression are being put in place by the very defenders of its freedom. Indeed, today's war on terror has led to the most concerted reduction of such freedom in decades.

In the meantime, Muslims are inventing new forms of ethical and political practice for a global arena. Such were the remarkable boycotts of Danish goods in many parts of the Islamic world. However unfair or unjust they might have been, these peaceful and individualized boycotts of unprecedented extent were, like the controversial cartoons, perfectly legal and even democratic. Indeed,

they derived from a tradition of non-state or civil society boycotts that include the movement to divest from apartheid-era South Africa. Both these boycotts operated through transnational capitalism to create a global ethics and politics outside the cognizance of states. We have already moved a step beyond the banning and burning of the Rushdie Affair here.

More important, however, is the fact that this global mobilization of Muslims should have represented itself neither in the old language of imperialism and oppression, nor indeed in that of resistance and *jihad*. Instead, it took its rhetoric from the arsenal of liberalism itself, merely extending categories like democracy and civil society into a global arena. But this extension also transforms such categories, which seem finally to have achieved the universality that liberalism invested them with, if only outside the nation-state and its legal forms. What has resulted from these protests and boycotts, then, is not simply damage to the Danish economy, but rather a complete reversal of the primal scene of liberal freedom as it was staged by *Jyllands-Posten*.

The scenario envisioned by *Jyllands-Posten* was of a poor immigrant minority being 'tested' for its tolerance by an entrenched and wealthy majority. (But isn't the classical doctrine of liberal tolerance meant to protect minorities from majorities and not the other way around?) Having gone on to fulfil the newspaper's prediction by failing its test, this wretched minority could then be accused of threatening the majority's liberal constitution. I will not go into the unpleasant task of speculating about the newspaper's motives in creating its own news by scooping itself in this way, nor ask about the rise in its sales afterwards. The denouement was a sudden implosion of the paper's national audience into a global Muslim one, within which the unfortunate Danish majority unexpectedly became a minority. Did these boycotts, then, signal the slow movement of democratic practices from a national to a global arena—one in which there exist as yet no institutions to anchor them.

8

A Pattern for National Modernity

Politics in Pakistan

Ian Bedford

Modernity is easier to pursue than to define. Diagnostic criteria taken as guidelinesw—in the spirit in which generations since Weber have distinguished 'modern' from 'traditional' forms of legitimate authority—may encourage too petrified an understanding, most of all by implying that modernity is a condition that 'awaits' societies and cultures. It is true that modernity (however we define it) is something that overtakes people. But it is also taken up. Its manifestations everywhere are accompanied by vehement, sometimes explosive, manifestations of affect: of attachment and repudiation.

In a country like Pakistan, founded explicitly as a homeland for the Muslims of India, notions of modernity and of the modern have been quite as prevalent as elsewhere. Two areas of application

may be singled out. At the state level, the civil bureaucracy and, more particularly, the Army have represented themselves as institutions uniquely fitted to monitor a framework of administration for a deserving people. But besides these, spokesmen and gatekeepers of Islam have been much exercised with the modern. In some respects, their concerns have simply echoed those of comparable groups of Muslims all over the world: in Indonesia, for example, where a 'scriptural' modernity has been prized[1] and the traditional has come more and more to be identified with the unfounded and the irrational. At the same time, the circumstances of Pakistan have been unusual in that there, of all places, since the insertion

---

[1] John Bowen, 1993, *Muslims through Discourse*, Princeton: Princeton University Press.

of the 'Objectives Resolution' (1949) into the Preamble of the Constitution—long before that constitution was proclaimed— the question of Islam has been represented as a central concern of the state.

In the account that follows, initiatives of the Army, and of some gatekeepers of Islam protected and promoted under military rule, will be considered as measures in the imposition of a brand of national modernity from above. To clarify this approach, the exemplary case of the Turkish modernizer, Mustafa Kemal, later Ataturk, will be taken as precedent—for his was a precedent which no subsequent Army modernizer could overlook. Ataturk, however, was a defiantly secular ruler. His legacy to the Turkish Republic—not an unmixed one—has been a combative form of secularism, which permeates civic life but is most at home in the Army.

The President of Pakistan and Chief Martial Law Administrator, General Zia-ul-Haq, seized power (July 1977) and ordered the execution of his predecessor, the elected Prime Minister, Zulfiqar Ali Bhutto. In the wake of the nationwide mobilization from below that deposed the Shah in Iran (1978–February 1979), General Zia sought to conciliate those *ulama* and lay Muslims who might otherwise cause trouble. These dangerous elements, as we will see, were encouraged, and enabled—but they were by no means conciliated. General Zia's gift to Pakistan—of which the Taliban may be considered an ingredient—is a version of national modernity in which the state, administered or closely supervised by the Army, serves as the vehicle for a reformed, emphatically non-'Indian' Islam which expresses the genius of the nation. This

modernizing vision was so enthusiastically welcomed by armed beneficiaries that the trauma of affect has proved all but impossible to hose down. Funding from outside, principally from Saudi Arabia, has contributed not only to the survival of the vision but to a brutal culture of violence. In the towns of south Punjab and elsewhere, Sunni *tehrik*s or 'movements' were terrorizing Shia and others long before the United States (US) overthrew Saddam Hussain in Iraq. In the last decade, Pakistan has become not so much a haven, as a bottomless reservoir for terrorists fuelled emotionally by an enormous *ressentiment* which is one aspect of a kind of modernity.

Dumont: The Acculturation to Modernity

Nothing could be further from secularism than this particular brand of modernity in Pakistan. Yet in what follows, it will be argued that it was by General Zia—and not by his Martial Law predecessor, General Ayub Khan, who was a secularist and knew his Ataturk—that one aspect, at least, of Ataturk's approach to nation building was most powerfully approximated. Put differently, there was more to the Ataturk model than its secularism.

Ataturk's achievement will be taken here not only as an empirical precedent, but as a term in a powerful, if idiosyncratic, thesis on modernity advanced by Louis Dumont. Dumont writes, in *German Ideology* (1994), of an 'acculturation' to modernity.[2] He carries his argument down to Lenin. Dumont takes as 'characteristic

---

[2] Louis Dumont, 1994, *German Ideology: From France to Germany and Back*, Chicago: University of

of modernity...a certain configuration of ideas-and-values...a relatively consistent configuration signalled by the primacy of the individual'.[3] Inasmuch as 'the individual' has come, in the modern West, to be taken for granted, Dumont sees that acceptance as an obstacle to the understanding of society.

Once the individualistic configuration is fully developed, as say in the eighteenth century, it sharpens its claim against contemporary society, and the belief appears, in some countries and certain social environments, that it is possible to realise a society that would entirely conform to individualism...Socially speaking, individualism then was a kind of utopian theory sheltered against any contact with actual social life.[4]

Where it did come to be implemented, as in France with the revolution, that implementation was selective, and could only be selective, as a society that was wholly founded on individualism would not survive. With the spread of economic liberalism, that direct expression of the individualist ideology which condemns

any intervention of the State, whose only role is to provide the conditions necessary for the free play of economic rationality in the enterprise and the market...no sooner is the system completely in force than it results paradoxically in a renewed intervention of the State in almost all the countries in question...Nobody, be he Mr Reagan, would dare to-day to return to Hoover's liberalism.[5]

Dumont, then, as we see, gets to modernity by way of individualism, a concept (thoroughly explored by him in

a number of works) whose claims may be well-nigh absolute, as in Hoover's or Reagan's liberalism, but which, in practice, is always adulterated with something else, with some ingredient of holism, to use a term from the Durkheimian tradition. Dumont uses the example of Germany—the Germany of Herder, rather than of Kant—to maintain in effect that when 'modernity' is presented to a nation or a people from without, as a complex of novelties that will not simply go away, that nation, if it is in a position to do so, will temper what it is bound to receive by bringing to it some ingredient of its own, from its 'holistic' resources. So, he speaks of an 'acculturation to modernity'.

In Germany, as contrasted with France, wrote Dumont, a 'counter-offensive' to the cosmopolitan notion of modernity was staged by Herder in the name of the German 'community', which it was feared would be overlooked.[6] This idiosyncratic combination of a veneration for the German *Gemeinschaft* with a devotion to the personal, 'inward' development of the individual, was a form of adaptation (here I state it without nuance) which Dumont argues was realized only in Germany.

The model Dumont attributes to Lenin, however, had less (though still a great deal) to do with cultural particularities, and was readily internationalized. Lenin's initiative concerned a 'people torn between Russian cultural identity and what we here call the individualistic configuration of the West'.[7] It conformed, than, to the general pattern for 'acculturation' sketched by Dumont; yet its content, unlike that of the German

---

Chicago Press (in French, *Homo Aequalis II*, Paris, 1991).

[3] Ibid., p. 7.
[4] Ibid.
[5] Ibid., p. 8.

[6] Ibid., p. 10.
[7] Ibid., p. 12.

model, could be detached from the original framework and taken up elsewhere, to begin with by 'communist parties all over the world'. Lenin's 'daring' initiative is set forth in an ostensibly Marxist document, the 'April Theses' of 1917. By overstepping a historical stage in the Marxist schema—precisely that stage which 'produced the conditions for intervening'—Lenin embraced "'the Populist dream of a direct transition from the overthrow of the tsarist autocracy to the building of socialism'"[8] (Walicki 1981 quoted in Dumont 1994).

The allure of this model—not only for nation builders, but for aspirants to modernity of many kinds—can be illustrated down to the present day. In Afghanistan in the 1970s, an engineering student, Gulbuddin Hekmatyar, read Lenin, and may have taken from what he learned the organizational structure of the Hezb-i-Islami.[9] Besides the notion of the party—a vanguard epitomizing, rather than representing, the people—the essential ingredient of the Leninist model was its extreme voluntarism. Nothing can have been further than Islamism from Lenin's mind; but in this case and others, it can be shown how ingredients of the model survived transplantation and continued to exercise a compelling effect the world over. Yet, because of its very indifference to cultural particularities, the specifically Leninist initiative does not in itself provide a comprehensive illustration of the intimate, cultural character of the double movement—

both an appropriation and an adaptation—sketched by Dumont.

Ataturk: More than 'Secularism' to His Achievement

Is there an instance of the 'acculturation to modernity' which, for all its particular character, has exerted an influence comparable to Lenin's outside its immediate context? An instance of this kind would have to draw in its own way on the existing cultural inheritance of a people, or a people-to-be, magnifying some elements, reducing others, in shaping a public ideal which would be taken up in the name of modernity. Such aspects of the Leninist model as Bolshevik party structure, and, even more, of an 'April Theses' voluntarism—which could be successfully urged only at the political level—are far too general, far too easily detached, to do proper justice to Dumont's insights.

I believe there is such a model. The achievement of Mustafa Kemal—Kemal Ataturk—in making a secular nation out of a Muslim population in Turkey has been widely admired, and emulated, in other Muslim countries, particularly by military leaders. This is not to say that all applications of the model have been successful. It is not to say that the model itself has been properly understood—but, rather, that it has irresistibly commended itself in circumstances where a military leader has appeared to occupy a position similar to that of Mustafa Kemal in 1924. The most explicit example is the modelling of his own actions on those of Ataturk by the founder of the Pahlavi dynasty in Iran, Reza Shah, after he seized power in 1925.

---

[8] Andrej Walicki, 1981, *A History of Russian Thought*, quoted in Dumont, *German Ideology*.

[9] Olivier Roy, 1985, *Islam and Resistance in Afghanistan*, Cambridge: Cambridge University Press, p. 78.

Mustafa Kemal, as he then was, was a successful World War I general serving the Ottoman Empire. In the early 1920s, before the election of the Grand National Assembly in Turkey and for a short time after, he was mistaken, at least in the West, for a pan-Islamist;[10] but he changed his tune very rapidly. As students of the Freedom Movement in India well know, collaboration between Hindus and Muslims against the British was founded in the early 1920s on Gandhi's acceptance of the Khilafat movement as an expression of the nationalist cause. Then anti-colonialist Hindus, as well as Muslims, protested against the supposed intention of the British, after the Ottoman defeat in the war, to abolish the Caliphate in Istanbul. Yet, it was Ataturk himself who, from 1924, as President of the Turkish Republic, abolished the Caliphate, secularized the Islamic courts, banned Islamic headdress, and carried out a variety of measures which had the force of an abrupt declaration of symbolic (and real) war on Islam. The obstacle was not so much dogmatic, as cultural; Islam was viewed less as a religion than as the shared culture of a community, resistant to modernization.

This headlong assault would not have been possible, of course, without the control of the resources of the state by a single party, by a single man and his government. But, on a lasting perspective, it would not have been possible without the substitution, or in a sense the discovery, of a cultural identity which could be defined in such a way as to compete with and, ideally, to supplant the Muslim identity of the vast majority

of Turkish subjects. For this reason, the truncation of the imperial domain, the loss of the Arab provinces, and the concentration of an ideal of autonomy on the remnant province, now the heartland, of Anatolia, can be viewed not as a calamity but as a solution, the solution of a new problem altogether.

It seems to us, today, all but axiomatic that a 'Turkish' identity would first have been known, and inhabited, in Turkey. But Turkism had been formulated, as a cultural identity and as a political programme, among several minority populations—not just one—in the late nineteenth-century Russian Empire,[11] and even as a strand within Bolshevism,[12] before Mustafa Kemal turned it to such definitive use.

The Turks of the Ottoman Empire were not a minority. They were, as yet, barely even 'Turks'. Yet, without this possibility of a substitution, and indeed of a replacement of identity on a national plane and in the name of 'modernity', Mustafa Kemal would have been just another military commander at the helm of state. After a decade or so, no one would have remembered his model, whether or not he had had the audacity to dismantle Islam. He would have had nothing to replace it with. Without this substitution of identities, his famed secularism—an ingredient as fundamental as ethnicity to

[10] Jacob M. Landau, 1990, *The Politics of Pan-Islam*, Oxford: Clarendon Press, p. 178.

[11] Tadeusz Swietochowski, 1985, *Russian Azerbaijan, 1905–1920: The Shaping of a National Identity in a Muslim Community*, Cambridge: Cambridge University Press, pp. 31–2. Also, see Adeeb Khalid, 1998, *The Politics of Cultural Reform: Jadidism in Central Asia*, Berkeley: University of California Press.

[12] Alexandre Bennigsen and Chantal Lemercier-Quelquejay, 1960, *Les mouvements nationaux chez les musulmans de Russie: le 'sultan-galievisme' au Tatarstan*, Paris: Mouton.

the mystique of Kemalism—would have acquired no lasting purchase. 'Ataturk' or not, he would have worked no magic and founded no precedent in the world. The challenge he mounted would have been little different from that proclaimed the world over by twentieth-century military dictators. His conviction would simply have resembled theirs: that the Army alone had the vision and the determination to carry a people enslaved by tradition into a modern world.

Vicissitudes in Pakistan of the Ataturk Model

In August 1948, one year after the proclamation of the new nation of Pakistan, a memorandum was forwarded to the Government of Pakistan by Muhammad Asad, Director of the Department of Islamic Thought. This document was recalled over forty years later as Pakistan faced its legacy of 'Islamization' after Zia ul-Haq.

…The picture of Islam drawn by the majority of our 'professional' ulama does not correspond to the needs of our present-day society, being entirely rigid and chained to ideas about the law which were held by great scholars of the early centuries of Islam. It follows, therefore, that this picture cannot possibly reflect the true intentions of the Law-Giver. For these juridic conclusions were surely not 'final' in the sense of having absolute validity for all times…Two ways are open to Muslim society in our days: either to go back to the original Message of Islam and to start thinking anew about its implications—with a view to making Islam once more a practical basis of our social and cultural life—or to banish Islam entirely from political life, as Kemal Ataturk did in his country…[13]

It was to the first of Asad's alternatives—but not the second!—that the avowed 'secularism' of the Ayub Khan regime (1958–69) weakly corresponded. General Ayub Khan, even before he was President, let alone Field Marshall, plunged the country under martial law (October 1958). He was unwilling to involve the ulama, or indeed anyone else, in the administration of Pakistan, but he harboured no ill designs on Islam as such. The Islam he favoured had a 'reform' ingredient, and he set up institutions to clarify its nature. His choice as director of the Institute of Islamic Research was the scholar, Dr Fazlur Rahman, already the author of a notable book[14] which proposed a critique of orthodoxy and paid considerable attention to the views of the medieval *falasafa*, heretics to some Muslims. Fazlur Rahman was the first and last of his kind to occupy such a high position. He was forced to leave Pakistan (for the University of Chicago) in 1968.[15] The Ayub regime crumbled soon after. Its secularist character was wanting, but was, in some ways, more substantial than that of his elected successor, Zulfiqar Ali Bhutto, who began as a socialist (1971) but went on to frame legislation, supported by fundamentalists, against the small Ahmadiyya community (1974).

General Ayub, then, was no Ataturk—even in respect of his secularism. In a state founded by and for Muslims, Ayub did not try to confine the scope of Islam. He left popular religion as he found it.

[13] Muhammad Asad, 1992, 'Memorandum to the Government of Pakistan of August, 1948', *Frontier Post*, Lahore, 10 April.

[14] Fazlur Rahman, 1958, *Prophecy and Islam: Philosophy and Orthodoxy*, Chicago: G. Allen and Unwin.

[15] Jamal Malik, 1996, *Colonialization of Islam: Dissolution of Traditional Structures in Pakistan*, Lahore: Vanguard Books, p. 44.

He certainly did his best to keep some prominent Muslims and their organizations out of public life,[16] but he would have challenged Islam at his cost. There was no counterweight identity to which he could appeal, as Kemal had appealed to Turkism. Ayub's abiding policy objective was to prevent Bengalis—East Pakistanis—from acquiring the influence their numbers deserved. To this end, he constituted West Pakistan as 'One Unit', a unit of four provinces granted administrative parity with the East wing. This pleased Punjab but upset the minor provinces. Eventually, military rule—Ayub's version of it—foundered on the rock of Bengal. Religion had very little to do with this outcome.

Yet, the Ataturk model was pertinent in his case. It was pertinent in one respect—and to define that respect, we may visualize the precedent of Ataturk as consisting of two, detachable parts. This dual aspect of the model is essential to my argument, especially as it concerns General Zia-ul-Haq, to whom the model is pertinent in quite a different aspect. Ayub Khan found in Ataturk the same precedent as had Reza Shah in Iran. This inheritance is available wherever the Army represents itself as the true upholder of national values and as morally entitled to intervene in the political process when these values are dishonoured or neglected. It is true that Ayub, explicit in his contempt for 'anti-national' politicians, did not proclaim his indebtedness to Ataturk. To have done so would have drawn attention to his secularist programme (limited though it was). His

Foreign Minister Bhutto, who when he first came to power was more open than Ayub could afford to be in his profession of secular values, founded a Kemal Ataturk Memorial in Larkana, his native town.[17] During the martial law years, when I was studying in Lahore, the 'Ataturk' precedent for Ayub's exaltation of the Army was recognized in many places, particularly among politics and law students, his restless opponents.

The most recent authoritative work on 'Pakistan's military economy', that of Ayesha Siddiqa, places Ayub's Pakistan securely in the lineage of 'Kemalist Turkey, [where the] military considered itself responsible for nationbuilding and integrity of state'.[18] To Ayub, however reluctant he was to proclaim them, Ataturk's military–secular values were at least congenial: but to General Zia, some twenty years later, they were anathema. Here, no conscious adaptation of Ataturk can have been intended: quite the opposite. Secularism was defeated. Yet, the Ataturk model was not exhausted. This model, I will show, has a structural logic which is at work—as in General Zia's case—even when the cultural values are reversed.

Under Ataturk, the break with the past was dramatized by a declared war, both institutional and symbolic, on Islam. Yet to fulfil this purpose, the principle of secularism was not enough. Rather than a principle, government set out to provide the people with an entire disposition, a way of life, and a new identity: the identity of Turk, which

[16] S.V.R. Nasr, 1994, *The Vanguard of the Islamic Revolution: The Jama'at-i Islam in Pakistan*, London: I.B. Tauris, chapter 7.

[17] Stanley Wolpert, 1993, *Zulfi Bhutto of Pakistan: His Life and Times*, Oxford: Oxford University Press, p. 226.

[18] Ayesha Siddiqa, 1993, *Military Inc.: Inside Pakistan's Military Economy*, Oxford: Oxford University Press, pp. 49, 132–3.

was less familiar in Ottoman Turkey than in the Turkic-speaking provinces of the Russian Empire and which, because it was unknown, could be construed as a modern identity, deep-rooted, but untrammelled by the past. This model will help to understand Zia's achievement. But it could not, with Zia, be a matter of simply replacing 'secularism' with 'Islam': we would then have 'Islam' on both sides of the equation. Zia had no intention of following Ataturk. Yet he did so, I will argue, and the Ataturk model prevailed, in at least one fateful respect, though its logic escaped him. This raises the question of Zia's agency.

To address this question, I will provide two forms of the argument. The first, though otherwise valid, depicts Zia as a rather more clear-sighted political actor than in fact he was. The second form will involve a severe qualification of the first. This approach, though oblique, will help do justice to the factors truly at work in the 'Pakistan' distortion of the Ataturk model.

A Fault Line in Islam

The first form of the argument is as follows. General Zia-ul-Haq, detested by partisans of the civil government and alarmed by the news from Iran, where a similar autocrat, far better supported internationally, was overthrown by a popular uprising, strove to legitimize his power. His only real ideological conviction was his notion of the Army as a modernizing force, a force for good. But equipped with this commonplace idea, he was led by circumstances to a new idea, to the vision of a new and attainable kind of modernity for Pakistan. He identified

a constituency with which to achieve this vision, while buttressing his personal rule.

Zia resembled Ataturk, and differed from Ayub, in this respect: he identified a vital constituency outside the Army. His Pakistan would be an Islamic Pakistan. There was nothing new about that; what was new was General Zia's exploitation of a rift that had opened within Islam, the world over, but more conspicuously in Pakistan than elsewhere. In Pakistan, a Muslim population had been exposed by government to a bewildering transition, from one conceptual framework to another: from the sphere of 'India' to that of the sovereign nation of Pakistan.

In Pakistan, as in India, not all Muslims were acquainted with the fundamentals of Islam. Up to the 1940s, the districts of what became Pakistan had been only feebly inclined to the Pakistan movement, which was the invention, for the most part, of an educated cadre, the consciously orthodox Muslims of the United Provinces. These Muslims, predominantly urban dwellers, had to migrate to Pakistan and were billeted on the provinces, where the history of their reception would take a volume in itself. The Pakistan they found was in many respects no different—empirically speaking—from the India they left behind. In both countries, Islam had many registers. One of these was Sufism. An Islam of the shrine coexisted with an Islam of the mosque in the towns and countryside. This diversity was not appreciated by all Muslims. Throughout the subcontinent, from the days of Ahmad Sirhindi in Akbar's Delhi, orthodox opinion had, at times, distanced itself from popular practices and had condemned their toleration by Muslim rulers.[19] Unwelcome practices were ascribed to Hinduism, though perceptions often erred.[20] More often, *ashraf* (higher status) Muslims had simply held aloof from popular currents. With the coming of Pakistan, orthodoxy sensed a new opportunity. The relative secularism and liberalism of the actual founders, insofar as these were constitutional democrats like Muhammad Ali Jinnah, proved less of an obstacle to the prospects of an orthodox revival than did the actual practices of Pakistan Muslims, both rural and urban.

There was, then, a fault line in Islam, which was magnified in Pakistan by an affronted nationalism, the need for radical differentiation of the new country from an India which Islam had outgrown. This, in itself, was a matter of advantage to General Zia, whose pressing need was to stay in power. Forces in Islam troublesome to Bhutto, and to Ayub before him—both secularists—had never received the encouragement they hoped for in Pakistan. What opened Zia's eyes was the advance on Pakistan, from outside the country, of a new—and internationally befriended—source of encouragement for these native forces. What worked to save him was a wholly contingent factor, the war on Afghanistan.

There are many aspects to this story. The one that concerns us here is not that of the US dependence on a stable ally to serve as recruiting sergeant and quartermaster in the fight against the Soviet Army—though that helped save Zia's skin, particularly in his confrontation with the home-grown Movement for the Restoration of Democracy in 1982–3. What concerns us here is a by-product of that alliance. Saudi money and Saudi advisers: this essential lubricant to international effort came with its own brand of Islam. The Saudi brand of Islam found eager adherents within the country, not least in the Army and the Intelligence Services. As Coll remarks of the process by which links were established, 'soon after the Soviet invasion of Afghanistan', between the Saudi and Pakistan intelligence agencies in a meeting attended by President Zia in Rawalpindi, 'a Saudi quickly became accustomed to being treated like a bank teller'.[21] It was 'five I.S.I. (Inter-Services Intelligence) generals', in Coll's narrative, who counted the money. But Zia's projects were already matured. The money was counted at an advanced stage in their implementation. In 1978, by President's Order, Shariat Benches had been set up in the four provincial high courts and in the Supreme Court to pronounce on the conformity of enacted laws to the injunctions of Islam.[22] The Fundamental Rights guaranteed in the 1973 constitution,

[19] Muzaffar Alam, 2004, *The Languages of Political Islam in India 1200–1800*, New Delhi: Viking, pp. 77–8.

[20] Marc Gaborieau, 1989, 'A Nineteenth-Century Indian "Wahhabi" Tract against the Cult of Muslim Saints: *Al-Balagh al-Mubin*', in Christian W. Troll (ed.), *Muslim Shrines in India*, New Delhi: Oxford University Press, pp. 198–239.

[21] Steve Coll, 2004, *Ghost Wars: The Secret History of the CIA, Afghanistan and bin Laden from the Soviet Invasion to September 10, 2001*, London: Penguin, p. 72.

[22] Rashida Patel, 1986, *Islamisation of Laws in Pakistan?* Karachi: Faiza Publishers, p. 87.

including that to freedom of religion, were set aside.[23]

Zia's push to Islamization was always subordinate to his need to shore up afresh the powers conferred on him by constitutional amendment and by referendum. His constituency of ulama saw this clearly. For all his exertions on their behalf, Zia never won their trust.[24] But in those first years, the pace of reform, directed from above, was relentless. In 1979, President Zia promulgated the 'Hudood' Ordinances. 'For the first time in Pakistan women became punishable for adultery and fornication, and both became a crime.'[25] In 1982, however, the Federal Shariat Court found that stoning to death for adultery (*rajm*)—as prescribed under the 'Hudood' Ordinance—was not grounded in *Sunnah* and was 'repugnant' to Islam.[26] In consequence, four judges of the Court were replaced, and rajm was declared Islamic by the new appointees.

Zia's ostensible values could not have been more different from those of Ataturk, whose intention was plain: to build his country into a modern, secular nation. To do so, Ataturk used all his capabilities—including main force—to substitute one kind of self-understanding for another. He implanted Turkism at the expense of Islam. It was to the structure of this assignment—an adversarial structure, eradicating one set of values—that the Zia-ul-Haq undertaking corresponds.

At this point, let us return to Dumont's notion of an acculturation to modernity.

Something new is conceived, something that will endure as a modification of culture when the moment for innovation has passed. Dumont, for his part, guided by his 'individualism' thesis, sees modernity as pitting itself against tradition in such a way that it 'posits its [own] values independently from society as it finds it'.[27] Now, the enormous affect modernity excites—one is attached to it, one deplores it, one is consumed by it—stems from this circumstance. No twentieth-century programme for action is less disposed to accept society 'as it finds it' than the new brand of political fundamentalism. The reconstitution of Islam in recent times, founded principally on the idea—absent from tradition—that an Islamic society grounded in shari'a law, governed wholly by the norms of the shari'a, can and must be realized by Muslims in the here and now, is a profound expression of the ethos of modernity. That expression was nowhere to be found during the last great mobilization of Indian Muslims before the Partition, the Khilafat movement. When Pakistan was conceived, the programme existed, it had already been proclaimed in the world, but its proponents in the subcontinent, like Maulana Mawdudi, kept wisely on the sidelines.

Up-to-date military technology; architectural masterworks; demanding intellectual projects (such as Islamic banking) debated at international conferences in glistening halls in the streamlined new capital of Islamabad with its Saudi-funded mosque; an Islamic university, its glossy journals and brochures; and the constant

---

[23] Patel, *Islamisation of Laws in Pakistan?* p. 18.
[24] Malik, *Colonialization of Islam*, pp. 139, 151.
[25] Patel, *Islamisation of Laws in Pakistan?* p. 41.
[26] Ibid., pp. 118–9.

[27] Dumont, *German Ideology*, p. 7.

coming and going of affably disposed American diplomats and oilmen: these formed the material counterpart of the Islamic modernity so promptly converted into an administrative programme by President Zia-ul-Haq. Yet, even where an 'Islamic' modernity can be shown to correspond in Pakistan to the 'secular' modernity proclaimed in Turkey, we are still far from the dynamism of the Ataturk model. In Turkey, secularism had been won—a precarious achievement!—at the expense of Islam. But what was to be the substitution in Pakistan? Islam was the very substance of Zia's ideology! In the nation of Pakistan, which was formed for Islam and which consisted, almost entirely, of Muslims, what, then, was to be replaced? I am arguing, then, that Zia's programme of substitution was obtained, in Pakistan, at the expense of popular Islam. But was this ever Zia's intention?

Popular Islam and the 'Substitution of Identity'

The evidence on this point suggests otherwise. It is true that over the eleven years of the Zia ascendancy, the forces of popular Islam (to be characterized in a moment) were progressively marginalized. The new institutions passed them by. In the most influential circles, they were discredited. Throughout the country, a militant orthodoxy, 'Wahhabi' in spirit, tailored only a little to meet the *fiqh* requirements of Hanafi Islam (which had long prevailed on the subcontinent) imposed its ethos and language, and invaded the sphere of policy and the affairs of state. But was this outcome what Zia 'meant'? In a sense it was highly

consonant with all he 'meant', but I will argue next that it was not what was planned but was rather an unintended, or dimly intended, consequence of forces which the president unleashed, but could not govern.

This requires a second form of the argument. By 'popular Islam', I refer above all to the Islam of Sufism, or to those varieties of Islam that took Sufism into account. Sufism in Pakistan was not (for the most part) an esoteric practice but was the Sufism of spiritual leaders (*shaikh* or *pir*) and of the shrines (*dargah*; but there are many kinds of shrine, and many terms in use).[28] To some in Pakistan, this is 'Indian' Islam; but it has been at home in the Punjab and Sindh since long before the Partition. Its domain is the countryside, but there are notable urban shrines. Popular Islam, to the orthodox—to moderate 'scripturalists' as well as to neo-fundamentalists—is discreditable: it is thoroughly infiltrated with music (*kafian* and *qawalli*), with public celebration, and with superstitious practices such as *ziyarat* (visits in reverence), weeping at shrines, and asking the pirs of shrines to intercede for the dead. In party polemics, it is confounded with 'feudalism'.

It is unlikely that Zia-ul-Haq formulated a deliberate policy of containing popular Islam. Like his predecessors, he sought to bring private endowments (*waqf*), which funded many shrines, under government control. But he sought to control most things, including the curricula of schools

[28] See Pnina Werbner, 2003, *Pilgrims of Love: The Anthropology of a Global Sufi Cult*, London: Routledge, chapters 1 and 2; Katherine Pratt Ewing, 1997, *Arguing Sainthood: Modernity, Psychoanalysis, Islam*, Durham and London: Duke University Press, pp. 41–6.

(*madrasa*) run by orthodox ulama.[29] Even his enthusiasm for an Islamist political programme was not enough to win him unqualified support among ulama. Indeed, Zia was prepared to make compromises which neither his Sunni Islamist constituency nor his Saudi benefactors saw a need for. One such compromise weakened his legislation on *zakat* (which authorized the state to collect and distribute funds for charity—supposedly an Islamic measure). When this ordinance offended the Shia, he exempted the Shia from compulsion, while other Muslims were compelled to pay a zakat levy on their bank accounts.[30] Zia did little to protect the Shia from the terrible depredations in store for them, as supposed heretics (in the eyes of home-grown Deobandi fundamentalists) and as a fifth column for Iran (in the eyes of the Saudis, who hated them anyway), but he did not want any trouble from them. Nor did he want any trouble from the countryside or the shrines.

Zia's legislative interventions left little to chance. Attempts since his death, to revive parliamentary activity in Pakistan have been crippled by the enormous weight assigned to the executive power by his constitutional amendments, and by the practice those authorized. Yet, this authorized damage at the political level is the tip of the iceberg. More ruinous (and just as enduring) has been the harm done in the name of Islam to coexistence among Muslims, and to the fabric of community in the new nation.

It is not so much what Zia authorized, as what Zia allowed. An early example of what was allowed was the pitched gun battle at Faisalabad Agricultural University in September 1981, following the address to students by the Afghan Mujahidin leader and noted recipient of Saudi funds, Gulbuddin Hekmatyar, who was there at the invitation of the Jama'at-i-Islami.[31] A chain of Saudi-funded madrasas, stretching along the Iran border, incubated the Taliban-to-be. In the south and central Punjab, tehriks (activist movements) terrorized the Shia populations, who responded in kind. The town of Jhang—burial place of the epic poet Waris Shah, whose tomb is a cherished site for lovers—has given its name to one of the most murderous of these terror bands, the Lashkar-i-Jhangvi.

Throughout Pakistan, dedication to the ideal of a shari'a Islam nurtured by the state left no room for the sufferance of popular error. The Barelwi tendency of Sunni Islam, rooted in the shrines, was placed on the defensive as tehriks of the rival tendency, the Deobandi, which sought to move into Barelwi territory, sprouted in the Punjab towns. A renewed spirit of orthodoxy flourished on campuses. At the University of Karachi in the early 1990s, I was told by a professor: 'No student of Islam today would be interested to study Sufism.' City students reiterated their contempt for pirs. This was, partly, incomprehension: just as, in an affluent welfare economy being dismantled for the sake of the free market, like Australia, nobody 'understands' trade unionism.

---

[29] Malik, *Colonialization of Islam*, chapter 5.
[30] Mohammad Waseem, 1994, *Politics and the State in Pakistan*, Islamabad: National Institute of Historical And Cultural Research, pp. 353–4.

[31] 'Savage Students Lord It Over Faisalabad's Premier University', 1995, *The Friday Times*, 26 October.

The dangers to popular Islam of this new spirit of incomprehension were perceived early. A striking example is afforded by Malik. In 1980, 'a new institution was set up under…the Auqaf Department…to conduct studies on Sufis and mysticism'.[32] The Chairman, appointed in 1982, Dr Yusuf Guraya, was a published author, whose views were known. To Dr Guraya, 'the shrine cult represented the feudal character of the country and the concomitant exploitation of the people and their alienation from true Islam'.[33] In response to his appointment, Barelwi rallied around the shrine of Data Saheb in Lahore, clashing with Deobandi, and successfully demanding the dismissal of the chairman. Malik himself shows sympathy for the dismissed chairman. It is certainly the case that his view on what constitutes 'true Islam' was widespread in Pakistan long before 1982 and that there is nothing novel, or even inflammatory, about the opinion as such. The only new feature—and it is this feature that constituted the event—is the heightened sensitivity of worshippers at shrines (here, the Barelwi demonstrators) to the institutionalization of that opinion under rapidly changing circumstances. In depicting the Barelwi as the aggressors, Malik overlooks the shift they were witnessing in the country at large, the provisioning of new institutions for the definition of Islam, and the will (and the financial means) to deploy them. It is notable that the government as such played no role in this event. The tide was running in a certain direction. Zia-ul-Haq and his advisers saw no reason to antagonize the shrines, but, by now, the

vessel was unstoppered and the genie was out. The consequences were no longer in their hands.

Paying the Full Cost of a 'Substitution'

The term 'acculturation to modernity', taken from Dumont, applies well to the experience of transformation willed on the people of Turkey by Ataturk. Our model here is that of the proclamation, by a military leader, of a modern, national identity to a people who are meant to be reborn to that identity, forsaking another which had been theirs all along. 'Modernity' is the word, not for a particular content or a specific goal (for these can vary) but for the embrace of new values which are distinctive, above all, for the rhetoric of their justification and for the affect they generate. The obstructers of modernity—passionate or bewildered—are always wrong.

I have argued that General Zia-ul-Haq, in Pakistan, imposed on his country a brand of Islam which he, as Chief Martial Law Administrator, could not realize without contradiction but which others sought to realize in his place. The downfall of the Shah of Iran, the accident of the Soviet invasion of Afghanistan, and the goodwill and the motivated blindness, respectively, of Saudi and American advisers, inspired General Zia to a course of action whose effects survive him and have made of Pakistan a country in which the traditional Islamic culture of the majority has remained under siege. Zia had nothing like the audacity of an Ataturk. The repudiation of popular Islam was not his intention. But the logic of the modernity he willed, drawing on elements which had only a small following in the country at

[32] Malik, *Colonialization of Islam*, pp. 68–9.
[33] Ibid., p. 69.

large but had been waiting in the wings ever since Pakistan was proclaimed as a nation of Muslims, has led to a slowly smouldering civil offensive by passionately motivated subjects wherever tradition, heresy, or anomaly offer their resistance, an offensive pursued with violence, if need be, with or without the state.

Was Zia, then, a kind of dazed Ataturk, an Ataturk by default? He was not even a secularist. Yet, his achievement approximates more closely to the Ataturk model than do the more prudent achievements of the secular elites of other nations who aspire to take 'only the good things' of modernity, leaving the culture of the masses undisturbed. This aspiration can never be realized. It is simply not possible to add modernity to what is already there. The

originality of Ataturk lay in his more or less clear-eyed determination to pay the full cost of a substitution. General Zia had no such vision. Half-trampled by circumstances, panicked by the Iran example, he sought to impose, from above—and god gave him such powerful allies!—a radical Muslim identity for Pakistan. The tragic irony of this example is that his project succeeded. Pakistan was transformed. A substitute Islam was imposed on an already Muslim country that had never prayed for it, and all this in the cause of a modernity which is entirely unlike that of W.W. Rostow and David McLelland (ideologues of the 1960s). Yet, here is a distinctive modernity nonetheless, which does not herald a Pax Americana. Far more than in Turkey, Islam itself has been wounded by this substitution.

III

Critical Cultures

9

Ripening with the Earth
On Maturity and Modernity in South India

Anand Pandian

In the wake of the European Enlightenment, modernity has been widely associated with the attainment of maturity. Kant famously described enlightenment in 1784, for example, as an emergence from the condition of a 'self-imposed immaturity', that is, from an 'inability to use one's understanding without guidance from another'.[1] It has by now been well established that this image of a possible maturity must be greatly revised to account for the specific conditions of colonial and postcolonial modernity. Colonial subjects in South Asia and elsewhere encountered the prospect of such freedom under the shadow of despotic authority. Widely engaged as childlike in their essential nature, colonial subjects grappled with insistent relations of guidance taken as essential to the very possibility of their development. Their capacity for such development under such conditions was judged explicitly and implicitly against the authority of universal standards of maturity, in relation to which the particular immaturity of their character and customs could be assessed and potentially overcome. The developmental imagination which

---

[1] Immanuel Kant, 1983, 'An Answer to the Question: What Is Enlightenment?' in Ted Humphrey (trans.), *Perpetual Peace and Other Essays*, Indianapolis: Hackett Publishing, p. 41. David Owen traces of a lineage of post-Kantian philosophical reflection concerning maturity through the work of Nietzsche, Weber, and Foucault in his 1994, *Maturity and Modernity: Nietzsche, Weber, Foucault and the Ambivalence of Reason*, London: Routledge. The question of maturity for these thinkers, he writes, concerns 'the relationship between the possibility of autonomy in modern culture and the realisation of this possibility' (Ibid.: 216).

Western colonialism shared has therefore depended upon an understanding of history itself as a general course of progress towards perfection.[2] Wherever exercised, that is, the association of modernity with maturity has relied upon an image of history as a universal trajectory of gradual transcendence.

In a series of lectures delivered in 2000, Ranajit Guha explored the limits of this image of universal history as 'World-history' in the sense elaborated by Hegel, that is, history as the actualization of a universal reason or 'spirit'.[3] Guha calls attention to the providential quality of this World-history: its freedom from arbitrariness, chance, or contingency. Therefore, while the actualization of spirit may appear analogous to the realization of the potential borne by a seed or germ, Guha emphasizes that history for Hegel represents a different order or principle of development than that of nature. In his *Lectures on the Philosophy of World History*, Hegel had distinguished the cyclical quality of natural change—'in nature there is nothing new under the sun,'[4] he wrote—from the linear and progressive production of newer and higher forms in the world of the spirit, the properly historical

development of these forms mediated by a struggle for self-consciousness. Hegel invests this structural distinction with a more concrete reality, Guha observes, through an elaboration of historical stages. Stages of 'World-history' may be distinguished from 'Prehistory' by their evident lack of 'immersion in nature' and the degree to which they affirm freedom—conditions attested by the empirical emergence of states. From this vantage point, the Orient, in particular, appears trapped in a state of 'spiritual infancy', with China and India excluded from World-history because 'they have not matured fully into statehood'.[5] An apparent absence of maturity in the form of self-conscious freedom, Guha argues, ultimately devolves into philosophical ground for 'right of conquest'.[6]

Guha probes the limit of such history by seeking to approach it and to think it from both sides: both from within and beyond the contours of its universality. Calling upon historiography to rid itself of its 'statist blinkers', Guha draws attention to 'the past as a story of man's being in the everyday world'.[7] Guha identifies this everyday life of the past in the present 'historicality', and he finds evidence of its presence in diverse vernacular traditions. In particular, he suggests, we may find such a quality at work in the reflections of Tagore on the childhood history of his own poetic impulse, which dwell upon unanticipated incidents such as the glimpse of dew in a coconut grove at sunrise, the sight of a gathering mass of

---

[2] 'Progress' itself became a singular and collective term in the eighteenth century, Reinhart Koselleck has observed: a name for the universal horizon of possibility towards which all humanity may develop under the right conditions. See Reinhart Koselleck, 2002, '"Progress" and "Decline": An Appendix to the History of Two Concepts', in *The Practice of Conceptual History: Timing History, Spacing Concepts*, Stanford: Stanford University Press, pp. 218–35.

[3] See especially, Ranajit Guha, 2002, 'The Prose of History, or the Invention of World-History', in *History at the Limit of World-History*, New York: Columbia University Press, pp. 24–47.

[4] Guha, 'The Prose of History', p. 33.

[5] Guha, *History at the Limit of World-History*, pp. 36, 39.

[6] Ibid., p. 42.

[7] Ibid., p. 6.

dark blue clouds, and the image of a cow licking the body of a donkey. Engaging such encounters with a world of inhabited nature, Guha implies, may lead us 'to look afresh at life in order to recuperate the historicality of what is humble and habitual'.[8] They do so by attesting to 'the incipience of sheer possibility', to 'a tendency that does not know where it is going'.[9]

Guha is concerned here with the relation between such ordinary events in a world of experience and the historical maturation of Tagore's being as a poet. I would argue, however, that we may take up this distinction between universal history and a more tangible and lived historicality as a way of posing broader questions concerning maturity and modernity as such. How to think about the prospect of maturity under modern conditions of life without referring this prospect back solely to either the inevitability of natural recurrence or to the necessity of a deliberate guidance? How may we restore to maturation the accident of encounter, while maintaining at the same time the commitment to process that maturation implies? Must we oppose the possibility of a mature autonomy to the determinations of natural character, or is there some way of finding ground for a different kind of freedom in the sheer incipience of natural life? How do we reconcile the collective horizons of deliberate intervention and intentional action at work in modern practices of development with the force and tendency of immanent processes of ongoing change? And through such developments, may we find a means

of conceiving postcolonial maturity neither as the attainment of a form already perfected elsewhere, nor as a failure of such realization?[10]

An organic language of growth and maturation suffuses the discourse of development. David Ludden has observed: 'The success of policies in promoting development can be gauged and steps prescribed to promote economic growth, as a biologist or doctor might prescribe a regimen to enhance the health and maturation of cells or people.'[11] This chapter seeks to invest such a language of natural and organic development—admittedly both pervasive and problematic—with a critical edge. I argue that the image of *ripening* in particular, may lend us a way of conceiving effectively the alterity of maturation under postcolonial conditions, insofar as we interpret this image against the grain of a conventional naturalization.[12] 'Ripening' brings the development both of subject and of nature—or, both of self and landscape—into a common frame. Ripening may be taken to invest both of these domains with an essential element of chance and contingency,

[8] Guha, *History at the Limit of World-History*, p. 94.
[9] Ibid., pp. 78–9.
[10] This last problem was posed with great acuity by Dipesh Chakrabarty, 1992, 'Postcoloniality and the Artifice of History: Who Speaks for "Indian" Pasts?' *Representations*, vol. 37, Winter, pp. 1–26.
[11] David Ludden, 1992, 'India's Development Regime', in Nicholas Dirks (ed.), *Colonialism and Culture*, Ann Arbor: University of Michigan Press, p. 247.
[12] On the political and conceptual stakes of conceiving of 'nature' other than as the ground for a 'naturalization' or essentialization of given conditions, see Donald Moore, Anand Pandian, and Jake Kosek, 2003, 'The Cultural Politics of Race and Nature: Terrains of Power and Practice', in D. Moore, J. Kosek, and A. Pandian (eds), *Race, Nature, and the Politics of Difference*, Durham: Duke University Press, pp. 1–70.

inasmuch as this process may be understood as a consequence of cultivating endeavours of diverse kinds. This language also highlights the convergence of multiple histories and practices of maturity in the postcolonial present, and the singular forms of life that may be pursued at these interstices. Put differently, rather than setting up a ready opposition between progress/development and ripening/maturity, I explore the pursuit of the latter in south India in order to underscore transformations in time and movements in life that insert into our horizons distinct articulations of modernity.

In what follows, I lend substance to these arguments by sketching three overlapping projects of maturation—their trajectories, limits, and displacements—in rural south India. Each of these finds expression on a single terrain of natural and cultural transformation: the agrarian environment of the Cumbum Valley in southern Tamil Nadu.[13] I found over the course of extensive fieldwork here that this was indeed a landscape of open incipience, one on which, as my interlocutors suggested, 'even the temple towers turn to garbage heaps' through the sheer force of natural contingency. What kind of maturity could such an earth sustain?

Citizens

A small building on the sprawling campus of the Madurai District Collectorate in southern Tamil Nadu hosts the office of the Special Deputy Collector (Kallar Reclamation): perhaps the only senior civil servant in independent India explicitly charged with the welfare and advancement of a single Hindu caste. The office is a legacy of the 1911 Criminal Tribes Act, and its enlistment in the colonial policing of Piramalai Kallar castefolk in hundreds of villages in the arid countryside west of Madurai. Blamed for habitual cattle theft, blackmail, and highway robbery by British officials throughout the nineteenth century, the entire caste was designated a 'criminal tribe' in 1918. For nearly thirty years, all Piramalai Kallar men were fingerprinted and prohibited from leaving their villages for any reason without written permission, radical measures supplemented by an array of experimental measures in 'Kallar Reclamation': compulsory schooling, grants of land, rural cooperatives and training centres, and occupational loans and other forms of rural credit. These diverse instruments were applied towards the realization of an official project in maturity articulated repeatedly in state annals from the closing years of the nineteenth century onwards: '*weaning* the criminal tribes in the Southern districts [of the Madras Presidency] from their predatory habits'.[14]

'[T]he best and probably the only way to reclaim the Kallars is by giving them property,' a senior Madras Presidency official insisted in 1910.[15] In the years that followed, many official observers described the Kallar predicament as an agrarian problem, taking the arid quality

---

[13] Many of the arguments that follow are developed more fully in Anand Pandian, 2010, *Crooked Stalks: Cultivating Virtue in South India*, New Delhi: Oxford University Press.

[14] Board of Land Revenue, Board's Proceedings (Misc.), No. 33, 6 January 1896, Tamil Nadu State Archives (hereafter TNSA); emphasis in original.

[15] Note by Cardew, 7 August 1910, G.O. No. 2683 Revenue, 15 August 1910, TNSA.

of their native landscape as a 'root cause' of criminality and proposing numerous agrarian strategies of moral pedagogy in response to this natural condition. In 1915, a 1,200-acre tract of government land at the head of the Cumbum Valley—surrounding the hamlet of Kullappa Gounden Patti—was identified as suitable for an agricultural reformatory settlement for Kallar households, to be managed by a missionary servant of the American Madura Mission. Revered E.P. Holton, who oversaw this endeavour between 1917 and 1918, portrayed himself as a 'Big Brother' working to lift his wards 'out of pettiness, laziness and the constant danger of slumping into mendicancy'.[16] He saw in agriculture the prospect of 'a better scale of living, for those who are willing to work for it, that is, development of character'.[17] The Department of Agriculture encouraged him to cultivate his own parcel of land as an object lesson for Kallar settlers and 'a model which the others can copy' on the lands they were granted themselves.[18]

Physical traces of the Kallar Voluntary Settlement on the landscape of the Cumbum Valley are by now very scarce. A virulent outbreak of malaria forced an early closure of the scheme in 1919; police officers were withdrawn from their local encampment, leaving behind the nineteen male Kallar convicts and their family members who had been brought to settle on the site. Retrospective narratives in Kullappa Gounden Patti suggest that almost none of the lands once assigned to these settlers now remain in the hands of their own descendents. 'They did not have the maturity to clear the land that they had been given,' one settler's grandson—a Head Constable himself at a local police station—told me one evening. 'Drinking, being rowdy…They just sowed some millets and took what came up.'

Within a few years, local officials doled out the lands once reserved for these Kallar settlers to hundreds of other Kallar and Dalit households inhabiting the region. Kallar Reclamation schools were established in Kullappa Gounden Patti and hundreds of other local villages, in accordance with a revamped state strategy for moral maturity adopted in the wake of the agricultural settlement's collapse. Kallar convicts had playfully named district jails as 'schools' in the early twentieth century, E.P. Holton reported in one of his letters on the 'Thief Caste' to his American friends.[19] Today, however, the compulsory schools of the colonial era are themselves recollected as 'jails' by the descendants of their Kallar wards, some of whom describe throwing rocks as children at their erstwhile teachers and running away to hide in the peanut fields.

The repeal of the Criminal Tribes Act in 1947 led towards the eventual suspension of all Kallar reform measures, except for the 265 government schools still administered under the aegis of Kallar Reclamation. These schools may be found now wherever

---

[16] E.P. Holton to Friends, 21 October 1918, and E.P. Holton to W.E. Strong, 6 July 1918, American Board of Commissioners (hereafter ABC) 16.1.9, v22, ABC for Foreign Missions Records, Houghton Library, Harvard University (HLH).

[17] E.P. and G.S. Holton to Friends, 29 May 1905, ABC 16.1.9, v17, HLH.

[18] Short note on the Kallar Settlement, G.O. No. 2092 Home (Judicial), 12 September 1918, TNSA.

[19] E.P. Holton to Friends, 21 October 1918, ABC 16.1.9, v22, HLH.

the Piramalai Kallar caste predominates, although they have since opened to students of all castes. 'We are cultivating children,' Headmaster Ramaraj suggested to me one afternoon in forceful English on the tidy grounds of the Kullappa Gounden Patti Kallar Elementary School campus. He described how the school aimed to make each student into a 'man of word' by teaching virtues such as honesty, propriety, duty, and sacrifice. When we first met, Ramaraj averred that education had indeed transformed the Kallars from thieving 'jungle brutes' into teachers and engineers. 'They have ripened,' he said. But on a later day, he leaned in close across his green steel desk for a quieter and more sardonic appraisal: 'They will never reform at all.'

'We shall make of the Kallar youth a fine race of stalwart, useful, well-behaved citizens who will live for and not on one another,' one local authority proudly stated in 1926 while the Governor of Madras laid the foundations for one of the Kallar boarding schools.[20] Partly due to the education provided by these schools, the Piramalai Kallar caste has won wide recognition as prosperous and respectable in recent decades. At the same time too, however, it is widely alleged that their newfound wealth and prominence depends upon their singular willingness to pursue 'crooked paths' such as smuggling, racketeering, and other illicit trades. In Kullappa Gounden Patti, such paths have crisscrossed most often the slopes of the state Reserve Forests surrounding the village, with the taking of hardwood timber,

blocks of sandalwood, poached animals, and even *ganja* cultivated on cleared forest tracts.

In the midst of fieldwork conducted in this village, I found that foresters had taken to camping out in the village to stage raids and intercept such goods smuggled down into the plains. One middle-aged forester likened the violence of such policing to the blows that parents and teachers would necessarily apply to children: 'A child raised without beating and a drumstick tree grown without pruning are of no use to society,' he insisted by recourse to a proverbial image of closely managed growth. We might find a contemporary echo here of the colonial project, but we must also recall that forest pilferage, like all such illicit paths, depends entirely upon state collusion. Crookedness, in other words, must itself be understood as the maturation of a cultivated disposition.

Teak

A strange sight presents itself with uncommon regularity throughout the arid uplands and hill perimeters of Tamil Nadu: row upon row of spindly and desiccated teak saplings stretching towards the horizon, each of their misshapen boles lending sustenance to no more than a handful of still-green leaves. One such withered carpet of teak spreads over 130 acres of land once reserved for the Kallar Voluntary Settlement in the early twentieth century, on an undulating tract lying between Kullappa Gounden Patti and the Reserve Forests of the High Wavy Mountains. A faded and battered sign planted against barbed wire fencing advertises in English the proprietors of this estate: 'V G P EVER GREEN PLANTATION (LTD)'. The

[20] G.O. No. 966 L, Public Works and Labor, 6 August 1926, TNSA.

enterprise defunct, a few watchmen once hired from the village now have the terrain to themselves. I intercepted them on a looping perambulation through the tract late one afternoon in 2002.

Passing between the spiny columns of teak, guard Rajendran casually tapped a bole here and there to knock off the crumbly red residue of termites. He pointed out saplings they had pruned themselves, and a few gaps in the barbed wire fencing that they had closed off with branches of thorn. 'Let the trees grow,' he said. It was their third visit to the plantation that day. 'The land is for us. The owners will not come. It belongs only to those who guard it, man,' Chinna Thevar declared before whistling a shrill warning to a gang of boys he had spotted in the distance. Concluding that the lads intended only to pilfer mangoes from in a nearby orchard, they returned their attention to me, and to my questions concerning the afterlife of an audacious and tragic venture that had transformed the landscape of this and hundreds of other Indian villages in the late twentieth century.

Glossy invitations to invest in corporate timber and fruit plantation schemes flooded the English and vernacular presses of India throughout the mid-1990s. In just a few years, thousands of companies popped up to capture as much as $2 billion in investment capital from the savings of hundreds of thousands of individual households, scattered throughout urban India and beyond.[21] Companies used these funds to acquire

massive expanses of rural land, typically upland tracts close to the margin of hills and forests: dry, fallow, and cheap on the market. Print advertisements bore detailed tables and testimonials, promising to potential investors both spectacular rates of return and the certainty of familial advancement through the scientific management of natural bounty. For example, one such testimonial for Golden Forests (India) Limited suggested, 'INVEST WITH AN ORGANISATION WHICH ENSURES "MATURITY"'. By 1999, these promises of natural, fiscal, and familial maturation had evaporated. Several newspaper exposés charged plantation ventures with widespread corruption and financial insolvency. The Securities and Exchange Board of India (SEBI) intervened by freezing the assets of many companies and banning them from soliciting new deposits without a legitimate credit rating. Advertisements disappeared, and countless offices shut their doors to hapless investors. The 'plantation bubble' had burst.[22]

VGP Evergreen Plantations was only one of these ventures. Initiated in 1994 under the aegis of Chennai retail magnate, V.G. Panneerdas, the enterprise persuaded 8,000 city dwellers to purchase small plots on one of their four teak plantations, newly established on several tracts in rural Tamil Nadu, including this plantation on the outskirts of Kullappa Gounden Patti. VGP advertisements represented arboreal growth as a secure and soaring fount of value, binding boles, money, and children together

---

[21] See George Mathew, 1998, 'Lost in the Forest of Deception', *Indian Express*, 16 February. These companies capitalized on booming export and domestic markets for fruit, government incentives for horticulture and wasteland development, and an

ongoing public discourse on deforestation that lent trees the solid assurance of soaring value.

[22] *Indian Express*, 1999, 'Plantation Bubble', 29 January.

in a common lattice of organic maturation. A 1995 Tamil notice published in *India Today*, for example, featured a bespectacled young man in a striped polo T-shirt, smiling at the stethoscope-laden infant he held up in his arms. 'To make your dear daughter a great doctor in the future, think and act right now,' advised the caption. Below the picture was a table promising the transformation of Rs 15,500 into Rs 600,000 over the span of twenty years.[23] The investment was scheduled to mature at the precise juncture when a child's future would need to be secured with the greatest educational or marital expense. Sketched below the projective table was the geometric growth that would underwrite these developments: the outlines of three teak trees, the apex of their canopies lending three points to an imaginary straight line headed up and out at 30 degrees (see Figure 9.1).

'Only if you have belief in future can you come up in life,' Evergreen Plantations Senior Manager Padmanabhan suggested one morning at the enterprise's headquarters in Chennai, describing how its owner himself 'came up from a downtrodden level'. Padmanabhan insisted upon the 'technical reliability' of the plantation endeavour, identifying teak as a 'commercially valuable tree' that had been cultivated here with the 'latest agricultural technologies'. However, the retired dean of the Tamil Nadu Agricultural University that had been hired by VGP to guide such usage was far less sanguine about their plantations' prospects for timely maturation. While he could forecast the 'genetic potential expressed in

nature' as an experimental scientist, the actual growth of plantation trees depended upon the vagaries of field conditions, the vicissitudes of local crop management, and the overall marketing strategy of the company. 'We are only planting, planting and managing the trees,' Dean Arumugam told me: 'We do not know how they are selling to customers.' The SEBI had, in fact, prohibited VGP from canvassing further investments by 1999, and the company was forced to suspend its plantation developments and arrange to compensate its thousands of investors. In spite of promised transformations, 'the land is as it was, the village is as it was,' Arumugam said.

In the village of Kullappa Gounden Patti, a Tamil proverb sometimes articulated by elder men and women presents an interesting counterpoint to VGP's advertised images of both natural and personal development. *Maram murrināl vairam, manitan murrināl putti [buddhi]*, the saying goes: 'If a tree matures, heartwood; if a man matures, judgement'. The proverb likens the stability of a mature and hardened tree in the face of winds and storms to the steadiness of a mature human being's life of desire. Maturity is identified here with virtues such as restraint and deliberation, as they are exercised with respect to the body and its sensual desires. From this standpoint, the failure of the VGP plantation in the village uplands is imagined more as a matter of personal failing rather than as an instance of corporate deceit. 'Thieving lad,' the local VGP watchmen and others here said about the young company manager who had looked after the tract. They described how he had succumbed to the pleasures of brandy, expensive cigarettes, and prostitution,

---

[23] *India Today*, 1995, Tamil edition, 21 July–5 August.

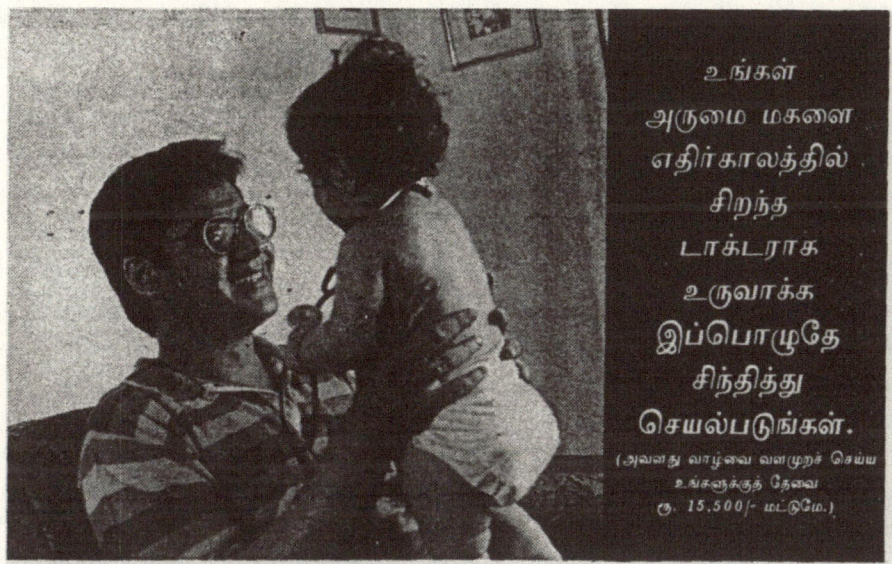

FIGURE 9.1 To Make Your Dear Daughter a Great Doctor in the Future, Think and Act Right Now

Source: India Today, 21 July–5 August 1995, Tamil Nadu.

selling off bits and pieces of the plantation infrastructure—stone posts, coils of barbed wire, gate valves, drip irrigation tubing, even titles to land—to meet his needs as his salary fell into arrears. Manager Suresh Kumar's body was discovered in the plantation guard shack one morning in 2002, hours after he had apparently taken his own life. Amidst the desiccated teak saplings, at least one tree close to the shack seemed to yield a strange fruit: a small bag of fried sweet dumplings, hanging from a sparse branch for several days until spooked herdswomen forced a watchman to cast them away.

Crops

For agrarian cultivators in the Cumbum Valley, there is no great difference between the maturing of crops and the maturing of children. One morning in the dry uplands just south of the VGP plantation, for instance, I stumbled upon cultivator Sekhar scattering seed beans over long red rows of freshly ploughed fields. He described how these plants would need rainwater to survive, in the same way that children needed milk. And the foreseen stages of their growth, he suggested, were akin to the stages of a woman's life: from a time of childhood to a time of maidenhood—puberty among girls is itself known colloquially as a 'flowering' in Tamil—and onwards into a time for fruiting and its harvest. Like most people in the region, he described such ripening into maturity as a process of coming into *pakkuvam*: a Tamil term derived from the Sanskrit *pakva*—to be cooked, ripened, refined, or perfected.[24] In the case of both

crops and children alike, maturity was a matter not only of a state to be attained but also of the ripeness or fitness of the conditions in which such maturity was sought. The maturation of children depended upon the maturity of their parents, a condition that could by no means be taken for granted in an environment of moral uncertainty. And the maturation of crops, by analogy again, depended upon the condition of the soil in which they were raised.

On another chilly morning expedition to these dry upland fields a few months later, for example, cultivator Vairam Pandian greeted me with the following words: 'A good pakkuvam'. He was speaking not of a crop—indeed, that morning he was supervising the movement of a tractor over three acres of fallow uncultivated land—but instead of the soil through which this machine was working. Pandian was pleased: one week after a hard rain, it was a good time to plough. To till the soil too soon after a rain was to struggle with thick blocks of clayey matter, but to wait too long on the other hand was to risk its untimely hardening. Crouching to pick up a small clump of soil and to show how it crumbled gently between his fingers, he explained how this softness of consistency would be obtained only if the soil was tilled at the correct time. The kind of ripeness or maturity at stake here

---

[24] The Vedas deploy the term *pak* figuratively to evoke a maturing, ripening, or perfecting of substance. In the ritual traditions of Vedic Brahmanism, the duty of the Brahmin is to 'cook' the world through sacrifice—Charles Malamoud, 1996, *Cooking the World: Ritual and Thought in Ancient India*, New Delhi: Oxford University Press. The argument holds as well for the selfhood of the sacrificer, he suggests: rituals of consecration, that is, subject the being of the sacrificer to a process of cooking through the alchemy of heat.

was therefore a question of both proper conduct and fortuitous timing: it concerned the 'disposition' to act appropriately, as well as the 'favours of nature' that would render such acts timely and effective. In this case, Pandian's sister-in-law had lent a portion of her salary the previous evening so that a tractor could be hired out at the right moment—'till it according to its pakkuvam,' she had told him. But in other instances, he explained, maturity was more clearly a matter of ripened inclination. Did a young girl have the pakkuvam to judge when to pluck ripening beans from a stalk? Or did a young man have the discipline to earn and provide for a family of his own?

As it happened, young men were collectively derided by their elders in the village as 'empty fellows' unable to distinguish idle pleasure from fruitful avocation. Therefore, when the Kullappa Gounden Patti 'Youth Club' decided to field candidates for the village panchayat elections in 2001, pakkuvam or maturity was a necessary topic of intense discussion among these young men. At a meeting called to canvass candidates for the upcoming contest, one of the leading youths in the organization evoked a proverbial image of immaturity to grapple with this problem. 'It is said that "A crop planted by young children will not reach the house",' Muthukumar reminded the others present, emphasizing a need for unwavering care rather than unreliable haste. These proverbial words, echoed by one other young man named Jegadisan that night, would have made some tangible sense to most of the youths attending the meeting: many worked as daily wage labourers in the grape orchards of the valley while their applications for salaried employment remained pending. And the advice would appear to have worked, as the Youth Club succeeded in winning two public offices in the elections that year, negotiating even for the post of village vice-president.

Muthukumar and Jegadisan—like most of the young men in the Youth Club meeting that evening, as well as the middle-aged cultivators, Vairam Pandian and Sekhar, mentioned earlier—belonged to the Piramalai Kallar caste, and one might identify in their common concern for maturity an echo of the colonial strategies imposed upon their predecessors. However, we cannot leap so easily here to conclude that we are faced with no more than an unanticipated reverberation of colonial moral pedagogy, however powerful that may have been. Their language of pakkuvam betrays a debt as well to south Indian religious traditions, and the ripeness of devotion they have elicited for centuries from pupils and devotees. Popular accounts of pakkuvam in the Cumbum Valley often dwell upon the possibility of an interior state of oneness: a steady and unwavering focus of the mind or heart upon a single object of attention, recollection, love, or struggle. Young Kallar men described, for example, their keenness for a romantic love that was mature and 'sincere' in its centring of thought, memory, desire, and sensual experience upon one locus of attention—one's own lover—rather than the sensory abandon of a more 'thievish' and meandering romantic indulgence. We may discern a similar concern at work even in the proverb voiced by Muthukumar at the Youth Club meeting that evening: the prospect of a harvest that would fail to ripen along a steady path home, compromised by the wavering attentions of its cultivator.

Although Tamil devotional literatures often rely upon the image of seed and fruit to sketch the trajectory of a ripening soul, these texts emphasize as well the necessary role of divine agency in returning to individuals the fruit of their deeds. In much the same way, cultivators and other rural citizens of the Cumbum Valley affirm the essential contingency of terrestrial ripening: devotion alone to agrarian endeavours does not suffice to ensure the realization of their ends. Farmers here routinely describe agriculture as a game of chance: subject to forces far beyond the toil of individual cultivators, and yielding as unpredictably as a lottery ticket, a dice game, or a round of cards. These analogies may be extended much more widely. In the raising of crops to maturity, as in the care of children, or the practice of devotion, or even the pursuit of election—this too a kind of 'agriculture', I was told—eventual returns of cultivating labour are a matter of inescapable accident and contingency. The firm convictions of colonial agrarian pedagogy notwithstanding, cultivators in the Cumbum Valley today find no guarantees that their work to ripen plants will ensure their own moral ripening as persons. The vicissitudes of organic development trouble any such faith in steady progress. People too may ripen out of time, like the vegetal stalks in which they find their doubles: some too early to yield any good, others too late for redemption.[25]

Earth

This chapter on modern south India has sketched three scenes, perhaps even parables, of maturity: its prospects and limits, its histories and afterlives, its unpredictability and openness when conceived and exercised as an organic course of transformation. These scenes have each presented distinctive faces and concerns, but they have overlapped as well, with respect to their themes and trajectories as well as with regard to their material terrain of cultivation, maturation, and development. Taken together, they are intended as means of rendering and sustaining an image of maturity as a kind of ripening. This image is one, I have suggested, that brings the potential development of both subject and nature into a common frame, rather than taking the maturation of one to entail a necessary transcendence of the other. We have also found a reminder, in these varied instances of ripeness both anticipated and confounded, of the inescapable contingency of maturation as a process of development, its inextricability from situations of encounter, accident, and chance. Evidence of maturity or its absence call for neither recognition of attainment nor condemnation of failure. Instead, these sketches of diverse and often unexpected outcomes are meant to convey the essential plurality of the modern subject under postcolonial conditions: its open constitution at the interstices of rival horizons of potential improvement, development, or transformation.

With each of these three instances, furthermore, I have confronted a teleological process of cultivation—a campaign of moral uplift, a project in financial gain, an endeavour to till the soil—with a Tamil proverb concerning maturation and the conditions of its realization. These proverbial images of pruned trees and beaten children,

[25] These arguments are further developed in the third and fourth chapters of my book, *Crooked Stalks*.

of ripening heartwood and maturing judgement, of immature cultivators and crops that fail to come home, may each be seen as assertions of natural truth: of turning to the permanence of nature in order to insist upon the firmness of certain kinds of cultural claims. I want to suggest, however, that each of these proverbs may be taken to bear their own historicality, their own openness to mediating a possible maturity. 'A proverb,' Walter Benjamin has written, 'is a ruin which stands on the site of an old story and in which a moral twines about a gesture like ivy around a wall'.[26] The image of nature cloaking this argument is meant to remind us that such utterances arise from traditions of storytelling founded upon the living authority of counsel.[27] Counsel, Benjamin suggests, 'is less an answer to a question than a proposal concerning the continuation of a story which is in the process of unfolding'.[28] For Benjamin, these stories are matters not just of folk or fairy tales but of experience as such, experience taken as a process of unfolding. In this sense, the proverbs to which I have turned may themselves be taken to affirm the historicality of the subject of maturity. They make possible, that is, arguments about incipience.

The openness of the incipient forms of maturation that I have described here may appear to rob us of any ground for faith in their eventual realization. But we must remember that for the rural citizens of the Cumbum Valley, the earth as ground is itself always ripening. Maturation does not simply happen to transpire upon its face, but is the very principle that yields its depths and surfaces. Diamonds ripen in the earth. Stone itself ripens. And the soil fails to burgeon forth overwhelmingly only because cultivators cut away its *sakti*, strength, or force through the crops they harvest from it. There are paths to be found among the forms of ripening that the earth allows. Some fail to flourish and they disappear—their lineages are said by their peers to have gone *tarisu* or 'fallow'. Many others leave this milieu to seek their prospects elsewhere, finding that to be a cultivator at this present moment is to be nothing more than a *patti kāttān*, a vestigial rustic or savage. But there are others still who remain and become cultivators, gambling with the earth for a possible fruit. This chapter is composed with the conviction that their experience— however shaken by the trials of the present— bears lessons for the modernity that we share. We may even find a certain resonance with these lessons on more familiar grounds. As Henri Bergson wrote in the early twentieth century, 'to exist is to change, to change is to mature, and to mature is to create oneself endlessly'.[29]

[26] Walter Benjamin, 2002, 'The Storyteller: Observations on the Works of Nikolai Leskov', in Howard Eiland and Michael W. Jennings (eds), *Walter Benjamin: Selected Writings, Volume 3, 1935–1938*, Cambridge: Harvard University Press, p. 162.

[27] On the place of proverbs and other elements of counsel in the moral traditions of south India, see Anand Pandian, 2008, 'Tradition in Fragments: Inherited Forms and Fractures in the Ethics of South India', *American Ethnologist*, vol. 35, no. 3, pp. 466–80.

[28] Benjamin, 'The Storyteller', pp. 145–6.

[29] Henri Bergson, 2005, *Creative Evolution*, New York: Cosimo Classics, p. 10. Bergson works here to extend the potential for open-ended change beyond the domain of conscious beings.

10

Modern Senses
Of Selves, Citizens, Nationals, and Subjects

Véronique Bénéï[†]

Have 'we' ever been modern? What is modernity? When and where does it begin? What kind of 'promise of future' does it hold for us? Who is modern, who isn't? These and many more questions about the ever elusive notion have nourished endless debates in recent years. The literature on the subject, the conferences held, courses taught, and theses written on related topics across the continents have reached astronomical proportions. If anything, our *relation* to the notion has pervasively come to define our epoch. Whether deemed postmodern or even 'postpostmodern', the latter is indelibly marked by a discourse about this '*rapport au temps qui est celui d'une promesse de futur*'.[1] As if modernity, too, were a foreign country... not only do they do things differently there, but it is forever out of reach.

Anthropology and Modernity

Historians have made no qualms about the fact that modernity is a largely fuzzy concept, difficult to situate both in its theoretical, spatial, and temporal dimensions. Even scholars laying greater emphasis on the role of state formation in the advent of a so-called 'modern period' continue to significantly disagree upon its datation: when, let alone

† Elements of this chapter are borrowed from the Introduction and the Conclusion to my 2009 book, *Schooling India: Hindus, Muslims, and the Forging of Citizens*, New Delhi, Permanent Black.

[1] Jean–François Lyotard, 1997, *Signé Malraux*, Conversation with Alain Gérard, available at http://www.grep-mp.org/conferences/Parcours-15-16/Malraux.htm (Last accessed on 22 May 2010).

where, does the state begin is still a moot point. The situation appears somewhat easier for those scholars privileging other factors of modernity, such as the decline of religion and the coming about of secularism. Regardless of this datational and definitional predicament, however, it is now an accepted fact that the concept of 'modernity' is not the sole prerogative of 'the West'. In many other societies and cultures, and at other points in time than those European ones arbitrarily universalized, there have been major moments of rupture that ushered in new modes—whether social, artistic, literary, or political—of producing, understanding, categorizing, and using knowledge.[2]

All of these new modes might be termed 'modern' by contrast to what preceded in the local *longue durée*. The difficulty, of course, is always to ensure that the historical lens adopted to envision the longue durée is, as it were, of a long enough scope. The colonial encounter and the advent of colonial modernity in South Asia is a case in point. On the one hand, one may see in this encounter a radical break from existing structures of social and political governance. The kind of state effects described by Foucault with reference to Europe have also been at play since the nineteenth century in India, albeit in a less totalistic form for historical reasons related to the limited expanse of the British Raj, a fact often left in oblivion in discussions of matters colonial in India.[3] On the other hand, some schemas,

especially linguistic and cultural, appear to have been redeployed through to the present day in postcolonial India, contributing to the shaping of contemporary political forms of modernity.[4] I will return to this. For the time being, I want to turn my attention to anthropologists' tardy engagement with the notion of modernity.[5]

Any anthropological reflection on 'modernity' must obviously ponder the relevance of this concept to the discipline's practitioners. At first sight, as was once pointed out,[6] the notion suggests a rather out-of-place and untenable absolutism in its apprehension of social change in any given society: the term implicitly furthers a dichotomy between 'traditional', or 'ancient', and 'modern', a dichotomy long punctured by the works spawned by Eric Hobsbawm and Terence Ranger's pioneering volume on

[2] See, for instance, Shmuel N. Eisenstadt, 2000, 'Multiple Modernities', *Daedalus*, Special issue, vol. 129, no. 1, pp. 1–29.
[3] Ian Copland, 1990, *The Burden of Empire: Perspectives on Imperialism and Colonialism*, Oxford: Oxford University Press.

[4] On language, see Sheldon Pollock, 2006 [2007], *The Language of the Gods in the World of Men: Sanskrit, Culture, and Power in Premodern India*, Berkeley and Delhi: University of California Press and Permanent Black.
[5] See Véronique Bénéï, 2009, *Schooling India: Hindus, Muslims, and the Forging of Citizens*, New Delhi, Permanent Black, for a fully-fledged discussion of this point, and C.J. Fuller and Véronique Bénéï (eds), 2009 [2001], *The Everyday State and Society in Modern India*, Delhi/London: Social Science Press/Hurst & Co., and Thomas Hansen and Finn Stepputat (eds), 2001, *States of Imagination: Ethnographic Explorations of the Postcolonial State*, Durham, NC: Duke University Press, for a discussion of the nation-state more specifically, and Joan Vincent, 1990, *Anthropology and Politics: Visions, Traditions and Trends*, Tucson: University of Arizona Press, for a discussion of the relationship of anthropology to the political more generally.
[6] Jonathan Spencer, 1996, 'Modernism, Modernity and Modernization', in Alan Barnard and Jonathan Spencer (eds), *Encyclopedia of Social and Cultural Anthropology*, London: Routledge, pp. 376–9.

the 'invention of tradition' some decades ago.[7] Tradition did not belong to the past. Rather, it was the fabric of the present, clothing many a nationalist project of modernity. Anthropologists and historians, then, appeared best equipped to explore and interrogate the relative and strategic value of such a concept. Yet, more often than not, they have seemed content to either reject, at first, or, more recently, embrace the notion wholeheartedly. That reflection on being modern has, in many instances, been intricately tied in with colonial processes may account for the initial disciplinary blindness, and conversely, the ulterior lack of critical distance towards the concept.

Let me explain. The avatars of (political) modernity in the form of the postcolonial nation-state were not considered 'authentic' objects of study until recently.[8] As is well known, anthropologists did not particularly shine through critical appraisal of the colonial situation until, precisely, the latter had become a thing of the past, or rather, 'post'. Meanwhile, historians, especially of South Asia, were already busy at work. Of course, there are many factors as to the initial disdain shown towards 'modernity' among anthropologists, and it is not the purpose here to retrace an intellectual history of the notion's coming to prominence among them. Arjun Appadurai's *Modernity at Large* certainly marked a watershed in the discipline and served to legitimize—whether as a reference

point or one of departure—discussion of a concept heretofore left to the other social sciences.[9] Today, it has been enjoying a currency unthinkable even ten years ago. Anthropologists have now become eager to register and document their informants' claims to 'being modern'; as if, perhaps, engaged in a collective, unconscious redeeming endeavour for earlier generations' blindness to the realities of colonialism. Regardless of any ethical justification, however, this has turned many anthropologists into unwitting mouthpieces of a discourse envisaging modernity as an unquestionable, tangible, palpable reality 'out there' in lieu of a relative ideological, historical, social, and cultural construct. Thus, the heuristic potential held by an anthropological appraisal of the notion of modernity has been lost on most of us.

Whether in anthropology or in the other social and political sciences, there remain many problematic assumptions and entailments in the notion of modernity as it is addressed today. Despite increased visibility of a critique of the Enlightenment and an emphasis placed on the very plurality of 'modernities', the Euro-American-centred narrative is still largely hegemonic. As is well known, according to this narrative, modernity is supposed to have originated in Europe and North America,[10] gradually reaching other parts of the world. Its avatars

[7] Eric Hobsbawm and Terence Ranger (eds), 1983, *The Invention of Tradition*, Cambridge: Cambridge University Press.

[8] For a full-fledged discussion of this point, see Bénéï, *Schooling India*.

[9] Arjun Appadurai, 1996, *Modernity at Large: Cultural Dimensions of Globalization*, Minneapolis: University of Minnesota Press.

[10] Japanese modernity, as has been well-documented, is as old as its European counterpart.

are known to have included nationalism[11] and democracy, as well as, more recently, globalization.[12] In political terms, modernity is often meant to refer to a concept cluster related to new modes of governance (for instance, Foucault's notion of governmentality), in which state formation nevertheless continues to play a predominant part. This is accompanied by the emergence of a civil society composed of social and political actors progressively freed from the shackles of so-called tradition—read ethnic, religious, and other kinds of inappropriate particularistic or communitarian ties—and who are henceforth expected to act as rational individuals.

Linked to these social and political developments, new modes of relations of production were brought about by a capitalist economy backed by industrialization processes dating back to the early eighteenth century. These processes have provided an explanatory model for the most empiricist and deterministic among us, with the idea that material, tangible, technological developments were bound to have particular impacts on social relations. The Marxist argument, today, reverberates in the one often made about globalization. 'Technological globalization', in particular, is in some ways the logical extension of industrialization processes which started two centuries earlier. So that, thanks to later technological redeployments, modernity—read 'Euro-North American modernity'—has

been made available to the Uygur peasant as much as to the Eskimo fisherman, the Kung cattle herder, the Andean nomad, the Italian entrepreneur, or the Japanese businessman, as suggested a few years ago by a famous advertisement for an internet service provider in Europe. That such a trope has been popularized to the point of becoming common sense is in itself interesting and certainly calls for more anthropological attention. For the moment, however, I wish to discuss some theoretical and disciplinary entailments of the notion of 'modernity', whether understood in the singular or in the plural.

What interests me more particularly is threefold. First, the implicit notion associated with modernity—especially since the Enlightenment period—of a unified self, which has come under heavy attack in postmodern times. Second, the rediscovery by anthropologists of topics political, not least of all state-related ones, has signified a new interest in the production of citizenship and a realization that educational matters no longer can be appraised through lifecycle events and initiation rituals only, but also through state institutions such as schooling. This has opened up spaces for anthropological reflection on the very site of school.[13] Third, in such reflection

[11] Benedict Anderson, 1991, *Imagined Communities. Reflections on the Origin and Spread of Nationalism*, London: Verso.
[12] Roland Robertson, 1992, *Globalization: Social Theory and Global Culture*, London: Sage Publications.

[13] For example, see the works of Kathleen Hall, 2002, *Lives in Translation: Sikh Youth as British Citizens*, Philadelphia: University of Pennsylvania Press; Gillian Evans, 2006, *Educational Failure and Working Class White Children in Britain*, London: Palgrave; Aurolyn Luykx, 1999, *The Citizen Factory: Schooling and Cultural Production in Bolivia*, New York: State University of New York Press; Amy Stambach, 2000, *Lessons from Mount Kilimanjaro: Schooling, Community, and Gender in East Africa*, New York: Routledge;

as well as in other discussions about the avatars of political modernity, the sensory dimension associated with the notion has often been more implicit than not, despite exerting substantial influence on current epistemologies of knowledge. Here, I want to make this sensory dimension explicit and show the benefits brought about by its exploration.

Fragmented Selves, Impossible Identities, and Nationalism

Much anthropological production of the past decades has occurred, willy-nilly, under the sun of 'deconstruction'. Thus have the major concepts used in the discipline been subjected to rightful decomposition, dissection, critique, and so forth. In the wake of the deconstructionist turn, the

and Padma M. Sarangapani, 2003, *Constructing School Knowledge: An Ethnography of Learning in an Indian Village*, New Delhi: Sage Publications. For a few pioneering, earlier examples, see Timothy J. Scrase, 1993, *Image, Ideology, and Inequality: Cultural Domination, Hegemony, and Schooling in India*, New Delhi: Sage Publications; Shirley Brice Heath, 1983, *Ways with Words. Language, Life, and Work in Communities and Classrooms*, Cambridge: Cambridge University Press; Robert W. Connell, 1975 [1971], *The Child's Construction of Politics*, Melbourne, Melbourne University Press; Paul Willis, 1977 [1981], *Learning to Labour: How Working Class Kids Get Working Class Jobs*, Farnborough, Hants: Saxon House and New York: Columbia University Press; George D. Spindler (ed.), 1955, *Education and Anthropology*, Palo Alto: Stanford University Press; Spindler (ed.), 1982, *Doing the Ethnography of Schooling: Educational Anthropology in Action*, New York: Holt, Rinehart & Winston; and George D. Spindler and Louise Spindler, 2000, *Fifty Years of Anthropology and Education 1950–2000. A Spindler Anthology*, London and Mahwah, NJ: Lawrence Erlbaum Associates; though the latter were considered more as sociologist and educationalists, respectively.

critique of an Enlightened, rational subject supposedly characterizing all projects of Euro-American—and, by diffusionist implication (see the earlier discussion), any other—political modernity has occupied centre stage. A resulting emphasis has been that placed upon both the importance of the self at the heart of any collective project *and* the irrefragable atomization of individuals. Who would deny, nay, who would dare question today the fragmentary character of all projects of socialization, be they national or else? Likewise, who would dispute the fragmentary nature of the very self? The postcolonial, postmodern subject has become a kaleidoscope ever refracting in the myriad of fleeting identity positionings s/he alternatively occupies in the world. To be sure, such a psychedelic vision served a welcome purpose over the past decades. It also remains an important safeguard for any study of socialization within the context of state processes, against attempts that would still want to see in 'The State' the monolithic beginning and end of all such projects.

Yet, such constant warning against the theoretical perils of homogeneity and full-fledged identities has brought about limitations in, precisely, reckoning with the latter's—even though fleeting—empirical materializations. Pierre Clastres's *Society against the State* may have contributed much to this critical scepticism by drawing attention to the pitfalls of state attempts at producing oneness and unity.[14] Today, it is as if the lessons learnt from Clastres's work had translated into theoretical abhorrence towards empirical oneness. I am, of course,

[14] Pierre Clastres, 1987, *Society against the State: Essays in Political Anthropology*, New York: Zone Books.

not arguing for a return to antiquated notions of the person or of culture as bounded, immutable wholes, if these ever existed.[15] But, I contend we should duly acknowledge that, despite identities being always impossible and in constant flux, there are collective projects around which identifications may revolve and, at times, crystallize rather powerfully. Granted, people do not necessarily unite under the same banner with the same understandings of what they are uniting for—or, as the case may be, against. Yet, there has to be some measure of common ground for even the possibility of coming together to be conceived at all. This is particularly obvious in the case of national(ist) projects of self-formation.

Social actors may ascribe different meanings to their senses of belonging to a nation, they may understand their parts as citizens differently, and have diverging aspirations, as I demonstrate in the case of western India at the turn of the twentieth century.[16] Yet, theoretical emphasis on the fluidity of social actors' categories and their multipositioning can exhaust neither the conceptual exploration of processes of self and institutional formation, nor their experientiality on the ground, least of all in relation to the nation-state and its citizens. For, whether openly acknowledged by anthropologists or not, what often emerges as importantly from their ethnographic narratives is a sense of a common ground uniting social actors, for instance in the form of a seemingly permanent or fleeting veneration for the cultural or historical heritage of their glorious national past', or in that of its total rejection. That this much may be commonly achieved as partial crystallization of identities, requires both acknowledging and exploration in its own right. It also invites further comparative work between the formal institutions of nation-states—whether in South Asia, 'the West', or elsewhere—not least of all on schooling. Indeed, one of the most potent state institutions penetrating everyday life and operating as both a prerequisite for its stability and a powerful means of national integration has been that of formal education.

Of Educated Subjects and Anthropologists: Rediscovering the Modern

For a long time, political anthropology neglected formal education as a process of social control and reproduction. Meanwhile, the topic was of interest to political scientists, sociologists, economists, and developmental planners.[17] They placed emphasis on formal education's 'modern' materialization, whether by examining overall institutionalized systems of knowledge production and transmission, or focusing on the minutiae of

[15] For an overview of the anthropological literature on 'issues of the "individual" and concepts of the "person"' in South Asia, see Saurabh Dube, 2004, *Stitches on Time: Colonial Textures and Postcolonial Tangles*, Durham: Duke University Press, pp. 121–3.

[16] Bénéï, *Schooling India*; see also, Samuel Kaplan, 2006, *The Pedagogical State: Education and the Politics of National Culture in Post-1980 Turkey*, Stanford: Stanford University Press, on post-1990s Turkey.

[17] For a pioneering example with specific reference to South Asia, see the work of political sociologists by Lloyd I. Rudolph and Susanne H. Rudolph (eds), 1972, *Education and Politics in India: Studies in Organization, Society, and Policy*, Cambridge, MA: Harvard University Press.

curricula and schooling processes supporting these systems. Sociologists working on schooling contributed to an understanding of social reproduction of certain groups (namely, the elite and the working class), and of processes of discrimination (social, racial, ethnic, and so on). By contrast, anthropology tended to relegate the field of education at its margins, confining it to departments and colleges of the same. The body of literature thus constituted, little affected the long tradition of anthropology in the (former) colonies. Generations of anthropologists, primarily interested in non-industrial societies, did not encounter mass educational systems. Even when they began to, their attraction towards 'traditional' areas of cultures—however constructed these were—remained stronger. This reflected in privileging the study of informal structures of knowledge transmission and socialization processes. Initiation and lifecycle rituals were among the most famous exemplars, illustrating and undergirding the discipline's implicit assumptions about pristine cultures and societies. Even as postcolonial societies soon after gaining independence started to build national systems of education, the then dominant regime of authenticity precluded envisaging postcolonial educational projects as truly authentic.

It was not until the postcolonial avatars of modernity, especially that of the nation-state, became crucial subjects of enquiry in the ever-expanding world order of nations that anthropologists in the 'mainstream' began turning their gaze onto these. Linked to a renewed interest in topics of political anthropology in the 1990s, the study of notions and practices of nationality and citizenship, in turn, generated a dynamic

field of anthropological studies of formal education. These studies give salience to the fact that children's socialization today is embedded in multiple culturally defined norms and rules from an early age, in which schooling has come to play a crucial part. Schooling has also, since its beginnings, been a highly contentious institutional process, often reflecting specific political projects, and often, too, subject to rivalling interpretations and appropriations within a given nation-state.

School has indeed been a privileged site for testing, even implementing projects—however utopian—of citizenship. Pedagogical missions lay at the very core of modernity projects both in 'Western' and 'non-Western' situations. Educational projects have, since the eighteenth and nineteenth centuries respectively, been sites for the expression of competing and conflicting visions of modernity. These were promoted by either colonial administrators and missionaries, or by indigenous educationalists and political and social leaders, at the level of public fora, newspapers, or other media participating in the construction of a public sphere. Governments, too, particularly envisaged pedagogical missions as crucial tools for safeguarding the viability of the state by producing 'responsible citizens'. Hence, the formal educational projects concocted in the nineteenth century by state officials and administrators, whether in Australia, with the establishment of school systems for the 'preparation of the young for their future responsibilities as citizens',[18] or in India, with the creation of separate schools for separate

[18] Stuart Macintyre, 1996, 'Citizenship and Education', in S. Rufus Davis (ed.), *Citizenship in*

communities in order to secure the latter's allegiance to the colonial state.[19] Today, this type of formal education often connotes the naturalization of a civil identification deemed the mark of an indisputable 'modernity'.

The terms of such 'modernity' have also received close scrutiny, thus furthering revision of old assumptions. Such is the case of the Gellnerian framework premised on a universalist sociological model of modernization, which is still so oft-encountered at the levels of state apparatuses and international aid agencies.[20] As is well known, this framework associates modernization with industrialization and secular nationalism: industrial division of labour is required, as well as a shared culture of nationalism that would hold together a society rendered atomized by the very processes associated with industrialization. This homogenous culture is aimed at being produced through schooling, especially at the primary level. In keeping with such a theoretical premise, all nation-states, whether 'older' or 'newer', have developed and implemented policies and programmes of 'universalisation of elementary education' to varying extents.[21] Not only is this framework problematic in view of its ethnocentrism precluding any alternative model of modernity, it also fails to register ordinary social agency. Analysing citizenship and education (schooling in particular) as state-centred strategies of social control and state-led projects serving the hierarchical structures of social reproduction[22] and of capitalist inequality does not do justice to the crucial role played by ordinary citizens. Indeed, if citizenship comprises the modern nation-state's range of attempts to define and produce 'ideal, loyal and dutiful citizens', no less does it also comprehend social actors' negotiated responses to these.[23] The view that states manufacture identities and citizenship at will[24] is, at best, too monolithic: it obfuscates social actors' intervention in the public sphere at different levels of mediation—whether state institutions, voluntary organizations, or even communalist outfits. How, then, can we critically provide alternative frameworks for envisaging the production of citizenship not only as a state project particularly located in key institutions and organizations for promoting the rights and responsibilities of citizenship,[25] but also as a site of citizens' agency? The answer lies in exploring and

Australia. Democracy, Law and Society, Melbourne: Constitutional Centenary Foundation, p. 229.

[19] Laura Bear, 2005, 'School Stories and Internal Frontiers: Tracing the Domestic Life of Anglo-Indian Citizens', in Véronique Bénéï (ed.), *Manufacturing Citizenship: Education and Nationalism in Europe, South Asia, and China*, London and New York: Routledge, pp. 236–61.

[20] Ernest Gellner, 1983, *Nations and Nationalism*, Ithaca, NY: Cornell University Press.

[21] Lê Thành Khôi, 2001, *Éducation et civilisations: Genèse du monde contemporain*, Paris: Bruno Leprince, UNESCO/Horizons du Monde.

[22] Pierre Bourdieu and Jean-Claude Passeron, 1977 [1970], *Reproduction in Education, Society and Culture*, London: Sage Publications.

[23] For a comparative illustration in South Asia, Europe, and China, see Véronique Bénéï (ed.), *Manufacturing Citizenship*.

[24] Pierre Bourdieu, 1999, 'Rethinking the State: Genesis and Structure of the Bureaucratic Field', in George Steinmetz (ed.), *State/Culture: The State-Formation after the Cultural Turn*, Durham, NC: Duke University Press, pp. 53–75.

[25] Thomas Humphrey Marshall, 1950, *Citizenship and Social Class and Other Essays*, Cambridge: Cambridge University Press.

registering the sensory modalities associated with modernity and the production of citizenship and nationality/nationalism.

Modernity, Nationalism, and the Senses

I referred earlier to the existence of major moments of epistemological rupture across cultures and societies. These new modes have often been linked to transformations occurring in sensory apparatuses, dispositions, and environments. Although these sensory apparatuses are often more implicitly assumed than explicitly discussed, they have nevertheless had considerable purchase on current epistemologies—anthropological ones in particular—with implications for the validity and definition of a notion of 'Indian modernity'. Senses and their registration are varyingly defined according to time, space, and culture. What sense(s) become(s) predominant and privileged over other(s) is a matter of cultural, social, historical, and of course, political circumstances. With respect to the Euro-American and South Asian contexts, the notion of sight seems of particular relevance, as discussed elsewhere.[26]

That sight became the primary mode of acquiring and producing knowledge during colonial times is evidenced by the ways in which both colonials and the indigenous population promoted—at times competing, at other times colluding—'performative displays' as well as 'visions', 'images', and 'visual practices' that progressively (re-) shaped a general episteme. Even newspapers bear direct relation to this process: not only

by virtue of Benedict Anderson's so-oft discussed argument of print capitalism (whereby a community of readers would imagine itself as a community of nationals),[27] but also because publishing was part of a process of making things *visible* in order to make them understandable. On another level, mapping and charting of all kinds, as Anderson and others have noted,[28] was also integral to cognitive operations of 'making visible'.

Sight thus acquired predominance in many appraisals of modernity, to the point of overshadowing all others in discussion thereof, at least in Europe.[29] In the colonial context, engagement with the sensory modalities entailed by the concept has largely remained peripheral, save a few exceptions. Walter Ong referred to the variegated ways in which sensory perceptions are privileged from one culture to another.[30] Earlier, Paul Stoller had developed a critique of Western epistemology attacking its major premise of visual and spatial cognition over any other, auditory one in particular.[31] Similarly, Ian

[26] Bénéï, *Schooling India*.

[27] Anderson, *Imagined Communities*.
[28] In particular, Bernard S. Cohn, 1987 [1967], 'The Census and Objectification in South Asia', in B. Cohn (ed.), *An Anthropologist among the Historians and Other Essays*, New Delhi: Oxford University Press, pp. 224–54.
[29] Bruno Latour, 1986. 'Visualization and Cognition: Thinking with Eyes and Hands', in H.A. Kuklick and E. Long (eds), *Knowledge and Society: Studies in the Sociology of Culture, Past and Present*, vol. 6, Greenwich, CT: JAI Press, pp. 1–40.
[30] Walter J. Ong, 1991, 'Shifting Sensorium', in David Howes (ed.), *The Varieties of Sensory Experience: A Sourcebook in the Anthropology of the Senses*, Toronto: University of Toronto Press, pp. 25–30.
[31] Paul Stoller, 1989, *The Taste of Ethnographic Things: The Senses in Anthropology*, Philadelphia:

Ritchie in his work on African sensorium suggestively argued that European cultures had gradually come to privilege sight over any other sense in the nineteenth century, both 'at home' and 'overseas'.[32]

This colonial sensory redeployment had bearing on the politics of British representation to the 'natives' where displays of imperial grandeur primarily involved the sense of sight, whether in Africa or in India. Thus, Andrew Apter has documented imperial assemblages as colonial state spectacles producing new epistemologies of knowledge (or at least, new redeployments in visual practices) in Africa,[33] while Mary Ann Steggles detailed the modalities of visualizing British imperialism in the Bombay Presidency in the nineteenth century.[34] The question is obviously complexified in the case of India, given the importance of the notion of sight prevalent in Indian society today. Derived from the Sanskrit root *drsh*, 'to see', the term *darshan* is often translated as either 'sight' (in the sense of an instance of seeing something or somebody) or the act of 'seeing'. The term may also refer to a 'vision', 'apparition', or even a 'glimpse'. One may ask whether the emphasis placed upon the term in Indian/Hindu culture today—both by popular common sense and by academics—might be a negotiated outcome of the colonial encounter standing as the closest equivalent to the sensory aspect central to a European conception of modernity.[35] Vindicating such a hypothesis is the comparative lack of understanding and tolerance demonstrated by the British in their fight against what they considered as an assault on other senses, especially the auditory one.[36] Even the fact that one of the commonest usages of darshan is a religious one today may fit with such a hypothesis. The term often refers to 'visions of the divine', of a god, a holy person, or even an artifact.[37] One can have darshan of a deity in a temple, or experience an inward awareness. Whether in popular post-independent India or Indianist anthropological common sense, the term's religious connotation is most salient. Yet, given the Orientalist vicissitudes, misunderstandings, and deceptive

University of Pennsylvania Press; and 1997, *Sensuous Scholarship*, Philadelphia: University of Pennsylvania Press.

[32] Ian Ritchie, 2000 [1993], 'African Theology and Social Change', PhD dissertation, Faculty of Religious Studies, McGill University. See 'Chapter 5: The Shifting Sensorium and African Orality', available at http://www3.sympatico.ca/ian.ritchie/ATSC.Chapter5.htm (Last accessed on 22 May 2010)

[33] Andrew Apter, 2002, 'On Imperial Spectacle: The Dialectics of Seeing in Colonial Nigeria', *Comparative Studies in Society and History*, vol. 44, no. 3, pp. 564–96.

[34] Mary Ann Steggles, 1997, 'Art and Politics: The Visualization of British Imperialism in the Bombay Presidency, 1800–1927', in Pauline Rohatgi, Pheroza Godrej, and Rahul Mehrotra (eds), *Bombay to Mumbai: Changing Perspectives*, Mumbai: Marg Publications, pp. 192–207. See also, among others, Chris Pinney, 2003, 'The Image in Indian Culture', in Veena Das (ed.), *The Oxford Companion Encyclopedia of Sociology and Social Anthropology*, New Delhi: Oxford University Press, pp. 625–53.

[35] Ibid.

[36] As suggested by Michael Roberts, 1990, 'Noise as Cultural Struggle: Tom-Tom Beating, the British and Communal Disturbances in Sri Lanka, 1880s–1930s', in Veena Das (ed.), *Mirrors of Violence: Communities, Riots and Survivors in South Asia*, New Delhi: Oxford University Press, pp. 240–85.

[37] Diana Eck, 1998, *Darshan: Seeing the Divine Image in India*, New York: Columbia University Press.

reappropriations that other concepts (such as caste[38]) have known in India, one may rightly wonder whether the contemporary religious emphasis is a relatively recent phenomenon stimulated by the colonial encounter. In other words, while simultaneously erecting darshan as the predominating sensory perception in the modern Indian reconfiguration of the senses—similar to the 'Euro-American' disposition—a spiritual and religious dimension may have been stressed congruently with an Orientalist mode of understanding 'the East', *in fine* providing a sensory illustration of the, 'but not quite' of, Bhabhaian mimicry.

Furthermore, such an emphasis on sight had repercussions on colonial as well as anthropological epistemes. Binary sets of categories, though the object of much discussion and disputation, largely informed modes of understanding 'otherness', from what resembled most closely Euro-American societies to what stood at its furthest. The point has repeatedly been made: what was being constructed by means of such dichotomous typologies was a ranking of 'other' societies according to their degree of commonality with European societies. Of particular interest here is the association of the notion of 'societies without writing' with a Weberian notion of stateless, more particularistic, irrational, and emotional political mode of governance. Its logical extension is that societies tending towards a more 'oral/aural' and 'auditory' mode have been implicitly deemed more irrational and emotional, and hence politically more

unstable. Even today, the analysis of 'ethnic conflict' and political violence (especially in African societies) is often tainted with such an assumption.[39] As if, too, the sense of hearing was the archaic remnant of an out-of-place, yet ever resurgent, primordialism that modernity should make sure to eradicate, or at the very least, keep in check. Yet, this obfuscates the fact that the sense of hearing is also integral to the constitution and lived experience of a 'modern' sensorium. Following Stoller's invitations, an anthropological perspective must acknowledge the importance and meaningfulness of other senses in a given 'modern' social, cultural, and political context.[40]

Here, it should be emphasized that the production of sensorium-s occurs jointly and *is not* specific to particular cognitive structures. Neither does a written/oral distinction nor a pre-literal/literal one successfully capture the pervasiveness and universality of the processes taking place right from infancy. In addition, as I demonstrate elsewhere,[41] the role of the state, especially through schooling, is crucial in the production and reshaping of sensorium-s. Indeed, national projects of self-formation largely rely upon the constitution of a 'national primary sensorium', as well as, in the case of regional states such

---

[38] See Nicholas B. Dirks, 2001, *Castes of Mind: Colonialism and the Making of Modern India*, Princeton: Princeton University Press.

[39] For a counter position, see Christopher C. Taylor, 2002, 'The Cultural Face of Terror in the Rwandan Genocide of 1994', in Alexander L. Hinton (ed.), *Annihilating Difference: The Anthropology of Genocide*, Berkeley: University of California Press, pp. 137–78.

[40] Stoller, *The Taste of Ethnographic Things; Sensuous Scholarship*.

[41] Bénéï, *Schooling India*.

as Maharashtra, that of a regional one. Characterizing the state of Maharashtra today is its pre-emptive take on the population's sensory world, a take putting at its service the sensorium developed from a recomposed musical tradition fusing devotional *abhanga*s, prayers, yoga, and physical education drills as well as martial rhythms. Such a recomposed tradition predicated upon existing sensory structures of feeling within regional society conversely both emblematizes and undergirds the regional state. It also articulates with the sensory transformations brought about by new technologies and industrialization in a variety of forms, from the sounds and fumes of cars, trucks, and tractors to the music belching out from loudspeakers outside temples, houses, theatres, and polling stations, and the visual redeployments of local patriotism and nationalism (flagged at the time of the war against Pakistan in Kargil). It is the recomposition of this sensorium that the state attempts to capture and which makes it so 'modern'.[42]

It should also be reiterated, however, that state attempts are only one side of the coin to the production of citizenship and nationality/nationalism. Citizens—including teachers in the very space of school—make seen, heard, and felt their negotiated responses to such attempts in the production of senses of regional and national belonging. They are social actors in the full sense of

the term, engaging with these projects through songs glorifying the Marathas, the independence struggle from the British, as well as other nationalist and postcolonial songs. Through these, the notion and lived experience of love for the mother-nation and its people is (re-)produced at school; not just on the occasion of annual gatherings and school competitions effecting a paroxystic conflation and telescoping of different historical moments (redefined in the process as foundational ones), but also in the daily conflation of different layers of sensory stimulations in the production of regional, national, and familial allegiance in ordinary school life. It goes without saying, of course, that such a notion and lived experience is a highly contested field among different communities.

The notion of sensorium thus elaborated has further heuristic potential for understanding the political and ethical implications borne by the emotional and linguistic structures of feeling daily (re-)produced in everyday life and the naturalization of senses of belonging effected in the process. Indeed, working with the notion helps bring into light the illusionary character of the 'public/private' dichotomy and the untenability of a distinction between the construction of social persons and that of interiorized selves.[43] Political modernity is often characterized by a sharp contrast between a public, democratic space, and

[42] See Benjamin's discussion by Scott J. Thompson, 2000, 'From "*Rausch*" to Rebellion: Walter Benjamin's *On Hashish* & the Aesthetic Dimensions of Prohibitionist Realism', *The Journal of Cognitive Liberties*, vol. 2, no. 1, pp. 21–42, available at www. wbenjamin.org/rausch.html (Last accessed on 8 March 2011).

[43] Jonas Frykman makes a similar point in his suggestive account of gymnastics as everyday lived production and sensory experience of modernity in Sweden in the 1930s. See Jonas Frykman, 1994, 'On the Move: The Struggle for the Body in Sweden in the 1930s', in Nadia Seremetakis (ed.), *The Senses Still*, Boulder, Colorado: Westview Press, pp. 63–85.

another, private one, the true realm of the authentic self. By contrast, the notion of sensorium helps us think through precisely the all-pervasive nature of all political and socialization processes. This, in turn, has implications for the formation of identities in light of the nature of a sensory-ridden democracy today.[44]

Classical analysis has it that identification takes place at three distinct levels, namely, the family; the professional, confessional and other institutions in which we might include schools, and the 'hegemonic' community, or nation. In the case of fascism, the first and third levels are usually flattened out. By contrast, I argue that this is not so only in the case of fascism. Rather, the three levels tend to coalesce in most projects of political modernity, whether frankly fascistic or not. Thus, the risk of fascism threatening most citizenries today, against which Etienne Balibar cautioned in his writings about the vicissitudes of identity as a gaze ('*identité*

comme regard')—a gaze through which the other becomes the demonized impossible co-resident[45]—is 'only' a matter of amplitude, rather than kind. In Maharashtra today, school, belonging to the second level of social organization, has become a very special *locus* both mediating and conflating the spaces of family and nation (of the first and third levels respectively). Rather than demonstrating that the state of Maharashtra is verging on fascism, this brings home the ideological perils inherent to any institutional, and particularly educational, modern nation-state project, especially when the powerful sensory resources it plays upon remain unacknowledged. In a sense, the fact that, rather than being analysed, the sensory resources upon which most aggressive and bellicose projects of national and self-formation have relied upon should have been taken for granted, may be the ultimate mark of 'our late modernity'.

[44] This is, of course, not to say that the senses have only come to acquire such importance in 'our late modernity'. For a remarkable and suggestive example of the importance of the senses in post-revolutionary France, see Sophie Wahnich, 2008, *La longue patience du peuple, 1792 naissance de la République*, Paris: Albin Michel. For a discussion of primary and secondary identities, see Étienne Balibar, 2005, 'Educating towards a European Citizenship: To Discipline or To Emancipate? Reflections from France', in Véronique Bénéï (ed.), *Manufacturing Citizenship: Education and Nationalism in Europe, South Asia, China*, London/New York: Routledge, pp. 37–56.

[45] Étienne Balibar, 1998, *Droit de cité*, La Tour d'Aigues: l'Aube, pp. 114–20.

11

The Intellectual's Hidden Body
Affect and Mood in Family Planning

Kalpana Ram

This chapter begins with an excerpt from an interview I conducted with a doctor in a large public hospital in the town of Chengalpattu, situated near metropolitan Chennai. Class and gender distance allow the doctor to speak, with prescriptive confidence, of planned fertility. However, it is not his own planned fertility of which he speaks. Nor is it the planned fertility of the male body in general. The body of fertility is exclusively projected onto women, and onto uneducated rural women in particular. This is not done through any overt reference—rather, the projection is implicit in the modalities of the technologies considered, and the assumptions about how seriously the 'woman in the body'[1] is to be

considered when this technology is 'inserted'.

Doctor: After the second child, we compulsorily insert a Copper T, or sterilize. We also have motivation by the nurses.

Q: Why is the diaphragm never used or suggested?

Doctor: The diaphragm is outdated.

Q: But there are also problems with the Copper T.

Doctor: Theoretically, there are no problems with the Copper T. The problems of back pain etc. have not been shown to be connected with insertion.

Q: How prepared are you to remove the Copper T if the woman is having problems?

Doctor: If the woman insists, we will remove it, but we will advise her, according to her medical history and family situation, as to what she should have instead. Copper T is best. If she wants oral pills, she can have them, but many

[1] Emily Martin, 1987, *The Woman in the Body: A Cultural Analysis of Reproduction*, Boston: Beacon Press.

forget to take pills. The Loop has problems of rejection, of allergy. These problems are not there with Copper T. Now the government has made Copper T compulsory after the second child. There is the human rights issue. But for the population in India, this is necessary.[2]

Over and above the finer details of the doctor's responses to my questions, what stands out is his absolute identification as a medical professional with broad directions of state policy, which is always being updated. This identification occurs at the expense of mere bodily experience. When the person who has the intrauterine device (IUD) inserted or a sterilization performed is a poor rural woman from surrounding villages, she has little hope that her pain or unease will count as sufficient reason to have it removed. Sterilization, the preferred alternative, is even more definitive. Once the woman has been 'motivated' into undergoing sterilization when the second child is born, the operation is irreversible. With the doctor, this perspective does not operate at the level of an explicit or systematized discourse. His inability to hear the voice of the poor woman is not because of any explicit preference on his part. What the doctor actually *says* is:

1. there are human rights issues, *but* for the population of India, compulsory insertion of an IUD is necessary after the second child;
2. there is 'motivation' by the nurse [for sterilization], *but* we compulsorily insert the IUD;
3. if the woman insists, we can remove the device, *but* it has been scientifically

shown that the problems women may experience are not related to the device ('Theoretically, there are no problems with the Copper T'); and
4. if the woman wants other methods, they are there, *but* the diaphragm is outdated, the Loop was full of problems, and the pill is too susceptible to lapses of memory.

Each of these propositions, as I have phrased it, oscillates between two kinds of considerations. On the one hand are human considerations, the woman's experiences, preferences, and choices; and on the other, considerations of the larger good (the nation) which can only be addressed by the rationality of planning, technology, and science. In each case, the second set of considerations far overwhelms the former. The distances of class and gender as well as the privileges separating metropolitan from rural people *build* on an equally fundamental gulf that is possibly less noticeable, that between subjectivity and the body. The body has been drained of agency—it figures only as the receptacle for IUDs or sterilization, its agency displayed at best by an equally mechanical reaction of 'rejection' or 'allergies'. Once body and consciousness have been separated in this manner, it is not so very difficult to conduct a second operation and relocate the consciousness that 'counts' in quite another body altogether. It is not the woman's experience of allergies, back pain, and rejections that count enough to make the doctor remove the device. Instead, the consciousness that 'counts' is that of the doctor, the bearer of science, who, above all, does not pose the risk of being out of alignment with current state policy.

[2] Interview with a doctor at public hospital, Chengalpattu, Tamil Nadu, 1996.

We must not forget that these formulations have been elicited in an interview situation by a university researcher's questions. They do not convey the everyday mode of the doctor's worldview, which is implicit in *action* rather than in statements. On my field trip to Tamil Nadu's villages near Chennai city in August 1996, while interviewing Dalit women on their experiences of puberty and maternity, I came across a woman who had had a Copper T inserted without her knowledge at a well-known government hospital in Madras. During her periods, she felt a protrusion and attempted to pull the obstacle, experiencing agonizing pain. She went to a different doctor who removed the remaining parts of the IUD but failed to inform her that this meant she could now become pregnant—as she soon did. She experienced an extremely difficult and painful pregnancy and delivery, since the uterus had barely healed from the previous laceration.

Doctors and nurses engaged in the actual dispensation and insertion of 'family planning' technology are not engaged in the business of providing systematized arguments, justifications, and theorizations. They characteristically *act* on certain assumptions, confident, as bearers of class authority and training, about their *right* to distance themselves from the voices and experiences of the women whose lives they intervene in. But their confidence also derives from an implicit reliance on the discursive work done by other kinds of intellectuals. And there is indeed a whole class of state intellectuals—demographers, economic planners, family planning experts, and even political scientists—who make it their full-time occupation to produce and

elaborate discourses that attempt to arrogate Reason on behalf of state policy. The very first Five Year Plan speaks with the voice of calm assurance, as if Reason has already been commandeered by those charting the course for a new independent India. Taking its place within the more far-reaching discourses of economics and bio-medicine, family planning adds a further elaboration to the process of applying the principles of rationality to the body itself, of coming to view the body as if it were like any other object in the world. The First Five Year Plan states its goals as follows: '(a) The reduction of the birth rate to the extent necessary to stabilise the population at a level consistent with the requirements of the national economy. (b) Family limitations or spacing of children is necessary and desirable in order to secure better health for the mother and better care and upbringing of children.'[3]

An extraordinary set of assumptions is set into motion here. The temporality of planning requires that ordinary people treat the temporality of the family just as the Five Year Plan conceptualizes the time of the nation: as empty homogeneous time, unresponsive to the particularity of any context, and measurable in the form of properly 'spaced' outputs (births) and inputs (cost of upkeep). Family planning discourse assumes it is possible to extend a purely economic subjectivity in order to gaze at the body, now denuded of all but biological powers, in abstract, rationalizing terms. For family planning to work, it is not enough for the mind to do the surveying,

[3] First Five Year Plan, cited in B.L. Raina, 1988, *Population Policy*, Delhi: B.R. Publishing Corporation, p. 10.

the ordering, and the choosing. It must also survey the body. The body, quite eliminated of its constitutive role in shaping human subjectivity, becomes part of the objective world. The category of 'fertility' presumes that the capacity to have children is understood primarily in terms of discrete biological propensities that can be located in specific organs. The natural laws which govern these organs can be learned by the mind and controlled, in the same way that any object in the world can. This rationalism imputed to the mind *requires* the body of biology to complete it. Rationalism works characteristically as a doublet. The more common critique, which accuses biologism of reducing the body to a biologically knowable entity like any other entity in the world, is incomplete in itself. For biologism contains implications for the mind too. The view of the mind and of knowledge sustained by biologism I will refer to as a *mentalist* understanding.

The Gap between Discourses of Planned Fertility and the Lived Body

How many of us can actually live up to this extraordinary version of the mind or of the body? We are reminded by a powerful tradition of phenomenology—associated with the work of Husserl, Heidegger, and Merleau-Ponty—that we do not primarily apprehend the world we inhabit as if it were abstract, featureless space. We 'instinctively' (that is, on the basis of past practice) know whether a certain object is reachable or not, without having to first measure the distance between ourselves and it. Nor is this knowledge something that can be said to reside exclusively in our minds. We do not carry purely mental maps of whether an object is reachable or not—it is our arms and hands that contain in them the practical measure of the 'reachability' of an object, and they carry this knowledge without actually having to reach out and test it. Far from the passive body that we have just encountered in the doctor's discourse, the body is radically entailed in this formulation of what it is to 'know' something. What is more, it is only on the basis of such a practical set of orientations that we are in turn able to 'grasp' the meaning of more abstract formulations of space such as we ourselves have created in disciplines such as geometry.

A concept such as 'fertility', let alone 'planned fertility' is again founded on too high a level of abstraction. As such, it cannot be assumed to be universal—it comes from a very specific discursive set of historical traditions and genealogies—nor can we assume that it can come to entirely supplant, for any of us, other more primary ways of living our relationship to our ability to conceive a child, give birth to it, and to nurture it. That potentiality is not lived as a discrete object of our consciousness, but rather as something on the horizon of *potentialities*. It takes quite specific social circumstances for it to become more concrete as a possibility. It takes even more specific circumstances—such as being imputed with an incapacity to bear a child, or a disturbance in the world around us—to make the desire for a child into an object of our conscious thoughts and desires, and in that context, it can, of course, turn into a very insistent and preoccupying project indeed. But even here, we cannot assume that we know how this situation will be *lived*. In rural Tamil Nadu, the inability to bear children, to nurture them past the precarious first years of infancy (which is also included in the diagnosis of 'infertility', always assumed to be a female incapacity), is lived neither as a purely mental process, nor as a purely physiological one. Instead, such volatility, if recurrent, may just as likely be lived as the intrusion and interference of malign spirits or maverick goddesses. And indeed, spirits and ghosts offer a perfectly apt modality with which to dramatize and live out the random and mysterious elements that will always persist as part of the human experience of conceiving and giving birth to a child.[4] Understood in this way, the experience of rural villagers is not limited to the airless world of 'superstition' to which it has been assigned by modernizers.

The Bodies of Demographers

In the account I have offered, the abstractions of family planning do not match *any* ordinary lived human relationship to the capacity to bear children; whereas maverick intrusions of spirits and ghosts at least captures one necessary element of that experience. But according to the discourse of demography, it is the 'superstitious beliefs', sociologically located among the uneducated, the rural, and the marginal in a society like India's, which prevents the nation from reaching its goals of population control. Let me quote from a group of demographers, planners, and political scientists who held a population policy workshop in 1978. The

workshop directly followed a resounding electoral defeat for Mrs Gandhi. Her authoritarian suspension of civil liberties (between 1975 and 1977) was repudiated. The prospect of ordinary Indians resuming the kind of agency awarded by civil liberties, and undertaking a 'voluntary' version of family planning not subject to coercion, strikes the editors of these workshop papers as a dilemma:

The most important question today is whether in a country where more than 70 per cent of the people are illiterate, where more than 80 per cent of the people live in villages with very inadequate facilities for sanitation, hygiene, medical care or pure water supply, where superstition, old beliefs as well as fanatic and dogmatic leaders and interested politicians rule unhindered, can we hope to fully achieve 'Voluntary Acceptance of Family Planning'?[5]

But are 'fanaticism', partiality, and non-rational affect the exclusive preserve of the 'illiterate' and their leaders? Extraordinarily emotional explosive images leap from the discourse of demographers in a way that nothing in their projected self-image would allow one to anticipate. The politics of caste and religion is described by Narayana and Kantner as 'a sack of writhing cobras... threaten[ing] to break through a dangerously threadbare social fabric'.[6] Electoral politics is described as the fire that 'keeps the cauldron of cultural antagonism bubbling'.[7] In the following account, a young researcher

---

[4] See K. Ram, forthcoming, *Fertile Disorder: Spirit Possession and Modern Projects of Subjectivity in the Lives of Tamil Rural Women*, Hawai'i: University of Hawai'i Press.

[5] M.M. Gandotra and Narayan Das, 1984, *Population Policy in India*, Bombay: Blackie and Son Publishers, p. ix.
[6] G. Narayana and J. Kantner, 1992, *Doing the Needful: The Dilemmas of India's Population Policy*, Boulder: Westview Press, p. ix.
[7] Ibid., p. 5.

employed by the Population Centre in Bangalore to conduct a qualitative village study treats the wary responses of villagers as nothing short of deception:

At the time of the fertility survey, a woman, with a son and a daughter, was in her first trimester of pregnancy. But she did not reveal the fact that she was pregnant thinking that I might ask her to accept tubectomy. She was basically afraid of the so-called post-tubectomy complications. But when her third child turned out to be a girl, she quietly accepted tubectomy. On being asked, she said that in order to avoid further daughters, who need large amounts of dowry she accepted tubectomy. All these were revealing to me as I thought that the respondents were truthful at the time of the collection of fertility history. In the quick, large scale surveys, many such facts are more likely to be missed.[8]

I use the trail of emotions and affects not simply to establish that intellectuals, too, have emotions and therefore, are also embodied creatures. This in itself is not much of a revelation. What gives this disclosure more urgency is the class attempt to project unruly emotions, deceit, and bodily excesses of fertility to others, be they villagers or Muslim minorities. But we can learn still more about the particular constitution of body image among intellectuals by attending to the peculiar place of the state in this body image. Others, such as Pandey, writing about modern historians, have drawn our attention to the identification between intellectuals and the state.[9] The term 'identification' wrongly

suggests we are dealing with two entities that are entirely separate from one another. Rather, we are dealing with a category of intellectuals who identify with the state in the sense that we identify with parts of our body, especially body parts such as our limbs, which are directly engaged with our motility, and our capacity to shape and affect the world. More precisely, the state could be said to fall into that special category of tools which, by virtue of acting as direct prosthetic extensions of our bodily agency, becomes thoroughly incorporated into the body image of the user.

A further consequence follows on from this. As an integral part of their own make-up, the identification is also not one which is visible to the intellectuals concerned. It never *occurs* to the woman doing the village ethnography to investigate what is revealed by the clearly attested fear of the village women that they might be pressured by the researcher to accept sterilization, nor to enquire into their reports that sterilization causes health disorders. Neither the state nor her own involvement with the state are open to question by the researcher because they are both part of the foundations that she takes for granted, much as we might take for granted the ground on which we walk.

We now begin to approach what is at stake for this group of intellectuals in the success of family planning. Discourse analysis is inadequate for the purposes of understanding what is at stake for the simple reason that family planning itself is not simply a 'discourse' for these intellectuals, it is a *project*. The powerful critiques of modernity, both Western and Indian, often note the divergence between 'modernity' and 'modernization', but have not adequately

[8] P.N. Sushma, n.d., 'Qualitative Village Study of Fertility', Unpublished paper, Population Centre, Bangalore, p. 9.

[9] G. Pandey, 1992, 'In Defence of the Fragment: Writing about Hindu–Muslim Riots in India Today', *Representations*, vol. 37, Winter, pp. 27–55.

taken stock of what is at stake in this difference. The mode of operation is itself different. This is a *watchword* rather than a word. The difference between the two conveys already the difference between a state of being and a *project*—a project that must be actively promoted. The language of rational planning is not a description, but a goal, or undertaking. Nehru's famous foreshadowing of India's 'tryst with destiny' at the midnight hour of 15 August 1947 simultaneously summons into being a people and a project: a people who are bearers of a *destiny*, something 'given', and also keepers of a 'tryst', to be *kept* by Indians, something to be lived up to. Compare this with the mood and emotion of unruffled composure with which Western intellectuals discuss modernity, as something that evolves out of an unbroken continuity with the cultural past. We may take as an example the slow evolution of the 'modern person' demonstrated by Marcel Mauss, who concludes his last essay with this flourish: 'From a simple masquerade to the mask, from a "role" (personnage) to a person, to a name, to an individual; from the latter to a being possessing metaphysical and moral value; from a moral consciousness to a sacred being; from the latter to a fundamental form of thought and action—the course is accomplished.'[10]

Such reposeful confidence in the unbrokenness of past, present, and future is quite foreign to Indian nationalism, as it must be to any nationalism forged as a 'derivative' but 'contestatory' discourse.[11] To be sure, Indian nationalism has consisted of many strands [and in one pervasive version], tries to seamlessly annex to the modern present, the glories of a continuous past, finding antecedents for scientific innovation in the Hindu epics,[12] locating in the 'classical' arts at least, a pure and continuous repository of spirituality.[13] But these attempts are far from resembling the serene and splendid majesty with which the past rolls down to the present of Western philosophers and intellectuals. It is this ability to *assume* the powerful presence of the past in the present, which is not only strange but enviable to the middle-class Indian postcolonial subject. By contrast, those nationalist discourses which claim to find a 'Hindu science' already prefigured in the Ramayana betray, in their anxious bellicosity, a hoarse insistence which is the product of well over a century of counter-discourse, a prolonged 'talking-back' to the West.

In his path-breaking work on Indian nationalism and the particular part played by state planning, Chatterjee distinguishes between the temporal and spatial linearity of developmental planning, and the temporality of politics: '"Developmentalism" implied

[10] M. Mauss, 1985, 'A Category of the Human Mind: The Notion of Person; the Notion of Self', in M. Carrithers, S. Collins, and S. Lukes (eds), *The Category of the Person*, Cambridge: Cambridge University Press, p. 3.

[11] P. Chatterjee, 1986, *Nationalist Thought and the Colonial World: A Derivative Discourse?* London and New Delhi: Zed Books and Oxford University Press.

[12] G. Prakash, 1999, *Another Reason: Science and the Imagination of Modern India*, Princeton: Princeton University Press.

[13] J. O'Shea, 2007, *At Home in the World: Bharata Natyam on the Global Stage*, Connecticut: Wesleyan University Press; and K. Ram, 2000, 'Dancing the Past into Life. The *Rasa, Nritta* and *Raga* of Immigrant Existence', *The Australian Journal of Anthropology*, Special issue on the Politics of Dance, vol. 11 no. 3, pp. 261–74.

a linear path, directed toward a goal, or a series of goals separated by stages. It implies the fixing of priorities between long-run and short-run goals and conscious choice between alternative paths.'[14] Politics, by contrast, necessarily entails the volatile time of shifting strategies. The Indian state had to manoeuvre, after independence, between the promotion of industrialization and responses to the threat of agrarian mobilization and conflict between social groups.[15] 'Development' itself sets in motion a sequence of political solutions, responding to new political jockeying and demands on the state. Yet, planning cannot show itself to be aware of any of this: '...the very form of an institution of rational planning located outside the political process is crucial for the self-definition of a developmental state embodying the single universal consciousness of the social whole.'[16]

The distinction undermines one aspect of developmental planning, but it does so at the expense of leaving intact the characterization of planning as linear rationality and that of politics as a thoroughly instrumental affair. By contrast, the emotions of planners makes it clear that planning itself is, and always has been, imbued with the affective investments and excitement of Indian modernization as a project of wresting autonomy and greater agency from those who would withhold it. I have explored this in greater detail elsewhere,[17] and will content myself

with one example. Writing on the eve of independence, Dwarkanath Ghosh in his book, *Pressure of Population and Economic Efficiency in India*,[18] certainly reduces people to economic costs and inputs. But there is more to his polemic than that. Unlike a pure bureaucratic rationalism, it also looks ahead to a vast expansion in agency in the newly independent nation: 'Great events have happened in this country. We have entered the penultimate stage of our political development, and acquired wide powers of shaping our future. In the construction of this future the size and growth of our population will play a large part.'[19]

Ghosh imagines the nation as composed of a multitude of 'intelligent laymen' whose reason, though obscured by emotions, will respond to facts and analysis, enabling them to voluntarily participate in the grand project of planning the nation by planning their own families. He is not alone in this assumption. The First Five Year plan makes the same generalized assumption of a shared rational outlook that unites the planners and the people, both undertaking to ensure that births are 'properly spaced in time and limited in number', safeguarding the nation's health and the health of the mother and child simultaneously.[20] The most striking feature of much of this period is the blurring of any distinction between the orientations

[14] P. Chatterjee, 1994, *The Nation and Its Fragments: Colonial and Postcolonial Histories*, New Delhi: Oxford University Press, p. 208.

[15] Ibid., pp. 210; also p. 205ff.

[16] Ibid., p. 219.

[17] K. Ram, 2001, 'Rationalising Fecund Bodies: Family Planning Policy and the Modern Indian

Nation-state', in M. Jolly and K. Ram (eds), *Borders of Being: Citizenship, Fertility and Sexuality in Asia and the Pacific*, Michigan: Michigan University Press, pp. 82–117.

[18] Dwarkanath Ghosh, 1946, *Pressure of Population and Economic Efficiency in India*, Bombay: Oxford University Press.

[19] Ibid., p. ix.

[20] Raina, *Population Policy*.

of the state, intellectuals, and the people. It is not Reason as such that dissolves all potential tensions between intellectuals and 'the people' in the becoming of the nation. Rather, it is an energetic field that leaps contagiously from body to body, dissolving distinctions even as it mobilizes those affected. If we follow the lead of Deleuze and Guattari, the term *affect* can be used precisely to signal this embodied dimension of mobile flows of energies and intensities, not only between human subjects but between human subjects and all that the world contains, including animals and objects.[21] Affect is described as either augmenting or diminishing the body's capacity to act. It is an improvement on the traditional associations with the term 'emotion' in that we tend to locate emotions in the interior of our consciousness. What I wish to highlight here, however, is the association of energies with *projects* of the most *public* kind. Mazzarella suggests something similar when he argues that affect be recognized as 'a necessary moment of any institutional practice with aspirations to public efficacy'.[22]

Once affect is taken into account, Chatterjee's distinction between politics and planning is harder to sustain. For the consideration of affect reveals that what may seem to be pure scientistic rationalism and bureaucratic managerialism is suffused, initially, with the excited political anticipation of a utopian future.

The agency associated with such a project does not resemble either the instrumental logic of strategic jockeying for power, nor the description of planning as imbued with linear temporality. Even as they anticipate five year 'stages', the planners *themselves* are living another temporality which is anything *but* linear. For the future they desire will not emerge in a linear manner out of the past in a country like India. Instead, it must be *wrested* away from the past that keeps reincarnating itself in recalcitrant subjects who threaten to drag modernity back into the constraints of collective identities such as caste, region, religion, and gender.

The Contagious Charge of Activist Modernity

I have argued in detail recently that many of the most powerful critiques of modernity have been too reductionist.[23] Following the powerful lead given by Foucault, postcolonial theory (among other forms of critique) has been content largely to characterize both the colonial and postcolonial state in terms of governmental rationalism. Such a characterization has, in turn, lent itself to a critique of modernity as sets of binary dichotomies that *excluded* 'the vast masses of people [from] the new life of the nation'.[24]

[21] G. Deleuze and F. Guattari, 1987, *A Thousand Plateaus. Capitalism and Schizophrenia*, Minneapolis: University of Minnesota, p. 178.
[22] W. Mazzarella, 2008, 'Affect: What Is It Good For?' in S. Dube (ed.), *Enchantments of Modernity. Empire, Nation, Globalization*, London: Routledge, p. 298.

[23] K. Ram, 2008, "A New Consciousness Must Come": Affectivity and Movement in Tamil Dalit Women's Activist Engagement with Cosmopolitan Modernity', in Pnina Werbner (ed.), *Anthropology and Cosmopolitanism: Rooted, Feminist and Vernacular Perspectives*, Oxford: Berg, pp. 135–55.
[24] P. Chatterjee, 1989, 'The Nationalist Resolution of the Women's Question', in K. Sangari and S. Vaid (eds), *Recasting Women. Essays in Colonial History*, New Delhi: Kali for Women, p. 251.

The two positions are intimately linked. If we characterize modernity primarily as a mode of *categorization*, then we necessarily have to understand it as one that includes some and excludes others, for that is what categories do, particularly when backed by the authority of a state. This tradition of critique leaves us unable to understand how so exclusionary a set of discourses could succeed in galvanizing poor Dalit women. I have argued that what is systematically missing from such characterizations is an adequate phenomenology of the *emancipatory* modality of *activism*. In this mode, where it appears primarily as a form of *mobilization*, modernity contagiously leaps from point to point, defying all attempts to pin it down sociologically, to see it as a mode of privilege that resides exclusively with particular social locations. Attempts to critique modernity as exclusively 'male', 'Western', or 'upper caste', as successive critiques have argued since the 1970s, have provided important sources of insight into the problems with universalist claims, but are also doomed to find themselves empirically disproved time and time again, as women, non-Western groups, and non-elite and Dalit castes take up modernity as active claimants rather than as excluded or abject elements. Rural Dalit women in Tamil Nadu, from fishing and from agricultural castes, draw on the collective effervescence of organized action, often under the aegis of non-government organizations (NGOs). These organizations may not in themselves be aiming at anything more than the propagation of hygienic practices and maternal health, but their mode of action is re-inflected by prior political histories and

by the very experience of mobilization itself.[25]

For rural Dalits in Tamil Nadu, the past in the present significantly includes the Self-Respect movement in Tamil Nadu and its mobilization against caste privileges and, more particularly, against Brahmanic priest-dominated forms of religion. That critique resulted not so much in the valorization of Dalit and non-elite styles of worship, as in the appropriation of a rational humanism as quintessentially 'Tamil' as well as 'modern'.[26] That past appears in the present in styles of reasoning and critique employed by young women, such as this young woman from a coastal fishing village in Kanyakumari district (Tamil Nadu) who stoutly rejects the 'beliefs' of her grandmother's day in terms that vividly recall the early Dravida Munnetra Kazhagam's (DMK) rationalist and humanist critiques. Here, she reinterprets the dangers of attracting the unwanted attention of spirits during menstruation as so many fears nurtured and imagined by the *human* mind: 'Well, this is what the grandmothers say—don't throw out the bloodied rag, it will bring the pey. But I think—well, I am the pey [spirit], I am the pishashu [demon], so why would they come

---

[25] Ram, 'A New Consciousness Must Come'.

[26] There is an analogy to be made here with Ambedkar's insistence on using the universalism and rationalism of science as a yardstick with which to judge and evaluate world religions, and his emphasis on the micro-politics of Dalits adopting modern dress and cleanliness. See G. Pandey, 2006, 'The Time of Dalit Conversion', *Economic and Political Weekly*, vol. xli, no. 18, 6 May, pp. 1779–88.

to me? My mind—that is the real reason for these *peys*.'[27]

Or take, for example, an excerpt from an interview with Victoria, a young woman who was working for an NGO in Chengalpattu district (Tamil Nadu, interviewed 1996). Her discourse vividly captures the heightened sense of agency with which she grasps modernity:

My family are Roman Catholic, and we owned a little land. In my village the dominant caste is Reddiar. Before I was born, my family must have worked on their land. We must have had to have give way to them, we must not have worn slippers in front of them, nor walked on the same path as them. Over the last thirty years or so, all that has changed. Maybe five out of every hundred still keep to the same habits and practices [*palakkam*]. In Porur, we have our own water supplies, pump-sets, hand-pump and new well. So we don't have to rely on the upper castes any more. We also know now that we are numerically dominant, and that frightens them a little.

Buoyed by this strength, Victoria was able to withstand the taunts she faced as she began moving around the district on her NGO work:

So I began to go around on my bike, taking doubles sometimes. I got insults from others. If I carried an umbrella, the villagers would say: 'Oh, look at her go with a *kutai* [umbrella], just like some big teacher.' I would ignore them, or retort: 'So what, have you paid for my umbrella?!'

[While we talk about marriage, she describes her own marriage] I have got a man such as I prayed for. He is not abusive, does not drink or

beat me, like so many women I counsel. We use the rhythm method of contraception advocated by the Sisters—so I watch my discharges, and know my fertile period. I was afraid of men when I first got married. I told my husband quite early that I did not want to be harassed [for sex] when my body is not feeling right, like during my periods. My husband agreed. Now sometimes he says he is tired and not wanting [sex], sometimes I say it.

The 'affective turn'[28] in social theory seems to be bringing some earlier formulations of postcolonial scholarship closer to what I am suggesting. Chatterjee, who earlier describes state planning in thoroughly 'governmental' terms as 'the concrete embodiment of the rational consciousness of a state [that] can promote the universal goal of development by harnessing within a single interconnected whole the discrete subjects of power in a society'[29] now describes governmentality as a 'de-politicised' concept, and draws specific attention to the 'passionate and often violent agitations to protest discrimination and to secure claims'.[30] Let me quote more fully:

The fact that the objectives of such agitations are framed by the conditions of governmentality is no reason to think that they cannot arouse considerable passion and affective energy. Collective actions in political society cannot be de-politicised by framing them within the grid of governmentality because the activities of governmentality affect the very conditions of livelihood and social existence of the groups they target. At least that part of Indian democracy

[27] For details, see K. Ram, 1998, 'Uneven Modernities and Ambivalent Sexualities: Women's Construction of Puberty in Coastal Kanyakumari, Tamilnadu', in Mary E. John and Janaki Nair (eds), *A Question of Silence? The Sexual Economies of Modern India*, New Delhi: Kali for Women, p. 294ff.

[28] Veena Das, 2008, 'Foreword', in Saurabh Dube (ed.), *Enchantments of Modernity: Empire, Nation, Globalization*, London: Routledge, p. xi.
[29] Chatterjee, *The Nation and Its Fragments*, p. 207.
[30] Ibid.

that falls within the domain of political society is definitely not anaemic and lifeless.[31]

But his formulation retains a certain compartmentalized approach to modernity. The depoliticized grid of governmentality still stands in contrast to the politics of collective action. The affective volatility of subaltern politics stands in contrast with a 'civil society' composed of the Indian urban middle classes, who are virtually 'indistinguishable from other western democracies'.[32] In all formulations, however revised, there appears to be at least *one* part of modernity which is doomed to remain 'anaemic and lifeless', while the other gathers to itself all the volatility and excitement of affect. However, my point is precisely that affect cannot be sociologically contained and compartmentalized in this way. Nor does the emancipatory excitement of modernity confine itself to a group politics—for Victoria, it inhabits the way she talks about her marriage, the reshaping of the meanings of marriage, maternity, and sexual relations. Her description of family planning is very different from that of the doctor with which we opened this chapter. The method is that favoured by the Catholic nuns who gave Victoria her entree into a wider world, namely, the rhythm method. The rhythm method at least relies on equipping the woman with a knowledge of her own body, as opposed to reliance on health personnel who have received external forms of 'motivation', and it here takes its place in a very different ensemble of

discursive elements that remind us of other genealogies of birth control as an aspect of women's struggle to secure greater autonomy and agency. This is a genealogy that, once again, demonstrates the contagiousness of emancipatory modernity, as it leaps from the middle-class location of the discourses of the women's movement in the 1930s to the voice of Dalit women such as Victoria:

...addressing the Indian Economic Conference in 1934, Alarmelmangathayar Ammal, a member of the Madras Legislative Council and of the AIWC [All India Women's Conference], said 'the problem of population with its concomitant of birth-control could not be solved by the deliberations of an assembly of males, but as mothers, women must be given a large voice in any future legislative measure on the question.' Similarly, some women activists of the AIWC countered the anti-birth-control campaign of male nationalists, on the ground that they had no experience of childbirth and that birth-control was the right of women to control over their bodies. For instance, Kamaladevi Chattopadhyaya, the first organising secretary of the AIWC and an active member of the Indian National Congress, told Satyamurthi that birth-control was 'the sacred and inalienable right of every woman to possess the means to control her body and not God or man can attempt to deprive her of that right without perpetrating an outrage on womanhood'.[33]

From Affects to the Mood of Family Planning Policy

A certain drama, of claiming political agency, of appropriating a modernity initially

[31] P. Chatterjee, 2008, 'Democracy and Economic Transformation in India', *Economic and Political Weekly*, vol. 43, no. 16, 19 April, p. 61.
[32] Ibid., p. 57.

[33] S. Anandhi, 1996, 'Reproductive Bodies and Regulated Sexuality: Birth Control Debates in the Early 20th Century Tamilnadu', in John and Nair (eds), *A Question of Silence?* pp. 149–50.

imposed from without, never entirely leaves the discourse of family planning. The historical fact that the Indian state was one of the first nation-states to adopt family planning as official state policy in 1951 continues to be cited as a marker of India's 'early' arrival as an ex-colony on the stage of modernity. According to the vice-president of the Family Planning Association of India, it is an indication that the Indian state 'was certainly ahead of its time'.[34] But the excitement of utopian anticipation that we find in Ghosh's discourse before independence, that contagious affect which dissolves any distinction between intellectuals and 'the people', is not the affect we came across in the discourse of contemporary demographers and planners. Instead, we found explosive affects of fear (at the threadbareness of the nation-sack), and frustration with various 'backward sections' (the writhing cobras that threaten to escape the nation-sack). The horizon of the imaginary unity of the nation, the utopian aspiration for a people working in harmony towards the same goals, have not simply disappeared. For what troubles the demographers is precisely *the gap* between the present in all its messiness and the utopian expectation of unity. I have suggested already that state often disappears from the investigations of demographers because it functions like a tool, as an extension of one's own bodily agency. But this is only when matters are proceeding

smoothly for state intellectuals. When the assemblage of materials needed to build and plan the nation-house is not to hand, however, then the state itself, once again, becomes an explicit object, not only of attention but also of solicitude and concern. The emotion which is to be detected in the discourses on population control can therefore be understood as occasional outbursts of anger, and more generally, the irritation and vexation of those whose work cannot proceed because *something is out of place*.

The materials they need to build the nation-house are malfunctioning. A function in which they took pride, as a token of India's claim to modernity—electoral democracy—has turned into a tool that is, quite literally, 'in the wrong hands'. Such an occasion arose, quite spectacularly, before the 'Emergency' of 1975. Faced with a confluence of urban movements opposing price rises, the 'Bhoodan' movement under the Gandhian leadership of J.P. Narayan, directed to land redistribution, and a national railway workers' strike, Mrs Gandhi declared the suspension of civil liberties lasting between June 1975 and January 1977. The effects of the Emergency were registered in many areas of civil life, but as is well known, one of the principal government initiatives permitted by the abrogation of civil liberties, was a particularly authoritarian version of 'family planning'.

I have argued elsewhere,[35] as have others, that the Emergency should be treated not as an exceptional measure, quite outside the norm, but as a means of making visible, by virtue of its exaggerations, what is normally

[34] R. Soonawala, 1993, 'Planning the Indian Experience', in P. Senanayake and R.L. Kleinman (eds), *Family Planning: Meeting Challenges–Promoting Choices*, The Proceedings of the IPPF Family Planning Congress, Lancaster and New York: The Parthenon Publishing Group, p. 77.

[35] Ram, 'Rationalising Fecund Bodies'.

invisible because it functions in a more muted fashion. In this chapter, I have used affects to guide us to the hidden body of intellectuals, buried under the discourse of Reason. That discourse, we have found, is punctured by eruptions of affective rage and frustration. But the work of identification between intellectuals and the state is not necessarily achieved at the level of explicit discourse at all. Rather it occurs at the level of *practice*. If we are not to be dazzled by the 'excesses' of Emergency and are to look to the continuities in attitudes, we need to shift our attention from the level of discourse to the level of practices where patterns show up. At the same time, we need tools other than the concept of 'affect' to capture the existential emotion of these practices.

The doctor in the public hospital does not take his cue simply from the discourses of demographers. He takes his cue from the practices, orientations, and technologies that have already been pre-selected for his use by the policies of family planning. I have detailed these policies elsewhere,[36] but would summarize their tenor by saying that they have typically encouraged only one method at a time, usually in short and intensive phases. More revealingly still, the sequence of contraceptive technologies that have been favoured by the state can be seen to illustrate a progressive diminution of choice for the user. The overwhelming reliance of state policy has been on sterilization, the method least able to be reversed. Sterilization accounts for 70–80 per cent of contraceptive protection.[37] Until the period of Emergency, male sterilization was four to five times more common than female sterilization. The reaction to male sterilizations during the Emergency, combined with the introduction of new forms of female sterilization—mini-laparotomy and laparoscopic sterilization—has led to an almost exclusive focus on women in policies since the early 1980s.[38] Contraceptive technologies allowing reversibility, and greater choices in preventing pregnancies, have been underemphasized, and have lacked infrastructural support.

These patterns in practice are also, simultaneously, continuities at the level of emotion. Rather than the affective intensity that is apparent in discourses and in activist practices, I would use the more enduring and inconspicuous concept of *mood* to describe the tone of state practices. Like affects, moods need not be considered an attribute of the individual subject. 'A mood assails us. It comes neither from "outside" nor from "inside",' says Heidegger.[39] Instead it pervades a particular way in which we find ourselves oriented to the world. The 'mood' of family planning practices reveals something about the existential style and way of being in the world of state intellectuals. They reveal, even more pervasively than the statements of demographers and political scientists, a mood of profound distrust, on the part of policymakers, of the social world they have inherited. While the official

---

[36] Ram, 'Rationalising Fecund Bodies'.
[37] Narayana and Kantner, *Doing the Needful*, p. 106.

[38] Ibid., p. 108; V. Soni, 1984, 'The Development and Current Organization of the Family Planning Programme', in T. Dyson and N. Crook (eds), *India's Demography: Essays on the Contemporary Population*, Atlantic Highlands, NJ: Humanities Press, pp. 151; Soonawala, 'Planning the Indian Experience', p. 83.
[39] M. Heidegger, 1992 [1962], *Being and Time*, Oxford: Blackwell, p. 176.

discourse reforms itself, with the demise of the Nehruvian state, to address a world of individual users and consumers, the practices silently continue to differentiate the world along older lines. Trust and distrust are elicited and distributed differentially according to class, according to gender, and according to whether a social group is perceived as modern or traditional. The affective intensities in discourses, the taken-for-granted assurance with which the doctor inserts an IUD into the body of a woman after childbirth, as well as the measures we single out as belonging to periods of 'Emergency', all draw inconspicuously on this pervasive mood of distrust.

The Moods of Silent Practices

In this chapter, I have utilized affects and moods as a 'trail'. A trail is visible (although one has to half-know what to look for in order to see it). It takes you on a journey of disclosure. It helps you uncover something that might otherwise remain covered over and hidden. In this instance, the trail has been used to disclose and restore a dimension often lacking in discussions of modernity, which for some time have largely taken the form of critique. The result has been a narrowing in the range of phenomena attended to, and of the kinds of concepts generated. Where do we turn, for instance, should we wish to move from a critique of Western modernity for its sham universalisms to an account of why a young Dalit woman speaks the language of emancipatory modernity? How do we shift from critical theories that cut modernity down to size—reducing it to a matter of discrete and particular 'subject

positions' given by race, ethnicity, gender, and geopolitical location—to theories that can account for the capacity of modernity to move people? In particular, the dominance of the model of modernity as governmentality has left us with little ability to appreciate, or even register, the affectively charged energies of modernity, even where these are most in evidence, as in activist projects and social movements. This is not surprising, given the fact that the entire point of Foucault's study of power in governmentality is that there *is* no body to be discerned any longer in the operation of power, only procedures that classify, distribute, analyse, and spatially fix the object of governance. Along with Foucault's analysis, we have inherited also his style of writing which, as de Certeau describes it, is *itself* often 'marvelously "panoptic"' in the way it sets about naming and classifying the rules, conditions of functioning, techniques, and procedures of governmentality'.[40] This allows governmentality to retain and reproduce some of its own orientations, which reside nowhere more than in the *style* with which it deals with the world. This style, doubly reinforced, has come to pervade our own scholarly habits of thought about modernity.

In attempting to come up with a better description of activism,[41] I have been led to pay wider attention to the role that

[40] M. de Certeau, 1984, *The Practice of Everyday Life*, Berkeley: University of California Press, p. 46.

[41] K. Ram, 2006, 'Temporality and Sorge in the Ethical Fashioning of the Feminist Self', in E. McMahon and B. Olubas (eds), *Feminist Temporalities*, Crawley, Western Australia: University of Western Australia Press, pp. 191–220; and 'A New Consciousness Must Come', 2009, 'Modernity as a "Rain of Words": Tracing the Flow of "Rain" between Dalit Women and Intellectuals in Tamil Nadu', *Asian*

affect can play in disrupting such habits of thought. Affects generally stand out from the everyday habitual level of existence 'through the force of altered, juxtaposed or disordered sensations'.[42] They are also visible. In ordinary life, our affects are visible to others as reactions one cannot hide even if one wished to. They are visible as the tears of distress and anguish, the curling upper lip of contempt, the downcast eyes, and drooping head of shame, all of which, and more, Tomkins describes in '*What are Affects?*'[43] Both these qualities of affects—their disruptiveness and their visibility—play a part in arresting the ordinary flow of intellectual habits, and in attuning us to the unusual and the novel.[44] Affective images of the nation as beset by writhing snakes and bubbling cauldrons fairly leapt off the page at me, not only by virtue of their intensity, but because they were so oddly out of place. In this chapter, I have suggested, not simply that we stay with these affects, but that we use them to lead us to other, less visible dimensions. They can lead us to a body. They can show us that there is indeed a bodily dimension to governmentality itself. In the rage and frustration of state intellectuals, we discern a class distance from the bodies they seek to regularize, as well as

a nearness and solicitude for the state which is suggestive of an intimacy that goes beyond the relationship between subject and object.

Even when we move away from the explicit discourses of demographers and family planners, to consider what I have described as silent state practices—an analytic pioneered by Foucault—we still find there a level of affectivity, which is better described as 'mood'. The concept of mood matches the inconspicuousness of the practices themselves. I would suggest that 'moods' are better suited to the study of those considerable dimensions of modernity which operate as silent practices, while we might reserve 'affects' for understanding the heightened drama and mobility of projects such as activist undertakings and social movements. The concept of mood—even more than affect—deserves to be described as 'impersonal' and 'pre-subjective'.[45] Yet, in itself, this description is incomplete. For if mood is not subjective, neither is it 'objective'. It is not something that is entirely external and 'given' in the way that nature is represented in the physical sciences. Mood is as much 'pre-objective' as it is 'pre-subjective' in the sense that it intimates a form of orientation between subjects and the world they inhabit, and as such belongs exclusively neither to one nor to the other. Heidegger finds its precedents, for example, in Aristotle's treatment of rhetoric rather than in the framework of 'psychology' and 'feelings'. Orators must correctly divine a mood that pre-exists their point of entry. That mood belongs to a generality, a state of being-with-one-another that Heidegger

Studies Review, Special issue on Dalit Cultural Politics, vol. 33, no. 4, pp. 501–16.

[42] M. Paterson, 2006, 'Feel the Presence: Technologies of Touch and Distance', *Environment and Planning D: Society and Space*, vol. 24, no. 5, pp. 1–18.

[43] E.K. Sedgwick and Adam Frank, 1995, *Shame and Its Sisters. A Silvan Tomkins Reader*, Durham: Duke University Press, p. 74.

[44] Cited from K. Stewart, 2009, 'Atmospheric Attunements', forthcoming in *Society and Space*, Special issue of Environment and Planning, edited Mark Jackson.

[45] Mazzarella, 'Affect: What Is It Good For?' p. 291.

describes as 'publicness'.[46] Heidegger thus seeks to rescue us from the problems that arise from placing emotions and feelings in the framework of individual subjectivity and psychology. To place them in this framework is, once again, to leave us with the problem that haunted Descartes: how can what is 'inside' the subject be verified from 'outside'? In the case of emotions, how can one person know what another feels, let alone come to share that feeling? How does the feeling get 'out' of one individual into another? We resort to appeals to extraordinary qualities such as 'empathy' to explain this problem. By appealing to an extraordinary quality, not available to many, we leave the problem intact. The ordinary experience of the communicability and contagiousness of emotions remains, on this account, a mystery, and cannot account for what are, pre-eminently, shared forms of engagement in the projects and practices of modernity.

[46] Heidegger, *Being and Time*, p. 178.

12

Ethno-logics
Paradigms of Modern Identity

Townsend Middleton[†]

Early Morning, July 2006. In the cramped offices of the Lekh Ethnic Association,[1] an ethnic leader frantically scribbles his final revisions of a memorandum to be submitted to the Government of India, arguing for the Lekhs' inclusion into the list of Scheduled Tribes (STs) of India. Fanned out over his desk lays an array of scholarly books, opened to the particular pages from which he is to glean the information to bolster his community's quest for ST recognition. As the elite ethnic leader works, his colleagues bid me welcome in whispered hellos, letting

me know he is not to be disturbed. The leader's eyes dart from one book to another, cross-referencing sources, then back again to the memorandum. He makes a slight change. Someone checks the clock. Beads of sweat begin to stand up on his nose. He waits for the whiteout to dry, then pencils in yet another citation.

Minutes later, three suit-clad men leave the office with the completed memorandum in tow. Knowing I am an anthropologist, they have invited me along for the day, so I do my best to keep pace as they navigate their way through the crowded bazaar to a microvan idling nearby. It will take us to a distant corner of the district, where their 'model community' is to be found. Upon arrival, these leaders will rendezvous with associates who have worked through the night coaching the locals and making other

---

† My thanks to Dominic Boyer, Jaideep Chatterjee, Jason Cons, Viranjini Munasinghe, and Saurabh Dube for their comments on earlier drafts of this chapter. All shortcomings remain my own.

[1] At the time of publication, the group's application for ST status was still pending. 'Lekh' is, thus, a pseudonym.

last minute preparations. The day demands a perfect similitude between what their memorandum says and what their people do, and thus everything must be in order. After all, they *will* be tested.

Somewhere along the same road plies a government-hired jeep heading for the same model community. Inside rides a team of government anthropologists armed with clipboards, criteria, and questionnaires. They have been sent from their offices at the Cultural Research Institute, Kolkata, by the Government of West Bengal to conduct an ethnographic survey of the Lekh. Ultimately, the report they write on the day's events will be a pivotal factor in determining whether or not the Lekh become an ST, thereby qualifying its members for the reservations and affirmative action benefits that, ostensibly, might lift them from their 'backward' condition.

As the ethnic leaders' microvan lurches down the heavily eroded road, conversation meanders from theories of primordial ethnic history, 'tradition', and 'culture' to related concerns of 'backwardness' and ethnic 'uplift'—all signature topics of modern-day identity-speak. Finally, after three gruelling hours, we arrive at a small hamlet straddling the now dwindling road. Gathered there stands a community bedecked in their most traditional attire—men to one side, women to the other—waiting to perform, waiting to convince whomever that they are proper 'tribal' subjects. As the van parts the throng of people, uneasy faces peer in. Just then one of the suit-clad men inside looks out and declares with satisfaction, 'Ahhh...ou see. There is a *tribal* community!'

Within minutes the government anthropologists arrive and the community springs into action, transforming this hillside village into a veritable ethnological lollapalooza. Folk songs waft across carefully arranged 'primitive' artifacts. Women dance and serve 'indigenous' foods. Drums roll, as shamans shake and hover erratically over their full array of ritual paraphernalia. There is exorcism and sacrifice, even blood drinking, not to mention bows, arrows, and troops of adolescents howling savage cries into the thick monsoon skies. All the while, the men in suits roam the perimeter orchestrating the encounter. These ethnic leaders make sure the anthropologists are looking in the right direction at the right time, and properly recording what they see. When necessary, they intervene to speak on behalf of interviewees, displacing their agency for the 'good of the constituency'. With so much at stake, it is imperative they provide the perfect representation of the 'tribal' subject.

Ethnology at Large

For the Lekh, the day held immense promise. A crucial step towards ethnic uplift, 'tribal' recognition represented a gateway into the world of citizen-based rights, equality, and progress—values enshrined in the Constitution of India and liberal democracies the world over. The ethnographic survey was their chance to be singled out from India's multitudes and administered the needed dose of positive discrimination to bring them up to speed with a rapidly progressing national mainstream. For them, this day was, above all, a moment to become modern.

Yet, it was also a *modern moment in and of itself*—an event structured by signature paradigms of modernity. When we analyse this classificatory moment further, we see this day of recognition was imbued with decidedly ethnological paradigms, at once integral to the making of modern communities and constitutive of the human landscape of modernity itself. Accordingly, the Lekh's quest for ST status was laden with not only opportunity and promise, but also paradox and antinomy, thus epitomizing the seductive trappings of contemporary identity formation. As one ethnic leader expressed to me in frustration while his community performed the day's demonstrations, 'To fulfil this tribal criteria, this is a ridiculous thing! You know Hegel? Hegel said man has reached the heights of civilization. But now look at us! We are going back to the cave!' That said, he continued to champion the quest for ST status.

In India, the paradoxes of secular nationalism have been under scrutiny now for some time from both the left and the right.[2] Particularly in the post-Mandal Commission era, India's reservation system and related affirmative action policies have proven especially contentious. That such policies demand 'backwardness' in the name of progress at the same time they champion difference and inequality in order to provisionally eliminate prejudice from public life bespeaks fundamental contradictions at the heart of liberal governance. These policies create the incentives to put identity to political work, yet at the same time, they set the terms and conditions through which communities may be recognized as entities within the secular nationalist order. By mandating the criteria for legal recognition, these policies thus involve their own cunning of recognition.[3] In the coming pages, we shall see just how deeply these mandates affect communities. In the exaggerated cultural displays of the Lekh though, we already see how particular ethnological attributes may be a conduit for political and socio-economic rights. Upon further review then, the secular impulse in India turns out to one of particular ethnological persuasions.

To investigate these persuasions, we must venture an understanding of 'ethnology' beyond the bounds of academic anthropology. Yet, in engaging with these and other 'found' anthropologies out there in the world, we also cannot ignore the impact that the discipline has had in shaping the socio-political possibilities of 'identity' in contemporary India and beyond. A wealth of recent scholarship has illustrated the overt and subtle collusions of ethnology and colonial rule.[4] These collusions largely laid the groundwork for contemporary systems of recognition, positive discrimination, and the like—including that within which the Lekh and hundreds of other communities are currently vying for 'tribal' status. Importantly though, ethnology was not simply brought to bear on socio-cultural diversity in the colonies. The disciplinary

---

[2] An excellent overview of these debates may be found in Aditya Nigam, 2006, *Insurrection of the Little Selves*, Oxford: Oxford University Press.

[3] See Elizabeth Povinelli, 2002, *The Cunning of Recognition*, Durham, NC: Duke University Press.

[4] See, for instance, Talal Asad (ed.), 1973, *Anthropology and the Colonial Encounter*, London: Ithaca Press; Jan van Bremen and A. Shimizu (eds), 1999, *Anthropology and Colonialism in Asia and Oceania*, Richmond, Surrey: Curzon Press; Bernard Cohn, 1996, *Colonialism and Its Forms of Knowledge*, Princeton, NJ: Princeton University Press; and Nicholas Dirks, 2001, *Castes of Mind*, Princeton, NJ: Princeton University Press.

form of knowledge also emerged out of the greater colonial encounter with socio-cultural difference itself. Scaled more broadly, it was this ever-increasing encompassment of human difference (or at least the pretensions thereof) that then gave rise to both modern ethnology and modernity's characteristically ethnological attributes.

Taxonomic categories such as 'race', 'caste', 'tribe', and later 'ethnicity', all were ways to apprehend and make sense of this myriad of difference. We know now that many of these categories were instantiated and/or reworked by colonial regimes in South Asia and elsewhere, yet, despite their loaded histories, today these terms have become naturalized into the landscapes of modern identity. Beyond simple categories, modernity also involved the institutionalization of particular logics of what it means to be a community and how a community operates. Designations like 'caste' and 'tribe' were yoked to concepts such as 'culture', 'religion', and 'tradition', and these concepts were in turn supported by more underlying rationales and discriminatory sensibilities, many of which inhered in the potent binaries through which modernity mapped itself onto human subjects. 'Tradition', as opposed to 'modern', thus became that which was unchanging and ahistorical, while the 'backward' became those yet to 'progress' into the arenas of rationalism, education, development, etc. Though couched as historicist judgements, these binaries also smuggled in an array of ethnological suppositions.

Over time, these schemes became operative paradigms not only in the policies of liberal governance—especially those concerning development and multiculturalism—but also in the popular imaginations of 'community' more generally.[5] In mutual accord, these institutional and informal reckonings of identity thereby made normative particular *ethno-logics* of how people inhabit the world. The case of the Lekh demonstrates how enabling, yet prescriptive these paradigms can be. Through other cases we shall see that modern ethno-logics are neither totalizing nor closed to negotiation with alternative rubrics of belonging. Yet, these same cases also make clear the socio-political implications of these schemes, as well as their seductive appeal.

By prying the inner workings of these conceptual systems, we can see how this has come to be. Take, for instance, the seemingly ubiquitous concepts of 'culture', 'religion', and 'tradition'. In today's world, it would be hard to imagine ethnic identity without them. As these concepts were institutionalized formally and popularized informally, they brought with them concordant rationales of subtle yet profound import. 'Culture', 'religion', and 'tradition' came to denote not just what people *did* in their daily lives; they also became something people *had*—as though they were in some sense objects, henceforth to be used as markers of human difference. The imperatives to apprehend difference fostered the tendency to freeze processes into objects—that is, to take conceptual snapshots of what, in actuality, were dynamic social phenomenon. The subjects of modernity were tagged accordingly. The great irony is that modernity, ostensibly a

[5] On imagined communities and nationalism, see Benedict Anderson, 1983, *Imagined Communities*, London: Verso Books.

phenomenon of historic transformation, was, in fact, predicated on particular assumptions of stasis and historical immutability. Modernity, in short, demanded its own anachrony.

Even a cursory glance at the astounding proliferation of identity politics in India over the past century signals major shifts in the grounds of communal possibility. As has been the case elsewhere in the world, this proliferation in India has been especially pronounced since independence from colonial rule. Various theories have partially explained the global explosion of ethnic movements during this time by pointing to, among other instigating conditions, open competition for political power, new avenues to sovereignty, entitlements provided by the welfare state, increasingly transnational ethnic networks or 'ethnoscapes', etc.[6] Keeping these contextual elements in view, this chapter pursues a different tack. Turning critical attention to the knowledge practices through which identity is conceived and legitimated in its modern valances, we may begin to understand how modernity has entailed a fundamental reworking of how we come to know ourselves, our community, and the others with whom we share the world. This is not to say that practices which today we might deem 'cultural', 'religious',

or 'traditional' did not predate and transcend the onset of modernity. Rather it is to call attention to the manner in which institutions of modern governance, along with the discourses of liberalism, and more recently multiculturalism, have conceptually fixed the ideas of 'culture', 'religion', and 'tradition', making them cardinal requisites of 'ethnic' identity and its rightful recognition. These elements now seem so natural that they tend to be taken for granted. Cases like that of the Lekh, however, throw these seemingly 'natural' paradigms into sharp relief. To question these frameworks is neither to supplant primordialist assumptions of ethnic identity with constructivist theories of ethno-genesis, nor is it to deny the real material and socio-political incentives of communal mobilization. Rather, it is to ask how the terms and conditions of modernity have reworked the very question and possibilities of identity itself.

To advance this line of questioning, this chapter traces the following critical trajectory. The first section, 'Ethnology Instituted', interrogates the colluded history of academic ethnology and colonial governance in order to expose the early institutionalization of particular ethnological rubrics in India. The next section, 'Identity Now', shifts attention to the instrumental role ethnological knowledge plays in the contemporary identity politics of India. The following section extends this line of enquiry down into the intimate worlds of 'Everyday Ethnology', where we encounter some of the deepest, most important, reaches of modern ethno-logics. The chapter closes with an invitation for further consideration of the integrality of ethnological knowledge in the modern world.

[6] Exemplary studies include Clifford Geertz, 1973, 'The Integrative Revolution: Primordialism and Civil Politics in the New States', in *The Interpretation of Cultures*, New York: Basic Books, pp. 255–310; H.R. Isaacs, 1975, *Idols of the Tribe*, New York: Harper and Row; and R. Fox, C. Aull, and L. Cimino, 1981, 'Ethnic Nationalism and the Welfare State', in C.F. Keyes (ed.), *Ethnic Change*, Seattle: University of Washington Press, pp. 198–245. On 'ethnoscapes', see Arjun Appadurai, 1996, *Modernity at Large*, Minneapolis: University of Minnesota Press.

Ethnology Instituted

As colonialism and the spread of capitalism pulled the disparate peoples of the world into unprecedented, uneven relation with one another, the attending political economies put a premium on knowing and utilizing human difference. In colonial India, overwhelming diversity and the prerogatives of imperialism upped the ante of ethnological reckoning to such a degree that ethnology quickly became essential to colonial rule. In time, particular kinds of ethnological distinction would come to reconfigure much of the human landscape on the subcontinent.

By the middle of the nineteenth century, the demographics of labour migration within India and overseas were already displaying obvious ethnological preferences. Certain *types* of people were seen as ideal for certain *types* of labour. Thus, 'dark', 'tribal' bodies were targeted for *jungli* and *coolie* labour, while 'martial races' like the Sikhs and the Gurkhas were tapped for armed service. Particular 'castes' were sought out to fill clerical niches in the colonial administration, while 'criminal tribes' were those communities deemed to be perpetually on the wrong side of the law. Many of these categories, and the prejudicial logics underpinning them, did not emerge out of thin—or European—air. Colonial officials often worked with existing classifications, sensibilities, and hierarchies in order to most effectively order and capitalize on India's diversity. In this regard, colonial rule often compounded pre-existing relations of advantage among its subjects at the same time as it opened alternative avenues for social mobility.

For the British, the Sepoy Mutiny of 1857 underscored the need to better understand India's multitudes. Towards this purpose, the British Raj increasingly relied upon ethnological means to effectively know and rule its subjects. Historical anthropologists, Bernard Cohn and Nicholas Dirks, have convincingly argued that anthropology became a modality of colonial rule in what was increasingly becoming an 'ethnographic state'.[7] As is evidenced by the occasional ethnological reports found in the colonial archive, the ethnographic inclination was there well before the Mutiny. However, in the latter half of the nineteenth century, these curiosities mushroomed into more ambitious and instrumental projects like *The Census of India* (1872 onward), W.W. Hunter's *Statistical Account of Bengal* (1876), *The Imperial Gazetteers of India* (1881 onward), as well as H.H. Risley's extensive ethnographic studies as part of the *Census of 1901* and his later, *People of India* (1915).

We must remember that this was the time when academic anthropology (primarily under the banner of 'ethnology') was calving itself off from philosophy to become its own discipline.[8] Significant correspondence between colonial bureaucrats like Risley, Hunter, and Brian Hodgson and pioneers of European anthropology (and related fields) like E.B. Tylor, Sir Henry Maine, and Paul Topinard reveals just how entwined this emerging discipline was with colonial rule

[7] Cohn, *Colonialism and Its Forms of Knowledge*; Dirks, *Castes of Mind*.
[8] See John Zammito, 2002, *Kant, Herder, and the Birth of Anthropology*, Chicago: University of Chicago Press.

in India.[9] Without question, enumerative studies like the census impressed upon colonial subjects categories, paradigms, and sensibilities of nineteenth-century European thought. However, we must also remember that these projects were staffed by Indians whose native ethnological sensibilities were depended upon for appropriate classification of India's masses. These studies were hence sites of negotiation between native ethno-logics of India and those of the British (albeit on an uneven playing field), and as such, were in their own formalized way emblematic of colonial encounters of difference writ large.

A historical overview of the *Census of India* shows quite clearly that the diversity of India gave the census makers fits. Categories like 'caste', 'tribe', 'aboriginal', and 'race' were frequently confused and conflated with concepts like 'religion', 'occupation', and 'country', to reveal the convoluted logics underpinning these demographic studies. Despite decennial efforts to refine the rubrics of enumeration, the census inevitably inscribed some categories and rationales and not others. As they were concretized in the policies of the British Raj, many of these distinctions made rigid socio-cultural boundaries that were, in reality, more fluid.[10] Predicated upon overly determined

understandings of social practice, these distinctions temporally froze the dynamic content that allegedly filled community forms like 'castes' and 'tribes'. Insofar as these official rubrics became the guidelines for community-based policies of governance, they simultaneously became ascriptive vehicles for communities seeking sovereignty, political representation, economic advantage, and other entitlements increasingly being dolled out by the government. In this way, the enumerative categories, concepts, and rationales used to parse the population of India became not only *models of* diverse identities, but also *models for* identity's becoming.[11] In subtle and not so subtle ways, these ethno-logics would become constitutional paradigms of Nehru's post-independence, developmental state.[12]

Identity Now: The Scheduling of Tribes

The Cultural Research Institute in Kolkata is a vacuous government building where communities' memorandums, ST applications, and ethnographic reports flutter incessantly from beneath the paperweights that pin them to the bureaucratic table. In the concrete stairwell of this mildewed monolith hangs a lone portrait of Dr B.R. Ambedkar. Disproportionately small, the portrait seems too modest to preside over the happenings of the department, but it is there nonetheless—hanging quietly, slightly askew.

It is especially apt that Ambedkar's image would deck these stark walls. On the one

[9] This collusion also obtained through other institutional arenas such as the Asiatic Society in Calcutta, The Royal Anthropological Institute of Great Britain, and other scholarly institution across Europe. Exemplary correspondence found in Gov. of Bengal, Fin Misc. Head Misc. Coll 1 File 1 Proceedings 1–55 March 1887.

[10] Sudipta Kaviraj, 1992, 'The Imaginary Institution of India', in P. Chatterjee and G. Pandey (eds), *Subaltern Studies VII*, Oxford: Oxford University Press, pp. 1–39.

[11] On 'models of' and 'models for', see Clifford Geertz, 1973, 'Religion as Cultural System', in Geertz, *The Interpretation of Cultures*, pp. 87–125. On the census, see Anderson, *Imagined Communities*.

[12] See Jaideep Chatterjee's chapter in this volume.

hand, as the Chairman of the Constitution Drafting Committee, Ambedkar oversaw the formation of policies that granted exceptional powers of recognition to the Indian government. The constitutional provisions for Scheduled Castes and Tribes, and the ethnic-based autonomies guaranteed to those listed in the 5th and 6th Schedules, lent considerable credence to the Indian government's role as an Archimedean arbitrator of modern identity. These provisions, furthermore, created lucrative incentives for communities to mobilize specific kinds of identity for political purposes. On the other hand, Ambedkar's activism for the Depressed Classes (Dalits) established key paradigms for the politics of minority in South Asia. His steadfast critiques of social, political, and economic inequality, his subsequent calls for positive discrimination, and his tactics of community mobilization, all became exemplary measures for an increasingly dynamic, increasingly participatory, political society in twentieth-century India. Reading Ambedkar as both bureaucrat and activist, we may thus learn a great deal about the history of identity politics in India. Reading Ambedkar as organic anthropologist, we may learn even more.

Ambedkar was a luminary of acute, if problematic, anthropological sensibilities. His attacks on Brahmanism continually ventured into socio-cultural terrain in order to critique the logics through which Hindus justified their castigation of Dalits. Excellent work by Anupama Rao has examined how Ambedkar evoked an antagonistic alterity between high-caste Hindus and Dalits.[13]

However, another degree of alterity lurks in Ambedkar's worldview. By his own admission, his politics virtually disavowed the so-called 'tribal' or 'aboriginal' peoples of India. Ambedkar justified this by proclaiming: 'The Aboriginal Tribes have *not as yet* developed any political sense to make the best use of their political opportunities and they may easily become mere instruments in the hands either of a majority or a minority and thereby disturb the balance without doing any good to themselves.'[14] In other words, they were 'not as yet' ready to be responsible participants in the world of liberal democratic rights. In this quintessentially modernist logic, 'tribals' were not only Hinduism's other-beyond-mention, they were modernity's. Though Ambedkar the bureaucrat eventually steered in special constitutional provisions for 'tribal' development, his anthropological sensibilities remain emblematic of liberal thought in India more generally. Indeed, similar rationales of radical alterity may still be found in the formal and informal mechanisms of 'tribal' recognition today.

Recall the Lekh, who, both in their written application and during their ethnographic survey, chose to suppress any signs of Hindu influence—this despite the fact that previously they have proudly claimed Brahmanic and/or Kshatriya status in the varnic order. The current criteria for STs make no formal mention of 'tribals'

R. Majumdar, and A. Sartori (eds), *From the Colonial to the Postcolonial*, Oxford: Oxford University Press, pp. 137–58.

[14] B.R. Ambedkar, 1945, 'Communal Deadlock and a Way to Solve It', in *Babasaheb Ambedkar Writings and Speeches* (hereafter *BAWS*), Bombay: Government of Maharashtra.

[13] Anupama Rao, 2007, 'Ambedkar and the Politics of Minority', in Dipesh Chakrabarty,

vis-à-vis Hinduism. However, the binary is now firmly entrenched in the public imaginary, where the radical opposition between tribes and castes continues to structure the ways in which communities conceive of, recognize, and occasionally even perform, the category.

Beyond the arenas of informal othering, the caste/tribe binary sneaks its way into official corridors of recognition through well-meaning discourses of assimilation into a presumptively Hindu mainstream, as well as through more prejudicial adjudications. Documents obtained from one high-level source in Delhi denied one community's application for ST status on the following grounds: 'Though [community X] had tribal origin, with the passage of time and due to their contact with exogenous people and their contacts with the Hindu tradition, they are gradually assimilating into the Great Tradition. It will be then a retrograde step if they are included into the list of Scheduled Tribes.'[15] When coupled with the more ambient ethno-logics of the popular imagination, formal statements such as this justify the Lekh's decision to accentuate their animistic tendencies while burying any traces of Hinduism. Though it is tempting to write off such performative tactics as opportunistic pandering, a more sensitive interpretation might understand this stilted interface between the government and its citizens to be symptomatic of the ways in which particular forms of ethnological knowledge have taken root in modern India.

In India, sanctioned categories of recognition bring with them their own

requisite conditions of singularity and purity. In such a logic, a community must have one culture, one religion, and one tradition that is uniquely their own. Both the government and communities tend to index 'culture' as though it were a hermetically sealed entity, a discrete object metonymic of an equally discrete people. It is a telling antinomy that in an era of increasing hybridity and intercultural flow, the strictures of recognition would involve such conceptual purity, yet they continue to insist on distinctiveness in the most rigid terms. The criteria for STs offer a compelling case in point. Laid down by the Lokur Commission in 1965, the current criteria are as follows:

1. indication of primitive traits;
2. distinctive culture;
3. geographical isolation;
4. shyness of contact with the community at large; and
5. backwardness.

The two requisites—'distinctive culture' and 'geographical isolation'—inscribe the aforementioned logics of singularity and conceptual purity. 'Tribes' are to have distinct cultural attributes and live in isolation from the rest of society, as though both culturally and socially their ways of being were sealed off from the murk of the modern mainstream. Requisites 1 and 5 evoke related logics: 'tribes' are to have 'primitive traits'—that is, characteristics not of this time. Furthermore, they are to exude 'backwardness'—in other words, attributes counterposed to the standard alignments of the modern day. In the grammar of Ambedkar, 'backwardness' marks the 'tribal' subject as s/he who has

[15] Government of India, 'Comments of the ORGI', Ministry of Tribal Affairs.

not *as of yet* progressed into the normative arenas of rationalism, education, democratic participation, etc. Affirmative action thus becomes the tonic of their historical incipience. This calls to mind Dipesh Chakrabarty's eloquent critique of the 'not yet', historicist logics through which particular peoples have been relegated to what he calls the 'waiting room of history'.[16] Only here, we see how historicist logics and ethnological thought have, in fact, worked hand and glove in the ordering of the subjects of modernity.

Beyond taxonomic designations, this issue of temporality extends to supporting concepts as well. The Lokur Commission's criteria for STs presume a static, objective quality of 'culture'. 'Tribal culture' is *out there,* waiting to be found—a certifiable reminder of modernity's past. In such a calculus of historical progression, 'culture' stands in as the fixed variable and is thus no variable at all—not through time and certainly not within a given community on any given day.

The discipline of academic anthropology today generally understands 'culture' to be a dynamic, contested process, rather than a static, unanimous object. Unfortunately, this view cannot be said to be *en vogue* in modern identity politics, where the dynamic processes of hybridity are presumed to undermine the distinctiveness of a community. 'Culture' thus comes to be conflated with 'tradition' as that which is pure and unchanging. This is precisely the rationale through which communities like the Lekh choose to downplay—if not outright deny—the traces of the inevitable cross-pollination of cultures. For purposes of identifying a community, a fluid, processual notion of 'culture' simply does not cut as sharply as a static, fixed one.

It is without question that ethno-logics of singularity and cultural purity afford aspiring ethnic groups powerful tools for moulding and mobilizing identity from within the proverbial melting pot of the modern age. In the best cases, the conceptual purity of the 'culture' concept can be a source of unity, a platform for rights, and a calling card for the preservation of human diversity across the globe. In the worst cases, rigid determinations of 'culture', 'religion', and 'tradition' foster precisely the types of fundamentalism and ethnic absolutism that have led to so much violence in recent decades.[17] Articulations of such a violent order should give us pause to consider precisely how ethnological knowledge is being operationalized in the world today.

Towards that end, let us then turn to the intimate spaces of everyday life where identity hits home. A brief look into the experiences of today's ethnic subjects signals fundamental changes in the ways people identify and belong to modern communities.

---

[16] Dipesh Chakrabarty, 2000, *Provincializing Europe*, Princeton: Princeton University Press. Johannes Fabian has made a similar argument. However, Fabian focuses primarily on how academic anthropology denies coevalness to its object communities. See Johannes Fabian, 1983, *Time and the Other*, New York: Columbia University Press.

[17] See Paul Gilroy, 1990, 'Nationalism, History, and Ethnic Absolutism', *The History Workshop Journal*, vol. 30, no. 1, pp. 114–220.

Everyday Ethnology

It is Sunday on the tea estate where fifteen villagers have gathered at the local schoolhouse for their monthly ethnic association meeting. Inside the small corrugated aluminum building they sit at crudely fashioned wooden desks too small for adults. At the front of the classroom, facing them, sits an older gentleman wearing a pin-stripped suit, a pressed cotton shirt, and polished leather boots. He is an elite of the ethnic association and this is clearly not his turf. As a Central Committee member of the All India Tamang Buddhist Association (AITBA), he is part of a vast apparatus of ethnic mobilization stretching across India and beyond. Though visibly uncomfortable, he commences the meeting in business-like fashion. It mustn't run late; his car and driver are waiting.

Protocol is soon thwarted though when local members start to complain about the political entanglements of the association, its controversial cultural policies, and the emergence of a rival faction with more lenient policies. With a minor mutiny on his hands, he begins to proselytize on the conjoined importance of a unified political and cultural front. He and AITBA speak from experience. It took them two decades to secure ST status for the Tamang community. Their quest included *bandh*s, hunger strikes, and seventy-seven delegational visits to Delhi alone. Closer to home, the association initiated extensive cultural engineering programmes to revitalize the 'pure', 'original' form of Tamang culture. These focused primarily on: (i) the elimination of Hindu elements from their repertoire; and (ii) the accentuation of uniquely Tamang Buddhist attributes.

As he pontificates on the inseparability of political solidarity and cultural singularity, the central committee member makes a compelling case: for unity, Tamangs must have one culture. This is precisely why the association has implemented such strict rules as to what is 'authentic'—and hence appropriate—cultural practice. In the past, those who violated these rules have been socially ostracized, even fined. Those who are still unsure of 'traditional' attire and appropriate 'religious' practices may refer to the plethora of DVDs, books, magazines, and notices put out by the association documenting what it means to be a true Tamang. Culture should be a source of pride, not tension, he reminds them. May they thus set their differences aside!

That these tea workers would spend their day off deliberating the nuances of 'culture' shows the currency of ethnological knowledge in their lives. The scope of homegrown ethnology, however, transcends their monthly meeting. Afterward, when the elite returns to town via car, they will descend by foot back into the recesses of the tea estate, stopping along the way to share with friends and neighbours the main points of the meeting. These casual conversations are a part of daily life, yet it is through these informal interactions that the niceties of AITBA's brand of Tamang 'culture' take root in the local community.

Importantly, AITBA's rigid renderings of 'culture', 'religion', and 'tradition' have met with mixed response. Some Tamangs embrace the efforts of cultural revitalization as a return to what is pure and authentic.

When questioned, these proponents often frame their devotion through narratives of modernization and cultural loss; recuperating 'tradition' and 'culture' thus becomes a means to stability in a time of incessant change. Opponents, on the other hand, see AITBA's rules as an infringement upon their private traditions. In their familial practice, Buddhist and Hindu elements have mingled seamlessly for generations and thus, these familial practices are their lived tradition, their continuity, and stability. Between these extremes, there are still many others for whom these new renderings of 'culture' are a source of confusion, increasingly laden with social and political consequences.

Since 2002, the Tamang's ST designation has increasingly set them apart from their neighbours such that their inter-ethnic relations are now often marked by competition, resentment, and jealousy. Unbending definitions of Tamang 'culture', 'religion', and 'tradition' have only sharpened such distinctions. Meanwhile, the imperatives of singularity and cultural purity have created rifts within the community itself where born-again ethnics chastise those who continue their syncretic religious practices as ignorant and uneducated. Neighbours who once celebrated popular holidays like Dusserra together now refuse to join one another. On Diwali, homes that used to glow through the night now go dark. Even families have been torn apart by divergent ethnological persuasions. In public life, these subtle dynamics are normally outshined by the more colourful celebrations of ethnic achievement, yet they are part and parcel to the same modality of modern self-making.

Here, we see how sanctioned categories, concepts, and logics of identity can profoundly affect how individuals come to know and associate with their communities and others. In a matter of years, normative ethno-logics (particularly those delineating the 'tribal' norm) have become ready-at-hand paradigms for everyday othering and identification. Through these everyday practices, the exigencies and attendant paradigms of recognition have reconfigured the Tamang's very sociality, often in divisive, unintended ways. These shifting contours of inclusion and exclusion accordingly represent the lived terrain of ethnological distinction where categories, concepts, and logics enter into the realm of social experience—reworking modes of social differentiations, and ultimately individuals' notions of the self. Such dynamics remind us that everyday ethnology entails much more than overt discourses of 'culture'—be they in the café or in the village schoolhouse on a particular Sunday every month. Everyday ethnology also happens when we draw the lines between 'Us' and 'Them' in our daily lives. Whether actualized through careful deliberation or split-second judgements and stereotypes, these are the practices through which we parse our social worlds, through which we recognize and render difference at the most intimate levels.

At the level of the individual too, the affects can be profound. Born-again Tamangs speak as though something in them has been rekindled; they now engage the world with a newfound sense of pride, purpose, and belonging. For opponents, these new paradigms of the 'old' are an affront to their very being, a source of disgust, an ideology that may have divided their community but shall never penetrate their individual core. In both cases, these are affective, embodied sentiments—articulated as though they came from within, be it from the heart or from the gut. Spanning devotion, defiance, and middling degrees of indifference, these wide-ranging receptions signal the mercurial dialectic of modern ethno-logics and belonging. On the one hand, they expose an important incongruence between conceptualizations of 'culture', 'religion', etc., and the actual experiences of identity. Whereas on the other, they encourage us to consider how ethnology functions as an epistemic modality for knowing and ordering socio-cultural difference and community forms. Here, too, we may ask how ethnology is coming to affect people's very being-in-the-world.

At the End

In the words of the political scientist Sudipta Kaviraj, in the nineteenth century, 'history breaks out everywhere'; 'History becomes the great terrain of politics. Because history is a way of talking about the collective self, and bringing it into existence.'[18] With Kaviraj's insight in mind, it is worth considering whether we have entered into a similar time for ethnology. Beyond the confines of the ivory tower, ethnological thought has seemingly broken out everywhere: in the offices of ethnic associations and the corridors of government; on stage, where authentic 'culture' is danced away;

in museums, where the 'primitive' stands encased in Plexiglas; in libraries and even the beauty isles of your local supermarket where each ethnicity finds its own place on the shelf; on the Internet; at the United Nations; and on the street, where people march and bleed everyday in the name of ethnic difference. Whether at the café or the capital building, 'culture', so it seems, is indeed the word on everyone's lips,[19] and ethnology a form of knowledge on everyone's minds.

Within this increasingly unbound field of thought, the cases of the Lekh and Tamang prove especially apt for exploring contemporary ethno-logics. However, we must remember that the politics of reservation, particularly those involving STs, are exemplary in this regard. Thinking more broadly, it is important to bear in mind that such normative forms of community distinction can never be the end-all, be-all of contemporary identity formation. In a nation haunted by Partition, history simply cannot be forgotten. However, history now shares the stage with other modalities of identification, most notably ethnology, but also the politics of development, economics, environmentalism, and even a strengthening penchant for mythology in the case of Hindutva. Beyond these modalities though, we are still left to ponder those aspects of identity that escape the purview of knowledge—namely, the intensity and fervour with which identity is experienced and expressed in the modern world. Approaching the enigma of identity,

[18] Sudipta Kaviraj, 1995, *The Unhappy Consciousness*, New Delhi: Oxford University Press, p. 108.

[19] Marshall Sahlins, 1993, 'Goodbye to Tristes Tropes: Ethnography in the Context of Modern World History', *Journal of Modern History*, vol. 65, no. 1, March, p. 3.

we would thus do well to seek out the ways in which ethnic distinction and other modalities of identification work with—that is, augment, corroborate, and accentuate—one another on their way to producing affects of a more embodied order. Without precluding related generative conditions, the select cases offered here attest to the integrality of ethnological knowledge to modern identity formations. They thereby remind us that while ethnology has not become *the* great terrain of politics, it certainly has become an indelible feature of the political morass.

The conditions of modern life continually press upon us the need and opportunity to step outside of ourselves and define ourselves with and against others. In the policies of positive discrimination and elsewhere, we find palpable incentives for such reflection and objectification. Daily encounters with transformation and difference also precipitate similar, albeit less formal, types of reckoning. These conditions help explain *why* the issue of identity has become so accentuated in recent times. Yet, modernity has also entailed a fundamental reworking of *how* we step outside ourselves, *how* we reflect upon the social world, and *how* we come to know and recognize the self and others. Going forward, the key issue then becomes not

that modernity encouraged ethnological awareness. Rather, the bleeding question is: *what kinds* of ethnic consciousness have taken root in the human landscape of today, and through which categories? Bolstered by which concepts? And according to what logics have the social and political possibilities of communal identity been refashioned? Through such questioning, we may come closer to understanding how particular abstract qualities of knowledge can have such worldly, corporeal consequences.

From our vantage point, we may never know what it meant nor how it felt to belong to a pre-modern community. And yet, as the cases of the Lekh and Tamang again illustrate, contemporary systems of recognition, and the normative ethno-logics they entail, often beg us to do just that—to define ourselves and others in the rigid primordial truths of 'culture', 'religion', 'tradition', etc. When we do that, we embrace both the enabling paradigms and troubling antinomies of modern identity, becoming at once modern subjects and subjects of a peculiarly ethnological modernity.[20] Surveying the turbulent contours of identity in South Asia today, it seems that such a prospect may hold as much danger as it does promise.

---

[20] Here, I work with Saurabh Dube's distinction between 'modern subjects' and 'subjects of modernity'. See Saurabh Dube, 2009, 'Introduction', in Saurabh Dube (ed.), *Enchantments of Modernity*, New Delhi: Routledge, pp. 8–13.

IV

Affecting Arts

13

Advertising in India
Genealogies of the Consumer Subject*

Arvind Rajagopal

The construction of life at the moment lies far more in the power of facts than in convictions... [Such facts] are for the gigantic apparatus of social life what oil is for machines: you do not go up to a turbine and pour machine oil all over it. You spurt a bit of it in the hidden rivets and joints that you must know.

—Walter Benjamin[1]

The fundamental substance of an epoch and its unheeded impulses illuminate each other reciprocally.

—Siegfried Kracauer[2]

Weimar era intellectuals in Germany argued that if the domains of economy and polity were increasingly administered and controlled, the realm of culture afforded a measure of freedom. In a sense, capitalism was proving to be more democratic than the political institutions of democracy. In the space of expression afforded by commodity consumption, it was possible to arrive at a diagnostic critique of capitalist modernity. We may both theoretically extend and

* Part of this chapter derives from an earlier article; see Arvind Rajagopal, 1998, 'Advertising, Politics and the Sentimental Education of the Indian Consumer', *Visual Anthropology Review*, vol. 14, no. 2, Fall–Winter, pp. 14–31.
[1] Walter Benjamin, 1979, 'Filling Station', in *One Way Street and Other Writings*, trans. Edmund Jephcott and Kingsley Shorter, London: Verso, p. 45.

[2] Siegfried Kracauer, 1995, 'The Mass Ornament', in Thomas Y. Levin (trans. and ed.), *The Mass Ornament: Weimar Essays*, Cambridge, MA: Harvard University Press, p. 75.

historically qualify their analyses, as I do in this chapter, to argue that ads for consumer goods perform the labour of articulating culture and economy, thereby allowing us to track historically specific subject forms and the mentalities they give rise to.

First Considerations

When capitalist markets were established in colonial India, they did not necessarily stand in the same relationship to polity and culture as the market did in Western Europe. Markets had of course pre-existed European arrival, and regional trading cultures spanned the Indian Ocean.[3] In this context, the development of a colonial market, we know, was geared to exporting raw materials and importing manufactured goods. This market was racially and culturally segregated in its forms of circulation and consumption. It was part of an economy maintained through a rule of difference between British and natives, and legitimated as a civilizational lag that was reproduced—even as it was supposed to be negated—by colonial rule.[4]

English-language advertisements of the period tended to see the native market as both inefficient and unsanitary, while confirming deleterious aesthetic and moral preferences. Goods were exposed to the elements and sold with poor packaging at best; suspicions of adulteration and other forms of chicanery were frequent. By contrast, the colonial market that catered to the British in India, and to well-to-do Indians, understood itself as superior in its norms and tastes, setting the standard that natives ought to aspire to but could ill afford. The work of civilizational uplift, such as it was, placed the colonial state—through ameliorative legislation and public works—at its centre.[5] In this sense, at least on the evidence of Anglophone ads, the colonial market was an enclave market, insulated from the larger society and unable to ensure that its example was followed.

Meanwhile, new indigenous practices of consumption were noticeable in the ads for various goods, such as women's clothing and fashion accessories, and pills and potions enhancing the sex lives of both men and women. Patent medicine promising miraculous cures for various afflictions were also widely advertised. Criticized in the native press as licentious and immoral,[6] such ads might have confirmed apprehensions about the vernacular market as requiring to be restrained rather than encouraged.

---

[3] Sugata Bose, 2006, *A Hundred Horizons: The Indian Ocean in the Age of Global Empire*, Cambridge, MA: Harvard University Press; K.N. Chaudhuri, 1978, *The Trading World of Asia and the English East India Company: 1660–1760*, Cambridge: Cambridge University Press; Ashin Das Gupta and Uma Das Gupta, 2001, *The World of the Indian Ocean Merchant 1500–1800: Collected Essays of Ashin Das Gupta*, New Delhi: Oxford University Press; and Dwijendranath Tripathi, 2004, *The Oxford History of Indian Business*, New York: Oxford University Press.

[4] See Partha Chatterjee, 1993, *The Nation and Its Fragments*, Princeton, NJ: Princeton University Press, 1993.

[5] See Sir Arthur Cotton, 1854, *Public Works in India: Their Importance. With Suggestions for Their Extension and Improvement*, London: Wm. H. Helm; and David Ludden, 1992, 'India's Development Regime', in Nicholas Dirks (ed.), *Colonialism and Culture*, Ann Arbor, MI: University of Michigan Press, pp. 247–87. I am grateful to David Ludden for directing me to Cotton's writing.

[6] Charu Gupta, 2002, *Sexuality, Obscenity, Community: Women, Muslims and the Hindu Public in Colonial India*, London: Palgrave Macmillan.

However, the new forms of caste, class, and gender subjectivity hinted at in such messages were subsumed within a growing nationalist movement. It was the anti-colonial critique that dominated the public sphere, muffling other, internal social conflicts being generated.

Among the first initiatives of the nationalist movement was, of course, the boycott of foreign imports and the promotion of domestically made products, such as the making and wearing of *khadi*.[7] Khadi was conceived to symbolize the way nationalism revalorized consumption, signalling the intent to create a virtuous national economy, to replace the destructive materialism imposed by colonial rule.[8] It was imagined as the first step in the programme of making subjects of the nation that was to come, rather than in indulging creatures who sought to assure their own comfort.

Now, the growth of nationalism within civil society and against the colonial state illustrated the divided character of the public sphere. Such a divide characterized Indian advertising too, between a vernacular domain whose moral status varied, depending on its fit with patriotic nationalist values, and an English-language realm catering largely to the colonial elite and to relatively affluent city dwellers. The former very likely had a larger audience, but was more entrepreneurial and dispersed in its production, and the archive of publicity resulting from it is slighter.

The disparity between vernacular and colonial public domains was so great as to pose the question of definition: when was advertising to be understood (roughly) as we see it today, and what was it before or besides that? Wall calendars with pictures of gods, promoting a particular merchant or a store, and chromolithographs commemorating the use of khadi as well as certain Congress leaders served the function of advertising just as much as messages in periodicals publicizing consumer goods.[9] The distinctions between religious imagery, political propaganda, and messages promoting commodity consumption were fluid and perhaps not seen as relevant. This can be understood as the analogue of an important aspect of Hindi writing before independence, and perhaps for years afterwards as well: journalism, political pamphleteering, and literature were not necessarily insulated from each other in practice or regarded as distinct, and they were often practiced by the same individuals.[10] Unlike English-language advertising, vernacular advertising was likely

[7] A 1930 letter written by Gandhi illustrates the point: 'It is not enough to wear khadi. The wearer should also realize that khadi symbolizes the spirit of patriotism and modesty. Wearing khadi does not give one the license to enjoy all kinds of liberty, but is the first step in the direction of self-restraint and a sign of our desire to curtail other unnecessary freedoms. [For example] [t]ea is never a necessity of life...' 'Two letters', *Navjivan*, 2 March 1930, in *The Collected Works of Mahatma Gandhi*, vol. XLIII, March–June 1930, New Delhi: Publications Division, Government of India, 1971, p. 2.

[8] Emma Tarlo has shown however, that khadi's success was as a mobilizational medium available to express a range of meanings and social class positions, rather than as a narrowly defined set of values. See Emma Tarlo, 1996, *Clothing Matters: Dress and Identity in India*, Chicago: University of Chicago Press.

[9] See Christopher Pinney, 2003, *Photos of the Gods*, London: Reaktion Books.

[10] See Francesca Orsini, 2002, *The Hindi Public Sphere 1920–1940: Language and Literature in the Age of Nationalism*, New York: Oxford University Press.

produced by entrepreneurs, for whom there was little impetus to declare it as a genre separate from other forms of writing.

English-language advertisers, in contrast to their vernacular counterparts, not only trafficked in the market. As well, they lobbied the state and gained contracts for governmental propaganda, and for engaging in developmental publicity, before as well as after independence.[11] In this transaction between the state and advertisers, the work of the advertising agency was central. It is perhaps this fact that, more than any other, distinguishes the two domains of publicity. Indian-language advertising was no doubt served by the agency form as well, but the archives that remain are largely, I suspect, those of Anglophone advertisers. The story they tell, perhaps not surprisingly, excludes any sense of the work of Indian-language agencies.

Advertising's Modernity

Anglophone-advertising agencies, subsidiaries of British or American firms, and increasingly over time, Indian firms, came to define the work of advertising, reproducing the modernizing rhetoric of their Western counterparts. In their understanding, the advertisement was a means of promoting market efficiency and assuring that the interests of producers and consumers both would be realized. Like the commodities they promoted, ads too were understood to transcend the conditions in which they were produced, and in fact, created their own context and were thus able to be read and circulated without requiring further mediation. It was the rise of the agency that permitted this distinct form of communication that could generate its own citational authority, and which was, in a sense, state-like in its effect. Viewed in this light, it is less surprising that vernacular publicity could not easily rise above its context in the way English-language advertising could.

In this, ad agencies in India were enabled by their catering mainly to an enclave market, occupied by the urban well-to-do who (for them) represented the model consumer, capable of actualizing their aspirations through their purchases.[12] On the other hand, the majority of Indians seemed condemned, for the foreseeable future, to a penurious existence so that elite advertisers saw little prospect of returns in addressing them.

What came to define the work of advertising was a certain hothouse character, a protected profession within a protected economy, albeit one that claimed to be both cosmopolitan and national. For proof of the former one did not have to look very far; Indian ads did not stray very far from the copybook of Western agencies, and assumed that Indian culture was little more than a veneer on the *homo economicus* already familiar to them. And nationalism for these advertisers was reduced to a stock selection

---

[11] World War II propaganda accounts were actively solicited and obtained by advertising agencies. And a glance at the in-house publications of ad agencies such as J. Walter Thompson and Co. and Lintas confirms the importance of developmental and public service contracts with the Indian government.

[12] For an excellent discussion of advertising in the contemporary period, see William Mazzarella, 2003, *Shoveling Smoke: Advertising in Contemporary India*, Durham, NC: Duke University Press.

of sanitized images connoting '*swadeshi*' or national distinction, that could be inserted into the symbolic repertoire of the urban consumer without necessarily engaging either with the Gandhian programme of moral rejuvenation, or for that matter, with the implications of Nehruvian developmentalism.

Colonial modernity, when it began to be adapted and domesticated, as, for instance, when intellectuals—from Rammohun Roy to Gandhi—sought to overcome the imagination of cultural inferiority. It responded to feelings of shame and humiliation that were often intensely personal, which they also perceived as a collective circumstance. The urgency of their imaginings of the possibility of change gave them a distinct quality: theirs was a polemical and embattled modernity, struggling to assert legitimacy and not certain of achieving their aim. The contrast with the attitudes and assumptions evinced in what I am calling the archive of Indian advertising, into the 1980s, is striking. It is not surprising therefore, that a recent historical account notes that the passage of independence in 1947 left little or no observable trace on ads.[13] The existing archive of advertising made available by Anglophone ad agencies, is one that displays little evidence of interest in engaging with the motives and sentiments of the indigenous market.[14]

Anglophone ad agencies arguably identified their work as modernizing.[15] And yet, we witness a relatively serene and unruffled mode of assertion in the images, for example, in ads for products such as Brooke Bond Tea, Lifebuoy Soap, Tata Swastik Bootpolish, Parle biscuits, or 7 o'clock blades. Whether the images contained religious iconography—as they might have done when promotional material circulated in the districts at the behest of regional wholesale merchants and local distributors—or figured individuals and objects identifiably 'modern' in appearance, there is seldom the sense of a sceptical interlocutor, or a rival drawing unfavourable comparison. If elsewhere modernity had the sense of an emergency about it, of responding to an existential and cultural crisis, Indian consumer modernity, on the evidence of Anglophone agencies, was sedate by contrast. From images of the Taj Mahal used to sell tea bags, to the mustachioed maharaja promoting flights on Air India, there was little in them that conveyed the tumult of an emerging market, let alone a developing nation. An advertising executive in Mumbai observed: 'Analyse the history of advertising in India and you'll realise that it was, till recently…the last whistle stop of English colonialism…[and]…until

---

[13] Vikram Doctor and Anvar Ali Khan, 1997, '*Kyon Na Aazmaye? A Brief History of Indian Advertising*', vol. XVIII, January, pp. 46–55.

[14] In some respects, the native market was actually in competition, for example, through imitation and counterfeit goods that the larger companies tried to fight back through a variety of means. Glimpses

of such action can sometimes be seen in ads, where information is provided about the trademark customers were supposed to look for, with warnings about fraudulent copies.

[15] See in this context, M.G. Parameswaran, 2001, *FCB-Ulka Brand Building Advertising: Concepts and Cases*, New Delhi: Tata McGraw-Hill.

the advent of television…the privy of the
English-speaking crowd….'[16]

The Vernacularization of Advertising Culture

The Indian advertising industry grew slowly
from its inception in the British era. Senior
members of the industry described it as
having been a kind of insiders' fraternity,
not engaged in a great deal of creative work
but, for the most part, using American ads
in Indian settings.[17] Little market research
was carried out, and given the limitations
of the market and the lack of competition,
it was perhaps not considered necessary.
Advertising was a haven for many English-
language poets, artists, and film-makers,
from Satyajit Ray to Shyam Benegal, but it
included some Indian-language poets too,
for example, Arun Kolatkar. Numerous
advertising executives testified to the heavily
urban, English-language biases of Indian
advertising. Most original advertising copy
was written in English, with companies
shifting to 'language copywriters' only several
years after the introduction of national
television.

The major break in post-independence
Indian advertising occurred *not with national
independence*, but decades later, with the
onset of nationwide television broadcasting
and market liberalization. The relaxation of
the licence–permit *raj*, and the establishment
of a communication platform that permitted
reaching consumers at negligible incremental
cost, was central to the new developments.
It was when it became possible to address a
mass market cheaply that newcomers could
forge price–value equations that challenged
the enclave market model being reproduced
by existing ad agencies. For example, laundry
detergent and cell phones, to name only
two products, were assumed by the agencies
to be affordable only by the premium
market—and in both cases, they were proven
drastically wrong. Infrastructural growth
and political change were leading to an
undermining of the status quo in which ad
agencies had become established.

The way in which this change came
to be understood and negotiated was
through a change in the terms of nationalist
discourse. Congress nationalism had been
ambivalent about consumption as a means
of self-actualization. Such an attitude could
be sustained in a protected, enclave market
catering to the restricted consumption
capacities of urban classes, where there
was little to be gained by contesting the
prevailing Nehruvian consensus. For
example, in a limited domestic market
where there were few imports, there was
little cause for ad agencies to utilize themes
from national culture as a marker of product
difference; multinationals, who spent the
most on advertising goods, were not anxious
to draw attention to their origins. The
advertising industry itself hardly operated
with exposure to the full rigours of a market,
and was only poorly professionalized. Since
the domestic market was itself understood
as small and homogeneous, and this then
further simplified the work of the advertising
industry. The mass market was tacitly
excluded from this definition, since it was
believed to require logistics of distribution

[16] Kiran Khalap, 1995, 'Chasing the Rainbow: A Two-colour, One Decade Catechism on the Hunt for Advertising Excellence in a Pseduomature Market', *Advertising & Marketing*, 30 June, p. 27.

[17] Field notes, Mumbai, June–August 2000.

rather than creative communication to ensure the sale of goods. In sum, ad agencies created an image of the market, as they could be expected to, reproducing certain assumptions about the market that dovetailed with the prevailing political consensus. With globalization, each of these assumptions came to be exposed, and its limitations revealed.

The growth of a consumer market is a political as well as an economic process, resignifying as it does the relations of production and consumption within a given historical context. If individuals are coached in new habits of consumption, they must, at the same time, be taught to conceive of the affective relations within which these practices are enacted. Given the austerity of the hitherto prevailing public culture, as well as its limited reach, it was to religion that advertising reached, obedient to the example of the electoral sphere. This is because, at least in the Nehruvian context, the market was simultaneously expressive of a particular political balance of forces and helped to reproduce it. And thus, the significance of the shift from an elite secular culture to a more Hinduized national culture was able to be registered, as ads themselves fashioned specific idioms from indigenous culture to cast more specific and targeted appeals to consumers.

Marketers in India often referred to the homogeneous character of the market before liberalization, as opposed to its more stratified aspect thereafter. This is misleading unless we realize that what they referred to was a middle-class market—not the middle class *per se* but the middle class of the marketers' imagination, which was indeed homogeneous. The market itself

was highly segmented, but what allowed the illusion of homogeneity was its price segmentation—and price was the principal means by which the Indian market was segmented. The difference between economy and premium brands in many categories could be three times as high as that obtained in the West, for example. What resulted with the institution of television and commercial sponsorship, especially after satellite television in mid-1994, was, of course, that the economics of conveying messages changed completely, with one platform becoming available for all price segments. Simultaneously, the relationship between income and affordability that had earlier been established was disrupted, as consumers in low-income segments reached out for products advertised for higher-income groups.

Until recently, elite advertisers did not attempt to go beyond patronizing modes of address in selling goods to lower-income sections of society, when they did address this segment of the market. Thus, for instance, in ads such as for Wheel detergent, Hindustan Levers' low-cost answer to their competition from a new regional entrant into the market, Nirma, women were 'shown' that their earlier soaps were ineffective by a man lecturing to them, and that the new soap was the answer to their unceasing struggle for whiter and cleaner clothes. Ads adopted an explicitly pedagogical strategy, and if any aesthetic value was contained in the ads, it was in terms of the score, usually something approximating a folksy jingle or a Hindi film tune. If one could risk an overly general statement, one might say that utility was presented as the most salient aspect of consumer messages for the lower middle and working classes, while aesthetics remained the province of their betters, the middle and upper classes. It was for them that the finer particulars of appearance, individual satisfaction, and self-actualization were important. Not that these aspects were entirely omitted in ads for lower-income segments, but if we examined the amounts of money spent in creating those ads, a clear stratification would emerge. What occurred with the expansion of the market was that attention finally began to be paid to the market potential at the 'bottom of the pyramid', noticed because of its ability to reward businesses for the effort.

As downmarket consumers weaned themselves from unbranded and regionally branded goods, they entered a new regime of consumption whose contours were not self-evident or readily available. Rather, it had to be constructed, by dint of advertising and marketing effort, through new modes of signification and styles of reading that consumers had to learn to deploy efficiently. Ads over the years reveal not merely a class-stratified range of texts to match a price-stratified array of products. We can find, as well, appeals that can be distinguished in terms of different audio-visual semantics, according to the character of the publics sought to be addressed or constructed (the assumption of a particular kind of address tending over time to form its own object). If advertisers envisioned the establishment, sooner or later, of a universe populated entirely by international brands, the pathway forged for the purpose still had to negotiate specific national histories. Ads within a protected domestic market evinced

a clear stratification, between a visual aesthetic for the upper classes and utilitarian appeals for downmarket customers. The distinction of the latter, more inexpensive ads emerged rather in the audio, through the jingle, which would be based on Hindi film or folk tunes. With the growth of the market and the entry of new consumers into different price-strata of consumption, the relationship between appeals to different class-strata changes, in ways that are to some extent shaped by the medium of communication.

Advertising and Commodity Culture

Now, the conversion of traditional relationships of patronage and clientism and of truck and barter, into relationships of commodity exchange and cash transactions traces one of the most fundamental dynamics of modern social transformation. The transformation is, however, never complete, and for important reasons. Commodity relations are seldom introduced or extended in terms of naked self-interest. Rather, they tend to be described as particular instances of larger networks of mutual dependence and obligation. Since the nature of this mutual dependence undergoes change at the same time, however, the terms in which individuals enter into them are themselves ceaselessly being revised. Ads provide a valuable record of the ways in which businesses seek to negotiate social contradictions while expanding markets, and thus illuminate the ongoing process of transformation.

In doing so, however, advertisers face a problem. Advertisers seek to show individuals in situ as it were, cross-hatched with prevailing caste, community, and gender relations, to create a reality effect, and enable viewers to recognize themselves in the ad narratives. At the same time, however, they must necessarily transcend existing reality if new practices of consumption are to be introduced. How are they to do so without losing their audience? The efforts of businesses to coach consumers in the appropriate styles of expenditure, and to render ubiquitous the signposts that equate consumption with the good life, make it clear that the outcomes are thought to be anything but inevitable.

The difficulty of this tutelary task confirms that no merely abstract exercise is involved here; rather the challenge is to engage embedded social relations. The transformation and expansion of the domestic market is a political as well as an economic process, resignifying as it does the relations of production and consumption within a given historical conjuncture. If individuals are trained in new habits of consumption, they must, at the same time, be taught to visualize the context within which these practices are enacted. If consumer longing must be evoked, like any desire, it has to be couched in a particular language. A given market configuration is simultaneously expressive of a particular political balance of forces and helps to achieve it. It is here, as I have said, that the significance of the shift from an elite secular culture to a more Hinduized national culture can be registered, as ads themselves fashion specific idioms from indigenous culture to cast more specific and targeted appeals to consumers.

Coda

In the now famous correspondence between Theodor Adorno and Walter Benjamin on the latter's work, Adorno wrote of the fruitful tension between his theory of the consumption of exchange value and Benjamin's theory about empathy with the soul of the commodity. Because Adorno understood commodity consumption as being not so much about the things in themselves as the idea they stood for, his response called for unmasking the forms of displacement, substitution, and equivalence through which commodities acquired their desirability. In response to Adorno, Benjamin observed that empathy with the commodity was nothing other than empathy with exchange value itself.[18] By this, he meant that in consuming exchange value, ideas of equivalence and an open-ended availability were hardly apparent as conscious or palpable benefits of consumption. Rather, individuals could identify with the commodity and the sense of promiscuous possibility it connoted, of a many-sided and costless engagement with an infinitely various world.

I take the insight resulting from this debate as crucial in understanding the task of ads, which work by proffering identification with shifting objects of desire. Although the

[18] Walter Benjamin, 1977, 'Reply. 9 December 1938', in Theodor Adorno, Walter Benjamin, Ernst Bloch, Bertolt Brecht, and Georg Lukacs (translation editor, Ronald Taylor), *Aesthetics and Politics*, London: Verso, p. 109. For the interesting debate between the advocate of the overarching necessity of theory (Adorno) and the adherent of an approach influenced by surrealism (Benjamin), wherein truth could be glimpsed via a confrontation with the objects themselves, see Ibid., pp. 110–41.

commodity opens out into an endless series of equivalences, the commodity cannot, in fact, be signified without mystification through particular images of longing. Hence, the effort here to historicize ads as well as the contexts in which they emerged. More broadly, this is a reminder that although commodification is universalistic in conception, it can only be a phase in 'the social life of things', becoming thereafter, gifts in exchange, and/or objects in use or disuse, and part of affective networks of interdependence and domination. Advertisers, however, maintain the fiction that the space of the commodity is one of freedom, and that to draw consumers into the realms of branded goods is to set in motion a process of improvement. The more consumers are drawn up to the heights of upmarket privilege and sophistication, the more realized they are, in this view, as they learn how to perceive their own needs. But even if advertisers seek to improve consumers in the mass market as a whole, they at the same time reproduce the cultural dynamics that maintain class differences, and thus act as a brake on any pedagogical process. Thus, they tend to mirror a given configuration of consumption patterns without acknowledging their complicity in the political balance of forces that any such configuration must represent.

In his widely cited book on the US advertising industry, *Advertising: The Uneasy Persuasion*, Michael Schudson asks the question of whether the real function of advertising is to promote individual consumption. Rather, as Schudson provocatively argues, advertising can be understood as capitalist realism, and as the counterpart of Soviet propaganda, which can be termed as socialist realism. Realism is, in this usage, not realistic of course. It is rather a one-sided accentuation of those aspects of reality that accord with the prevailing socio-political system. Capitalist realism, in Schudson's definition, thus focused on individual achievement and material fulfilment, prophesied improvement and progress through striving for increased consumption of goods.[19] Schudson thus alerts us to the formal and generic aspect to representations of commodity culture as essential to the particular forms of empathy that Benjamin more generally identified.

During the Cold War, the ubiquitous signs of commodity culture for decades symbolized the affluence of the 'free world' as against the controlled economies of the Eastern bloc. For those in the developing world, the contrast between 'their' advertising and 'our' advertising was both a statement about national sovereignty and a reminder of underdevelopment. Advertising in India, for instance, had folk jingles for Kirloskar pump sets, Vicco Vajradanti tooth powder, and Tinopal washing powder. For many years, the most circulated advertising in India was acoustic, broadcast in radio jingles or by streetside barkers, and rooted in ethnic specificity, while much advertising remained regional and local, and did not enter the archives, even of the national ad agencies. The division is not only geographical; the gulf between rural and urban advertising only amplifies the distance between vernacular and English-language cultures, where the latter has been allied and associated with

[19] Michael Schudson, 1984, *Advertising: The Uneasy Persuasion*, New York: Basic Books.

status symbols, whether for cars, cigarettes, or colas. As self-styled modernizers, those at the helm of the advertising profession tend to regard what goes on in the hinterland, and in regional and non-metropolitan languages, as insignificant in relation to what they themselves are engaged in.

Schudson's discussion provides a means of specifying some key distinctions in the Indian case. With an abundance of Hindu mythological imagery, capitalist realism was at best slow to enter Indian advertising. In any case, between agrarian, industrial, and mercantile capital, the public sector and small businesses, the Indian economy was not all capitalist, and hardly of a piece. For the relatively small urban middle class that existed until the 1980s, with the growth of television, Indian advertising might provide memories of 'the long afternoon of underdevelopment' as they look back from the more prosperous vantage point of the new millennium.[20] But for the bulk of the population, Indian advertising, until recently, represented a kind of overhead transmission, an exchange of goods and symbols beyond their reach. In such a situation, advertising was perhaps more likely to succeed as fantasy than as realism.

Advertising culture in India in the 1980s and before was marked by the absence, by and large, of a popular visual aesthetic for the majority of the consuming population. This was symptomatic of an elitist politics that Hindu nationalism—the dominant political challenger to Congress

developmentalism—both capitalized upon and overcame, by drawing on religion and ritual to indigenize the languages of politics in efforts to forge a new hegemonizing ideology. Advertisers in India, long identified with a colonial box*wallah* culture, have begun to follow this lead. Today, ethnocultural imagery offers valuable resources in endowing brands with the aura they lack for new entrants into the global market. A spectrum of uses of symbolism can be noted, ranging from fetish imagery for inexpensive goods, and demotic invocations of the vernacular influenced by MTV, to abstract Sanskritic/classical evocations for premium products. Advertisers thus retain their assumption of different modes of reading for different classes while they adapt their erstwhile approach to the constraints of a single visual regime. Earlier, ads for premium products were most explicit in acknowledging the pleasures of the text, and the gaps and slippages to be negotiated in arriving at its meaning. Indigenous symbols tended to appear here as class markers, burnishing the aura of the brand rather than creating it, adorning the narrative rather than underpinning it. This was in contrast to ads for mid-market and downmarket products, where such symbols were used as mass markers (to coin a phrase), and to form a kind of reference or ground, absorbing and reconciling the trajectories of different segments of the text. In the latter ads, then, indigenous imagery was read in a relatively literal manner, corresponding to the literal character of belief attributed to the intended readers of these ads. In this way, advertisers continued to imagine a public whose internal divisions were harmonious with respect to each other. However, the objective

[20] See Kai Friese, 2007, 'Slow Speed: The Long Afternoon of Underdevelopment', *Bidoun*, vol. 11, Summer, available at http://www.bidoun.com/issues/issue_11/04_all.html (Last accessed on 30 January 2009).

production of a unified visual field across an antagonistic social terrain (consisting not only of contradictory class, caste, and gender formations, but of Muslims and other minorities as well) complicates such assumptions.

The pedagogical project of making subjects into citizens is assumed not only by the state, I suggest, but as well and increasingly, by the market, in an age of economic liberalization. The state seeks to utilize the rhetorical device of nationalism, through which local tradition is acknowledged while orienting individuals towards an indigenous modernity. But the state's inability to carry through on the rhetorical possibilities of nationalism, and the resulting ossification of an official nationalism, strengthened market-led initiatives in this respect. Advertisers' progress as pedagogues quickly reaches its limits, however, given their parasitism on the prevailing political dispensation on the one hand, and their misleading conception of the market as an autonomous space of freedom, on the other. Religious imagery is reformulated to provide a class-stratified sign system, as advertisers seek to accommodate diverse reading styles in one visual arena. In this process, the symbolic limits of a public based on Hindu imagery are reinforced rather than opened up, as advertisers endow these images with an iconic status to reach new consumers. As a result, even as the project of Hinduizing the nation appears to have reached an impasse, and Hindu nationalists fail to secure the kind of political power it was feared they would achieve, we may have images of 'soft Hindutva' circulating in public life, representing the unreconciled contradictions of Hindu orthodoxy with modern social reform. If new publics then take shape under the dispensation of older images of caste Hindu authority, the internal contradictions developing in the process are likely to increase over time. While advertising narratives of desire and fulfilment are powerful in germinating modern forms of consciousness, it is only in the political realm that the logic unleashed by them can find their resolution.

14

Architectonic Improvisations
Modernity and Design in Postcolonial India

Jaideep Chatterjee

Reflecting upon the human crisis that erupted in the streets of New Delhi in 2006 in wake of the state-sponsored citywide building demolition drive, this chapter asks: in spite of protracted resistance by citizens, why is there not any critical questioning of the state's enduring faith in a 'design' for the city?[1] I claim that there is more at play here than mere oversight. Instead, I argue that this 'lapse' is due to a particular genealogy of design through which it transcends the 'particular' design(ing) of any building, or even the Master Plan, to emerge, in conjunction with 'Progress', 'Development', and 'Modernity', as a 'universal' and 'rational' concept that is crucial to India's self-imagination. Following this line of enquiry, the chapter presents, in the final section, ethnographic vignettes from an ongoing project of '(re)designing' an urban village in Delhi sponsored by the state. It examines these to unpack conventional wisdom about design's 'universality' and 'rationality' and thus, its relationships to questions of modernity in postcolonial contexts.

Delhi Is Burning! Who Is to Blame?

In September of 2006, 'in a retaliatory action', the Delhi Police opened fire and killed four people protesting against the

---

[1] By the end of 2005, Municipal Corporation of Delhi's (MCD) report had swelled to some 80,000 individual violating properties that included high schools, institutes, government buildings, shopping malls, etc. Astonishingly, 1,600 out of Delhi's 2,300 residential colonies were 'unauthorized', and there were some 200 roads in the capital on whose edges land was being illegally used.

destruction of their workplace by the Municipal Corporation of Delhi (MCD). Seelampur, where this incident took place, is not exactly new to such Faustian measures. For that matter, neither is the city of Delhi. To (re)produce a 'modern' (and now, global) identity for the capital city, the Government of India and the Delhi state have often used the 'Delhi Master Plan' to 'relocate and rehabilitate' sections of the city's population (read: poor) to the margins.[2] Yet, what *was* striking about the present situation was the extent of the state's actions and the violent and open battle between the Supreme Court, Delhi government, the public works authorities, and the citizens that followed. This was a battle whose effects resound till date.

This state-sponsored 'demolition drive', in addition to all the resistance it faced and the crisis it generated, also gave rise to all kinds of deliberations in various media. Especially prominent amongst these was the heated debate between the Delhi government and the Supreme Court of India over the question of what and who precipitated the crisis. Briefly paraphrased, the exchange went something like this.[3] According to the Supreme Court, the blame

for the crisis lay on the Delhi government. The latter, the Court argued, had not only failed to implement the Master Plan, but also undermined the design of the Master Plan when it allowed 'illegal' construction and land usage to proliferate in an ad hoc manner. It was a combination of these two, the failure to implement and the ad hoc actions of the government that undermined the design of the Master Plan, which, in turn, led to the crisis.

Not surprisingly, the Delhi government blamed the Supreme Court in return. According to them, the 'crisis' was not precipitated by their actions, but rather by the Supreme Court's decision to demolish all buildings violating the Master Plan. The Delhi government argued that the production and implementation of the Master Plan was their purview and the Supreme Court had exceeded its mandate when it ordered the demolition of buildings violating the Delhi Master Plan. It was this 'cavalier' decision that was destabilizing the populace of the capital city.

Framed in such a manner, the dispute seems to be one of mandates specified by the Indian constitution for the judicial, legislative, and executive branches of the state. In fact, the central question that emerged in the various discussions in the media underscored precisely this issue: whose actions (the Court or the government) were unconstitutional.[4] To my mind, however, a more involved examination of the exchange between the two august bodies reveals

---

[2] Suparna Chatterjee and Judith Kenny Chatterjee, 1999, 'Creating a Capital: The Ninth Delhi Plan and Decolonization', *Historical Geography*, no. 27, pp. 73–98.

[3] For a detailed coverage of the exchanges between the Supreme Court of India and the Delhi government, see news dailies in Delhi from September 2005 till date. See especially, *The Times of India*, 2006, 'B.J.P. Blames Congress-Led Delhi Government', 11 October, p. 6; *The Times of India*, 2006, 'Supreme Court Rebuts Center, Delhi Government', 7 November, p. 6; and *The Times of India*, 2006, 'What If Residents Start Protesting?' 7 November, p. 7.

[4] See *India Today*, 23 October 2006; especially see, Neeraj Mishra, 2006, 'Face Off: Judiciary vs Legislature', *India Today*, 23 October, pp. 20–30.

something quite other, and perhaps more enduring, than this immediate problem of exceeding one's constitutional mandate.

Take, for example, the central argument made by the Supreme Court that the crisis was occasioned because the Delhi government had not followed the design of the Master Plan. By implicitly claiming that there would be no crisis in the city if everything had gone according to 'design', this seemingly innocuous statement actually serves as front for certain historically entrenched ideas about design. First, it assumes that the design of the city as it is imagined in the Master Plan can be unproblematically and seamlessly translated into the actual city. I shall have more to say about such a view of the translative process later on. Second and more importantly, however, this statement asserts a belief in the ability of design to: (i) 'foresee' each and every future possibility that might occur in the city's development; (ii) accordingly make adequate provisions for such 'innumerable' possibilities in the design document; and finally, (iii) therefore be an antithesis to adhocism/improvisation and so prevention against crisis. In other words, undergirding the arguments of the Supreme Court is the notion in which the design for the city appears, not simply as a guideline for future actions, but rather as that which has already mapped out the future (history) of the city. In this sense, design is understood as an omnipotent and omniprescient phenomenon that is both the beginning (since it is presumed that the city will 'develop' according to its design) and the end of a process which is also concurrently imagined as unfolding linearly and unproblematically.

But what is even more remarkable is that such a conception of design seems to structure the Court's arguments far beyond the ambit of the Master Plan. Thus when, for example, Jaipal Reddy, the Minister for Urban Development, convinced the Parliament to pass the Delhi Laws (Special Provisions) Act 2006 which would provide a one year 'grace' period for all illegal properties, the Chief Justice of India stayed this provision of the Delhi Laws Act 2006.[5] His logic was that the Delhi government's actions are not governance. As he claimed, '[I]t is their manner of handling the issue, which is causing totally unavoidable harassment to the residents of Delhi… every time you [the Delhi government] issue notification a day before, you bring to nought [sic] the order of this Court.'[6] For the Supreme Court, it would seem, not only Delhi, but even governance cannot be *strategic*, *improvised*, and dealing directly with the things as they happen. Rather, their position is one in which the city and its governance, all have their individual design(s) which have already mapped out the (future) history of what they ought to be.

The Delhi government's position, when re-examined, is not much different. In fact, implicit in their very act to pass a 'special law' to provide grace period to the 'violating' buildings *is* an acceptance of the premise that the city *was* 'deviating' from and *was* 'breaching' that already mapped out future of New Delhi, exemplified in the design document. If anything, the government

[5] See *India Today*, 23 October 2006; especially see, Neeraj Mishra, 'Face Off'.

[6] *The Hindu*, 2006, 'Supreme Court Slams Center, Delhi Govt.', 14 September, p. 5.

comes across as being even more steadfast in its beliefs about design, as they were in the best position to revise the Master Plan and bring it in line with the reality of the city. But again, like the Supreme Court, they were quite content to not question their belief in design in spite of continued resistance by the residents of Delhi against the diktats of the Master Plan.

Furthermore, that the Delhi government shares an orientation similar to the Supreme Court towards the idea of design in general is attested in the former's inability to reply to the Court's accusation of ad hoc governance. Their silence and subsequent withdrawal from any measure to stop the demolition drive shows that they also believed that their actions were not in line with the 'design(s)' of governance, and that adhocism and improvisation have no place in governance. Finally, the shared ideas about design are also evident in the government's counterclaim that the Supreme Court had exceeded its authority. For how can one make this statement without also implicitly claiming that all future (possible) actions of the Supreme Court were already mapped out in its 'design' as contained in the Constitution of India, which one might add, following this line of logic, would seem to be the 'design' for the nation. In fact, if one were to continue this analysis, such a conception of design seems to extend it *ad infinitum*.

In light of this, the crisis that gripped Delhi, one could argue, is not so much about the immediate actions of the Court, the government, and least of all the citizens, but rather springs from this particular conception and claim of design as a 'universal' phenomenon that is rational, antithetical to adhocism, is what precedes all existence, guiding its development, while simultaneously being the end (identity) towards which all existence is to be directed. Given this tall order, a pressing question to ask is, perhaps, from whence this understanding in design? From where its claim to universality, autonomy, givenness, and authority? How come such faith in its predictive, retrodictive, and transformative capacities?

Unpacking these questions in any significant manner would require more space than is available. What I would like to do here, however, is present two things. First, a provisional sketch of some discursive and institutional contexts, both in India and globally, where the above-mentioned claims of design have been elaborated, (re) produced, and sustained. Such a 'sketch', I hope, will help us realize the depth and the enormity of the problem at hand when addressing entrenched ideas about design. Second, I examine an actual exercise of (re) designing some parts of New Delhi. My aim through the latter is to unpack two purported attributes of design which are central in sustaining design's larger claims: its neutrality as a process; and its rationality and status as the dialectical 'other' of adhocism and improvisation. I begin with the sketch.

Design: A Fragmented Genealogy

To be fair to the Delhi government and to the Supreme Court of India, design's universal project(ions) is neither of their making nor one whose discussion is foremost on their minds. This 'project' has a long, complicated, and fragmented history that weaves itself in and out with other similarly 'universal project(ion)s' such as history, progress, economics, development, modernity, nationalism, and identity.

Prominent, though implied, articulations of 'design' and its relation to existence and identity are visible in the philosophical elaborations of German idealism in the late eighteenth and early nineteenth centuries. For instance, the history of world, for Hegel, was nothing other than the design (*Geist*) of the world working itself out from potentiality to actuality.[7] Furthermore, design figured prominently in terms of particularities too, especially through terms such as *Bildung* that came to signify a somewhat similar process of individual development.[8]

A parallel articulation, though one that was perhaps far more potent in its implication, about design appears in the activities of the Department of Science and Art (DSA) of the British Empire. As the architectural historian Arindam Dutta has persuasively demonstrated, the ideologues and ideologies of the DSA sought nothing less than to restructure economic stratification through aesthetic means.[9] Towards this end, the DSA, Dutta argues, enlarged the discursive scope of design by presenting a creative combination of not only utilitarian philosophies of John

Stuart Mill and Jeremy Bentham, but also the aesthetic theories from Kant to Burke together with mature ideas of British workshop-based pedagogy.[10]

India's singular status in the British Empire ensured that it was constantly imbricated with(in) the workings of the DSA. In fact, DSA's theories about design owe as much to German idealism as they do to the British colonial state's cartographical efforts, its generation of elaborate taxonomies, museums, and anthropologies of its subjects, and in the efforts of the Public Works Department (PWD) to '(re)design' the existence of their colonial territory.[11] Take, for example, the restructuring of Lucknow after the Revolt of 1857, or the institution of the PWD to 'manage' the 'unhygienic and dismal' conditions of native Indian cities.[12] In each case, the colonial effort was to not only understand India through design(s), that is, through large 'objectively' identified socio-cultural 'patterns', but also to use these 'patterns' to

[7] Georg Wilhelm Friedrich Hegel, 1929, 'Introduction to the Philosophy of History', in Jacob Loewenberg (ed.), *Selections*, New York: C. Scribner's Sons. For a detailed discussion of German idealist philosophy, see Theodore Ziolkowski, 1990, *German Romanticism and Its Institutions*, Princeton, NJ: Princeton University Press.

[8] Hans-Georg Gadamer, 1989, *Truth and Method*, 2nd edition, New York: Crossroad.

[9] Arindam Dutta, 2007, *The Bureaucracy of Beauty: Design in the Age of Its Global Reproducibility*, New York: Routledge.

[10] Ibid.

[11] See among others, Bernard S. Cohn, 1996, *Colonialism and Its Forms of Knowledge: The British in India*, Princeton Studies in Culture/Power/History, Princeton, NJ: Princeton University Press; Nicholas B. Dirks, 2001, *Castes of Mind: Colonialism and the Making of Modern India*, Princeton, NJ: Princeton University Press; and Veena Talwar Oldenburg, 1984, *The Making of Colonial Lucknow, 1856–1877*, Princeton, NJ: Princeton University Press.

[12] See, for example, Veena Talwar Oldenburg, *The Making of Colonial Lucknow, 1856–1877*. See also, Peter Scriver, 2007, 'Empire-Building and Thinking in the Public Works Department of British India', in Peter Scriver and Vikramaditya Prakash (eds), *Colonial Modernities: Building, Dwelling and Architecture in British India and Ceylon*, London and New York: Routledge, pp. 69–92.

objectify India *and* determine a course for its development.

A little later, in the initial decades of the twentieth century, some of the central ideas of the DSA that were the precursor to the British Arts and Crafts movement combined with the German *Werkbund* to give rise to what is called the Modern Movement in architecture.[13] Here, the ideas of German idealism and that of commodity production received much further fillip. Indeed, at the La Sarraz Conference in 1928 and the subsequent Athens Charter drafted in the 1930s, the 'universality' of architectural design emerges by aligning it with 'rational' principles of economics, industrial standardization, town planning, as well as claiming an inherent universality of architectural design.[14] Echoing Hegelian ideas, Gropius, one of the chief ideologues of modernism in architecture, frames such a reformulation of design with utmost clarity when he notes: '[*W*]*e have begun to understand that designing our physical environment does not mean to apply a fixed set of esthetics, but embodies rather a continuous*

inner growth, a conviction which recreates truth in the service of mankind.'[15]

Additionally, the La Sarraz Declaration, and the Congrès International d'Architecture Moderne (CIAM) it founded, also advocated for an explicitly political role of architecture and design. Leading this charge was Le Corbusier, the prophetic master of architectural modernism, who called for a direct intervention by the state on behalf of architects. His rationale was that nation-states had to heed the advice of its architects in order to develop their modern identity.[16] Like the DSA, perhaps even more so, CIAM ideas about urbanism and design, as many scholars have argued, became the basis for a series of urban experiments that ranged from Brasilia to Islamabad. In India, Gropius, CIAM, and Le Corbusier, as we shall see momentarily, enjoyed especial esteem.

This period also saw the emergence of another apparatus that served to prop up the platform for design in unprecedented ways. This was the 'official' launch of the global discourse on 'development' that stemmed from the gathering at Bretton Woods, where the International Monetary Fund (IMF) and the World Bank were created. The effects of this discourse, as we know, have been nothing short of remaking the entire geography of the world. As scholars have argued, development quickly materialized into a way through which nations and peoples viewed themselves and

[13]   Marie Ann Frank, 1996, 'The Theory of Pure Design and American Architectural Education in the Early Twentieth Century', thesis submitted to Department of History of Architecture and Urbanism, Cornell University, Ithaca, New York.

[14]   For a detailed analysis of the discourse generated during the La Sarraz Conference, see Eric Paul Mumford, 2000, *The Ciam Discourse on Urbanism, 1928–1960*, Cambridge, MA: MIT Press. For an analysis of the different political views within the La Sarraz Conference, see Martin Steinmann, 1972, 'Political Standpoints in Ciam 1928–1933', *Architectural Association Quarterly*, vol. 4, no. 4, pp. 49–55.

[15]   Walter Gropius, 1955, Scope of Total Architecture, 1st edition, New York: Harper; emphasis in original.

[16]   Steinmann, 'Political Standpoints in Ciam 1928–1933'.

'others'.[17] According to the anthropologist Akhil Gupta: '"[D]eveloped" and "underdeveloped" are not terms that indicate the position of nation-states in an objective matrix defined by quantitative indicators as the development apparatus—exemplified by the tables of the World Bank—would have us believe. They are also…forms of identity in the postcolonial world.'[18]

Sharing philosophical roots tracing back to German idealism, development and design dovetailed with each other quite seamlessly at the level of constructing identity in general; of producing and controlling existence and being at the individual, collective, and philosophical level. For, how else could one begin the process of development or achieve a specific national, urban, or even personal identity if not through: (i) having a 'design/plan/blueprint' at the outset; (ii) developing (translating and concretizing) that design; and finally, (iii) using that 'design' as the benchmark to measure progress.

In fact, this resonance between development and design already had much currency in India. It was, as mentioned earlier, a strategy present in the governing tactics of the British colonial state for decades, a part of the pedagogy put in place by the DSA in India too. It is not surprising then, as many scholars have noted, that these ideas were also taken up within articulations of anti-colonial nationalism—the first stirrings of which appeared in the meeting

of Congress Working Committee in the 1930s that was to serve as the precursor to the Planning Commission of India. Indeed, in postcolonial governance, the Planning Commission of India has become *the* place where experts actively 'design' and decide the future of the nation. As Partha Chatterjee has persuasively argued in his work on development and state planning in India, economic planning in postcolonial India appears as concrete forms in which state power is exercised, as well as that economic planning is the form of determining state policy.[19]

However, the emphasis was not only on economic planning. Nehru, perhaps aptly called the 'architect' of modern India, was sure that 'designing' the built environment played a direct role in (re)fashioning India's identity. He believed that this would enable India to be viewed as a nation fulfilling its 'tryst with destiny' to be modern. The most compelling example of such a union of architectural design and national identity is probably Chandigarh, designed by the 'master' of modern architecture, Le Corbusier. For both Nehru and Corbusier, Chandigarh was to showcase to the world the capacity of design to transform India and catapult it to the world stage. Indeed their mutually respectful relationship and personal correspondence attests to this. Take, for example, a letter to Nehru from Corbusier in 1959 in which the latter writes,

I have the honour and pleasure of offering you very simply this album concerning Chandigarh,

[17] See, for example, Arturo Escobar, 1995, *Encountering Development: The Making and Unmaking of the Third World*, Princeton Studies in Culture/Power/History, Princeton, NJ: Princeton University Press.

[18] Akhil Gupta, 1998, *Postcolonial Developments: Agriculture in the Making of Modern India*, Durham, NC: Duke University Press.

[19] Partha Chatterjee, 1994, 'Development Planning and Indian State', in T.J. Byres (ed.), *The State and Development Planning in India*, New Delhi: Oxford University Press, pp. 51–72.

which assumes the form of the 'CIAM Town Planning Grid.' This album contains only a part of the tremendous work I have realized for Chandigarh...I hope this album will still let you feel that a valuable work is being undertaken which will perhaps astonish wealthier and more powerful nations.[20]

Nehru for his part was no less complimentary about Corbusier and agreed fully with the latter's views on Chandigarh and its place in the history of the mankind. Speaking at the Seminar and Exhibition of Architecture in March 1959, Nehru observed:

Architecture to a large extent is a product of the age. [T]he static conditions in regard to architecture in India in the last 200 years...really was a reflection of the static conditions of the Indian mind or Indian conditions...A society which ceases to go ahead necessarily becomes weak...We should not be afraid of innovations. I have welcomed very greatly one experiment in India, Chandigarh...[21]

Furthermore, Corbusier was not only the only member of CIAM who came to India. The final team that designed Chandigarh contained four such members.[22] Each went on to train and influence generations of Indian architects, urban designers, and urban planners in the intricacies and the rationality of design. In addition to this, scores of architects and urban planners from India were sent abroad, especially to

the United States (US), to be trained in modern methods of city and urban design. Many came back with firm convictions about the (re)generative and prophetic powers of design and made it their agenda to apply their knowledge to India.[23] In the general meeting of the Indian Institute of Architecture in 1954, the President of the institute, Mr M.K. Jadhav, expresses just such a sentiment. 'The introduction of Town Planning,' he notes, 'both in urban and rural areas in its legitimate form is a very healthy idea and cannot be brushed aside...the tremendous job for the planner and architect who must be a collective entity and not an individual, is to make all the elements in the programme work to effect *pre-determined results*....'[24] In the same speech, he also adds:

Our efforts in this great country will be measured by what we have all done together, and the profession will have to be in the vanguard. The architect and the men in the profession having used their sinews shall build so that it may be said that they had built well. In the words of Ruskin, 'therefore as we build, let us think we build for ever. Let it not be for the present delight, nor for the present use alone. But let it be such work that our descendent will thank us for. And let us think, as we lay stone on stone, that a time is to come when these stones will be considered sacred, because our hands have touched them, and that men will say as they look upon the wrought

---

[20] Le Corbusier, Letter to Nehru, 11 November 1952, cited in Ravi Kalia, 1987, *Chandigarh: In Search of an Identity*, Carbondale: Southern Illinois University Press.

[21] Government of India, 1964, *Jawaharlal Nehru's Speeches: September 1957–April 1963*, New Delhi: Ministry of Information and Broadcasting.

[22] Kalia, *Chandigarh: In Search of an Identity*.

[23] Jeffrey W. Cody, 2003, *Exporting American Architecture, 1870–2000, Planning, History and the Environment Series*, London and New York: Routledge. See also the short autobiographical essays of prominent architects in India in Association Francaise d'Action Artistique, 1985, Architecture in India, Paris: Electra.

[24] M.K. Jadhav, 1954, *Presidential Address*, Bombay: The Indian Institute of Architects, p. 3; emphasis added.

substance on them, See! This our fathers did for us.'[25]

The given excerpts from M.K. Jadhav's speech are extremely significant. Apart from their obvious paternalism and gendered underpinnings, they also encapsulate many of the notions we have been tracing so far:

1. 'Legitimate' design and town planning is essential and vital for the development of a nation.
2. More pointedly, they are an 'objective' and 'assured' way to bring about not only results that are wanted but, more importantly, those which are destined.
3. Architecture (read design-as-built) due to its concreteness, tangibility, and permanence is posited as texts through which one could effectively read and create the history of a nation.
4. That the actual task of building (whether the nation, its character, identity, or its built environment) should be left to those who are best equipped in the science and art of design, namely, architects.

Apropos we discover in Jadhav's comments something else that is extremely significant. This being that design (and its synonym planning) in Jadhav's comments also seems to emerge as, what Gramsci calls, the 'common-sense' of a society.[26] That is,

within these comments we discover that principle of design has at once become an indelible part of the 'worldview' for those sectors of India's society *and* emerged as integral to the external and internal constitution of the modern Indian nation and subject. Indeed, it was precisely such ideas that became the basis for the first Master Plan of Delhi as it was formulated in 1962 with the help of the Ford Foundation.[27] Furthermore, as I have argued elsewhere, these ideas were further strengthened in the 1960s and the 1970s when they became the basis on which architects and urban planner gained their own legitimacy from the Indian state, as well demanded that they be treated at par with statesmen, that is, with those who would refashion India.[28]

The complex imbrications between design, progress, development, modernity, and national identity in India makes unpacking this nexus a tall order. Such a review would not only involve evaluating certain 'givens' within the disciplines of urban planning and architecture, but would also involve readdressing our very orientations towards the relationship's knowledge and selfhood in general. Yet such

[25] Jadhav, *Presidential Address*, p. 5.
[26] Antonio Gramsci, Quintin Hoare, and Geoffrey Nowell-Smith, 1999, *Selections from the Prison Notebooks of Antonio Gramsci*, New York: International Publishers. Gramsci uses the term common sense to mean the uncritical and largely unconscious way of perceiving and understanding the world that has become 'common' in any given epoch. This understanding of 'common' sense corresponds quite fittingly to what this chapter argues is the status of

design within certain sections of Indian populace. For these sections, mostly urban, well-to-do, and educated in private schools, design is at once associated with rationality and with good taste. Planning (a synonym of design), thanks to India's 'Five Year Plan' style of development, is far more in common usage, and has covered much more ground.
[27] Jyoti Hosagrahar, 2005, *Indigenous Modernities: Negotiating Architecture and Urbanism*, The Architext Series, London and New York: Routledge.
[28] Jaideep Chatterjee, 2011, 'The Gift of Design: Producing Architecture-Culture in Contemporary India', Doctoral dissertation submitted to Cornell University, Ithaca, New York.

a critical enquiry is, however, long overdue. The remainder of this chapter presents one step towards the former, that is, I specially focus on two claims that structure the universal edifice of design: (i) its claims to neutrality and, thus, its position beyond the trappings of power and politics; and (ii) its claim to rationality and, thus, its identity as being antithetical to ad-hocism and immediate ingenuity. I interrogate these claims through an analysis of a project conducted by architects and urban designers under the auspices of the Delhi Urban Arts Commission (DUAC) and the Lieutenant (Lt) Governor of Delhi's office to regenerate and redesign an 'urban village' in the capital city of New Delhi.

Khirki: A/The Model Village

Flanked by Delhi's arterial Outer Ring Road to its north, and by Saket, an upscale residential locality to its south, the 'village' of Khirki today lies in the heart of posh south Delhi. Initially settled in 1327 adjacent to the Khirki mosque, the village grew around the mosque and together with the Satpula dam formed a part of Firoze Shah Tuglaq's Delhi. Traditionally, its inhabitants eked out their living through farming on the land near the village. Soon after India's independence in 1947, the village faced a massive upheaval. It was mostly abandoned by its Muslim residents who moved to Pakistan in the wake of riots following the partition of India. Like many other places in Delhi, Khirki was then used as a rehabilitation colony for Hindu refugees who crossed over from Pakistan. Later, Khirki was incorporated into the National Capital Region (NCR) of Delhi

that was itself created under the first Master Plan of Delhi, 1962. It is since then that Khirki is labelled an 'urban village'.

This naming has proved to be a double-edged sword for Khirki. On the one hand, it has ensured that Khirki remained exempt from many a heavy-handed urban experiments of the state under the umbrella of developing and modernizing Delhi. Additionally, Khirki has also escaped the various land tenure systems, developmental guidelines, and building bye-laws framed within Delhi's Master Plan. Consequently, at least until now, Khirki's environ remains somewhat idyllic, and its residents claim that they enjoy a greater degree of security and cohesion than is otherwise present in other parts of Delhi. On the other hand, however, calling it a 'village' has also resulted in its neglect by the public works authority. For example, Khirki has been largely sidestepped by the MCD in terms of providing water, sewerage, and other facilities regularly provided to other plotted and 'purely' urban areas within the NCR. Also, significantly, official and state rhetoric about Khirki has consistently been through a rubric of lack: lack of planning, lack of control, lack of infrastructure, and so on and so forth.

It is this 'negative character' of Khirki that now seems to be a problem for Delhi, a city that is busy refashioning a new rhetoric for itself as a world city in line with India's new identity as major player within global economy and politics. According to this new expression of development, variously phrased by politicians and the media, Delhi has seen unprecedented growth in last decade, and like India, it is time for Delhi to take its place on the global stage of metropolises. Thus, it is said that if the US has New York, the United Kingdom (UK) has London, Japan has Tokyo, India will have Delhi; a world-class city replete with modern infrastructure and facilities. Needless to say, within this scenario, places like Khirki which seemingly developed exempt from urban bye-laws and codes (re)present an anachronism (and embarrassment) within a picture of Delhi as a modern, beautiful, and global city.

To circumvent this 'problem' and bring Khirki in sync with Delhi's modern image, the state set up a task force comprising various municipal bodies, the DUAC, residents of Khirki, and architects from TVB, a college of architecture and a non-governmental organization. The aim of this task force, of which I was a part, was to study Khirki and create a 'model/vision' that would not only dictate the future development of Khirki but would provide a blueprint for similar action to be undertaken in the 136 (or so) 'urban villages' that come under the NCR of Delhi.

After working intensively for three months with the residents of the village and the concerned authorities, the task force presented its findings and proposals to the Lt Governor of Delhi and Minister of State for Urban Development in a highly publicized event. The suggestions and methods of the task force got much praise from all quarters. The Lt Governor of Delhi heralded it as a new stage in urban planning and development of the country, a stage in which experts and people worked in close partnership. All agreed that it was the combined effort of the residents and the experts that had managed to turn a 'negative'

space within the city into a template and vision for development that could be followed not only in Delhi, but perhaps across similar situations all over the country.

At first glance, the Khirki experiment appears to justify all the claims about design's universal capacity, its truth, and its claims to rationality. Indeed, it appears as a textbook example of a process that is beyond the realm of politics, strife, and adhocism. First, a 'problem' area is identified. The state takes the initiative and attends to it. A task force comprising all associated authorities and experts is created, and a higher authority, in this case the DUAC, is made in-charge to oversee the performance of the various agents involved. Additionally, in a departure from previous top-down planning processes, the residents of the locality are also 'included' in the decision-making process. The design team visits the 'site', works with the Resident Welfare Association (henceforth RWA), and produces a design that will ostensibly work as a template for the future development of the locality. This design is submitted to the DUAC, which ratifies it and sends it back to the design team who finalize it. The 'finished' design is then shown to the residents and to the state authorities, who incorporate it into their 'Master Plan' with the intention of implementing it in due time. Each step of the design process seems to neatly dovetail into the earlier one. There is, on the face of it, no scope for mere opinion, rivalry, and makeshift-ness.

Yet, the practice on ground tells quite a different story. Take, for instance, the politics governing the exchanges between the members of the RWA and the design team. Initially, the notion that residents of Khirki should be included in the design was a step welcomed by all. However, in actuality, this remained limited to a few self-selected members of the RWA, all of whom were men belonging to the upper caste(s), and who were major landowners in the village. Thus, right from the onset, the project became one in which vested interests emerged and battled with each other. In fact, at the very first meeting between the members of the RWA and the design team, the secretary of the RWA told us, quite categorically, '[Y]ou please do your work. I request you to not go around asking too many people what they want. Most people here are ignorant and villagers...If you go around asking them then hundred people will have hundred opinions and no work will get done...you interact with us. That is all.'

This directive by the RWA put the design team in a rather perplexing situation. On the one hand, to sidestep the RWA and interact with other residents of the locality would have been to undermine the primary organization of the locality as well as undercut those whose cooperation the design team greatly needed. On the other hand, we felt that to limit our understanding and exchange with the village to what the 'elders' told us would hamper our ability to propose a viable plan for the locality. Thus, strategy after strategy followed on how to uncover information without offending any of the parties concerned. At the end, the design that was produced was not some rationally worked out objective design that could be implemented, as the state presumed, all over Delhi or the country. It was instead, a document that was carefully *(re)crafted* and, more importantly, *(re)negotiated* a number

of times to reflect different and extremely 'local' and particular interests. Moreover, it generated more questions than a 'vision' for future development. In fact, when I returned to the field six months later and asked the head of the design team about the status of the project, he candidly replied, '...nothing at all, look that was merely an exercise... there is a huge gap between what we think will happen and what happens...It's not so simple...there are just too many things that happen simultaneously...too many interests and parties involved when even one action in a small part of a city is concerned.'

Now, it may be pointed that even though 'politics' is present, it is not necessarily a part of the actual design produced by the experts. Though enveloped in political manoeuverings, the design(ing), that is, the act of producing the design, was itself still rational, neutral, and a universal process. One could even take it a step further and argue that, in fact, design-as-process not only provided for a safe haven from the politics of the village but also took those disparate set of conditions, subjected them to a rational and formal (read: universal) knowledge to synthesize a solution (design) that would enable predestined and desired results.

However, that this too was not quite the case can be gleaned from the next example of the interactions between two sets of experts: the architects from the design group; and the architects and planners committee within the DUAC to whom the former methodically reported. In the first such meeting, the presentation made by the field workers was completely consigned to the dustbin. The Chairman of the DUAC, an internationally renowned architect, told us that our entire approach to the problem was wrong. Rebuking us all, he advised that instead of gathering more data, we should have spent time trying to identify viable urban-level design projects within the village. He then asked us go back to the drawing board and present something 'concrete' two weeks later.

By the time the date for the second meeting came along, the group had unfortunately been unable to progress any further in their work. Amidst all the tension the night before, we decided that two changes were to be made to the presentation. First, we would rearrange the order of the slides to be presented. That is, we would first present the 'product' of our work instead of the 'process' like we had done previously. Second, instead of a junior member of the team, the group leader, who was himself a prominent architect and the head of the overall task force, would make the presentation. To our surprise, this time the result of the presentation was the exact opposite. We had a very 'productive' discussion and the dignitaries present were extremely happy with the work done. The Chairman of the DUAC lauded our progress claiming that we had indeed hit upon the crux of the problem of development in situations such as Khirki village.

As we exited the conference room, the entire team felt extremely elated. We were doubly satisfied since we had not only evaded the fiasco of the last meeting but also pulled one over on the DUAC committee. Soon after, the head of the team turned to me and said, 'See today...we did not get scolded. Why do you think that happened? What is your analysis?' Confessing that I was quite baffled by the progress of the meeting, I turned the question(s) back on him. I

asked him, why did he think we were not reprimanded? 'Well,' he said,

[T]here were two ideas on the board. Ours in which we wanted to let the residents have a say in the direction of development for their village. Look the business of the administration and the planning process is the protection of civic life. But now these guys, the Chairman and the administration have a different approach to development. They want the rate of growth to grow. Thus more incentive for more money to be made, with this in mind they want to invest in those areas which they feel will grow and produce more…I do not agree with this. Our ideas don't belong to that school of thought. We want to go about it differently. But I know him (the Chairman) for a long time. I know what he expects in a presentation. I know how to phrase it. Plus you all had also told me what had transpired in the previous meeting. What I did was to turn the whole thing around! We didn't have any real solutions or ideas. But then neither did he.

The group leader's summary of what occurred in the meeting gets us to the heart of the design versus adhocism debate. As mentioned earlier, in this debate, adhocism, improvisation, and the like are posited as being diametrically opposite to design; it is design's Other. Consequently, design is seen as an apparatus, a form of knowledge that is ordered, already formulated, singular, free of tension and strife. Additionally, it is conceived as a resource to resolve the arbitrariness of a 'make it up as you go along' attitude.

Yet, as the observations of the lead architect of the group shows us, this is quite far from what took place in a meeting between experts. His comments testify that far from being a seamless body of knowledge, design is, in fact, as much in the process of defining itself as the very thing it seeks to problematize and conceptualize. Additionally, his comments bespeak the existence of different kinds of expertise-as-knowledge that may exist within a body of expert practitioners. According to the group leader, the chairman's expertise-as-knowledge subscribed to the idiom of trickle-down model of economic progress. Consequently, the role played by his form of expertise-as-knowledge within his expertise-as-practice was one of finding profitable urban-level design projects within Khirki. In other words, finding the kind of opportunities that would generate what he felt as 'growth' and 'progress' within Khirki. The group leader's expertise-as-practice, on the other hand, adhered to a different model of expertise-as-knowledge which takes a separate and somewhat critical stance against the chairman's expertise. This, in and of itself, forces us question any simplistic model of design expertise.

But there is more here. There was, it would seem, a resolution and a triumph of design principles at the end of the second presentation. Yet, what is interesting is that: (i) this 'resolution' was not one in which different ideas fused together flawlessly in the form of a final design (clearly the group had walked out knowing that we still differed from the chairman's view on how to approach Khirki); and (ii) this 'resolution' was not also a synthesis between two forms of design expertise. In fact, the resolution did not even come about through any recourse to expertise. It happened by resorting to a sleight of hand, to improvisation, and adhocism, all of which are considered anathema to design. It was like the group leader said: he knew, due to his association with the chairman, what the latter expects in a presentation. Given this, he ingeniously turned the whole thing around to make it appear that not only was the group hard at work in the grace period given to it, but also that we had indeed arrived at a rational solution to the 'problem' of how to regenerate Khirki, which we had not.

In fact, the more I worked with architects, the more I became attuned that this adhocism is present in all kinds of situations; a kind of thinking on one's feet. Throughout my fieldwork, it would crop up in all kinds of contexts. If the waterproofing on a roof did not work, architects do not tear down the roof and begin anew. Instead, they use plastic sheets as a new layer of waterproofing. If students ran out of adhesive while making a model the night before submission of work, they would use toothpaste instead. Perhaps *the* central example of improvisation was the concept sheet that every student, and later a 'professional', would present during a design evaluation. Ideally, this sheet is considered to be the starting point of one's work. Indeed, the first question during the process of criticism would often be, 'What is your concept from which you have evolved this building?' The notion here being that an idea (read: design-in-mind) precedes and guides the appearance of a design-on-paper, which, in turn, guides the production of the actual building. But in practice, just the opposite was true. They, me included, would wait till the last moment to make this sheet. And then too, the sheet was not made by retracing their steps from beginning to end. More often than not, and in spite of an education that is heavily predicated on making this process transparent, transmissible, and translatable, this retracing was not even possible as the process remained completely nebulous to architects. Resultantly, the sheet would be made with the following question in mind: how can I create a concept to explain what I have done? That is, the rationale would emerge *post mortem* and *as improvisation*, not a priori to the doing of the work as is 'ideally' expected from 'experts' who embody 'design' as a logical, rational process.

There is even a word that architects use for this adhocism, *jugar*. And, there too I realized that jugar was not the purview of architects alone. There are several such synonyms, *tarkeeb*, *upay* (strategy, strategic), *thor* (literally, to break), etc. These words (and thus a way of doing things) have much currency in Delhi and the northern parts of India. Jugar and its synonyms figure regularly as examples of ingenuity. They appear in jokes, anecdotes, and sayings in which jugar appears as a metaphor and a metonym for individual action, or something that structures an individual, a collectivity all the way up to India as a nation, and indeed the 'world'.[29] But what is most important, at least for our discussion, is that jugar would always index some very essential things: (i) it always appears in the form of practice, accompanying it, attending to it, and somehow structuring it; (ii) mind and body, knowledge and practice are seen as a compound and not as disaggregated parts within jugar; (iii) it is intimately tied to

experience; and finally, (iv) importantly, it is seen as a symbol of hope, as a way around a conundrum which may prove impossible using 'conventional' (read: formalized and standardized) methods.

Design and Jugar or Jugar and Design

The attempt of this chapter to present jugar (improvisation, extemporization) as something that constantly accompanies design is not to berate design, nor is it to 'expose' architects as unprofessional and insincere. To the contrary, many architects I worked with were highly knowledgeable and extremely sincere in their efforts to change what they felt were pitiable conditions for some residents of Delhi. And not only that, many had earnestly devoted their careers to mediating and remedying the heavy-handed 'develop-mentality' inscribed within the practices of the state authorities. Furthermore, the aim is also not to do away with the notion of design; perhaps doing away with it is not possible. If anything, the chapter shows that design and its attendant values are deeply ingrained and have become integral to India's claim to modernity, to the constitution of the national self, and to expert identity. Moreover, the putative universality of design has not been all negative; much like other 'universals', it, too, has enabled many a nation, individual, and thing to carve a specific identity for itself. Thus, jettisoning it completely may not even be desirable. Finally, the chapter also does not claim that jugar is an autochthonous form of knowledge with its own logic that is to be counterposed against design, or that it is even separate from and untouched by design.

---

[29] A fascinating example of a saying involving jugar is: *jugar pe duniya kayam hai* (literally, jugar makes the world go around). What is particularly interesting about this saying is that it is a take on a more highbrow saying according to which it is *umeed* (hope) which makes the world go around. That jugar transposes and appears as a synonym of hope is extremely telling.

The aim of the chapter is far more modest. It is, at the least, to recognize, as one architect and friend remarked, that the brilliance of architects is that they are the greatest *jugaroo*s (those who do jugar). And thus, to banish or deny the presence of jugar is to limit the potential of design and architects themselves. More specifically, the chapter is also a call to recognize that in spite of claims to universality, scientificity, rigour, and formality, attending design (whether as an idea, a form of knowledge, design-on-paper, or design-as-built) at every instance is jugar, improvisation, adhocism; in other words, design's 'Other'. To not acknowledge this, is to fundamentally misunderstand design itself.

At a more 'abstract' level, the article also questions a related 'universal', that is, modernity. As the chapter has shown, modernity and design have long, complex, and intertwined histories. Much of this dialectical narrative is buttressed by design's (and perhaps, even modernity's) pivotal

claim(s) that: (i) it is the rational universal self; (ii) everything, whether this be a person, a thing, a city, an action, or indeed a nation, has a 'design'; (iii) the identity of this '(any) thing' is merely the design working itself out from its ideational, potential stage to a palpable, real, and concrete stage; and finally, (iv) whose value (whether positive or negative) is derived from how closely it adheres to that 'linear' progression.[30] By acknowledging jugar and improvisation as something that always accompanies design (and thus, by extension modernity), the chapter hopes to emphasize the pluralities inherent in what we (can) label 'designed' and 'modern'.

At the end, this chapter is, in the very least, a pragmatic appeal to the Indian state and its develop-mentality to rethink the unflinching faith and assumptions about 'design(ing)', whether a neighbourhood, a city, or indeed the nation. To not do so is to watch as Delhi, and perhaps the nation, erupts time and again.

---

[30] For an argument regarding the linear temporality invoked by modernity, see, among others, Dipesh Chakrabarty, 2000, *Provincializing Europe: Postcolonial Thought and Historical Difference*, Princeton Studies in Culture/Power/History, Princeton: Princeton University Press; and Timothy Mitchell, 2000, *Questions of Modernity*, Minneapolis: University of Minnesota Press.

15

Making Art Modern

Re-visiting Artistic Modernism in India

Sanjukta Sunderason

In September 2005, Tyeb Mehta (1925–2009), the veteran Indian artist and one of the prime modernist painters in the country, set a new record with his painting *Mahisashura* (1997) selling at a whopping $1.584 million at the Christie's auction of modern and contemporary Indian art in New York, the first time for a contemporary Indian artist to cross the million dollar mark.[1] I cite this event not only to underscore the recent high noon of modern and contemporary Indian art in the global market, but more importantly, to evoke the primarily modernist apparatus of Tyeb Mehta as a point of entry into what

can be seen as a space of ambivalence in India's artistic modernism. The *Mahisashura* is a typical Mehta composition; the artist uses strict formalist economy in juxtaposing colliding planar surfaces of flat colour to symbolize the conflict between the Mother Goddess and the mythic buffalo demon; dramatic fragmentation of the central figure captures the mythic conflict within the rigid simplicity of form, the minimalist treatment of pictorial space signifying the 'essence' of social catharsis.[2] In an interview given to *The New York Times* correspondent following the auction, the octogenarian artist made a set of connections between his art, memory,

[1] Shoumini Sengupta, 2006, 'Indian Artist Enjoys His World Audience', *The New York Times*, 24 January, available at http://www.nytimes.com/2006/01/24/arts/design/24tyeb.html (Last accessed on 15 February 2010).

[2] The *Mahisashura* series was made by Tyeb Mehta over the 1990s. The picture mentioned here was made in 1997; acrylic on canvas (signed, titled, and dated on reverse: 150 × 120 cm).

and violence. Reflecting on the communal genocide during the Partition of India in 1947, Mehta noted, 'That violence gave me a clue about the emotion I wanted to paint. That violence has stuck into my mind.'[3] The memory of Partition remained a lasting concern with Mehta, and time and again, he has been quoted saying: 'I don't work on events but prefer to create an image which becomes a metaphor.'[4]

This rather brief foray into Tyeb Mehta's art suggests a set of issues for form-making in twentieth-century art in India, namely, memory, metaphor, and conflict; these further point towards a set of overlapping spaces—the mythic and the modern, the personal and the public, the formal and the social. My effort here will be to follow these into the decades between the 1940s and the 1970s. Rather than retrace a stable narrative of Indian 'modern art', I will foreground an ambivalence within the 'modern'. Modernism in the plastic arts in India has inhabited multiple constellations throughout the twentieth century, developing at various points, as a dialectical process of invoking, resisting, or negotiating questions of tradition, identity, and experience. 'Pure subjectivity' and 'pure form'—hallmarks of the high modernism of post-1945 Western art—have often, in India, remained entangled in such dialectics, with artistic metaphor itself becoming a

double text of the personal and the public, the formal and the contextual. To enter ambivalences within the modern not only does one need to loosen fixities of pure form or subjectivity, but recognize more clearly, the persistence of the 'non-formal'—the contextual, the ideological, the historical— albeit in amorphous mutations, in the making of the modern in Indian art. Some questions that surface hence are: how can the historical be mapped into the formal, the ideological into the idiomatic, the collective into the subjective?; or rather, in what ways could anxiety, discontent, or resistance be identified within the rarefied autonomous frames of modernist art?

Geeta Kapur, in her critical take on 'third-world modernisms' dislodges the viability of pure internationalism in Indian art, arguing for a curious hybridity determined by cultural politics of postcoloniality. The artist as an individual, she suggests, subject to the project of modernization and grappling, consciously or unconsciously, with the postcolonial predicament, remains implicated within the experiences of the collective: 'Even the tasks of subjectivity, so long as they are unresolved, require acts of allegorical exegesis, often via the nation.'[5] The modernist quest for unbridled self-expression in India, she thus argues, has been reinscribed by the lived experience or inherited memory of the anti-colonial struggle; modernism here is 'deeply politicized and carries with it the potential for resistance'.[6] Since the late nineteenth

---

[3] Tyeb Mehta in conversation with Shoumini Sengupta, 'Indian Artist Enjoys His World Audience'.

[4] Tyeb Mehta in conversation with Radhika Rajamani, 2003, 'Artist For All Times', *The Hindu*, 22 January, available at http://www. thehindu.com/thehindu/mp/2003/01/22/ stories/2003012200460100.htm (Last accessed on 15 February 2010).

[5] Geeta Kapur, 2000, *When was Modernism: Essays on Contemporary Cultural Practice in India*, New Delhi: Tulika, p. 297.

[6] Ibid., p. 301.

century, questions of artistic subjectivity and stylistic innovation in Indian art were interspersed with cultural projections of the 'nation'—within rhetorics of taste, cultural 'renaissance', and artistic self-consciousness, as well as anti-colonial, anti-capitalist, ruralist counter-modernisms.[7] Rather than an ideology of *antipassatismo*, or absolute break with the past, modernism in India related to history and tradition both in derivative and innovative modes, fusing thus, notions of tradition, artistic subjectivity, and nationalist politics. While the 'Indian-style' paintings of the Bengal School delved deep into mythology and precolonial 'classical antiquity' in a nostalgic historicism, pastoral romance characterized idyllic images of village India in the ruralist endeavours at Rabindranath Tagore's university at

Shantiniketan and the art school, Kala Bhawan.

Post-1920s, the 'formal' initiatives in the works of Gaganendranath Tagore, followed by Rabindranath Tagore, Amrita Sher-Gil, and Jamini Roy, introduced fresh possibilities for a modern art in India, loosening considerably the nationalist consensus of the first two decades. The 1930s was marked by conscious attempts by artists at Shantiniketan to address the 'local' within the national—Nandalal Bose, Ramkinkar Baij, and Benodebehari Mukherjee, the celebrated trinity of Kala Bhawan—and the active visual culture of ruralist environmentalism in art, institutionalized at the school in curriculum, instruction, and practice, created a constellation of modernism that was rooted in landscape, habitation, and the everyday, characterized famously hence as 'contextual modernism'.[8] In the 1940s, the modern was evoked in yet another configuration, now celebrated as 'progressive' art based on the 'popular', the 'social', and the 'real'—a 'concrete contextuality' in art, invoked by writers, artists, and critics associated with what became known as the Marxist cultural movement.[9] Post-independence, the modern in art became all the more fractured, now becoming at once, institutional/infrastructural investment of the state, the idiom of promise and freedom for

[7] See Tapati Guha-Thakurta's pioneering study, 1992, *The Making of a New 'Indian' Art: Artists, Aesthetics and Nationalism in Bengal, 1850–1920*, Cambridge: Cambridge University Press, for a historical treatment of questions of changing art instruction, patronage, artistic identity, and ideology against the backdrop of the art movement led by Abanindranath Tagore and his students, christened as the Bengal School of painting. Also, see Guha-Thakurta (1995) on early modernist engagements with the national in 'Visualizing the Nation: The Iconography of a "National Art" in Modern India', *Journal of Arts and Ideas*, Special issue on Modern Indian Art, nos 27 and 28, March, pp. 7–40, through the works of Raja Ravi Varma, Abanindranath Tagore, and Nandalal Bose. Looking at a similar time frame, Partha Mitter, 1994, *Art and Nationalism in India, 1850–1922, Occidental Orientations*, New York: Cambridge University Press, looks at colonial art institutions with the ideologies of the nationalist and intellectual movements around the turn of the century. In his latest book, 2007, *The Triumph of Modernism: India's Artists and the Avant Garde, 1922–1947*, London: Reaktion Books, Mitter follows the modernist idiom through the stylistic nodes of primitivism and naturalism.

[8] R. Siva Kumar, 1997, *Santiniketan: The Making of Contextual Modernism*, New Delhi: National Gallery of Modern Art.

[9] For manifestoes and documents on various platforms of the left-wing cultural ferment, see Sudhi Pradhan (ed.), 1979, *Marxist Cultural Movement in India, Chronicles and Documents 1936–1947*, vol. 1, 1st edition, Calcutta: Pustak Bipani.

individualist 'self-expression' of the new 'citizen–artist', as well as longings and spaces for anxiety and critical dialogues with the material, lived experience.

In this chapter, as mentioned earlier, my focus is on the decades between 1940s and 1970s, particularly images from post-independence Calcutta. The 1940s as the closing decade of British rule in India, with its heightened socio-political catharsis, wrought the first rupture in the lyrical calmness of the Indian-style paintings of the previous decades. As politics entered visual frames more violently, the modern was destabilized somewhat in a bid to accommodate not nostalgia but critical dialogue with context. Taking a bird's eye view of the century, similar tensions in the modern can be seen in the late 1960s–1970s, this time through a radical reorientation of the notions of the social and the political in art to accommodate the multilayered politics of postcoloniality. My focus here is framed by the critical importance these decades share in reorienting the discourse of artistic modernism in India. I do not claim to present an in-depth stylistic analysis of any singular artist or group, or narrative on each modernist initiative in Indian art, rather, to introduce a conceptual complex around the making of the modern form in Indian art—its pluralities and tensions. We can proceed with the premise that the work of art is, after all, the '...nodal point of several different causal lines...psychological, sociological, stylistic',[10] that an artist's creation or selection of styles cannot do away with both sociological and psychological

causation, dialogues between which might again lead us to the tensions between pure subjectivity and social determination of art. Artists discussed here can be placed within the complex matrix of the social, the formal, and the political in art making. Despite their individual approaches to art practice, they suggest alternative understandings of form and subjectivity in crafting the 'modern', opening up further more fractured dialogues between art and politics.

Memory, Metaphor, and the Modern Form

Between 1971 and 1979, Somnath Hore (1921–2006), one of the ace printmakers in India, and a sculptor of repute, made a series of paper pulp prints, white on white, dramatized with sudden ruptures and incisions, often with red paint trickling along pierced or scraped surfaces. The moulds were first made on clay or wax sheets, transferred thereon to cement matrices, and paper pulp poured on them, to create a highly textured surface, with undulations, freckles, pores, and fissures. The surface was then gashed or split open with a knife, or scarred with a scorching rod, burning or melting the wax. The series bears the generic title, *Wounds*. Hore's paper pulp series were extensions of his intaglio prints from engravings done on acid-lacerated metal plates. These were figurative prints with minimal gestures, their sharp and skeletal geometrical contours bearing marks of hunger. In an interview, Hore explains the idea behind his *Wounds* series:

I am all the time involved in one concern. What I call the Wounds. Social wounds you may call it. Whether it is famine or refugees, or the riots, or whatever it is. For this concept I don't have to

[10] Arnold Hauser, 1959, *The Philosophy of Art History*, London: Routledge and Kegan Paul, p. 13.

think, it is there inside me. I don't have to think in terms of the material…I remember seeing the metal plate in nitric acid, and the bubbles of anger, making wounds on the metal. I thought this was a most appropriate means to express my own ideas, by this etching process.[11]

Wound as an idiom and motif recurs time and again—in his lithographs, etchings, intaglio prints, and paper pulp series, and finally his sculptures (Hore preferred calling these *Bronzes*). All along, Hore has persistently engaged in creating a form that would reflect the corporeality of violence. In his *Bronzes* (mainly from late 1970s), he created concave, hollow figurines— emaciated, limp animals and human forms, by suspending and wrapping over one another, flattened, warped, or gashed wax sheets. In the low-relief paper pulp prints in the *Wounds* series (primarily in the 1970s and early 1980s), the sharp incisions and gashes on the surface are symbolic of scars inflicted by a knife, or a bullet shot, rupturing the organic body of the print. What we see is the complete plasticity of form that transmutes the representational realism of violence. Bypassing pictorial realism in the conventional sense, it arrives at an expressionistic abstraction of 'trauma' in suggested corporeality. Each element, the porous organic surface, the deep incisions or trickling red paint, as well as stark sparseness of the pictorial space with its minimalist iconicity, all create a unity, which captures the dramatic moment of violence.

What is important here is the making of abstraction—a radical simplification of form—whereby the artist is seen to distance himself from the factual tangibility of lived experience. Memory is objectified through the erasure of situational details; the material form captures the essence of malady and anguish. In the 'significant form' of the final image *Wound*, experience in the phenomenal world is thus remembered, captured, and frozen in a striking abstract composition, where the form becomes the signifier of violence, its moods and memories: 'They look abstract, but in fact, they truly are wounds, inflicted on sheets of clay or wax…It was but an extension of the wounds a burin or acid could make on surfaces like wood or metal sheets.'[12] This act of making abstraction involves not simply an elimination of the event, but its internalization and sublimation. The minimalist rendering in the 'pure form' is also thus the distilled essence of the experience of violence: the metaphor of scarred surfaces connects the formal to the social and the political, and artistic objectification creates a form which is indeed the 'form of the content' and the content, 'the form in which it happened'.[13] The result is surely a masterpiece of expressionistic abstraction, reoriented against the contextual politics of decolonization.

The nature of abstraction arrived at thus—the silent presence of the *Wounds* in the understanding of modernism in

[11] Somnath Hore, in conversation with Neville Tuli, reproduced in Neville Tuli (ed.), 1997, *The Flamed Mosaic, Indian Contemporary Painting*, New Delhi: HEART in association with Mapin Publishers, p. 308.

[12] Ibid., pp. 15–16.
[13] Suggested by art critic, Pranabranjan Ray, with regard to the abstract works of Somnath Hore; see P. Ray, 1983, 'Somnath Hore and the Wounds', in *Somnath Hore*, New Delhi: Lalit Kala Akademi Series of Contemporary Indian Art, p. 8.

Indian art—requires much more critical art historical scrutiny than it has received so far. The *Wounds* resonate with a metaphorical presence of memory and violence, much akin to what we heard from Tyeb Mehta at the outset. Following memory and metaphor into Mehta's art, we enter a completely different arrangement of pictorial space, in this case, large oils with flat surfaces, arranged in controlled suspension. Figures occupy a dramatic grandeur in Mehta's massive canvasses. Like projectiles of flat angular surfaces, Mehta's figures collide, split, and entangle, disrupted, as in his *Diagonal* series,[14] by a fissure across the spectrum, rupturing as well as containing the colliding figures in a grand symmetry. His figures are precise in their neat dismemberments, the limbs dislocated as the figures fall on their heads in sustained agony. Whether in his *Falling Figure* series, or works like *The Gesture*,[15] or the *Mahisashura* series we began with, the persistence of dislocation and collision is a hallmark of Mehta's art: it represents, as the artist reflects, a 'cosmic tragedy'.[16]

The 'diagonal' appears in Mehta's canvas as a 'pictorial device' to focus more on the expressive qualities of colour as an element than lines.[17] He uses the diagonal to fragment the image, prompting thereby its own movement, and defining the pictorial space for colour to be applied. The planar characteristics of Mehta's dislocated figures, striking in their solid flat masses of colour, make his work essentially minimalist. Yet, in constructing a splintering surface, both in the figures themselves and the pictorial space at large, Mehta continues to grapple with a fractured memory of the Partition; split surfaces and figures resonate with the memory of conflict and artist's quest for a monumental metaphor of violence.[18] The resultant image leaves us with a set of suggestions, the 'significant form' becomes, once again, a symbolic entry point into the realm of memory and trauma.

This disciplining of personal anguish to the rigidities of form is the critical point in the abstract, minimalist compositions of both Somnath Hore and Tyeb Mehta. In both their works, we see a marked centrality of form, a radical erasure of details in strict adherence to the dictates of compositional elements. However, the pure form is arrived at through a conscious engagement with lived experience; while history and memory mutate into the 'significant form' through the use of metaphor, the artists adhere to

---

[14] Tyeb Mehta, *Diagonal* series, oils on canvas, made during the 1970s.

[15] *Falling Figure with a Bird,* 1988, oil on canvas. Mehta began making *Falling Figures* way back in 1965. After his visit to New York, his canvasses underwent a significant change in terms of composition and application of colour. He returned to the *Falling Figure* in the 1980s, using the suspended projectiles of coloured surfaces. The *Diagonal* series, for example, *Diagonal,* 1973, oil on canvas, 175 x 175 cm, and paintings like the *Gesture III*, 1977, oil on canvas, 120 x 150 cm, as well as the *Mahisashura* series fall in the post-1960s period, with a high point from mid-1970s.

[16] The artist, quoting Kandinsky, in Geeta Kapur, 1978, 'Introduction', in Geeta Kapur (conceived and compiled), *Pictorial Space: A Point of View on Contemporary Indian Art*, an exhibition held at Lalit

Kala Akademi, New Delhi between 14 December 1977 and 3 January 1978.

[17] Mehta in conversation with fellow artists, reproduced in Ursula Bickelmann and Nissim Ezekiel (eds), 1987, *Artists Today/East–West Visual Arts Encounter*, Bombay: Marg Publications, p. 93.

[18] Shoumini Sengupta, 'Indian Artist Enjoys His World'.

the distinctly modernist idiom of formal purity. For Somnath Hore, it is the material and the texture, which is moulded, carved, spilt, or stitched time and again to bear the scars of wounds. For Tyeb Mehta, it is the purely formal use of colour, 'without being hampered by textures or brush marks'.[19] The diagonal that divided his canvas was an essentially formalist device, though it can be seen as connoting fracture. As the artist points out himself, 'I realised that the diagonal gave me two separate areas to work on. I could display the image the way I liked, not only in terms of pure design, but also for emotive purposes.'[20] Thus, Mehta asserts, despite the persistence of the social in his art, that his paintings should be held '… only on formal terms'.[21] It is precisely this implicit politicality of strict formalism in the works of these two artists, which makes them crucial signposts in entering modernism in post-independence Indian art.

The symbolic presence of memory and angst in the works of Somnath Hore and Tyeb Mehta in the 1970s, takes us back to the critical decade of the 1940s, which has a recurring metaphoric presence in the works of both these artists. Both artists were direct products of the forces released in the 1940s; and, their initial years as artists lead us to two critical nodes in Indian art practice in the 1940s–1950s, namely, progressivism and modernist internationalism. Hore was a young artist–reporter of the Communist Party of India (CPI) in the heydays of the left-wing cultural ferment in the 1940s.

Schooled by fellow comrade and artist, Chittaprosad, in making sketches of peasant rebellion and popular resistance, Hore was to become an integral, albeit silent, worker of the progressive culture in the 1940s that the CPI patronized. Tyeb Mehta was a student of the J.J. School of Art in Bombay. In the late 1940s, he became a close associate of the part of the Progressive Artists' Group of Bombay which spearheaded the distinct internationalist modernism in the Bombay art circuits. The Progressive Artists were formed in 1947, a product of both 'progressive' ethos of critical realism and the staunch individualist zest for the international avant-garde.

Progressivism and internationalism in Indian art appear, and with reason, as two divergent trails in the pursuit of modernism in Indian art. The former, with its legacy of left cultural activism of the 1940s, dwelt more on social signification and popular accessibility of art, thus stressing social realistic idioms for the artist. Internationalism, also a cherished ideal of the 1940s, rebelliously argued for the artist's freedom from contextual politics in an untarnished exploration of pure formalism, *sans* politics, either nationalist or socialist. Yet, historically, they share a common root in the 'crisis' of the 1940s, and it is in this common contextual legacy that both have a claim as 'modernist' moments in Indian art. Although the social concern of progressive art and the individualist formalism might appear to be two mutually opposing practices, I will suggest here the precise overlaps of the two, what I have earlier mentioned as ambivalence of the individual and the collective, the formal and the social. Both Tyeb Mehta and Somnath Hore, in

[19] Bickelmann and Ezekiel (eds), *Artists Today/ East–West Visual Arts Encounter*, p. 94.
[20] Ibid.
[21] Tyeb Mehta, in conversation with Neville Tuli, reproduced in Tuli, *The Flamed Mosaic*, p. 332.

their respective manners, lead us into this ambivalence in the Indian modern.

The 'Place for People' in Modern Art: The Progressive and the Political

Against the backdrop of World War II and British India being roped into the imperial war effort, the 1940s began with a catastrophic famine in Bengal, killing more than two million and displacing yet more. While vast stretches of rural Bengal fell victim to hunger and epidemic, pushing millions to the streets of Calcutta and the subdivisional towns in search of food, urban landscape altered completely with hitherto unseen sights of hunger, destitution, and death. As mass politics burgeoned in strikes and increased political violence, the most tarred experience of the decade was the communal riots and genocide, culminating in partition in the wake of independence. The Bengal Famine of 1943 and the Partition, it can be argued, had set the tone for artistic figuration in the decades to come. Henceforth, the image of the famished and the displaced would appear time and again in the works of artists in Bengal, disrupting the lyrical contours of the previous decades, patronized largely by the Bengal School. What was introduced in the 1940s, whether in progressive art circles or in the works of the internationalists, was a visual vocabulary of unrest, conflict, and resistance. In the works of the latter, this unrest would appear as individual angst of the alienated artist, whereas progressive art sought to reflect socio-political moorings of the day.

Merging art with politics more directly and violently rather than in implicit terms, the 1940s created the context where

modernism as a dialectical practice in art production could surface. It was enmeshed in languages of 'realism', 'progress', 'popular', and 'revolutionary'. In art, the idea of progressivism made itself felt in the debates around the nature of literature, or representation in visual arts, forwarding what was seen as 'revolutionary humanism', the 'popularization' of art, taking art 'to the people'. This idea of the progressive was informed by a socialist reading of cultural production, if not direct political affiliation of its members with the CPI. In their first bulletin, captioned *People's Theatre Stars the People*, the Indian People's Theatre Association (IPTA), formed in 1943 under the direct patronage of the CPI, declared the emergence in art, of 'new methods of production, new social relationships and patterns, new social conflicts and problems'.[22] Earlier, in the late 1930s, a similar issue was voiced by the Manifesto of the Progressive Writers' Association, one of the earliest spaces of what would henceforth develop as the Marxist cultural movement. The manifesto sought to bring in Indian art 'something more real, something more in harmony with the facts of our existence today, something which will make our art full bodied and virile'.[23] With the formation of IPTA, this was given an active mobile resonance, with the cultural squad of IPTA travelling to the villages, factories, and small towns. The people's theatre movement also sought to reinvent art as 'a potent force for the creation of future', a bid to address

[22] First Souvenir of the IPTA, p. 2.
[23] Sajjad Zaheer, 1979, 'Preface to "Towards Progressive Literature"', in Pradhan (ed.), *Marxist Cultural Movement in India*, p. 36.

the 'divorce between arts like dancing and painting and the revolutionary *motifs* and attitudes of the masses'.[24] The left cultural movement sought to create in art a distinct 'popular'—'national in form, socialist in content'—and in its wake, it brought together artists, writers, and performers in a common platform to fashion the idiom of progressive art.

Progressive art in the 1940s was meant to be primarily figurative, a significant iconographic development of the decade being the physiognomy of hunger and depletion, most brilliantly explored in the works of artists in Bengal like Zainul Abedin, Chittaprosad, Gobardhan Ash, Deviprasad Roychoudhuri, *et al*. The 1940s also brought about a dramatic alteration in the artist's search for his models. From here onwards, urban spaces and landscapes would come to constitute one of the dominant imageries in art, shifting the erstwhile focus on the idyllic village India as the site of the 'national'—the fissured cityscape and the individuals caught in it would now become the dominant icons in art. Within the rhetoric of progressive art, recognition was also given to art making as critical cultural practice, which necessitated artists to address the socio-political context in which they were operating. The search for a new vocabulary in art, which could reflect the mood of the times, further prompted the formation of artists' groups across the country: in 1941 was formed the Young Turks in Bombay; in 1943, the Calcutta Group of artists in Calcutta; and in 1947, the Progressive Artists' Group in Bombay and the Dilli Silpi Chakra in Delhi. These groups, though in most instances dissolved

by the mid-1950s (except the Silpi Chakra), were spaces of ardent internationalism in Indian art. Artists who emerged in these groups not only sought to experiment in new formal idioms of international modernism in their respective manners, they grappled at the same time with issues of individualistic and formal autonomy, seeking, in some cases, even a complete divorce from the social. In post-independence India, these groups were to emerge as bastions of modernism in Indian art, in their search for a new artistic language and identity in the new nation-state.

Both the Calcutta Group and the Progressive Artists' Group in Bombay had a fraught relationship with progressive art movement, more specifically, the left culture movement of the 1940s. Fashioning themselves as urban professional artists, members of both groups began their manifestoes by addressing questions of identity, the crisis of the times, and charting a clear departure from both academic naturalism as well as lyrical mysticism of the early decades of the twentieth century. Some of the founder members of the Calcutta Group like Rathin Maitra were closely associated with the Anti-Fascist Writers' and Artists' Association (established in 1941). Likewise, Francis Newton Souza, a founder member of the Progressive Artists' Group, had a Communist Party membership in the mid-1940s and began with a left leaning.[25] However, in their artistic quest, they were seeking not merely a radical break with the past, but indeed, an autonomy of the work

---

[24] First Souvenir of the IPTA, p. 2.

[25] Yashodhara Dalmia, 2002, *The Making of Modern Indian Art: The Progressives*, New Delhi: Oxford University Press, pp. 79–80.

of art itself: '…absolute freedom for content and technique, almost anarchic'.[26] Given the crisis of the 1940s, and the parallel 'progressive' will to portray the common man, most artists from these groups began their careers in this decade with images of the poor, marginalized, and downtrodden.

Yet, their insistence on formal experimentations and modernist internationalism was not always in keeping with the social realist underpinnings of the visual arts of the left progressive movement. For a movement that projected popular access to culture, taking art 'to the people', formal elitism was bound to prompt a rupture. Members of both the groups eventually denounced any political content or inspiration in their art in the 1940s, more importantly any leftist influence, which became tantamount with Stalinist propaganda.[27] Yet, as Geeta Kapur comments, the Marxist cultural movement of the 1940s, in its attempts in breaking elitism of art practice and defining a place for the people outside the 'classical', remains one of the earliest mutations of Western avant-garde in India. But the movement also defined the spaces of tension in modernist art practice—between the collective and the individual, the realist and the formal, the progressive and the modern.

In post-independence India, this tension tilted largely towards the formalist modernism caught in the euphoria of the new nation-state, a status quo that was soon to be disrupted in the heady political turbulence of the 1960s–70s, particularly in Bengal. From the mid-1960s onwards, the political milieu of Calcutta and the region at large was caught in a frenzy of agitational politics and radical people's struggle, culminating in the Naxalbari uprising. Agrarian revolt was coupled with widespread student agitation and daily violence in the city, followed by notorious official repression.[28] As the economy continued to sag, the war with Pakistan and the Bangladesh Liberation War (1971) brought in a fresh spate of refugees to the city, and before long, the disillusionment of a national emergency in 1974 ruptured the political fabric once more. In art, these decades resurrected the tendencies released in the 1940s. The progressive art movement had successfully located art in the public sphere in a critical functional role, opening up spaces for the artist as an activist and his art as socio-political dialogue. In the 1960s and the 1970s, this resurfaced with a re-emergence of iconographies of violence and wounds, particularly amongst the artists working in Bengal, for whom the quest for the modern form could not preclude artistic sensibility of the social, lingering most persistently against the backdrop of

---

[26] *Introducing Progressive Artists' Group, Bombay* catalogue to the joint exhibition of the Calcutta Group and the Bombay Progressives, 1950 (from the private papers of Rathin Maitra, founder member, Calcutta Group of artists).

[27] Artists like Prodosh Das Gupta and Newton Souza, founding members of the Calcutta Group and the Progressive Artists' Group respectively, denied in later years, any direct political motivation in their works in the 1940s, stressing the primacy of formal experimentation. See Prodosh Das Gupta, 1981, 'The Calcutta Group: Its Aims and Achievements', *Lalit Kala Contemporary*, vol. 31, April, pp. 5–12.

[28] The Naxalite movement in Bengal and Bihar marked a cathartic phase in radical left politics. Beginning with the issue of land redistribution in north Bengal, it brought in its wake violent student politics and political catharsis in Calcutta in the 1960s.

continued economic decline and urban chaos in post-independence Calcutta. What recurred time and again in the works of artists in the 1960s and the 1970s was the engagement with context—the search for form became entwined with the crisis of the everyday. Political and social sensitivity in various mutations would mark artists working in Calcutta from late-1950s, creating for the artists a different engagement with and sensibility around the modern in art. The eerie disquiet of the Naxalbari movement brought in distinct totems of the grotesque and the uncanny; expressionism and grotesque realism emerged as dominant stylistic idioms, with surrealism providing the ideal idiomatic device to engage with the dark political turmoil of daily life.

After a brief interlude in the 1950s, figurative art was to emerge more prominently in these decades, with an intense turn towards the social and the political in art. In Calcutta, the 'social realism' of the 1940s gave way to new experimentations with the grotesque, the surreal, and the existential. While satire was evoked through caricature and fantastic exaggerations of the human form in the works of artists like Paritosh Sen (1918–2008) and Jogen Choudhury (*b.* 1939) to capture both the ridiculous and the sinister, in Somnath Hore, the abstract form itself became a text for the wounded corporeality of violence. In the works of artists like Bijon Chowdhury (*b.* 1931), Nikhil Biswas (1930–66), and Robin Mondol (*b.* 1929), the human figures are labyrinthine, truncated, and distorted, caught in the sullen despair of a burgeoning cityscape. Thick expressionist impastos of colour in dark hues accentuate urban chaos

and gloom. Dislocated figures in grotesque excesses or cubistic fractures dominate the works of these artists in a constant recurring motif of struggle and conflict, creating once more, physiognomies of pain and alienation. Particularly engaging here are Nikhil Biswas's *Combat* series and *Clown and Circus* series,[29] and Robin Mondol's *Brothel* series. The tragic consciousness in the works of these artists spanned from expressionist degeneration to evoking the ridiculous, the sinister, and the fantastic. Another artist who made the human predicament his central concern in large pictorial surfaces was A. Ramachandran (*b.* 1935). Between the 1960s–70s, Ramachandran explored a critical realist idiom in his mammoth canvasses, which he described quoting Dostoevsky, as one 'extending into the fantastic'.[30] His figures in gigantic canvasses are headless, male and female, lumped together against dead space, compressed into distortion, disease, and pestilence, offering a 'grim ontology of human existence'.[31]

From the monumental compositions of action and disarray one sees in Ramachandran, one can move to the frozen exactitude of the realist oils of Bikash

[29] *Combat* series, 1965, drawings and watercolour and ink on paper; *Clown and Circus* series, 1965, oil on rolling paper.

[30] Classic compositions from this period include monumental compositions like *The Cells*, 1964, oil on canvas, 365.8 x 152.4 cm; *Indian Resurrection*, 1965, oil on canvas, 381 x 177.8 cms; *Encounter*, 1967, oil on canvas, 731.5 x 182.9 cm; *Vision of War*, 1977, oil on board, 365.8 x 182.9 cm. A detailed study of Ramachandran's art is given in Siva Kumar (ed.), 2003, *Ramachandran: A Retrospective, Vol. 1*, National Gallery of Modern Art in association with the Vadhera Art Gallery, New Delhi: Vadhera Art Gallery, p. 72.

[31] Ibid., p. 79.

Bhattacharjee (1940–2006). In a radically different treatment of the much-fraught style of realism, Bikash Bhattacharjee comes with his heady photo-realistic compositions in the 1970s, using very successfully the stylistic device of surrealism. The artist is a master of realist oils; he constructs an exactitude of a street, an interior, or individuals in classic naturalistic verisimilitude. In this he introduces, in a dramatic intervention, an abrupt element of juxtaposition that subverts the calm familiarity of the realist image. The naturalistic is juxtaposed with the uncanny, the real transmuting to the surreal. Thus, rendering the familiar uncanny, the artist stages the violence within the everyday. For example, the *Doll* series Bhattacharya made in the 1970s holds up before the viewer flashes from the dark days of the Naxalite movement in Calcutta, wrecked by political strife and police atrocities. The doll hangs suspended from a half open drawer, or lies abandoned in a desolate street corner. The viewer is immediately left with a feeling of both presence and absence, throbbing with the eerie lingering of a recent violence.[32] Artistic subversion of the perceived 'normality' in society is transported in Bikash's canvas in an essentially modernist juxtaposition of form, illusion, and perception.

Some of these artists came together to form the Society of Contemporary Artists in Calcutta in 1960, and in 1964, the Calcutta Painters, the latter splitting from the former. Some of them, though not directly involved in politics, nonetheless rooted their works from this period in the essentially fraught

political context of Calcutta in the late 1960s and the 1970s. The city itself provided idioms of catharsis in their works, the organic form they explored became idiomatic of the chaos they lived in. An interesting distinction is drawn by Ratan Parimoo in his comparison of the 'expressiveness of the young Calcutta painters' and the 'expressionism' of the Progressive Artists' Group of Bombay. The Bombay progressives, he maintains, used figural distortions, thick impastos, or the fracturing of pictorial space, maintaining a controlled treatment of formal stylistics and emotional communiqué. Their formal idioms drew heavily on German expressionism, keeping the preponderance of the plasticity of form and style over the dramatic social content. In contrast, Parimoo sees in the works of the Calcutta artists, 'the image and the environs in which it is placed evoke uncanny effects'.[33] Thus, more than abstract expressionism, surrealism comes more handy as a pictorial device. The persistence of the 'environs' and the 'uncanny' in the work of these artists underscores the socio-political fractures within which they worked.

As agitational politics and left extremism of the 1960s brought back the rhetoric of fractures in the works of artists in Bengal, at a national level, the 1970s rendered the political in art more intense and integrated. Through the 1960s and the 1970s, the reeling impact of the Sino-Indian War, the Bangadesh Liberation War, and the national emergency in 1974 laid bare the fissures in the postcolonial state, striking

---

[32] *Doll* series, oils on canvas, the series made through the 1970s–80s.

[33] Ratan Parimoo, 1975, *Studies in Modern Indian Art: A Collection of Essays*, New Delhi: Kanak Publications, p. 98.

at the root of the modernist dream of nationhood. It also prompted artists across the country to respond to a fresh political crisis. Nationwide, artists like Gieve Patel (*b*. 1940), Vivan Sundaram (*b*. 1943), and Sudhir Patwardhan (*b*. 1949) responded to the crisis through their own satirical, grotesque, or surreal figurations. Sundaram and Patwardhan were a part of a new political turn in Indian art since the late 1960s, based largely in Baroda. Along with other artists like Bhupen Khakkar (1934–2003), they launched a frontal attack on post-independence non-figurative art as being a part of a conformist international formalism in the cultural politics of the Cold War. The journal, *Vrischik*, published from Baroda, became the mouthpiece of radical ideas in art making, spearheaded by the polemical writings of the art critic, Geeta Kapur. Significantly also, in the late 1960s and the 1970s, artists like Nalini Malini (*b*. 1946), Nilima Sheikh (*b*. 1945), and Arpita Singh (*b*. 1937) were to bring in the dialectic of gender and the everyday in making the 'modern' in art.

These were artists who developed their experience and art making in the politically charged decades of the late 1960s and the 1970s. In their compositions, sites/sights of modernism in Indian art get all the more fractured, with the autonomy of the form and the artist getting mediated not only by national and local politics, but most significantly, by the politics of the everyday, of gender and class. The urban landscape surfaced once more as dominant idiom and these artists engaged directly with the social as the goal in art making. In a bid to democratize art, they sought to retrieve the space for the narrative and the

figurative in art, making the idiom sensitive and responsive to the multilayered cultural politics of postcolonial nationhood. By the 1970s, the politics of postcoloniality would surface most vividly, particularly against the hiatus of the national emergency. With artists like Bhupen Khakhar, Sudhir Patwardhan, and Nalini Malini, the figurative, narrative idiom typical to Indian art was revived. I will close here with a mention of the exhibition which saw a culmination of this few figurative turn in Indian art: the 'Place for People' exhibition in 1980–1 in Delhi and Bombay was put together by artists like Jogen Chowdhury, Bhupen Khakhar, Nalini Malini, Sudhir Patwardhan, Gulamohammed Sheikh, and Vivan Sundaram, based primarily in Baroda, but connected to the art worlds of Bombay, Delhi, and Shantiniketan. An exhibition of great critical importance, 'Place for People' (1981, Jehangir Art Gallery, Bombay) brought back ideologies of narration and the figurative, redefining the modern in Indian art. Post-independence euphoria of internationalist non-figurative modernism was revoked in polemic and practice, and the artists consciously used the narrative idiom to contain multiple existential politics of the postcolonial subjectivity.

'Concrete Potentiality': The Avant-garde and Its Social Contents

Developments in the 1960s–1970s open up questions on the possible narratives of modernism in Indian art. Can we dissociate the social figuration or politically responsive idioms from the narratives on artistic modernism in post-independence Indian art? Or should we the search for multiple spaces or alternative understandings of the modern, questioning not only a stable meta-narrative of the modern, but diffusing its habitations, grounding historically questions of artistic autonomy, agency, and sensibilities, social and political? Pushing tensions beyond the form/content binary, the issue of style needs to be considered closely, and a review of stylistic idioms used by artists discussed here might offer some directions. For young artists working in the 1940s, cubism and expressionism had served as important stylistic devices to portray subjective angst and rebellion against established canons, in their case, both the lyrical mythological bias of the already waning Bengal School of art as well as the rigid verisimilitude of academic naturalism. I will suggest here that not only were such experiments with style conducive to accommodate individual trauma and dislocation typical to the politically fraught years of the 1940s in India, but in the works of certain artists, these apparently 'formal' quests can also be seen to connect the social and the formal, the claims of progressive politics on art and its purely aesthetic determinations. As an interface between the artist and his object, the question of style remains wedged between the individual and the collective, the personal and the social, as the artist himself remains rooted, consciously or unconsciously, in the historical experiences of his times, what Lukács referred to as 'concrete potentiality— the inevitable location of the individual in his social context'.[34] Style, says Lukács, is not an autonomous formalistic category, but

connected fundamentally to the worldview, the *Weltanschauung* underlying the art work: 'It is the writers' attempt to reproduce this view of the world which constitutes his "intention" and is the formative principle underlying the style of a given piece of writing. Looked at in this way, style ceases to be a formalistic category, rather it is rooted in content; it is the *specific form of a specific content*.'[35]

In post-independence India, the modernist idioms of cubism, expressionism, or surrealism have proven particularly productive in containing the artist's subjective alienation and critical engagement with his concrete context. Fantastic, grotesque, or surreal figurations, or cubist fractures, became critical devices in capturing rupture in the works of many artists in the 1960s and the 1970s. In a way, the tension between social realistic figuration and formalist individualism, that had surfaced in the 1940s, can be said to have been resolved somewhat in the works of artists in these decades. The tension between the form and content, fostered largely by the left-wing cultural initiative in the 1940s, gets reoriented in the subsequent decades to contain an implicit critical consciousness, or a deep politicality. Artists like Somnath Hore or Tyeb Mehta, or even the new generation of Calcutta or Baroda artists, began grappling with purely formal elements in their art with a sustained engagement with socio-political subtexts, fusing the hiatus between pure form and social content. With them, debates

[34] Georg Lukács, 1963, *Meaning of Contemporary Realism*, trans. from German by John and Necke Mander, London: Merlin Press, p. 19.

[35] Ibid., emphasis added. Lukács was writing essentially on literature, yet, his observations remain pertinent in considering the tensions between realism and modernism in visual arts.

around artistic modernity came to concern not just form, content, or style, but indeed, the question of a 'reactive subjectivity' of the artist. The artist's selection or creation of a particular stylistic idiom points to a critical consciousness, which has marked the works of the artists discussed so far. This consciousness calls for a reconsideration of questions of artistic subjectivity, a space where we can also see the inherent tension between realism and modernism in Indian art in the twentieth century.

Critical here is the understanding of the avant-garde in India. The artistic avant-garde developed here through the fraught history of decolonization, more vividly articulated within the polemics of the 'progressive' left-wing cultural movement in the 1940s. Directing its rhetoric against revivalism and mysticism in art, the cultural movement privileged critical realism over pure individualism in art making, arguing for active reflection of social reality through a critical intervention of the artist–producer. Though the movement itself was diluted to a considerable degree in the immediate post-independence promise of the new nation-state, it had succeeded, within a decade of heightened struggle, in introducing in Indian art practices, the complex questions and possibilities around critical realism and modernism. In fact, it is the persistence of the memory of decolonization, particularly the crisis of the 1940s, in the imageries of the subsequent decades that demands reorientations in the understandings of modernism in Indian art.

Writing in 1978, Geeta Kapur argues that it is the persistence of the memory of decolonization which would provoke fresh experimentations in artistic sensitivity

and formal experimentations, and create possibilities for radical avant-gardism in India beyond purely technical finesse.[36] But this memory of anguish, she says, needs to transmute through the pulls of the contemporary, 'the memory of experiences imbibed as much as lived...It is the present and the value we give to it or, shall we say, the conscience we bring to it that forms the content of both memory and imagination.'[37] While conscience is more an ethical quality than aesthetic, Kapur projects authenticity as the nodal criterion for artistic practice. Personal authenticity, she says, needs to accommodate both conscience and reckoning of experience, the need being what she justly calls, an 'emotive–intuition' function in an artist. Kapur draws heavily from what K.G. Subramanyan—the artist, scholar, and prime modernist in post-independence India—called the 'man–environment nexus', where man is 'the feeling man', and environment, 'the living environment'.[38] What connects the artist to his environment is artistic sensitivity and a deep sensibility of the environment in which he operates. Artistic purism is basic to internationalism, and this, he maintains, cannot be transported to the Indian context: 'there can be similarities in the end product, there cannot be similarities in the root without a sacrifice of personality'.[39] Personal authenticity is thus more than pure

[36] Geeta Kapur, 1978, *Contemporary Indian Artists*, New Delhi: Vikas Publishing House Pvt. Ltd., p. x.

[37] Ibid., p. xi.

[38] K.G. Subramanyan, 1987, *The Living Tradition, Perspectives on Modern Indian Art*, Calcutta: Seagull Books, p. 87.

[39] Ibid., p. 48.

subjectivity, it requires what Subramanyan calls an 'environmental resonance'.

Writing way back in 1917, Rabindranath Tagore had pointed out this precise tension between artistic subjectivity and environmental resonance. For Tagore, the prime amongst the earliest individualists in Indian art, art was 'the expression of personality', personality being knowing the world as a 'personal fact'. 'If this world were taken away,' he wrote, 'our personality would lose all its content.'[40] For Tagore, internationalism did not mean an erasure of the local and the particular. His art school at Shantiniketan practiced this confluence of art and environment, both in terms of engaging with the rural landscape and the communities inhabiting it, as celebrated in the individual styles of the first generation of masters at Shantiniketan: Nandalal Bose, Benodebehari Mukherjee, and Ramkinkar Baij. In the works of each of these artists, albeit through different interventions, the 'local' entered the 'formal' mediated by the subjective realization of the man–environment nexus. Partha Mitter sees this 'environmental primitivism' as a rhetoric of anti-urban, anti-capitalist counter-modernity—a 'return' to village India as against the dehumanizing principles of colonial modernity.[41]

The return to the local as the site of the national was a critical point in the developments of the modern idiom in Indian art, and in its inception since the early 1930s vis-à-vis demands for political democratization and Gandhian populism, it remains an intrinsically political project—not in portraying resistance and rupture, but rather, in the creative zeal to contain and project the forms, colours, and motifs, drawn from folk idioms of India. Ruralism or pastoralism, rather than primitivism, seem more apt for describing this generic tendency in art post-1920s. In their respective manners, artists across the twentieth century—Nandalal Bose, Ramkinkar Baij, Benodebehari Mukhopadhyay, Jamini Roy, Maqbool Fida Husain, and K.G. Subramanyan—have endeavoured to contain and transmute the 'local' in their art, through intrinsically subjective engagements with their material. Their perception of the human predicament as well as the intrinsic dialogic possibilities of pictorial space make them fundamental, particularly so in the ways these artists continue to be referred as the bedrock of modernism in India.

My concern in this chapter has been to highlight spaces where the modern form has emerged through artistic engagements with conflict and violence, and indeed memory; I have argued for approaching artistic modernism in India through historically rooted, socially conditioned subjectivities as well as the implicit politicalities of form and style. My material, I am aware, has been limited to paintings and graphic art. A more comprehensive treatment of sculpture, mixed media, or installations would have been too ambitious to be tackled within the scope of this rather introductory chapter, and as a coda, I will mention here the new experimentations with Dada and Pop-Art, and installations, which artists like Bhupen Khakkar and Vivan Sundaram brought in

[40] Rabindranath Tagore, 1961, 'What Is Art?' in P. Neogy (ed.), *Tagore on Art and Aesthetics*, New Delhi: International Cultural Centre, p. 18.

[41] Partha Mitter, 2007, *Triumph of Modernism: India's Artists and the Avant-Garde*, London, Reaktion Books.

from the late 1970s. Before jumping onto the bandwagon of the postmodern in Indian art, a historical reading of these 'moderns' needs to be conducted, such that the sites and claims of modernism are themselves adequately addressed.

Catalogues[42]

Manifestations II: Indian Art in the 20th Century: 100 Artists from the DAG Collection, Roobina Karode (ed.), New Delhi: Delhi Art Gallery, 2004.

Manifestations III: Hundred Artists from the Delhi Art Gallery, Roobina Karode (ed.), New Delhi: Delhi Art Gallery, 2005.

Masterpieces and Museum-quality Indian Modern and Contemporary Paintings, curated by Neville Tuli, Bombay: Osian's, December, 2002.

Masterpieces and Museum-quality III, Indian Contemporary Paintings with Rare Books and Vintage Film Memorablia, curated by Neville Tuli, Bombay: Osian's, March 2004.

[42] The catalogues and the exhibition catalogue *Art of Bengal* were used for accessing images and artist biographical details, which have been used to produce the text itself.

Afterword

Prathama Banerjee[†]

How does one read this volume on modernity? Is it just yet another work on the subject—one that comes after so much writing and rewriting—which has critiqued, decentred, provincialized, hybridized, differed/deferred, and such like, the very idea of the modern? Or to ask the same question differently, what critical purchase do we get by analytically staying with the modern now that the postcolonial has, apparently, irrevocably exposed the ruses of modernity?

Modern Makeovers has an answer. It argues that we must continue to engage modernity because the modern—as concept, name, and entity—survives in the world as part of the 'intimate lives of the popular and

the political'.[1] In South Asia, the modern is routinely invoked by hegemonic discourses as the sole ground for social transformation and governmental intervention. But it is also regularly invoked by resistant and everyday subjectivities, claiming rights, representation, development, and emancipation, all in the name of the modern. These enactments of the modern do not necessarily bolster up modernity as project—that is, as reason, progress, development, secularism, and so on—but, very often, produce 'recalcitrant traces and singularities that exceed the circumspection of the sociological and philosophical categories of modern European thought'[2] and one might add, regimes of modern, governmental technologies. In other

† I would like to thank Saurabh Dube for his comments on an earlier draft of this chapter. Also, my gratitude to Uday Kumar as always. The errors and the flights of fancy are all mine.

[1] Saurabh Dube, 'Introduction', this volume.
[2] Ibid.

words, much can and does happen in the name of the modern, even today.

Not surprisingly, the chapters in this volume do *not* have modernity as the *object* of their study. The writers neither critique (for that has already been done) nor rewrite (for that is ongoing anyway) the 'project' of modernity. Instead, they dwell on distinct sites—art, religion, disease, biography, ethnography, advertising, citizenship, and subjectivity—so as to foreground the different, even contrary ways in which the modern gets routinely enacted as well as self-consciously performed. Consequently, most chapters—even those reflecting on colonial histories—appear unhampered by the earlier kind of anxieties about the modern and the national, or even by the associated need to invent multiple modernities[3] or a kind of ownership to 'our' modernity.[4] In that sense, this volume is post-national in its intent[5]—not in the sense of ignoring the particularities of what has come to be the nation of India or the region of South Asia, but in the sense of having already traversed and moved beyond the nation as framing category.

[3] S.N. Eisenstadt, 2000, 'Multiple Modernities', *Daedalus*, vol. 129, no. 1, Winter, pp. 1–29.
[4] Partha Chatterjee, 1997, *Our Modernity*, Rotterdam and Dakar: Sephis and CODESRIA; also, note Dipesh Chakrabarty's critical use of a term such as the 'Bengali modern', for example. See Dipesh Chakrabarty, 2000, 'Witness to Suffering: Domestic Violence and the Birth of the Modern Subject in Bengal', in Timothy Mitchell (ed.), *Questions of Modernity*, Minnesota: University of Minnesota Press, p. 70.
[5] For an elaboration of the idea of the 'post-national', see Aditya Nigam, 2010, *After Utopia*, Delhi: Primus; also, see 2009, *Economic and Political Weekly*, Special issue on 'The Postnational Condition', vol. 44, no. 39, 2 October.

Some of the chapters are explicit accounts of the post-national. Thus, Mrinalini Sinha talks of how it was possible, till less than a hundred years ago, to demand political rights in the name of imperial subjecthood rather than national citizenship. Bodhisattva Kar talks of how the postcolonial remains forever deferred as the nation reproduces the colonial imperative in its own provinces. The other chapters too make it clear that the nation is not the only location in relation to which the modern can be thought. In fact, the modern is differently enacted in different locations, of which the nation is only one—other locations being the Empire, the Muslim diaspora, the East Bengal *mofussil*, and for that matter, the image, the city, the reproductive body the citizen, and so on. The point is to alter our perception of the modern by making it site or network-specific while thwarting the monopolistic claim of the nation over the modern. In other words, the implicit argument of the volume as a whole is that it is only from a post-national location that the modern can be re-viewed as series of political and strategic enactments rather than as *necessary* history. Or else, we remain forever caught up in the national vis-à-vis the modern binary, either in the form of an opposition (national versus modern) or in the form of a statist claim (national modern).

What the chapters also demonstrate in the process—and this, to my mind, is particularly important—is that these diverse enactments of the modern also differently constitute the non-modern for purposes of specific strategic and political deployments. This argument goes well beyond the established 'constructivist' historiography in South Asia that argues that the pre-modern, the archaic, the primitive, and the traditional here were constructed by colonial modernity. For the point here is to show that the non-modern gets produced not only through dominant statist and scientific discourses, but also in sites of the popular, the mass, the market, the image, the city, and so on. I think this is the critical though implicit point that the volume makes about the non-modern, namely, that it is not only a stable 'other' invented by and for the sake of the modern but also a contingent, changing, heteronomous thing, which emerges out of diverse enactments of the modern and takes on diverse trajectories. Should we then ask, by pushing the point further, whether one must actually write a narrative of the changing career of the non-modern—as we have written of the changing versions of the modern—through three or more centuries?

This is, of course, a big question and needs collaborative and long-term work. Let me merely say here that raising the question of the non-modern is not an invitation to rethink either the question of tradition (the foundational category of modern social sciences) or of the primordial (a grounding concept in much of modern Western metaphysics). Nor is it a call for renewed engagement with notions such as the pastoral, the rural, or the romantic, that is, notions that have historically lent themselves to anti-modern ideologizing, including in the South Asian Gandhian moment. How and for what purpose must we then think the non-modern in the first place? Do we think the non-modern as the *counter*-modern in the sense that Foucault meant it, that is, in the sense of an imperative, simultaneous and coincidental to modernity, that reactivates other pasts in the heart of the present so as to resist the modernist will seeking to

render other memories and lineages dead?[6] Or do we think of the non-modern as *extra*-modern, constituted in an agonistic relationship to the modern, which forever seeks to fall outside, exceed, and sometimes self-consciously transcend it, as in so much of modern anti-alienation rhetoric and aesthetics? Or is there a way to think (what perhaps one is mistakenly calling) the *non*-modern by going beyond a relationship of negation vis-à-vis the modern and raising the question of limits and ends of modernity?

In the rest of this 'Afterword', I shall briefly talk around this question. I shall ask if it is worthwhile rethinking the modern in South Asia by placing it alongside two other times, the early modern and the contemporary, which are being discussed in recent years in South Asia. These two temporalities are not quite modern but also not quite a negation of the modern—for these so-called other times are not 'other' in a dichotomous or oppositional sense. They do not operate in the way that temporal constructs such as the medieval or the archaic or the pre-modern do vis-à-vis the modern. That is, they do not simply bolster the idea of the modern by constituting grounds of tradition or culture in the name of the non-modern. Instead, the early modern and the contemporary raise questions about the limits of the modern, about its twilights and its fade-outs, as it were; and make us wonder if we have not become prone to imagining all times to come as modern, that is, to imagine a relentless present as an interminable modernity, a modernity

[6] Michel Foucault, 1984, 'What Is Enlightenment?' in Paul Rabinow (ed.), *The Foucault Reader*, New York: Pantheon Press, p. 39.

without end. I am suggesting that there is a productive ambiguity in thinking with the early modern and the contemporary. On the one hand, the early modern and the contemporary are often placed within the ambit of intelligibility provided by the modern. On the other hand, they also effect a division, a differentiation within the modern, at times enlarging the reach of the modern but also, at times, thwarting it. The early modern and the contemporary then help us raise the following question: *what do notions of the limit and the end do that notions of negation do not do, in relation to the idea of the modern*?

The question of the end is, of course, highly fraught and I must clarify what I am *not* doing here. I am not arguing for an imagination of the non-modern as postmodern, as a historical period coming 'after' the end of modernity. In any case, the prefix 'post' does by no means signal an end, only a reconstituted relationship to the modern—just as with terms such as postcolonial, post-socialist, post-national, and so on. Nor am I harking back to the 1990s when the rhetoric of the end of history—and so the end of philosophy, end of politics, and end of all such markers of the modern—took the post-Cold War world by storm. That moment is past and is now exposed for what it was, namely, a moment of unabashed capitalist cheering after the collapse of the Soviet Union. I am also not arguing for a renewed transition narrative that would see modernity ending to give way to another phase of history, thus rescuing the *non*-modern from the conceptual clutches of the *pre*-modern. In fact, transition narratives have hardly ever conceived of an end to modernity. They have imagined an

end to capitalism—or for that matter, to totalitarianism—but by that very count have promised the birth of a truer modernity, in the name of communism, democracy, and such like. In other words, in transition narratives, the category of the modern has remained stable and constant, implying that even though we conceptualize modernity through capitalism and democracy, these are by no means concurrent categories. After all, there seems to be something about the modern that always already exceeds both capitalism and democracy. (This is something we shall return to later.) Last, I am also not gesturing towards the rhetoric of the apocalyptic end that has marked our twentieth and twenty-first century modernity, through images of the nuclear holocaust, 9/11, and environmental disaster, for in such cases, the end of modernity is also made to appear as the end of the world itself.[7]

What can one then mean by raising the question of the limit or the end with regard to modernity? Precisely the recognition that, by its very linguistic constitution and temporal intent, the modern is meant to perpetuate itself *ad infinitum*—for everything that is and everything that is to come cannot but be grasped as modern. There seems to be a 'before' but no 'after' modernity; and even the 'before' falls under the shadow of

[7] See Faisal Devji's chapter in this volume which discusses the rise of a globality based on the imagination of simultaneous death, such as through nuclear conflagration, of entire humanity. Also interesting is how historians are trying to ask if it is possible to imagine a future 'without us' a la climate change today, and what it means for the 'historical imagination'; see Dipesh Chakrabarty, 2009, 'The Climate of History: Four Theses', *Critical Inquiry*, vol. 35, no. 2, Winter, pp. 197–222.

the modern. This is paradoxically true even today because—unlike the conventional narratives of modernization, which saw allegedly mismatched elements in the present as stubborn 'residues' of the past—we now recognize that the traditional and the archaic are very often modern inventions too. The non-modern thus becomes constitutive of the modern (and vice versa), leaving no imagination of narratives *indifferent* to the question of modernity. Thus, modernity becomes all the more engrossing, even as modernity itself gets more and more differentiated and hybridized. That is the paradox of working with modernity, or perhaps we can call this the 'modernity effect'.

The Contemporary

Let us then problematize modernity, not by setting up its negation, but by asking an altogether different question: what is the relationship between the modern and the contemporary? Does the contemporary, a neighbouring time as it were, in any way signal a temporality which is not exhausted by enactments and imaginations of the modern? Many of the chapters in the volume, without stating it explicitly, address the contemporary; even though, in the way that they are pitched, these chapters appear as part of the history of modernity. This might appear an incontrovertible fact in itself—the fact that our contemporary is very much an enactment of the modern. But what if we question this apparently self-evident nature of the present, and work with the hypothesis that while the modern is very much part of the genealogy of our present, the contemporary might very well be quite

different from what we call the modern? In other words, I am suggesting that we dwell on the contemporary not as another empirical instant in the mutating career of the modern but as possibly another, not-quite-modern time.

The modern, historically speaking, has been one amongst many ways of being contemporary. Modernity valorized the present by setting up a favourable contrast with the past—it was, as Foucault put it, the 'will to heroise the present'.[8] But that by itself was not entirely uncommon to other times and contexts.[9] What was specific to modernity was additionally a refiguration of the present as the necessary and logical future of the past. This modern contemporary was then made self-identical by conceptually exporting 'others' to the past and/or to the colony. It was then recast as eternal, such that all times to come—including utopian futures—appeared as always already modern. (Perhaps this is why the only name we have been able to invent for a present that is no longer quite modern is the derivative name of the postmodern.) If the modern is thus seen as one, particular historical way of grasping the contemporary, it then becomes possible for us to imagine other ways of being contemporary too. I have elsewhere written about one such instance of imagining the contemporary differently, amongst Santals of mid-nineteenth century Bengal and Bihar, who argued that familiar causalities no longer worked in their present, because this present no longer

[8] Michel Foucault, 'What Is Enlightenment', p. 35.
[9] Yigal Bronner, 2002, 'What Is New and What Is *Navya*? Sanskrit Poetics on the Eve of Colonialism', *Journal of Indian Philosophy*, vol. 30, no. 5, pp. 441–62.

seemed have a simple relation of succession to their past.[10] Another such instance of a different contemporary was the 'millenarian conjuncture' that operated over a good part of the Old World in the sixteenth century, to which both Akbar of India and Phillip II of Spain felt compelled to respond.[11]

In some ways, there is already a South Asian debate on the contemporary—though not quite explicitly staged in the way that I am formulating. Some scholars such as Dilip Gaonkar assert that there is a strong need to continue with the category of the modern in the contemporary; indeed that it is no less than ethnocentric to give up on modernity—in the name of the postmodern and such like—precisely at a time when non-European peoples of the world have begun to work out their own, alternative modernities.[12] In fact, there is even an argument amongst literary scholars that not only modernity, but different literary and artistic modernisms are critical to making sense of today's postcolonial world and must be acknowledged as such.[13] So, for instance, Caribbean modernism, Bengali modernism, Dalit modernism, and so on. In other words,

the contemporary is seen in this view as not just the *postcolonial* moment, but as the time of the *decolonization* of the modern.

Other scholars, however, believe that the modern is an inadequate name for the contemporary. Partha Chatterjee, for instance, argues that contemporary politics in India cannot be understood simply in terms of the advance of modernity, that is, through modernity's self-narrative of secularization and democracy, just as it cannot be understood in terms of cultural survivals of a 'pre-modern' past. According to him, the modern in India today is starkly delimited—a demographically confined, elitist, civic/state agenda for regulation and transformation of society, which had already reached its logical end by the late 1970s in the form of the failure of the authoritarian Emergency regime. Democracy—which Chatterjee delinks from modernity—however has, since the 1980s, deepened and flourished in the site of political society, in defiance of modern norms of law, secularism, and civility.[14] In other words, while it subsists in the contemporary in powerful ways, modernity is also often pitted against and retreats before democracy. We can extrapolate from this argument that the contemporary in India is somewhat in mismatch with the modern.

In a small essay titled, 'What Is the Contemporary?' Georgio Agamben says

[10] Prathama Banerjee, 2006, *The Politics of Time: 'Primitives' and History-writing in a Colonial Society*, New Delhi: Oxford University Press.

[11] Sanjay Subramanyam, 1997, 'Connected Histories: Notes towards a Reconfiguration of Early Modern Eurasia', *Modern Asian Studies*, vol. 31, no. 3, July, pp. 735–62.

[12] Dilip Parameshwar Gaonkar, 2001, 'On Alternative Modernities', in D.P. Gaonkar (ed.), *Alternative Modernities*, Durham, NC: Duke University Press, p. 14.

[13] Simon Gikandi, 1992, *Writing in Limbo: Modernism and Caribbean Literature*, Ithaca, NY: Cornell University Press; Laura Doyle and Laura Winkiel (eds), 2005, *Geomodernisms: Race, Modernism, Modernity*, Bloomington: Indiana University Press.

[14] Partha Chatterjee, 2005, 'Sovereign Violence and the Domain of the Political', in Thomas B. Hansen and Finn Stepputat (eds), *Citizens, Migrants and the State in the Postcolonial World*, Princeton: Princeton University Press, pp. 82–102; and Partha Chatterjee, 2004, *Politics of the Governed: Reflections on Popular Politics in Most of the World*, New York: Columbia University Press.

that to think of the contemporary is to divide, interrupt, and interpolate time, to transform it and put it in relation with other times—not in an act of history but in an act of 'citing' histories differently.[15] This is unavoidable since the present does not yield up to understanding in any simple, immediate manner, and we must imagine 'untimely' histories in order to return to that part of the present that we have been incapable of living. 'That which impedes access to the present is precisely the mass of what for some reason (its traumatic character, its excessive nearness) we have not managed to live. The attention to this "unlived" is the life of the contemporary. And to be contemporary means in this sense to return to a present where we have never been.'[16]

This formulation speaks interestingly to us. Agamben, of course, continues to label this contemporary as modern. For us, however, the point is precisely that our unlived present is that time which appears neither modern nor pre-modern, that is, the time that failed to make it into the narrative of modernity. In other words, going by Agamben's formulation, what we must do is to split our present into different times, of which the modern (and the traditional) would only be one, and reconstruct other times and histories of the present, perhaps even agonistically, outside and irrespective of the genealogy of the modern.

One of the directions in which we may move from here is to rewrite the genealogy of our present by disentangling the distinct histories that appear to come together to constitute the modern, such as the history of democracy, the history of capitalism, the history of public sphere, the history of the self, and so on. Hitherto we have worked with the presumption that these different histories necessarily articulate without surplus under the name of the modern. And yet, we are not entirely clear about the nature of these articulations. We almost always work by using epochal signifiers such as modernity, capitalism, and democracy interchangeably, or at most, through hyphenated concepts such as capitalist modernity, colonial modernity, capitalist democracy, and so on. This, however, is not for lack of theoretical rigour amongst us. In fact, this is in the nature of how modernity itself operates, in the nature of the 'modernity effect' as it were.

As Chapter 1 of this volume tells us, modernity is a unique category, in that it functions simultaneously as concept and as entity as well as, and I emphasize, subjectivity and as time. It is not accidental therefore that intellectuals have struggled endlessly with these varying manifestations of modernity—now a set of ideas (reason, enlightenment, progress); now a set of norms (equality, liberty, secularity); now an orientation of the self (secular, rational, individual, modernist, schizophrenic); now institutions and technologies (public sphere, governmentality, democracy); now capital; now an epoch (with a beginning but no end); and now an empty placeholder (filled with content by various peoples in various times and places). The point, however, is to note that in the way modernity has been historically constituted as a meta-concept/experience, it is meant to precisely work

---

[15] Georgio Agamben, 2009, 'What Is the Contemporary?' in G. Agamben, '*What Is an Apparatus*' *and Other Essays*, Stanford: Stanford University Press, p. 53.

[16] Ibid., p. 51.

in this way, as some as well as all of these. While, at one level, the modern is seen as analogous to and associated with other epochal signifiers such as the primordial, the classical, the ancient, or the medieval, none of these other times claim to work simultaneously and seamlessly across so many registers—conceptual, empirical, temporal, normative—in the way that modernity does.

In other words, the modern works precisely by subsuming all histories and all subjectivities of the present under its sign. So, whether we write the story of capital, or of democracy, or of the public sphere, or of faith, or of the self, they all seem to flow into the singular and capacious story of the modern. This is the self-perpetuating technique of the modern as idea and as performance. If, however, we imagine all these histories—of the state, of the demos, of self, of capital, of gods, of the modern itself—to be distinct or even contrary histories which nevertheless can and do intersect, then it becomes possible to also imagine a contemporary today that is other than the modern, that is not exhausted by the modern and its enactments.

The Early Modern

Along with disaggregating the many histories that appear pulled together under the name of the modern, we could also move towards a rethinking of the precolonial. In recent times, there has been a great deal of writing on early modernity in South Asia, which has sought to rescue the idea of the non-modern from always already appearing as 'pre-modern'. This new work is very unlike the earlier 'transition-debate' historiography

that discussed potentialities of indigenous capitalism in South Asia, an almost-transition, which was not-quite, to be later interrupted by colonialism.[17] This earlier historiography looked for capitalism—a modern formation—but interestingly, did not thereby claim modernity as such for South Asia. Today, the argument is different—that in South Asia, and other parts of the non-Western world, the period approximately between 1500 and 1800 saw the emergence of traits that could be termed modern by any count. Scholars have located history-writing traditions[18] and professional scribal cultures[19] in precolonial times, just as they have noticed the rise of public spaces/spheres as constituting the political. They have noted new state formations, which, though not absolutist in the Perry Anderson sense, sought military and fiscal centralization and deployed the rhetoric of universal empire. They have even noted an emergent sensibility of individual power and glory, which defied caste and community proscriptions. There have also been discussions on the growth of travel cultures

[17] Irfan Habib, 1969, 'Potentialities of Capitalistic Development in the Economy of Mughal India', *The Journal of Economic History*, vol. XXIX, no. 1, pp. 32–78.

[18] Raziuddin Aquil and Partha Chatterjee, 2008, *History in the Vernacular*, Delhi: Permanent Black; Kumkum Chatterjee, 2009, *The Cultures of History in Early Modern India: Persianisation and Mughal Culture in Bengal*, New Delhi: Oxford University Press; and Velecheru Narayana Rao, David Shulman, and Sanjay and Subramanyam, 2003, *Textures of Time: Writing History in South India, 1600–1800*, New York: Other Press LLC.

[19] See the Oxford Early Modern South Asia Project, led by Rosalind O'Hanlon, David Washbrook, Christopher Minkowski, and Imre Bangha, 2007 onwards.

and travelogues as a distinct genre of writing in these centuries, constituting a precolonial globalization along with professional and literary cosmopolitanisms.[20]

Clearly, the argument here is not so much about capitalism—though global trade networks and fiscal innovation do form the context of some of these histories—as about modernity as a social and cultural formation. More significantly, this argument is not a nationalist one, based on a comparative exercise across nations or across modern geopolitical regions. Therefore, this work on early modernity does not propose to match European modernity with South Asian, Chinese, or Arab modernities. Instead, it argues that precolonial modernity was really the product of global 'connected' histories, only later to be recast through bifurcations such as colonizer/colonized, centre/periphery, developed/underdeveloped, and so on, which emerged once modernity as a category got subsumed under the idea of (colonial/industrial) capitalism. In other words, this historiography seeks to delink capitalism and modernity.

The current volume does not really have chapters reflecting this new interest in the early modern. This is not accidental. The reason for this is the theoretically unresolved relationship between the early modern and the modern in South Asia. The early modern scholarship mentioned here is deliberately and militantly empirical, and believes that the way to thwart the hegemony of

colonial–capitalist modernity is to recast modernity as a completely empty category, waiting to be filled with local content generated by purely empirical work.[21] This, however, is really only a strategic and provisional move, for in this historiography too, the modern works as a substantive category—as a way of making claims to history, public sphere, supremacy of politics, renewal of the self, and so on—and not merely as a chronological bracket.

A specific chapter in this volume does gesture towards traces of what can be called an early modern imagination—that of universal empire—and indeed, makes the critical move of showing that such imaginations could mutate and go on to inflect later, and more explicitly, colonial–national times such as the early twentieth century. Mrinalini Sinha shows how there were codes of extra-national subjecthood—in the form of imperial, British citizenship and the right to travel and inhabit as citizens all lands of the Empire—which articulated political aspirations of many till very late. She even goes on to argue that 'national independence in the colonial world may have as much to do with the demands of anti-colonial struggles themselves as with imperial deflection of these demands onto the safer confines of the national–territorial space'.[22] I am sure many would agree that early modern imaginaries such as that of imperial and/or global subjecthood very much infused and confounded national modern times. This was true not just of early nineteenth-century

[20] Sanjay Subramanyam, 'Connected Histories: Notes towards a Reconfiguration of Early Modern Eurasia'; 1998, 'Hearing Voices: Vignettes of Early Modernity in South Asia, 1400–1750, *Daedalus*, Special issue on 'Early Modernities', vol. 127, no. 3, Summer, pp. 75–104.

[21] Sheldon Pollock, 2007, 'We Need to Find What We Are Not Looking For', *IIAS Newsletter*, no. 43, Spring, pp. 1 and 4.

[22] Mrinalini Sinha, Chapter 1, this volume.

individuals such as Rammohan Roy but also of so-called 'moderate' nationalists of late nineteenth century, living in a virtual relationship with the British Parliament as it were, and of globally dispersed militant/ anarchist revolutionaries of late nineteenth and early twentieth centuries. I am also sure that such a story is well supplemented by the story of the globalization of labour through slavery and bondage—both allegedly early modern forms of surplus extraction and yet, both continuing well into the national modern times—leading us to ask very interesting questions of the idea of global/ imperial subjecthood.

But what is important for us here is to note the unresolved relationship of such a putatively early modern moment with colonial–national modernity. It is striking, going along with Mrinalini Sinha's story, that the politics of global/imperial subjecthood has become part of neither the history of the pre-modern in South Asia nor of the national modern. The early modern, even when it seems to animate the twentieth century, falls through the crack, so to speak. Nationalist history, of course, tried to neutralize claims of imperial citizenship by calling it the 'proto-nationalist' consciousness of moderates, exiles, and diasporics, eventually and inevitably superseded by the properly modern nationalism of the *swadeshi* and *swaraj* variety. But clearly, this nationalist attempt has not been too successful. What we have then in the colonial modern times is the trace of the early modern, which is not easily put into the narrative of the history of the nation and the colonial modern.

Of course, it will be argued that all this is not quite the concern of the South Asian scholarship on early modernity. The point of that historiography is precisely to delink the colonial modern from the early modern, so as to rescue the latter from being seen as the causal antecedent of colonial–capitalist modernity. But, for historians of modern times in South Asia, questions must be asked about how to take on board the early modern. Such an early modern is neither modern—in the dominant sense—nor is it pre-modern, traditional, or classical—in the sense of a negation of the modern. Or does formulating something by the name of early modern necessarily lead to a quandary for us—because we neither have the historicist option of a modern–early modern continuity (the original European transition narrative), nor the nationalist option of imagining a perfect break in colonialism and of peddling a wistful story of 'our' (disrupted) modernity?

In fact, one could say that the question of the relationship between the modern and the early modern is an immediate, if unspoken, political question today. Unlike in the West, where a modern relationship to the early modern was constitutive of the career of modernity, in the dominant historical imagination of the colony, the early modern has always been haunted by its proximity, indeed by its imputed historical causal relationship, to the moment of colonial triumph. This is the reason why in the colony, the ancient has won over the early modern—through a temporal twist very different from the West's reclamation of classical antiquity through early modern mediation. Few would disagree with the fallout of this valorization of ancient India, at the cost of the medieval or the early modern. It has made possible militant Hinduism as a political force in modern times. It has also made possible conservative forms of post-liberalization, urban, middle-class enactments of the modern (see Arvind Rajagopal's chapter on advertising in this volume). But there are also more complicated questions regarding this.

Take, for instance, Dalit rewritings of history in the twentieth century. These critique the pre-modern, the early modern, and the national modern in the same breath in order to enact a liberation from 'tradition', project a certain global address, and produce a modernist subjectivity via discourses of rights, race, and indigeneity. And yet, these histories also often hold on to an idea of ancientness—Buddhist or pre-Aryan—for the sake precisely of the modern. We know that this is a political–intellectual manoeuvre to enact a critique of, indeed a secession from the nation, and exactly for that purpose, also shore up the nation, that is, shore up the nation as caste and caste as nation. We shall then have to ask of the early modern, with its disavowal of the nation as colonial and contingent, in what way it can speak to a Dalit subjectivity that sees an ancient, indeed eternal nation, unified under the sign of caste.

Coda

As must be evident, there is an interesting asymmetry between the ways that the contemporary and the early modern get problematized. While the latter gets anchored in discussions of a historical–empirical nature, the former opens on to a site of philosophical or conceptual interruption that concerns the very notion of historicity. In other words, there is an asymmetry in the modes of enquiry into the two times of the contemporary and the early modern. In conclusion, therefore, let me make a few provisional statements regarding the nature of this asymmetry so as reflect on the question I began with: in what way is it possible to think of time 'beyond' or 'irrespective' of narratives of the modern?

The contemporary—because it opens on to the future—cannot ever be fully grasped in an empirical mode. We know that the modern way of being contemporary sought to do exactly this (in spite of promises of revolution). Modernity sought to fully apprehend and control the future through notions of progress, modernization, and development, just as capital sought to predict and manage it through creditization, monetization, and speculation over time. We also know the limits of and the violence perpetrated by this mode of grasping the contemporary. For us therefore, the task is to approach the contemporary otherwise. We need to find ways of exploring the contemporary as a time which is not foreclosed, that is, in which the domain of facticity is not yet fully evident or established. By this, I am not trying to insinuate a kind of idealist philosophy of the contemporary. I am only saying that to do justice to the materiality of the contemporary, we must give 'form' to entities and practices that are *emergent* in time and which, therefore, cannot be rendered or grasped simply as a priori, given, self-evident 'facts'. Only thus can we move away from the modernist mode of grasping all times to come as always already known or knowable—that is, as derivatives and mutants of the modern itself. In other words, we cannot afford to be historicist or empiricist, in the conventional sense, about our contemporary.

I would even argue that we cannot be historicist or empiricist about the early modern either. If we seek to activate 'other histories' in our own contemporary—which is exactly what I see the South Asian early modernists as trying to do—we cannot simply proceed by emptying the modern of its (colonial/capitalist) content and refilling it with 'other' empirical content. For what we are struggling against is not only the colonial modern legacy of rendering all histories and pasts as *pre*-histories. What we are struggling against is the specifically modern mode of articulating pasts to the contemporary. Modernity sought to articulate 'other' pasts to its own present through specific categories of temporal mediation, such as tradition, custom, heritage, and even culture. For us then, the question is: what will be our categories of temporal mediation, what will be the appropriate narrative techniques that allow the activation of other pasts in ways that will eventually loosen the grip of the colonial modern over our present? In other words, South Asian early modernists cannot turn their faces away from the colonial modern. They too must engage in the conceptual work, indeed in the form-giving task, that students of the contemporary face vis-à-vis the modern.

In a way, this is to work with the 'untimely'. I invoke the sensibility of the untimely in the way that Gilles Deleuze did some decades ago, in his own bid to give form to the contemporary. He saw the untimely as a way of 'acting counter to our time and thereby acting on our time…for

the benefit of a time to come'.[23] Interestingly for us, Deleuze was offering a critique of truth, in the double sense of historical fact and eternal truth, even as he argued for a materialist philosophy. His argument, following Nietzsche, was that the critical opposition in terms of which philosophy must be realized is that of present and non-present, of our time and the untimely, '[for] in the untimely there are truths that are more durable than all historical and eternal truths put together: truths of times to come'.[24] For us, however, the untimely gestures towards not only the Deleuzian time to come, but also other, heterodox pasts that has had no future in modernity. Can one see the so-called early modern as such an untimely, heterodox past? Is the name 'early modern' then ironic, rather than literal?

The early modern then, if we must reactivate it in the contemporary, cannot be seen simply as a kind of lost, or forgotten, or abandoned past—being recovered painstakingly through acts of history and motifs of commemoration. In fact, we must struggle against idioms of loss and amnesia from pervading political subjectivities of our times, for that slips easily into the earlier modernist mode. We must also move beyond the task of simply showing up the present as contingent, which is important but not sufficient for rethinking the contemporary. In fact, we must ask, crucially, if it is possible to imagine a new relationship to

[23] Gilles Deleuze, 1997 [1968], *Difference and Repetition*, trans. Paul Patton, London: Athlone Press, p. xxi.
[24] Gilles Deleuze, 1983 [1962], *Nietzsche and Philosophy*, London and New York: Continuum, p. 107.

heterodox pasts, which must, of necessity, be a relationship across temporal interruption rather than succession. What forms can such relationships take (calling a past early modern is after all to already set up a relationship)? If this has to be relationship of knowledge, as it must be at some level, then the task will be also to imagine a disciplinary form and intellectual orientation appropriate to such knowledge. Only thus, by mobilizing pasts in the mode of the untimely, can we reanimate the contemporary and disrupt the alleged identity of our present with the modern.

Contributors

PRATHAMA BANERJEE is Associate Fellow at the Centre for the Study of Developing Societies (CSDS), Delhi.

IAN BEDFORD is Senior Research Fellow in the Department of Anthropology, Macquarie University, Australia.

VÉRONIQUE BÉNÉÏ is Senior Research Fellow in the Department of Anthropology, London School of Economics and Political Science, UK.

JAIDEEP CHATTERJEE is Visiting Assistant Professor at the School of Architechture and Planning, Indraprastha University, New Delhi.

ROHAN DEB ROY is Research Fellow in the Department of History and Philosophy of Science, University of Cambridge, UK.

FAISAL DEVJI is University Reader in Modern South Asian History at St Anthony's College, University of Oxford, UK.

SAURABH DUBE is Professor of History at the Centre for Asian and African Studies, El Colegio de México, Mexico.

ATIG GHOSH is Project Fellow at the Maulana Abul Kalam Azad Institute of Asian Studies, Kolkata.

BODHISATTVA KAR is Fellow in History at the Centre for Studies in Social Sciences (CSSS), Kolkata.

TOWNSEND MIDDLETON is Fellow in the Department of Anthropology, Duke University, USA.

ANAND PANDIAN is Assistant Professor in the Department of Anthropology, The Johns Hopkins University, USA.

ARVIND RAJAGOPAL is Professor of Media Studies and an affiliated faculty in the Departments of Sociology and Social and Cultural Analysis at New York University, USA.

KALPANA RAM is Senior Lecturer in the Department of Anthropology, Macquarie University, Australia.

ANUPAMA RAO is Associate Professor of History at Barnard College, New York.

MRINALINI SINHA is Alice Freeman Palmer Professor of History at the University of Michigan, USA.

AJAY SKARIA is Associate Professor of History at the University of Minnesota, USA.

SANJUKTA SUNDERASON is a PhD candidate in History of Art at the University College London, UK.